SATA Storage Technology

MINDSHARE, INC.

Training Courses

- Certified Wireless USB
- Core and Core2 Processor Architecture
- DRAM Architecture
- HyperTransport 3.0 System Architecture
- Opteron Processor Architecture
- PC Architecture
- PCI Express 2.0
- SAS Storage Technology
- SATA Storage Technology
- USB System Architecture
- Virtualization Technology

MindShare provides technical training at customer sites and periodically offers public classes (visit www.mindshare.com for an updated list).

MindShare Books (short list)

- PCI Express System Architecture
- PCI System Architecture
- SAS Storage Architecture
- The Unabridged Pentium 4
- USB System Architecture

SATA Storage Technology

MINDSHARE, INC.

Donovan (Don) Anderson

Contributions by:
Mike Jackson
Duncan Penman

MINDSHARE PRESS

Visit MindShare, Inc. on the web: www.mindshare.com

Library of Congress Control Number: 2006934887

MindShare Press
Attn: Maryanne Daves
4285 Slash Pine Dr.
Colorado Springs, CO 80908
Fax: 719-487-1434

Set in 10-point Palatino by MindShare, Inc.

ISBN 978-0-9770878-1-5

First Printing April 2007

Acknowledgements:

Special thanks must be extended to several people and organizations for their assistance and contributions in the preparation of this book.

Duncan Penman — for sharing his technical expertise and experience in the ATA and Serial ATA technologies, for preparing a review of the SATA command structure, and finally for editing this book for technical accuracy.

Mike Jackson — for preparing the chapters covering the SATA electrical interface.

COMAX — for providing photographs of SATA cables and connectors.

Hewlett Packard — for having graciously given permission to use several illustrations.

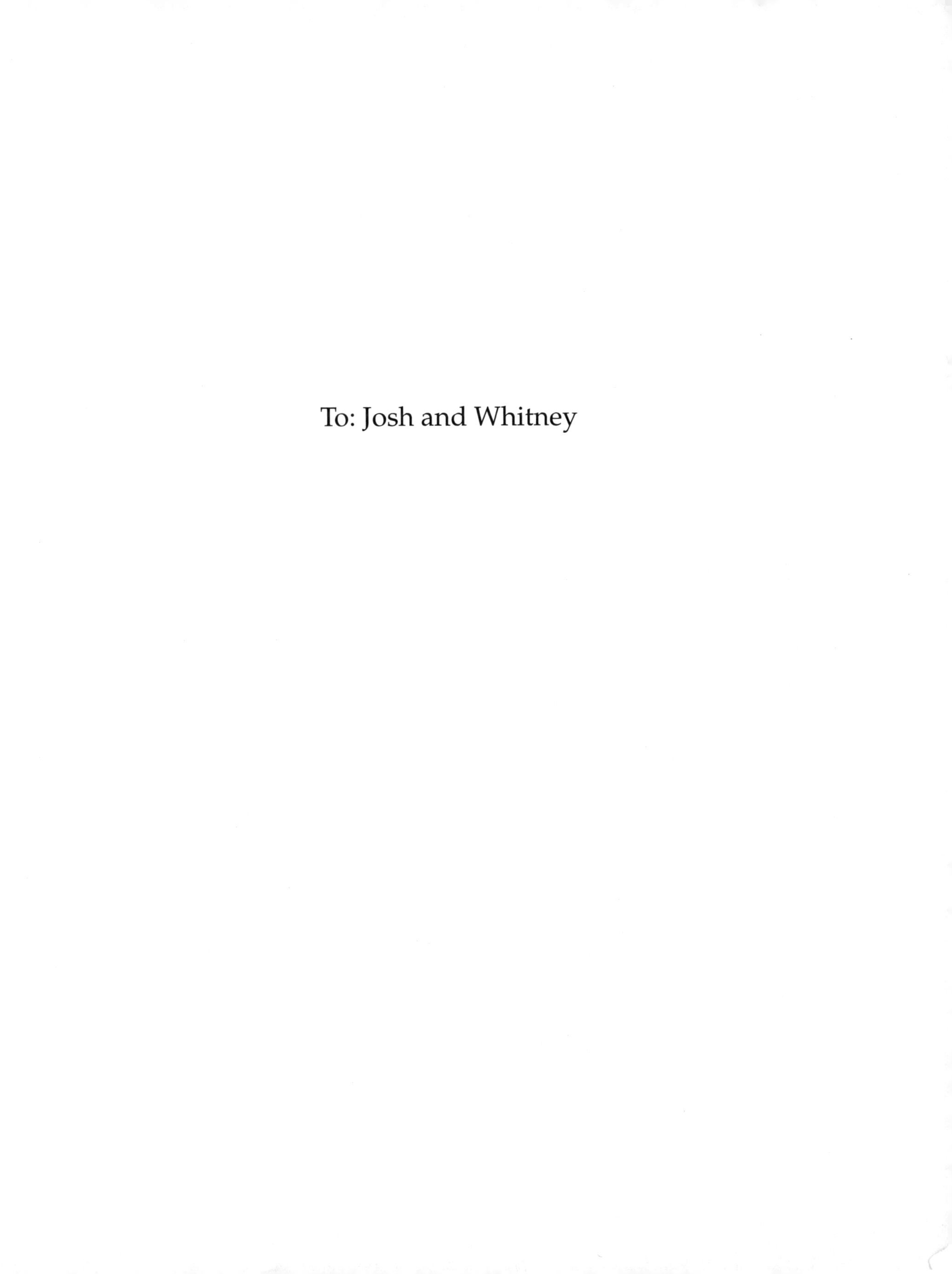

To: Josh and Whitney

Contents

Contents

Chapter 2: The Motivation for SATA

Chapter 3: SATA Overview

Chapter 4: Introduction to FIS Transfers

Contents

Part Two
FIS Transmission Protocols

Chapter 5: FIS Types and Formats

Chapter 6: Transport and Link Protocols

Chapter 7: FIS Retry

Chapter 8: Data Flow Control

Chapter 9: Physical Layer Functions

Chapter 10: Error Detection and Handling

Part Three
Command and Control Protocols

Chapter 11: The Command Protocol

Chapter 14: Native Command Queuing

Chapter 15: Port Multipliers

Chapter 16: Port Selectors

Chapter 17: Enclosure Services

Part Five
Physical Layer Details

Chapter 18: SATA Initialization

Contents

Chapter 19: Physical Layer

Chapter 20: Cables & Connectors

Chapter 21: Hot Plug

Chapter 22: Link Power Management

Contents

Chapter 23: BIST Features

Appendices

Appendix A: 8b/10b Encoding Tutorial

Appendix B: ATA & SATACommands

Contents

Figures

Figures

Figures

Figures

Tables

Tables

About This Book

Scope

The *SATA Storage Technology* book is intended as a tutorial and to serve as classroom materials for the training MindShare delivers on this subject. It should be considered a companion to the SATA specification, helping to clarify and explain the concepts and motivations for decisions that were made in the creation of the specification. This book does not attempt to recreate or duplicate reference material from the specification. Doing so would potentially introduce errors into information that is rightfully the sole domain of the specification.

The MindShare Architecture Series

The MindShare System Architecture book series includes the publications shown in Table 1.

Table 1: PC Architecture Book Series

Category	Title	Edition	ISBN
Processor Architecture	80486 System Architecture	3rd	0-201-40994-1
	Pentium® Processor System Architecture	2nd	0-201-40992-5
	Pentium® Pro and Pentium® II System Architecture	2nd	0-201-30973-4
	PowerPC System Architecture	1st	0-201-40990-9
	The Unabridged Pentium® 4	1st	0-321-24656-X

Table 1: PC Architecture Book Series (Continued)

Category	Title	Edition	ISBN
Bus Architectures	PCI System Architecture	4th	0-201-30974-2
	EISA System Architecture	Out-of-print	0-201-40995-X
	Firewire System Architecture: IEEE 1394	2nd	0-201-48535-4
	ISA System Architecture	3rd	0-201-40996-8
	Universal Serial Bus System Architecture	2nd	0-201-30975-0
	PCI-X System Architecture	1st	0-201-72682-3
	PCI Express System Architecture	1st	0-321-15630-7
Network Architecture	InfiniBand Network Architecture	1st	0-321-11765-4
Other Architectures	PCMCIA System Architecture: 16-Bit PC Cards	2nd	0-201-40991-7
	CardBus System Architecture	1st	0-201-40997-6
	Plug and Play System Architecture	1st	0-201-41013-3
	Protected Mode Software Architecture	1st	0-201-55447-X
	AGP System Architecture	1st	0-201-37964-3
Storage Architecture	SAS Storage Architecture	1st	0-977-08780-8
	SATA Storage Technology	1st	978-0-9770878-1-5

Cautionary Note

The reader should keep in mind that MindShare's book series often deals with rapidly evolving technologies. This being the case, it should be recognized that the book is a "snapshot" of the state of the targeted technology at the time that the book was completed. We attempt to update each book on a timely basis to reflect changes in the targeted technology, but, due to various factors (waiting for the next version of the standard to be approved, the time necessary to make the changes, and the time to produce the books and get them out to the distribution channels), there will always be a delay.

The Standard Is the Final Word

As with all of our books, this book represents the author's interpretation of the specification - in this case the SATA 2.6 specification. However, please note that during the time that most of the writing was done the 2.5 version of the specification was in force. Near the conclusion of the project, the 2.6 version was released. The author has updated the information to make the content current, but with the realization that some changes introduced by the 2.6 specification may have been missed. In any case, the specification must be considered the final word!

Documentation Conventions

The conventions used in this book for numeric values are defined in the sections that follow.

Hexadecimal Notation

This section defines the typographical convention used throughout this book. All hex numbers are followed by an "h." Examples:

```
9A4Eh
0100h
```

Binary Notation

All binary numbers are followed by a "b." Examples:

```
0001 0101b
01b
```

Decimal Notation

Numbers without any suffix are decimal. When required for clarity, decimal numbers are followed by a "d." The following examples each represent a decimal number:

```
16
255
256d
128d
```

Bits Versus Bytes Notation

All abbreviations for "bits" use lower case. For example:

- 2.5Gb/s = 2.5 Gigabits per second.
- 2Mb = 2 Megabits.

All references to "bytes" are specified in upper case. For example:

- 10MB/s = 10 Megabytes per second.
- 2KB = 2 Kilobytes.

Other designations:

Bit Fields

In many cases, bit fields are documented as [15:8], with this example referring to bits 8 through 15.

The # symbol designates that the field definition depends on the ATA/SATA command being executed.

Other Terminology and Abbreviations

Host/HBA — The term Host is used often by the specification and may refer to the SATA Host Controller Adapter (HBA) as well as the CPU, IO bus, memory, and software that plays a role in conveying information to or from the SATA link and devices. This book uses the term HBA when reference is being made to the SATA Host interface, such as AHCI.

Device/Drive — The specification routinely uses the term "SATA Device" when referring to devices that are attached to a SATA link. This text also uses the term drive. These terms can be used interchangeably except when reference is being made to devices such as Port Multipliers that attach to a SATA link, but are not drives.

Port Multiplier (PM) — The abbreviation "PM" applies only to the Port Multiplier.

Frame Information Structure (FIS, FIS's FISes) — These abbreviations apply to the singular, plural, and possessive forms of the term Frame Information Structure.

Double Word (DWord, DW) — DWord is used in the body of this book, and DW is employed in some diagrams where space is limited.

Visit Our Web Site (www.mindshare.com)

In addition to listing all of our courses and books, our web site contains:

- Technical information covering questions asked by class participants and readers of our books
- Errata for a number of the books
- Information on MindShare training courses
- Short courses available for viewing online
- Technical papers

We Want Your Feedback

MindShare values your comments and suggestions. You can contact us via mail, phone, fax or email.

Phone: (719) 487-1417 and in the U.S. (800) 633-1440.
Fax: (719) 487-1434.
Technical seminars: E-mail nancy.shanley@mindshare.com.
Technical questions: E-mail don@mindshare.com.
MindShare books: E-mail maryanne@mindshare.com

Mailing Address:

MindShare, Inc.
4285 Slash Pine Drive
Colorado Springs, CO 80908

Part One

SATA Overview

1 The Evolution of Parallel ATA

This Chapter

Background information regarding the parallel ATA (PATA) implementations is important for understanding the Serial ATA (SATA) implementation. The SATA design provides compatibility with the PATA legacy programming interface and with the commands defined for PATA. This chapter provides a base level of knowledge for the Parallel ATA implementation and is intended as a review or primer of the technology.

The Next Chapter

The next chapter introduces the motivation for implementing a serial version of ATA. Many recognized shortcomings of PATA are addressed in the SATA implementation. The chapter identifies these shortcomings and describes the solutions provided by SATA.

ATA transitions to Serial Interface

The parallel ATA (PATA) implementation, like many other IO interfaces, has a high-speed serial cousin simply named Serial ATA (SATA). SATA was designed for software compatibility with the ATA/ATAPI 6 specification. The motivation to migrate ATA to a serial interface includes a wide variety of issues, including:

- Cost reduction through reduced pin count
- Lower voltages for smaller silicon sizes
- Improved transmission speed between the drive and Host Adapter
- Enhanced reliability
- Improved cables/connector
- Aggressive positioning of ATA for the server environment

The next chapter discusses the improvements and new features brought about by the SATA implementation.

Origins of ATA

The origins of ATA can be traced back to Compaq Computer in the mid 1980s. At that time, Compaq was principally know for its portable computers. Compaq's first portables were based on the IBM PC and later the IBM PC-AT. Hard disc drives in PCs were initially implemented with a combination of hard disc controller cards that plugged directly into the PC expansion bus and the associated disc drives that were installed into drive bays. Figure 1-1 on page 10 depicts this hard drive controller and hard drive combination.

Figure 1-1: Controller/Disc Drive in Early PC Implementations

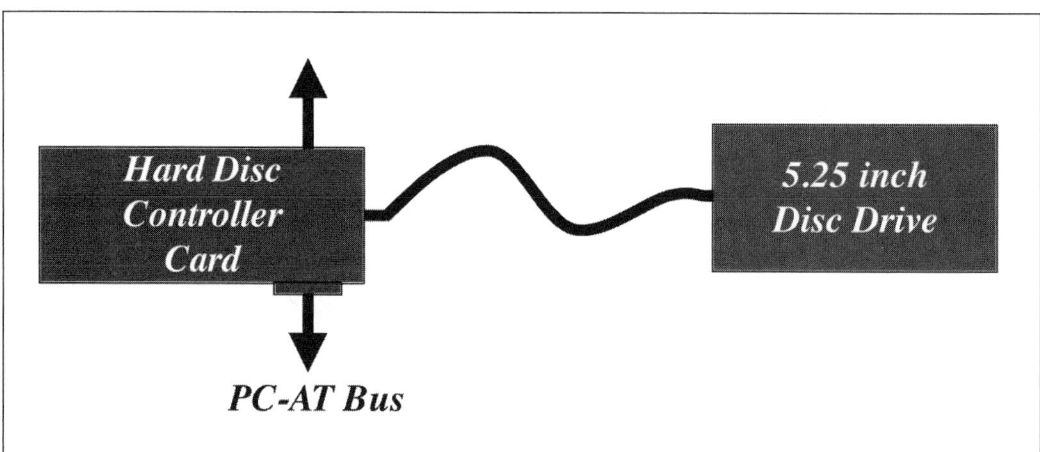

Compaq sought to create a portable computer that was smaller and lighter than the original portable (sometimes called luggables), which in some configuration weighed nearly 40 pounds. The Portable II design reduced overall size, in part, by integrating many of the IO functions directly onto the motherboard; thereby, eliminating the need for many expansion cards and associated expansion slots. These integrated functions included the floppy drive interface, serial interface, and parallel interface. Compaq also eliminated the hard disc controller as a plug-in adapter card and mounted it on top of the drive. This implementation of combining the disc controller and drive was called the Compaq Integrated Drive. In doing this, it was necessary to extend the PC-AT expansion bus to the drive bay. This was done via a ribbon cable and a small interface circuit called the Host Bus Adapter. See Figure 1-2 on page 11.

Figure 1-2: PC-AT Host Bus Interface (on motherboard) and Integrated Controller and Drive

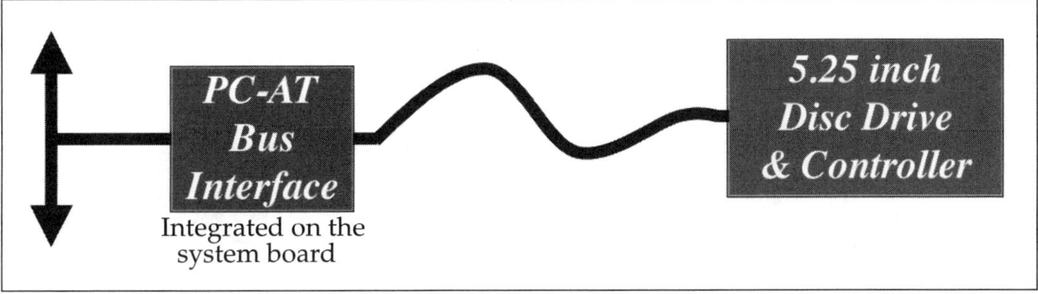

The next generation of the Compaq Integrated Drive was fully integrated when the controller was incorporated inside a Wren disc drive housing, manufactured by Imprimis.

Emergence of IDE (Integrated Disc Electronics) Drives

Other hard disc drive vendors began manufacturing integrated drives similar to Compaq's proprietary solution. These disc drives became known as IDE drives. What these initials actually mean is not clear. A few possibilities include:

- Integrated Disc Electronics
- Integrated Drive Electronics
- Integrated Drive Element
- Intelligent Drive Electronics

"My personal favorite is Integrated Disc Electronics, but what IDE originally stood for probably falls under the category of "Who cares?"."

Support for Two Drives

Another feature of the IDE drives is the ability to attach and address two devices via a single Host Adapter Interface and shared ribbon cable. See Figure 1-3 on page 12. Note that jumpers or switches on each drive must be set to designate which drive would respond as drive zero (0) and which would respond as drive one (1). See the section entitled, "Device Register - Selecting the Target ATA Device" on page 21 for a description of how these drives are independently addressed.

Figure 1-3: Two Drives Can Share the Same IDE Interface

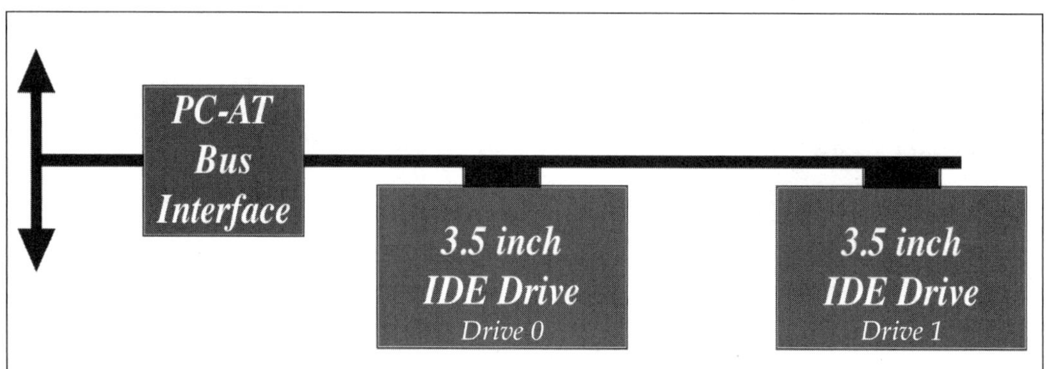

Compatibility Problems

One of the early problems associated with IDE was that no standard existed for implementing these drives. Consequently there were a number of compatibility problems. Perhaps the most common problems occurred when two drives from different manufacturers were connected to the same IDE cable.

The ATA Standard

Eventually a working group within the Common Access Methods group was formed to define a standard interface specification for the interconnect between the IBM PC-AT bus and IDE drives. The specification was ultimately called AT-Attachment or ATA. The first ATA specification was finally published as:

ANSI (American National Standards Institute) X3.221-1994

Today there is also the ATA working committee named T13 that defines the direction of ATA. T13 is chartered by the:

INCITS - Technical Committee for the InterNational Committee on Information Technology Standards

The ATA Signalling Interface

The ATA interface is represented in block diagram form in Figure 1-4 on page 14. The interface consists of 32 signals, 7 ground pins, and 1 reserved pin position for the key (See Figure 1-5 on page 16). Fundamentally, the ATA Host Bus Adapter (HBA) merely extended the IBM PC-AT expansion bus to the disc drive where the disc controller electronics reside. The interface consists of several major signal groups:

- IO Address-related signals
- Control signals
- Data lines
- DMA-related signals

These signal groups along with the other miscellaneous signals are listed and described in Table 1-1 on page 14. Note that many of the signals are not used in current ATA implementations. Power to the drive is delivered by a separate power connector.

Figure 1-4: Parallel ATA Block Diagram

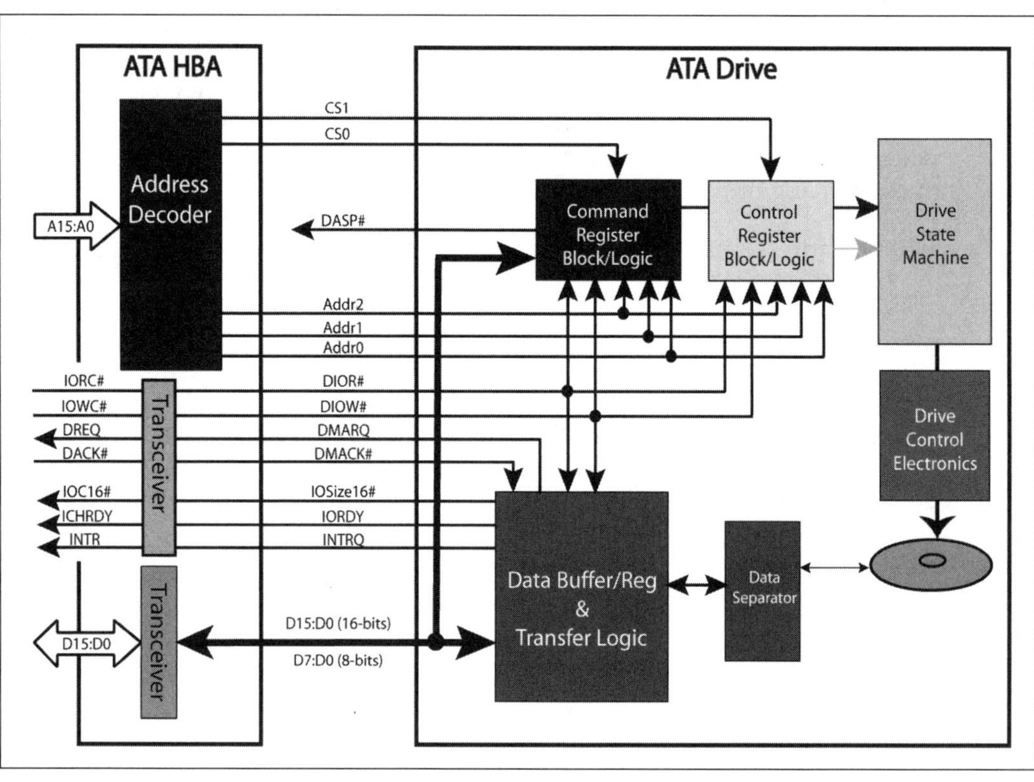

Table 1-1: Parallel ATA Signals

Signal Name	Description
Addr2:0	Lower 3 address lines — provides access for up to 8 registers within the command and control blocks.
CS0	Chip Select Zero — asserted when software accesses the Command Register Block within the HBA. The target IO address range was originally defined as 01F0h to 01FFh.
CS1	Chip Select One — asserted when software accesses the Control Register Block. The control registers were originally mapped into the IO address range of 03F0h to 03FFh.

Table 1-1: Parallel ATA Signals

Signal Name	Description
Data15:0	Data lines — used to transfer data between the PC-AT bus and the drive.
IOCS16	Control line asserted by the drive interface when a 16-bit register is being accessed, resulting in all 16 data lines being used during the data transfer.
IOW#	IO Write Command — asserted when a write transfer is targeting a register within the command or control block.
IOR#	IO Read Command — asserted when a read transfer is targeting a register within the command or control block.
IORDY	IO Ready — asserted by the drive controller to indicate that data has either been captured or sourced to the data bus.
INTRQ	Interrupt Request — asserted by the drive interface to call the software to handle a drive event (e.g., command completion).
DMARQ	DMA Request — used by the drive controller to request a 3rd party DMA transfer to or from the drive and main system memory.
DMACK#	DMA Acknowledge — returned by the 3rd party DMA controller to notify the driver controller that it's ready to transfer data.
DASP	Device Active/Slave Present — used as a drive activity signal and driven by device 1 to notify device 0 that a slave drive is present.
SPSync/CSEL	Spindle Synchronization/Cable Select — spindle synchronization is officially obsolete. Cable select is used to configure drive automatically by defining them as either a master or slave device.
PDIAG	Passed Diagnostics — asserted by a slave device (device 1) following reset to notify the master drive whether it passed internal diagnostics or not.
RESET#	RESET is asserted on the ATA interface as a result of the bus reset on the host bus (e.g., PC-AT Reset or PCI Reset).

Figure 1-5: Parallel ATA Connector Pin Definition

Signal	Pin	Pin	Signal
RESET#	1	2	Grnd
Data7	3	4	Data8
Data6	5	6	Data9
Data5	7	8	Data10
Data4	9	10	Data11
Data3	11	12	Data12
Data2	13	14	Data13
Data1	15	16	Data14
Data0	17	18	Data15
Grnd	19	20	N.C.
DMARQ	21	22	Grnd
IOW#	23	24	Grnd
IOR#	25	26	Grnd
IORDY	27	28	SPSync/CSEL
DMACK#	29	30	Grnd
INTRQ	31	32	IOCS16
ADDR1	33	34	PDIAG
ADDR0	35	36	ADDR2
CS0#	37	38	CS1#
DASP	39	40	Grnd

ATA Protocol/Performance Review

As illustrated in the previous sections, the original ATA bus was merely an extension of the IBM PC-AT bus, thus its performance was the same as the AT bus. The AT bus operated at a transmission rate of 8 MHz and transferred up to 2 bytes of information during each IO transfer, requiring a minimum of 3 clock cycles. This yielded a maximum throughput of approximately 5MB/sec. When ATA adapters were attached to the PCI bus, subsequent versions of the specification took advantage of the much better performance while using the same ATA interface. This section describes these advancements in performance.

ATA

The first version of ATA attached directly to the IBM PC-AT bus and supported two modes of operation:

- PIO (Programmed IO) - instructions executing on the host CPU are responsible for moving data between the drive and memory via IO operations. PIO involves two separate operations to move data between an ATA drive and memory:
    1. The first instruction of a PIO operation transfers 2 bytes of data from either memory or the drive to a processor register.
    2. The second instruction transfers data from the processor register to the drive or to memory. This resulted in considerable CPU overhead but completed transfers faster than the other available methods of the time.
- DMA — the ATA specification defined the IBM PC-AT method of DMA and due to the programming overhead and slow transmission rates, drive manufacturers did not support this legacy DMA solution.

The transmission rate across the ATA bus could be sustained at 5MB/s; however, actual transfer rates were slower due to the nature of the PIO transfers.

ATA-2/3

ATA version 2 introduced a new DMA transmission protocol based on the PCI bus burst transaction protocol. The ATA bus transmission rate remained at approximately 8MHz (one-fourth of the 33MHz PCI clock rate) but the protocol allowed the transfer of two bytes during every tick of the 8MHz clock. This of course yields a maximum data transfer rate of 16MB/s. This protocol requires the ATA adapter to implement a DMA engine and data buffer to support the DMA transfer. The DMA engine residing on the PCI-based HBA transferred data between its internal buffer and memory via PCI burst transactions.

ATA-4

The ATA-4 implementation defined a 16.5MHz transmission rate (one-half of the 33MHz PCI clock), resulting in a maximum throughput of 33MB/s when transferring two bytes during each clock. This new DMA transmission was termed UltraDMA 33.

ATA-5

The ATA-5 DMA protocol named UltraDMA 66 transferred two bytes of data for every cycle of the 33MHz PCI clock, yielding a transfer rate of 66MB/s. However, the ATA ribbon cable and connectors originally designed for an 8MHz transmission rate would no longer operate reliably. To solve the problem, additional conductors were inserted between each of the normal 40 conductors, thereby doubling the number of conductors to 80. These additional conductors are tied to ground, thus improving the electrical transmission characteristics (e. g., reduced crosstalk) of the ATA interface and set the stage for even faster transmission rates.

ATA-6

ATA Host Adapters and drives that supported the UltraDMA 100 multiplied the 33MHz clock used in ATA-5 by a factor of 1.5 to yield a transmission rate of 49.99MHz and a maximum throughput of approximately 100MB/s.

ATA-7

The latest and perhaps final step in performance enhancement for the ATA parallel interface is UltraDMA133. HBAs and drives using the ATA-7 DMA protocol use double data rate (DDR) clocking of the 33MHz clock to achieve an effective transmission rate of 66MHz. Two bytes transferred at the 66MHz rate of course yields throughput of 133MB/s.

Table 1-2 summarizes the DMA modes defined by the ATA specifications and the maximum transmission rates supported by each generation of ATA, along with the year of its first implementation.

Table 1-2: ATA Bus Maximum Bandwidths

Standard	Year	Speed	Transfer Modes
NA	1986		Pre-Standard
ATA	1994	5MB/sec	PIO modes 0-2 Multiword DMA mode 0
ATA-2	1996	16MB/sec	PIO modes 3-4 Multiword DMA modes 1-2
ATA-3	1997		
ATA-4	1998	33MB/sec	Ultra DMA modes 0-2
ATA-5	2000	66MB/sec	Ultra DMA modes 3-4
ATA-6	2002	100MB/sec	Ultra DMA mode 5
ATA-7	2003	133MB/sec	Ultra DMA mode 6

The Legacy Programming Interface

The disc controller programming interface consists of a block of registers mapped into the x86 IO address space. This register set is also known as the "task file," illustrated in Table 1-3 on page 29 The registers in use today include:

- Eight Command Registers — mapped starting at IO address 01F0h.
- One Control Register — mapped at IO address 03F6h.

Most HBA register addresses target the same registers during read and write operations. However, three register addresses target different registers when being read versus being written.

1. Feature/Error Register at 01F1h
   — Error register during reads
   — Feature register during writes
2. Command/Status Register at 01F7h
   — Status register during reads
   — Command register during writes
3. Alternate Control/Alternate Status register at 03F6h
   — Alternate Status register during reads
   — Device Control register during writes

Figure 1-6: Legacy ATA Taskfile

Cmd Reg	Reads		Writes		Notes
Address	7 0		7 0		
01F0	Data		Data		16-bit accesses
01F1	Error		Feature		8-bit access only
01F2	Sector Count		Sector Count		8-bit access only
01F3	Sector #		Sector #		8-bit access only
01F4	Cylinder Low		Cylinder Low		8-bit access only
01F5	Cylinder High		Cylinder High		8-bit access only
01F6	Device	Head	Device	Head	8-bit access only
01F7	Status		Command		8-bit access only
Ctrl Reg					
03F6	Alternate Status		Device Control		8-bit access only

HBA Register Descriptions

This section describes the HBA register functions. The original definition of the HBA registers changed over time. This text generally does not cover registers that are no longer in use. Some registers are discussed in groups, while others are discussed individually as follows:

- Device register
- Start Sector Address registers
- Transfer Size register (Sector Count)
- Feature register
- Command register
- Data register
- Status register
- Error register
- Control register
- Alternate Status register

Device Register - Selecting the Target ATA Device

"Support for Two Drives" on page 11 introduces the ATA bus's support for attaching two devices. Drive selection begins with jumpers or switches on the drive that must be set such that one drive is configured as drive 0 and the other as drive 1. Software must initialize the Device register (bits 7:4) by either setting or clearing bit 4 to specify the target drive. When the command is issued, each drive compares the value in its Device register (always the same in both drives) with its configured drive number. See Figure 1-7. The drive that detects a match is selected and proceeds to execute the command.

Figure 1-7: ATA Drive Selection

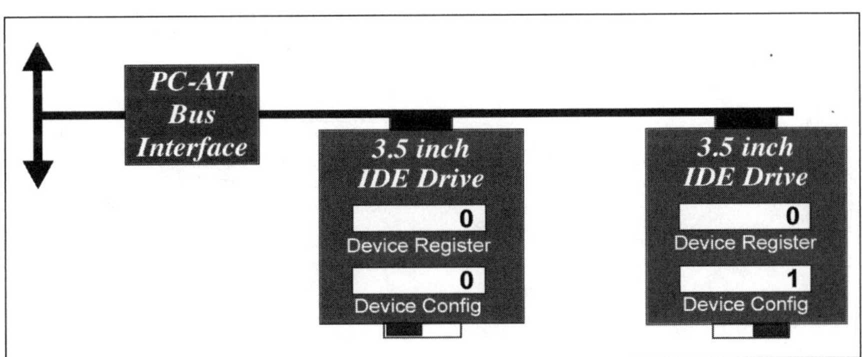

Start Sector Address

Part of the HBA register initialization involves specifying the start sector address on disc where data is to be read from or written to. The sector addressing used in early IDE and ATA drives was based on the physical organization of drives (refer to Figure 1-8 on page 22). Drives had a specific number of platters, head, and tracks. This was termed the drive geometry. A given track position associated with a stack of platters forms a cylinder within the drive, such that, any track "n" is present in the same relative position on all platters. This form of physical disc addressing identifies the sector start address and is often termed Cylinder, Head, Sector (CHS) addressing.

Figure 1-8: Physical Drive Geometry

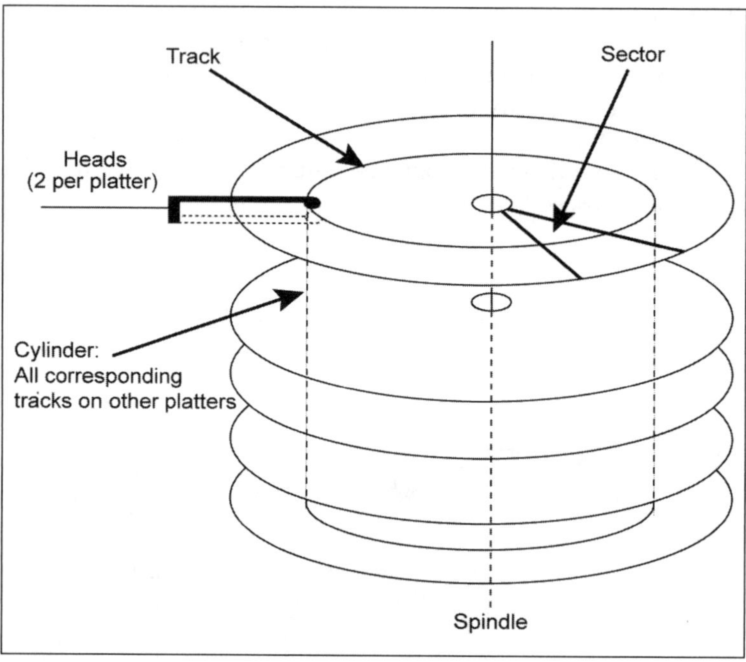

Physical Disc Address Registers. The early IDE and ATA implementations used physical disc addressing. This addressing scheme is based on the physical geometry of the disc as discussed in the previous section:

- Cylinder
- Head
- Sector

Prior to reading from or writing to the disc, software must initialize the starting sector address based on CHS registers highlighted in Figure 1-9.

Figure 1-9: Cylinder, Head, and Sector Physical Address Registers

Cmd Reg	Reads		Writes		Notes
Address	7	0	7	0	
01F0	Data				16-bit accesses
01F1	Error		Feature		8-bit access only
01F2	Sector Count				8-bit access only
01F3	Sector Number				8-bit access only
01F4	Cylinder Low				8-bit access only
01F5	Cylinder High				8-bit access only
01F6	Device	Head	Device	Head	8-bit access only
01F7	Status		Command		8-bit access only
Ctrl Reg					
03F6	Alternate Status		Device Control		8-bit access only

The total number of sectors that can be addressed by the HBA interface is based on the register sizes below:

- 8-bit Sector Number = 2^8
- 16-bit Cylinder Low/High Number = 2^{16}
- 4-bit Head Number = 2^4

The total equals 2^{28} sectors.

Because many different drives were built with different numbers of cylinders, heads and sectors/platter, software responsible for accessing the drives had to know each drive's geometry. This led to the designation of drive types that specified particular geometries.

A different addressing scheme was implemented in version 2 of the ATA standard where software views all sectors as a linear block of sectors. This addressing method is termed Logical Block Addressing (LBA) and eliminates the need for knowing drive types.

Logical Block Addressing. Logical Block Addressing (LBA) eliminates the need for software to address drives based on their specific physical organization. Software views drives as a single logical block of linear sectors. Drives of course still have a specific geometry and are tasked with performing the necessary translation from logical to physical addressing. LBA is enabled during task file initialization by setting Bit 6 within the Device register (at 01F6h).

Logical Block Address Registers (28 bits). The registers involved in logical addressing are the same as used with CHS addressing except the register names are changed to reflect the Logical Block Addressing mechanism as illustrated in Figure 1-10.

Figure 1-10: 28-Bit Logical Block Address Registers

Cmd Reg	Reads		Writes		Notes
Address	7	0	7	0	
01F0	Data				16-bit accesses
01F1	Error		Feature		8-bit access only
01F2	Sector Count				8-bit access only
01F3	LBA Low (7:0)				8-bit access only
01F4	LBA Middle (15:8)				8-bit access only
01F5	LBA High (23:16)				8-bit access only
01F6	Device	LBA (27:24)	Device	LBA (27:24)	8-bit access only
01F7	Status		Command		8-bit access only
Ctrl Reg					
03F6	Alternate Status		Device Control		8-bit access only

Logical Block Address Registers (48 bits). The ATA6 standard introduced 48-bit Logical Block Addressing. As illustrated in Figure 1-11 on page 25, the upper nibble of the 28-bit LBA is not used in the 48-bit implementation. Instead, only the low, middle, and high bytes are used for specifying the 48-bit address. This was accomplished by extending the LBA registers such that two writes are issued to each of the three byte address locations (01F3, 01F4 and 01F5). Figure 1-11 on page 25 shows that the initial write to these registers loads the upper 24 bits (47:24) and the second write loads the lower 24 bits (23:0) of the 48-bit address.

Along with these extensions the Sector Count register was also extended to accept two writes. In all cases the high-order byte is loaded first, followed by the lower order byte. To read the contents of the previously written register value, software must first set the High Order Byte (HOB) in the Control register. (See "Device Control Register" on page 28.)

The extended version of LBA is supported by a series new commands that have "Extended" appended to the command (e.g. ReadDMAExtended)

Figure 1-11: 48-Bit Logical Block Address Registers

Cmd Reg	Reads		Writes		Notes
Address	7	0	7	0	
01F0	Data				16-bit accesses
01F1	Error		Feature		Two 8-bit accesses
01F2	Sector Count				Two 8-bit accesses
01F3	LBA Low (31:24 then 7:0)				Two 8-bit accesses
01F4	LBA Middle (39:32 then 15:8)				Two 8-bit accesses
01F5	LBA High (47:40 then 23:16)				Two 8-bit accesses
01F6	Device		Device		8-bit access only
01F7	Status		Command		8-bit access only
Ctrl Reg					
03F6	Alternate Status		Device Control		8-bit access only

Transfer Size Register

Transfers to or from disc drives may consist of one or more sectors. Software initializes the Sector Count register to specify the size of the data transfer. Note that some commands use the sector count register for other information. For example, DMA Queued commands specify the "tag" value in the sector count register.

Feature Register

The Feature register is used in conjunction with a variety of commands. Software writes the desired feature value into the register during initialization to specify the feature that is to be set. Some commands such as DMA Queued commands use the Feature register to specify the sector count.

Command Register

After the task file has been initialized for a particular command, software writes to the command register, which triggers execution of the selected command. The actions taken by the drive and host during execution of the command are defined by the particular command selected. Specific actions are taken by the HBA when this command is written and software writes to the ATA registers is limited as follows:

- The Status register's BSY (Busy) bit is set indicating that the drive is executing the command and has taken control of the registers.
- No host software writes are permitted to the Feature, Sector Count, LBA Low, LBA Mid, LBA High, or Device registers.
- When the command completes the Status/Error registers are updated to report completion status and the BSY bit is cleared.

Data Register

The data register is accessed by software during execution of Programmed IO (PIO) commands. During PIO operations one or more word (2-byte) accesses are required to complete the command. Note that DMA operations target the DMA memory buffer within a drive and not the data register.

The original ATA registers were all implemented as 8-bit registers except the Data register, which is accessible as a 16-bit register. When performing a 16-bit access starting at IO address 01F0h, the 2-byte Data register is targeted, rather than the contents of locations 01F0h and 01F1h. An IO read or write with an address of 01F1h targets the Error or Feature register, respectively.

Status Register

The status register is updated by the drive to reflect the current state of the command being performed. If an interrupt is pending, reading this register clears the pending interrupt, resulting in the INTRQ signal being deasserted. The Status register contents are illustrated in Figure 1-12.

Figure 1-12: Status Register Contents

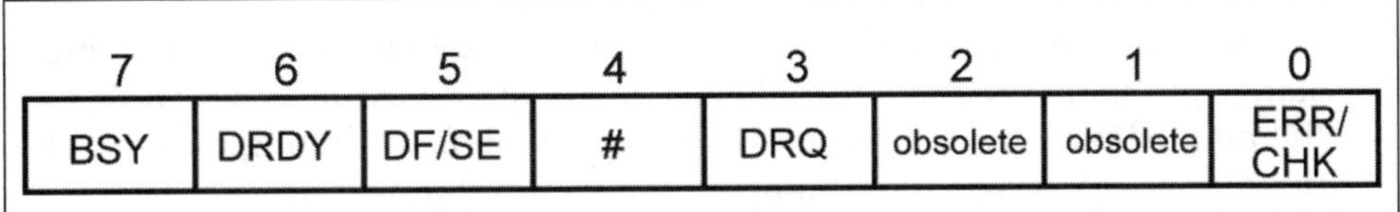

Following is a brief description of each bit:

- BSY (Busy) — indicates who has control of the Command Register Block; host software (BSY=0) or the device (BSY=1). When software writes a command into a device's command register (01F7h) the device must set the BSY within 400ns, which inhibits software from accessing the Feature, Sector Count, LBA Low, LBA Mid, LBA High, or Device registers during command execution. Once software detects BSY cleared write access to the registers is allowed (unless the DRQ status bit is set) and software may issue another command. Note there are numerous conditions under which the BSY bit will be set or cleared as commands are being executed.
- DRDY (Device Ready) — indicates that the device is ready to accept and attempt execution of all commands that it implements.
- DF/SE (Device Fault / Stream Error) — devices set this bit when they are unable to complete execution of the command in process, providing that the error is not reported in the device Error register (01F1h). Streaming errors are only related to the Stream commands.
- # — bits marked "#" are command dependent. This bit was previously defined as the DSC (Device Seek Complete).
- DRQ (Data Request) — a device typically sets the DRQ bit when data is ready for transfer between the host and device. In some cases, when DRQ is set at the same time BSY is cleared. When either DRQ or BSY are set software is not allowed to perform writes to the registers listed under the first bullet in this list.
- Obsolete — previously defined bits that are no longer used.
- ERR/CHK — indicates that an error occurred during execution of the previous command that has been reported in the Error register. This bit is also defined as CHK when PACKET and SERVICE commands are being executed and indicates an exception condition occurred during command execution.

Error Register

When errors occur during execution of a command, bits are set in the error register to reflect the nature of the error condition. The ERR bit in the Status register validates the contents of this register. Software is responsible for reading error status and taking the appropriate action. As illustrated in Figure 1-13, most of the bit positions are designated with the # symbol, indicating that the bit field definition depends on the command that incurred the error.

The ABRT (Abort) bit indicates that the command could not be executed due to command corrupt, command not supported, or other conditions required for command completion being wrong or missing.

Figure 1-13: Error Register Definition

7	6	5	4	3	2	1	0
#	#	#	#	#	ABRT	#	#

Device Control Register

The Control Register is used for a variety of miscellaneous functions that are defined below. Figure 1-14 on page 29 illustrates the bit field designations and locations.

- HOB (High Order Byte) — Recall that loading some of the register contents require back-to-back byte-sized writes to the same address location. Setting the HOB bit enables software to read the previous written byte from the selected 8-bit register.
- SRST (Soft Reset) — Software sets this bit (writes a 1) to reset the drive. Reset is not deasserted to the device until software clears the SRST bit, but only after reset has been asserted for at least 5µs. Note also that a write that sets this bit (1) also causes the BSY bit to be set within 400ns of the write operation.
- nIEN (Interrupt Enable, negative logic) when nIEN is cleared (0), interrupt request generation is enabled within the device, while setting the bit disables interrupt generation.

Figure 1-14: Control Register Contents

7	6	5	4	3	2	1	0
HOB	Resv	Resv	Resv	Resv	SRST	nIEN	0

Alternate Status Register

The Alternate Status register has the same bit field designations as the Status register. The primary difference is that this register does not clear pending interrupts when read as does the regular Status register.

Support for Multiple ATA Interfaces

The previous discussion focused on a single host adapter implementation whose registers were mapped to specific IO locations. As demand for systems with more than two drives emerged, support for multiple host adapters (or interfaces) was defined. This led to standardization of three additional ATA host adapter interfaces. Each interface has specific IO mapping for the Command and Control Blocks and separate interrupt assignments as listed in Table 1-3 on page 29.

Table 1-3: Legacy Task File IO Address Mapping

Channel	Command Block	Control Block	Interrupt Request
Primary	01F0-01F7h	03F6h	IRQ 14
Secondary	0170-0177h	0376h	IRQ 15
Tertiary	01E8 - 01EFh	03EEh	IRQ 11
Quaternary	0168 - 016Fh	036Eh	IRQ 10

Because each of the four ATA bus interfaces supports two ATA drives (one master and one slave), the maximum number of drives supported by legacy software is eight as illustrated in Figure 1-15 on page 30.

Figure 1-15: Legacy Software Supports Up to 8 Drives in a Single System

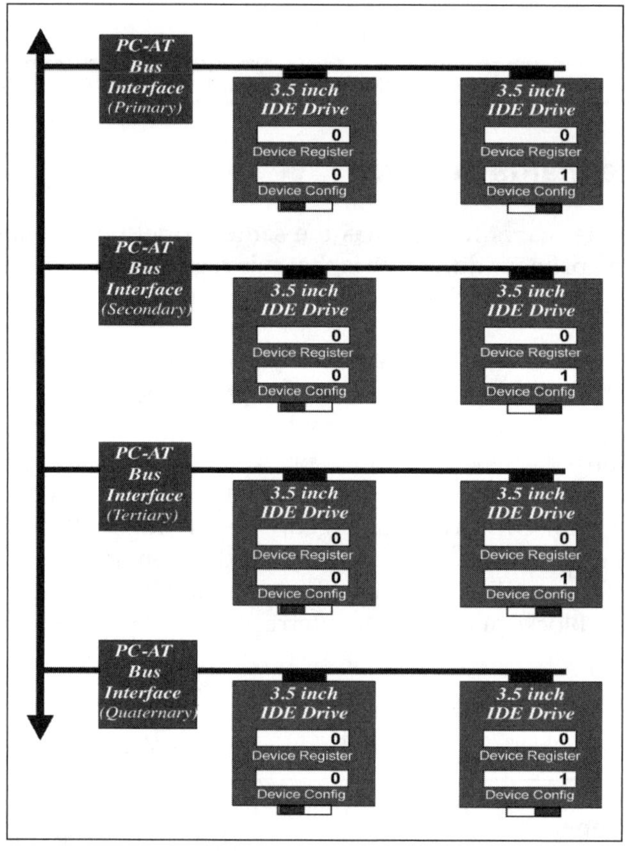

The ATA Packet Interface (ATAPI)

Some ATA devices were developed to support the SCSI command set. The SCSI commands are encapsulated within a block of data referred to as a packet. A special command called a Packet command transports the SCSI command to the device. ATAPI devices include CD-ROM and DVD drives,

Device Signature

Each ATA drive provides a device signature via the register set. Following device reset drives perform their initialization and the execute internal diagnostics. Upon completion of the diagnostics, drives load the ATA registers with the following information:

- Device signature — indicating the device as either an ATA device or an ATAPI device
- Diagnostic results — indicating whether the drive passed the diagnostics.

Figure 1-16 shows the specified register contents for ATA and ATAPI devices. The register values shown are those that identify whether the device is an ATA or ATAPI device, along with diagnostic status information reported in the Error and Status registers. Note that Figure 1-16 illustrates "good" status.

Figure 1-16: ATA and ATAPI Signatures — Register Content

ATA Devices

Register	Value
Data	
Error	01h
Sector Count	01h
Sector Number	01h
Cylinder Low	00h
Cylinder High	00h
Device	00h
Status	00h-70h

ATAPI Devices

Register	Value
Data	
Error	01h
Sector Count	01h
Sector Number	01h
Cylinder Low	14h
Cylinder High	EBh
Device	00h
Status	00h

Performing Commands

Disk operations are performed by setting up, issuing, and executing commands. The nature of the setup depends on the type of command to be performed. Commands are issued by simply writing the appropriate value to the Command register at IO location 01F7h and can generally be categorized as either:

- Commands Without Data Transfer
- Commands With Data Transfer

Note that the ATA specification defines eleven specific command categories. These are detailed in Table 11-1 on page 179.

Setting Up Data Transfers

Some commands require that the task file be initialized prior to issuing a command to the drive. Whether initialization is required and which registers are initialized depends on the particular command to be executed. In addition to task file initialization, DMA commands require the DMA engine to also be initialized.

Commands without Data Transfer. Some of these commands require some setup prior to the command being issued, while others do not. For example, the Set Feature command requires that specific values be written to the Feature register prior to writing the Set Feature command value into the Command register (01F7h).

Data Transfer Commands. Most Data Transfer commands require that the sector start address registers (e.g., LBA registers) and sector count be initialized prior to the command being issued. However, some Data Transfer commands such as the Identify Device Command do not require initialization prior to the command being issued.

Command Execution

When a drive executes a specific command, the actions taken are of course command dependent. However, in every case, completion status is posted in the Status and Error registers. Upon completion of a command, an ATA drive typically issues an interrupt (via the INTRQ line) to notify software to check status. Following are two examples of command delivery and execution; one Non-Data command example and one Data Transfer command example.

Figure 1-17 illustrates a typical Non-Data command being executed that requires no task file initialization. In this case, the command is simply issued to the drive controller, the drive executes the command, and updates the Status register. The example sequence is described in more detail below:

1. Host software issues the non-data command to the host adapter via an IO write transaction that is forwarded on to the drive.
2. The drive updates the command register within ATA (task file).
3. The drive decodes the command, triggering command execution.
4. Upon completing the command, the drive updates the status register to report success or failure of the command. Then the drive notifies software by sending an interrupt request to the host adapter.

5. The interrupt is delivered to the processor, which ultimately fetches the interrupt service routine.
6. The interrupt service routine reads the command's completion status from the ATA registers, thereby completing the command.

Figure 1-17: Flush Cache Command Sequence

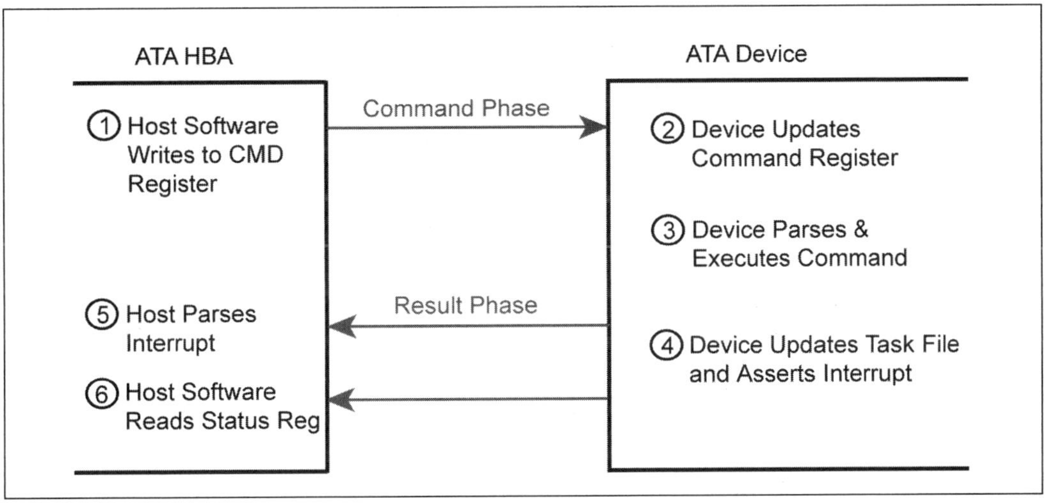

ATA HBA

ATA Device

① Host Software Writes to CMD Register

Command Phase

② Device Updates Command Register

③ Device Parses & Executes Command

⑤ Host Parses Interrupt

Result Phase

④ Device Updates Task File and Asserts Interrupt

⑥ Host Software Reads Status Reg

Figure 1-18 on page 34 illustrates a typical read command execution sequence beginning with register initialization as follows:

1. Host adapter forwards IO write transactions to the drive, causing
2. drive to update the ATA (task file) registers.
3. Host adapter forwards an IO write targeting the Command register
4. The drive decodes the command, triggering command execution
5. ATA drive processes the command and initiates the data transfer and notifies software by sending an interrupt to the HBA.
6. The HBA forwards the interrupt across the IO bus (e.g., PCI)
7. Upon command completion the ATA drive updates completion status within the ATA registers and generates an interrupt to notify host software.
8. The HBA forwards the interrupt, calling the interrupt service routing
9. The interrupt service routine reads good status from the ATA registers and the command is retired.

Figure 1-18: Parallel ATA Data Command Sequence

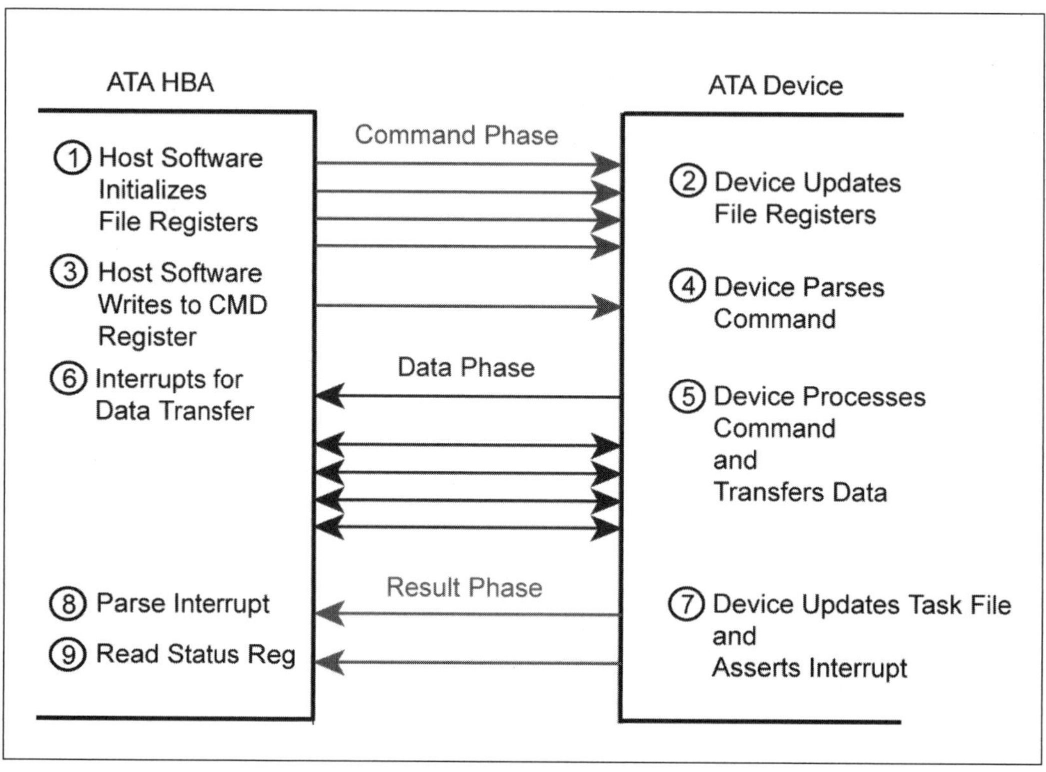

Overlap and Command Queuing

ATA4 introduced the concept of overlap and command queuing. These features were initially not widely used but are critical in some SATA command protocols.

Overlap

Overlap provides a method for drives to relinquish ownership of the shared ATA interface. For example, a slower ATAPI CD ROM drive could release the bus while processing a command; thereby making it possible for software to issue a command to a faster ATA drive. Thus, two commands overlap allowing simultaneous command processing.

A bus release is accomplished via a combination of hardware and software. First, software knows whether a drive supports the overlap feature via the Identify Device command that returns device capability information. Software may choose to enable this feature within the drive. Once overlap is enabled and upon receiving a command, the drive can release the bus by setting and clear the appropriate bit fields within the ATA Status register. Subsequently, software will poll the device to see if it has released the bus. If so, a command can be set up and issued to the other device. Software continues to poll both devices to determine which completes first.

Support for overlap is limited to small group of commands, including:

- NOP (with a subcommand code other than 00h)
- Packet
- Read DMA Queued
- Read DMA Queued Ext
- Service
- Write DMA Queued
- Write DMA Queued Ext
- Write DMA Queued FUA Ext

Queuing

A drive that supports queuing must also support the overlap feature. Queuing is a variation of the concept of overlay in that a disc drive may choose to release the bus as a way of notifying software that it is ready to receive another command. Once host software issued a DMA Queued command it is expected to poll the drive to detect that it has released the bus, and is therefore ready to receive a subsequent command that supports overlap.

Drives Capabilities - The Device Identify Command

A variety of features such as overlap and queuing are optional features that may or may not be supported by a drive. In addition, the ATA/ATAPI specifications have dramatically improved drive performance through a series of ATA interface protocols and modes of operation. Software can detect a drive's capabilities by reading its configuration information via the Device Identify command. The specification defines the content and format of the data returned when the command is executed. Note that much of the information returned by a Serial ATA drive conforms to the information provided by parallel ATA drive, thus providing compatibility with software written for the parallel drives. However, most of the ATA-related information from the parallel implementations have no meaning for a SATA drive.

Summary of ATA Standards

Table 1-4 summarizes the history of ATA including the year in which the standard was written.

Table 1-4: ATA Progression

Standard	Year	Speed	Key Features
NA	1986		Pre-Standard
ATA	1994		PIO modes 0-2 Multi word DMA mode 0
ATA-2	1996	16MB/sec	PIO modes 3-4 Multiwarhead DMA modes 1-2 Logical Block Address (LBA)
ATA-3	1997		SMART
ATA/ATAPI-4	1998	33MB/sec	Ultra DMA modes 0-2 Data CRC, overlap, queuing 80-wire cable
ATA/ATAPI-5	2000	66MB/sec	Ultra DMA modes 3-4
ATA/ATAPI-6	2002	100MB/sec	Ultra DMA mode 5 48-bit LBA
ATA/ATAPI-7	2003	133MB/sec	Ultra DMA mode 6

2 The Motivation for SATA

Previous Chapter

Background information regarding the parallel ATA (PATA) implementations is important to understanding the Serial ATA (SATA) implementation. The SATA design provides compatibility with the PATA legacy programming interface and with the commands defined for PATA. The previous chapter provides a base level of information as a review and or a primer on the parallel implementation.

This Chapter

This chapter introduces the motivation for implementing a serial version of ATA. Many recognized shortcomings of PATA are addressed in the SATA implementation. The chapter identified the problems with PATA and described the solution provided by SATA.

The Next Chapter

The next chapter provides a comprehensive overview of the SATA features and protocols.

Motivation and Design Goals for SATA

ATA, like so many other IO interfaces, now has a high-speed serial interface. Many compelling reasons led to this serial interface including the need for:

- Lower pin count
- Higher performance
- Simple drive configuration
- Better cables/connectors
- Greater reliability
- Low voltage support
- Migration to more server implementations

An extremely important aspect of a serial interface implementation is to maintain software compatibility with ATA. The following sections discuss the problems with Parallel ATA (PATA) and how SATA solves these problems, while maintaining software compatibility.

Lower Pin Count

The parallel ATA (PATA) implementation includes a large number of pins as illustrated in Figure 1-5 on page 16 (Chapter 1). Note that some of these pins are not used today or are not required, leaving 26 signal pins that are required. The problems with high pin count are numerous:

- high cost of implementing larger chips to accommodate the high pin count on both drives and HBA
- more board space taken up due to high pin count
- the 40 pin connectors take up much space and are costly
- cables take up more space, are costly, cumbersome to route, and inhibit air flow through a system

In short, many problems associated with PATA result directly from the high pin count. A serial interface with fewer pins solves many of the PATA-related problems. See Chapter 20, entitled "Cables & Connectors," on page 361 for details.

Performance

PATA implementations are limited by the physical connectors and cables originally used in conjunction with the IBM PC-AT bus that operated at transmission rates of 8MB/sec. Today PATA operates at transmission rates of 133MB/sec. To accomplish the higher PATA transmission rates ground pins are inserted between each signal, thereby doubling the connector size to 80 pins. Further increases in performance using the PATA cables and connectors will be more than difficult.

PATA's limited transmission capability is not suitable for the next generation of hard drives that will require much higher transmission rates. SATA's high-speed serial interface operates at 1.5Gbits/sec, which yields a maximum transmission rate of 150MB/sec (Generation 1). The second generation of SATA doubles the transmission rate to 300MB/sec and plans exist to increase performance even further.

No Drive Configuration Required

As described in "Support for Two Drives" on page 11, ATA drives required configuration jumpers to support two drives that share the same ATA bus. One drive must be selected as drive zero and the other as drive one. Failure to set the drives correctly typically prevent either drive from working.

There is no need for Drive Select switch/jumper on SATA drives because each drive resides on its own bus. Each SATA drive responds only as drive 0.

Cables and Connectors

PATA cables and connectors have many short comings including: high pin count that adds to their cost, increases space requirements, cables are cumbersome to manage, typical cable length is limited to 18 inches. In addition to these issues, PATA connectors use pin connections that are prone to bending and difficult to plug in the best of conditions. Finally, PATA connectors have no support for hot plugging. Figure Figure 2-1 contrasts the PATA and SATA drives and connectors.

Figure 2-1: Comparison of SATA and PATA Connectors

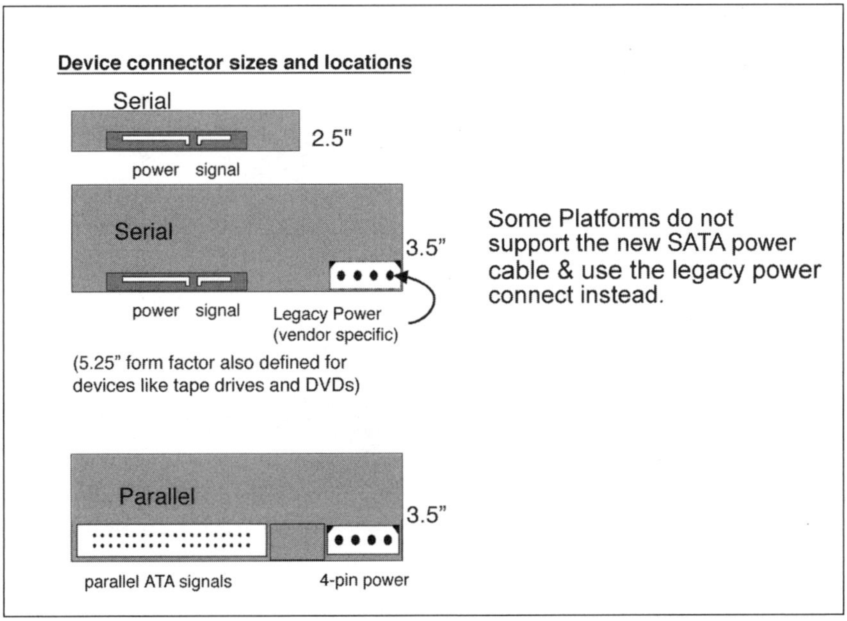

The SATA cable and connectors have the following characteristics that improve upon PATA:

- Signal cable has 7 conductors (two differential pair for noise immunity and three ground pins).
- SATA maximum cable length specified by the 1.0a standard is 1 meter (39.37 inches) compared with 18 inches for PATA.
- SATA cables are smaller, easier to manage, and less costly than the PATA solution.
- Connectors have contacts rather than pins.
- Connectors designed for easy connection, sometimes called blind mating.
- Connectors designed to support Hot Plug (aka, Hot Docking).
- SATA connectors are more easily adapted to backplane implementations

Figure 2-2 illustrates the SATA device (drive) connector and the connector at the Host Adapter. The connections can be made directly such that a drive can be plugged into a bay in backplane fashion or a cable can be routed between the two connectors. See Chapter 20, entitled "Cables & Connectors," on page 361 for additional information.

Figure 2-2: SATA DATA and Power Connectors

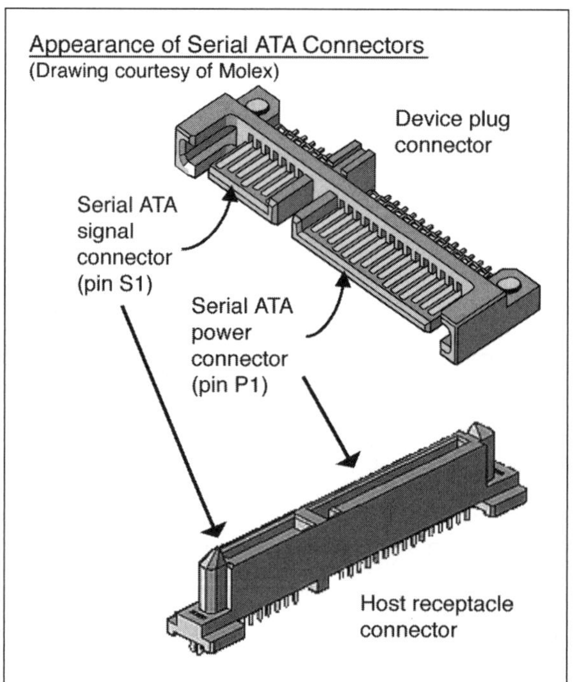

Reliability

The ATA bus does not incorporate any native transmission-related error detection and reporting capability. However, the UltraDMA transfers operating at transmission rates of 33Mhz and higher do support CRC error checking, but only during the transmission of data.

In contrast, every packet of information sent across the SATA bus includes a Cyclic Redundancy Check (CRC). These checks are designed to detect every single and double-bit error that occurs. There exists an extremely high probability that CRC will detect virtually every error.

When an error is detected the hardware is designed to perform an automatic retry, by sending the failed packet again. This retry mechanism is supported for all packet types except data packets. This restriction is due to the very large data packet size (up to 8KB) that would need to be buffered at the interface to support the retry mechanism. The large buffer size competes with the goal of keeping drive costs low, and therefore data packet retry is not supported.

Lower Voltages

As silicon manufacturing process sizes became smaller, they also require smaller voltages. Because the ATA signaling was done at 5 volts, it is not suitable for these smaller processes.

In contrast, SATA's signal voltages have been lowered to 0.7 volts. This permits much smaller drive interface chips, as well as reducing power.

Migration to Servers

ATA drives are compelling for server applications primarily due to the low price/megabyte of storage when compared with SCSI and Fibre drives. Many of the shortcomings associated with ATA drives can be mitigated with RAID implementations. RAID can provide additional flexibility, reliability and improve overall performance. The parallel interface limitations of two drives/cable, no hot docking support, and lack of support for other server-related features such as dual ported drives, make ATA server implementations problematic.

SATA drives improve on the ATA server environment in a variety of ways. RAID implementations coupled with the SATA enhancements can improve performance significantly over ATA and provide comparable performance to SCSI systems in some cases. A number of server-related features were introduced with the SATA II specification:

10. Improved performance via the 3.0Gb/sec high-speed serial interface
11. Port Multipliers that allow a single HBA port to support up to 15 drives
12. Port Selectors that provide dual-ported functionality
13. Hot Docking support
14. Drives with Native Command Queuing
15. Support for Enclosure Services and Management

Another potentially important issue is that Serial Attached SCSI (SAS) connectors permit attachment of SATA drives, and supports the SATA protocol.

Software Compatibility with Parallel ATA

A major goal associated with the SATA implementation is to preserve much of the existing investment in firmware and software as implementers transition to SATA.

SATA is designed to be backwardly compatible with ATA legacy software. To support this compatibility the ATA Task File registers (See "The Legacy Programming Interface" on page 19) are also implemented in SATA. When software performs the IO writes to set up and execute an ATA command, the SATA Host Adapter and drive perform the command just as it would have done in ATA, albeit via a different interface protocol. While the details of how protocol is implemented changes with SATA, the end result is the same from legacy software's perspective.

From a purist's perspective, SATA is not completely compatible with legacy software. For example, older versions of Windows designed to run early version of ATA may not work with SATA implementations. Some of the more jaded observers may even view the SATA implementation as SATAnical! The author will try to avoid this type of silly expression in the future.

3 SATA Overview

Previous Chapter

The previous chapter introduced the motivation for implementing a serial version of ATA. Many recognized shortcomings of PATA were addressed by the SATA implementation. The chapter identified these shortcomings and described the solution provided by SATA.

This Chapter

This overview provides a conceptual understanding of the operation of the SATA interface. This includes the basics of how SATA communication is handled and the primary functions of each layer as defined by the specification. How SATA maintains software compatibility with parallel ATA is also covered in this chapter, along with the new features introduced by the SATA II extension.

The Next Chapter

Communications across the SATA interface consist primarily of transferring Frame Information Structures (FISes). A FIS may deliver shadow or ATA register contents, data, control information, etc. This chapter introduces the reader to the basics of the FIS transmission protocol. Subsequent chapters detail the protocol further and discuss variations due to flow control requirements, errors, and related issues.

The SATA Specification

The SATA specification is developed and maintained by the Serial ATA International Organization. Member companies can download the spec from www.sata-io.org. Non-member companies must pay a fee (currently $25) in order to download a copy.

SATA version 2.6 was the latest version of the specification at the time of printing. The generic terms SATA I and SATA II are used in this book to describe the features defined by the first and second generations of SATA. It's important to note that while the SATA II features include the 3.0Gb/s transmission rates, drives based on the latest version of the specification can operate at either 1.5Gb/s or 3.0Gb/s. Furthermore, most of the features introduced by SATA II are supported at both transmission rates.

Summary of SATA Features

The last chapter introduced the major shortcomings of ATA and the improvements made by Serial ATA. Table 3-1 contains a more comprehensive list of features associated with the SATA implementations.

Table 3-1: Summary of Major SATA Features

Feature	Description
Serial Interface	The serial interface consists of two differential pairs for bi-directional signaling.
Scalable Performance	Transmission rates of 1.5Gb/s and 3.0Gb/s.
ATA Commands	Support for existing ATA commands.
Low Voltage Signaling	Signaling is performed at low differential voltages: 500mV peak-to-peak.
Improved Cable & Connectors	Implementation of thin flexible cable with maximum length of 1 meter and connectors that provide blind mating capability.
Error Detection and Retry	Each packet, or more properly, each Frame includes CRC generation and checking. CRC generation covers only the Frame Information Structure. CRC errors detected by the receiver are reported back to the transmitting node, perhaps resulting in an automatic re-transmission of the FIS (Frame Information Structure) via a hardware retry mechanism.
Link Power Management	The SATA serial interface can be placed into low power modes following lengthy periods of idle and can quickly recover to normal power and operation.

Table 3-1: Summary of Major SATA Features

Feature	Description
Hot Plug Support	SATA ports can optionally provide support for hot plugging drives. The SATA connector is designed so that 3 contact points can be implemented (1. ground pins, 2. current-limited power, 3. other power and signals) to support hot plugging drives.
Asynchronous Event Notification	Drives and port interfaces can signal the host of events that take place. As an example, a CD-ROM drive could report a CD ejection event to the host adapter.
Full Support for Native Command Queuing	Detailed protocols and new commands are defined to support Native Command Queuing (NCQ) on SATA II drives and hosts. NCQ permits drives to queue up to 32 commands and execute them in the order that will result in the best overall performance.
Port Multipliers	These devices expand the number of ports for attaching and accessing larger numbers of drives via a single HBA port.
Port Selectors	These devices permit two hosts to gain access to the same port/drive to allow fail-over implementations.
Enclosure Services	SATA defines the devices and structure for managing heat, power, error conditions, etc. related to large drive bays and other enclosure types.

The Serial Interconnect

Serial ATA defines a high-speed serial connection between the Host Adapter and each Drive. The SATA I version of the specification defined the transmission rate of 1.5Gb/s (Generation 1) and the SATA II specification increased the transmission rate to 3Gb/s (providing support for both speeds). The maximum bandwidth is easily calculated because each byte transmitted is a 10-bit value as a result of 8-bit to 10-bit encoding.

Gen 1 speed = 150MB/s
Gen 2 speed = 300MB/s

The SATA interface consists of 2 differential pairs implemented at the HBA port and at the SATA device. However, the SATA implementation is very different from high-speed serial bus implementations that operate in the dual simplex mode where data transfers can be performed in both directions simultaneously. The SATA implementation is based on a half duplex scheme where transfers can be performed in only one direction at a time. SATA implements one differential pair for transmission of data and the other pair for feedback from the receiving device. As illustrated in Figure 3-1 on page 46, the transmitting node (either Host or Device) obtains current transmission status from the receiving node (via the back bus) as the packet (also called a FIS) is delivered.

Figure 3-1: SATA Serial Bus Implementation

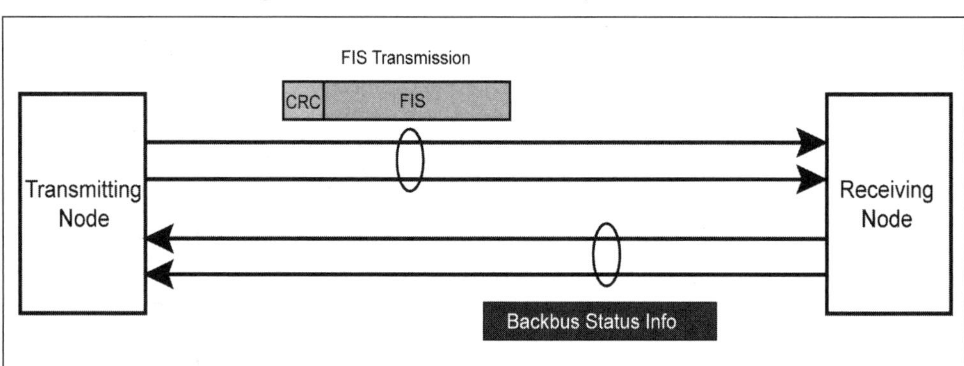

SATA Compatibility with Parallel ATA

SATA's software compatibility allows an improved hardware implementation without requiring a huge amount of new firmware and software. This goal places the burden on the hardware design to ensure compatible operation with PATA software. The following sections discuss several areas of software compatiblility.

The Legacy Programming Interface

The primary element of software compatibility is of course the ATA programming interface. Figure 3-2 on page 47 conceptualizes the approach taken by SATA to provide legacy programming support versus that of parallel ATA. Recall that ATA host adapters merely forward IO reads and writes, which originate from the CPU, across the ATA cable to the drive's registers (task file). In SATA implementations, a duplicate copy of the Task File, called "shadow registers," is located in the host adapter. Once software has loaded the shadow register, the HBA sends the register contents to the drive via a packet called a "Frame Information Structure" or FIS. All information exchanged between the SATA HBA and SATA drive is done serially via these Frame Information Structures.

Figure 3-2: Task File Implementations ATA vs. SATA

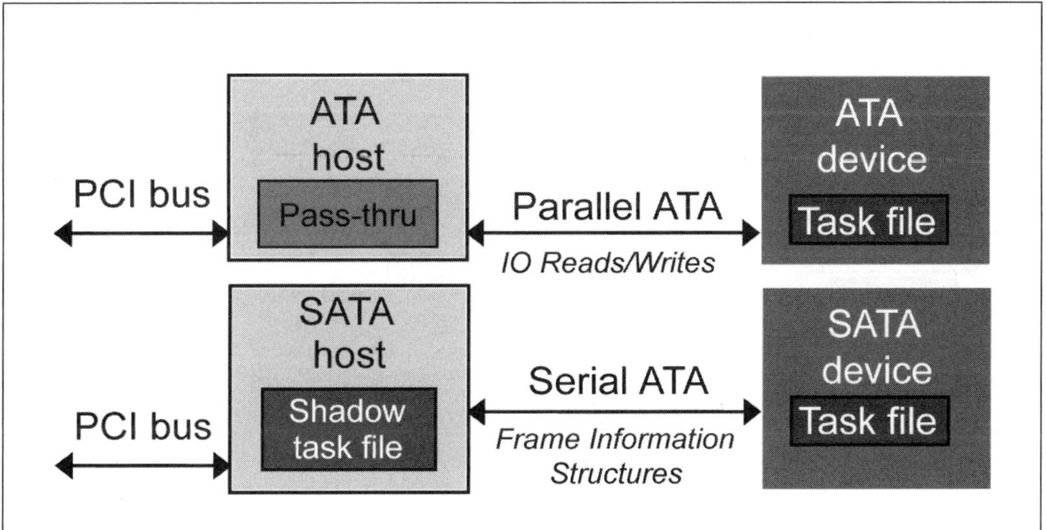

Refer to Figure 3-3 on page 48 for a more detailed view of the HBA and SATA drive implementation. Note that legacy software is unaware that its IO accesses do not directly target the task file within the drive. Consider the normal process of software initializing the shadow registers and issuing an ATA command to the drive for execution. When software issues the command by writing to the command register, this triggers the SATA HBA to perform the following sequence of events:

1. The SATA HBA sends a packet containing the entire contents of the shadow register (called a Register FIS) to the drive via the high-speed serial link.
2. The drive receives the Register FIS and updates its registers with the FIS contents.
3. Next, the drive parses and processes the command.

As the command is processed, the drive and HBA exchange a particular sequence of FISes needed to fulfill the command. This may include transferring data and concluding with the drive reporting command completion to the HBA by returning a Register FIS with completion status or error information. Note that the actual type and number of FISes exchanged between the HBA and SATA drive during command execution is command dependent.

More detailed examples of command execution in the SATA environment are shown in the section entitled "SATA Command Protocol" on page 61.

Figure 3-3: SATA Interface with Shadow Registers (HBA) and Task File (Device)

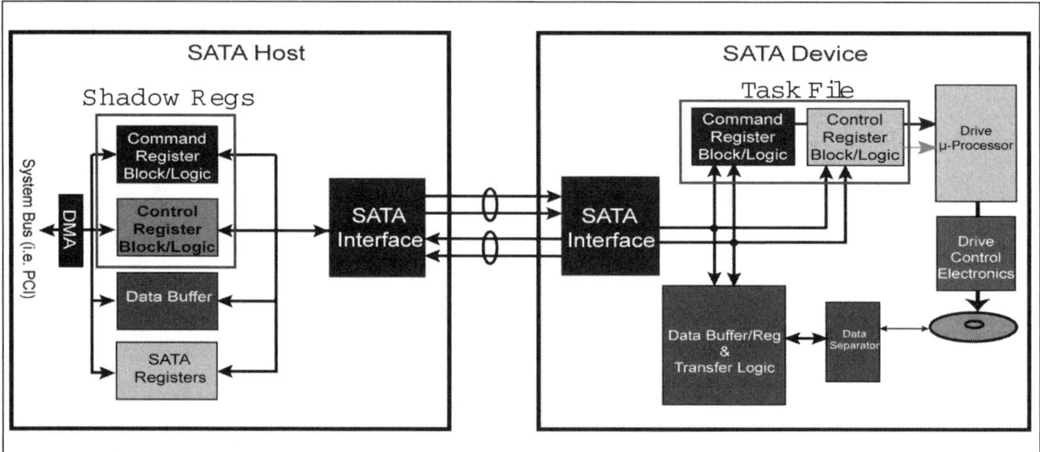

Legacy Drive Addressing with SATA

Parallel ATA supports up to four standard ATA host adapter interfaces in a single system. Each interface has specific IO mapping for the Command and Control Blocks and for interrupt assignments. Refer to the section entitled, "Support for Multiple ATA Interfaces" on page 29 for a review of ATA's standard interfaces.

Because each of the four ATA bus interfaces supports two ATA drives (one master and one slave), the maximum number of drives supported by legacy software is eight, as illustrated in Figure 3-4 on page 49. However, SATA drives connected to dedicated HBA ports respond to drive address zero (master) only. This limits the maximum number of drives that legacy software can access to one per legacy interface, unless the SATA HBAs are designed to emulate Master/Slave operation. These options are reviewed in the following two sections.

Figure 3-4: Legacy Software Supports Up to 8 Drives in a Single System

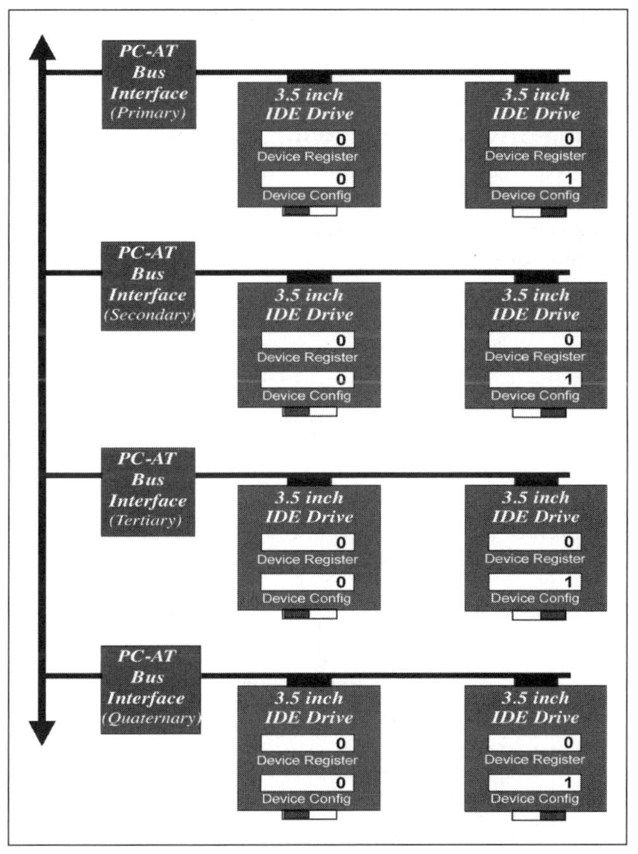

Drive Addressing Based on Single Drive Interfaces

A SATA HBA could support legacy addressing by supporting four sets of Shadow Registers mapped to the legacy IO locations. Without Master/Slave emulation only four SATA drives could be accessed by legacy software.

Port Selection Based on Master/Slave Emulation

The heading entitled "Device Register - Selecting the Target ATA Device" on page 21 describes the method used to address two devices in ATA. In summary, this technique requires that each device be assigned a unique address, usually via jumpers on the ATA devices. One device must be set to address zero (the master) and the other to one (the slave). Because both devices reside on the same bus, the task file registers within both devices receive the same programming. The device register contents select the target device based on whether a value of 0 or 1 is placed in the device select bit.

In SATA Master/Slave emulation the HBA must designate which SATA drive will be treated as 0 and which will be treated as 1. Figure 3-5 depicts a two port HBA supporting drive emulation with a single primary interface. Only one of the port interfaces will be accessed at a time based upon:

- the HBA's hardware designation of which port will be targeted as device 0 and which as device 1, and
- the state of the device selection bit.

This hardware emulation permits two SATA drives to be accessed as if they both reside on the same bus. The specification provides no standardized hardware implementation for this emulation.

Figure 3-5: SATA HBA Emulation of Standard ATA Device Addressing

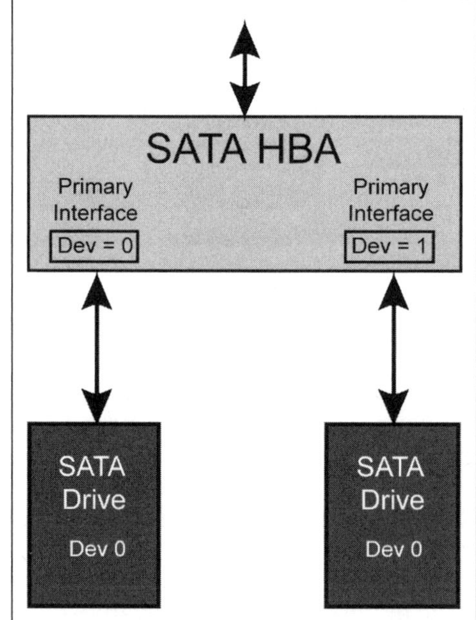

SATA-Specific Registers

SATA I defines a group of three Status and Control Registers (SCRs) that pertain specifically to the SATA interface, and SATA II adds two additional registers. These registers are implemented in host-side port interfaces. That is, in host adapter port interfaces (Figure 3-6 on page 51) and in the port interfaces of port multipliers (Figure 3-20 on page 67).

SATA I

- SStatus Register (SCR 0) — The SATA status register reports connection status, connection speed, and link power state.
- SError Register (SCR 1) — The SATA error register is segmented into two groups; error reporting based on severity and error reporting for diagnostic purposes.
- SControl Register (SCR 2) — This register controls link power transitions, resetting the link, forcing link speed changes.

SATA II

- SActive Register (SCR 3) — Used to support Native Command Queueing by tracking transactions that have been issued to the drive but not yet completed.
- SNotification Register (SCR 4) — Identifies which drive/port signaled an asynchronous event.

Figure 3-6 also lists the control register space from SCR 5 to SCR 15 that are reserved for future expansion.

Figure 3-6: SATA SCRs (within HBA)

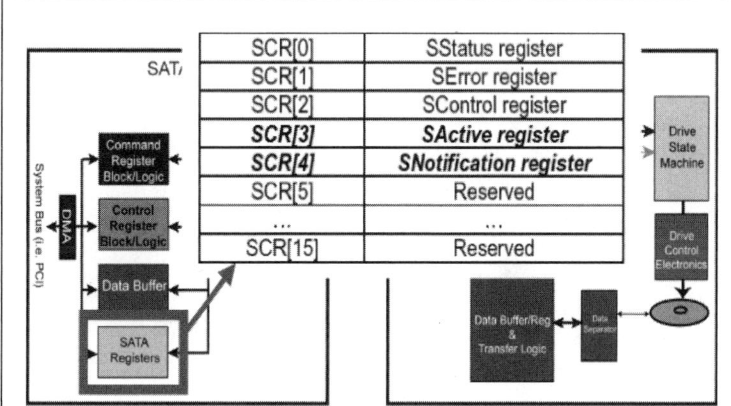

SATA Protocol Layer Overview

SATA protocol is defined by the specification as a series of layers. The list below introduces each layer and explains its primary functions.

- **Application layer** — consists of the programming interface to the SATA environment. In legacy implementations this is represented by the register set (Shadow Registers in the HBA). In the AHCI implementations the programming interface consists of a combination of the Shadow registers, HBA-specific registers and memory data structures located in main DRAM.
- **Command layer** — defines the sequence of FISs to be exchanged between the host adapter and the drive during command execution. Based on the command type and type of packet received the command layer determines the next packet to send and initiates its delivery, if a response is required.
- **Transport layer** — formats and requests transmission of FISs, manages flow control, detects FIS errors and retries some FIS transmission failures, and decodes each FIS received.
- **Link layer** — generates and receives primitives used in the link protocol. Responsible for preparing each Frame Information Structures (FIS) for transmission, decoding primitives, detecting transmission errors, etc.
- **Physical layer** — consists of the link transceiver used to send and receive all SATA link traffic, performs link initialization, link power management, and Hot Plug operations.

Figure 3-7 on page 53 illustrates the hierarchy of the layers. The following discussions describe the functions of each layer from the legacy software perspective. To contrast these actions with those performed when the AHCI controller is used, see "The AHCI Programming Interface" on page 69.

Figure 3-7: SATA Protocol Layers

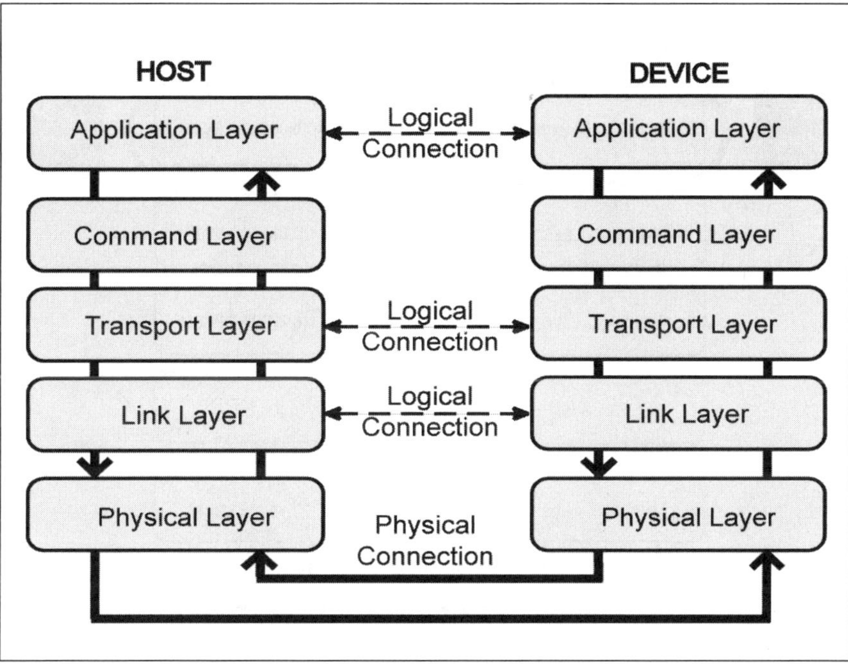

Application Layer

Communications across the SATA interface consist primarily of transferring Frame Information Structures (FISes). A FIS can be delivered from the HBA to the drive or from the drive to the HBA, and it may contain shadow or ATA register contents, data, control information, etc. In general, a FIS originates at the Application layer and is received by the Application layer at the opposite end of the link. Fig shows Application layer at the top of the hierarchy for both the HBA and SATA drive.

Figure 3-8: Application Layer Provides SATA Programming Interface

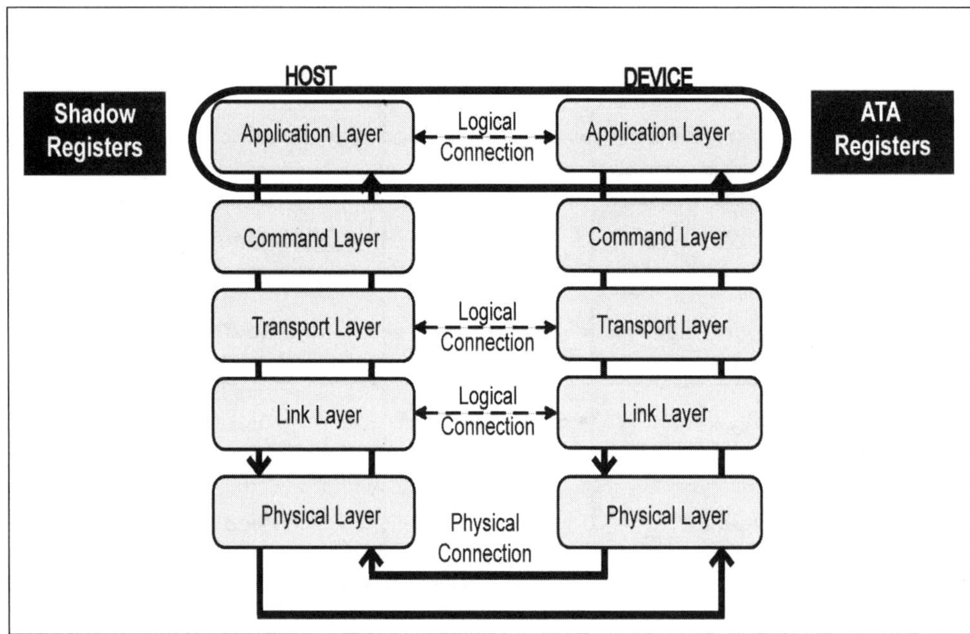

Host Software Issues each Command

Registers within the SATA host adapter must be initialized by host software when a command is to be performed. Depending on the command being issued by software, two groups of registers may need to be configured:

- DMA Registers (when a DMA command is being issued)
- Legacy ATA Registers

In SATA a copy of the legacy ATA registers, called "shadow registers" is kept in the Host Adapter. Host software initializes the shadow registers as required for the particular command to be issued. Software then issues the command by writing its corresponding value to the command register, which is also part of the shadow registers. This action causes the SATA Application layer to forward the shadow register contents to the Transport layer. This information must be forwarded to the drive where the actual ATA registers reside within the drive's Application layer. The logical communication shown between the application layers of the host and device promotes the concept of information being passed between the shadow registers and the ATA registers.

The SATA Drive Receives and Processes the Command

When the SATA Drive receives a FIS containing a new command, it processes the command, and once the command has completed, it forwards the contents of its ATA registers to the Shadow registers within the HBA's Application layer to report final status.

During command processing the HBA and the drive may exchange a number of FISes. When a FIS is received the contents of one or more registers within the Application layer are generally changed. In this way, the HBA and drive communicate and exchange information as a command is executed.

Command Layer

When commands are delivered and executed in a SATA implementation, two or more FISs are typically exchanged between the host and drive. The type and sequence of FISs exchanged is a function of the command being performed. The command layer is responsible for managing the high-level protocol, by verifying receipt of the expected FIS and by issuing any subsequent FIS to be returned in response. The command layer state machine defines the appropriate action required for each command type. The Application and Command layers are closely coupled and one could consider the Command layer as being part of the Application layer functionality.

Transport Layer

Requests to transmit a Frame Information Structure may come from the Application layer or the from command layer. In either case, the Transport layer is responsible for creating a compliant FIS. Figure 3-9 on page 56 depicts the Application layer sending shadow register contents to the Transport layer to initiate a command. The FIS created by the Transport layer is called a Register FIS - Host to Device because it contains the contents of the shadow registers that must be forwarded to the drive.

FISs are stored in small buffers within the Transport layer. This buffering supports retries of most FISs in the event of transmission errors. Note the logical connection between the Transport layers in Figure 3-9. This connection represents the movement of a FIS from a transmit buffer in the transaction layer at one side of the link to the receive buffer in the transaction layer at the opposite side. Note also that the Transport layers use a flow control mechanism to ensure these buffers do not overflow or underflow.

Figure 3-9: Transport Layer Creates and Decodes each FIS

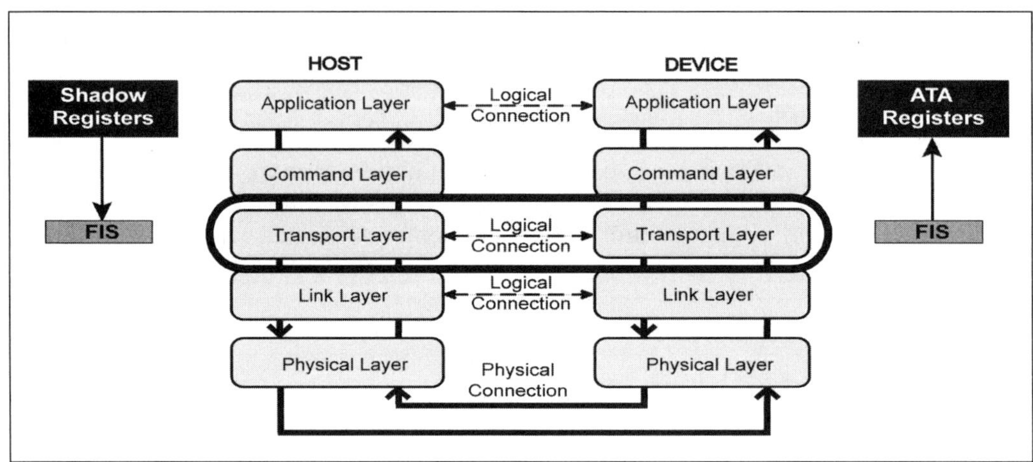

The format and contents of the 20 byte Register FIS is illustrated in Figure 3-10. Note that the FIS ID is 27h, several byte and bit fields are reserved and the other fields contain the contents of the ATA command and Control register fields. Notice that the fields in Figure 3-10 contain the legacy register names for backward reference as done in the 1.0a specification. For example, the diagram uses the Cylinder/Head/Sector convention for specifying the starting disc address. Figure 3-11 on page 57 shows the contents of the same Register FIS with the LBA labels, which are used in the later versions of the SATA specification.

Figure 3-10: Format and Contents of the Register FIS - Host to Device

	+3	+2	+1	+0
	7 6 5 4 3 2 1 0	7 6 5 4 3 2 1 0	7 6 5 4 3 2 1 0	7 6 5 4 3 2 1 0
DW 0	Features	Command	C R R Reserved	FIS Type (27h)
DW 1	Dev/Head	Cyl High	Cyl Low	Sector Number
DW 2	Features (exp)	Cyl High (exp)	Cyl Low (exp)	Sec Num (exp)
DW 3	Control	Reserved (0)	Sec Count (exp)	Sector Count
DW 4	Reserved (0)	Reserved (0)	Reserved (0)	Reserved (0)

Figure 3-11: Register FIS - Host to Device showing the LBA Field Definitions

	+3 (bits 7–0)	+2 (bits 7–0)	+1 (bits 7–0)	+0 (bits 7–0)
DW 0	Features	Command	C R R Reserved	FIS Type (27h)
DW 1	Device	LBA High	LBA Middle	LBA Low
DW 2	Features (exp)	LBA High (exp)	LBA Mid (exp)	LBA Low (exp)
DW 3	Control	Reserved (0)	Sec Count (exp)	Sector Count
DW 4	Reserved (0)	Reserved (0)	Reserved (0)	Reserved (0)

Link Layer

The Link Layer essentially manages the FIS transmission protocol. A major part of this protocol is generating and decoding small packets called primitives. These primitives are employed in a variety of ways to facilitate link transmission protocol, including:

- Indicate beginning and end of each FIS
- Bus arbitration
- FIS transmission status
- Flow control
- Link power management
- Clock compensation

Figure 3-12 on page 58 depicts the transmission of a packet from host to drive. Notice that the FIS shown adjacent to the link layers includes Start and End primitives that inform the receiver of the packet boundaries. Each primitive consists of a 4 byte packet of information that is generated within the Link layer and decoded by the receiver's Link layer.

The receiver detects these primitives and removes them from the FIS at the Link layer. Figure 3-13 on page 58 illustrates the format of a SOF primitive that is placed at the very beginning of the FIS. Note the values shown are the 10-bit encoded values. Details regarding the protocol and use of the various primitives are covered in subsequent chapters.

Figure 3-12: Link Layer Manages Link Protocol via Primitive Generation/Reception

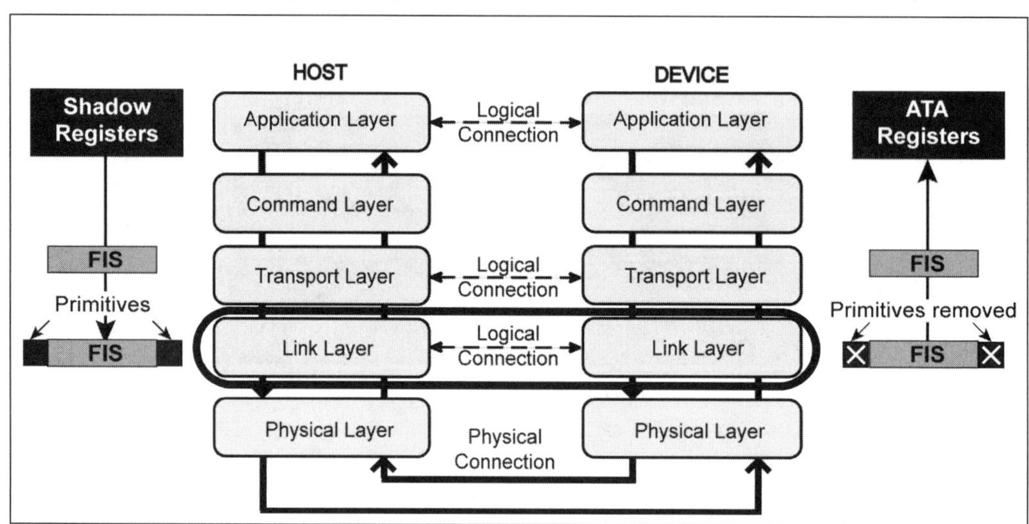

Figure 3-13: Example Primitive (SOF)

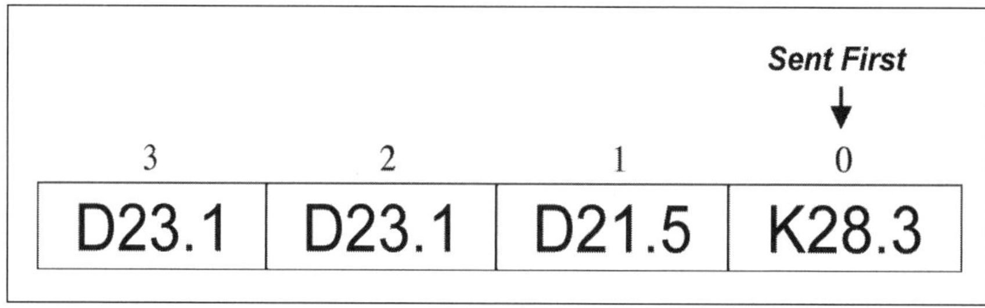

Physical Layer

This layer resides hierarchically at the bottom of the SATA layered architecture (see Figure 3-14 on page 59) and performs two general roles:

1. Establishing link communications following reset (via Out of Band, or OOB signaling)
2. Transmit and receive FIS and primitive traffic

Figure 3-14: Physical Layer Manages Link initialization and Transmits/Receives FIS Traffic

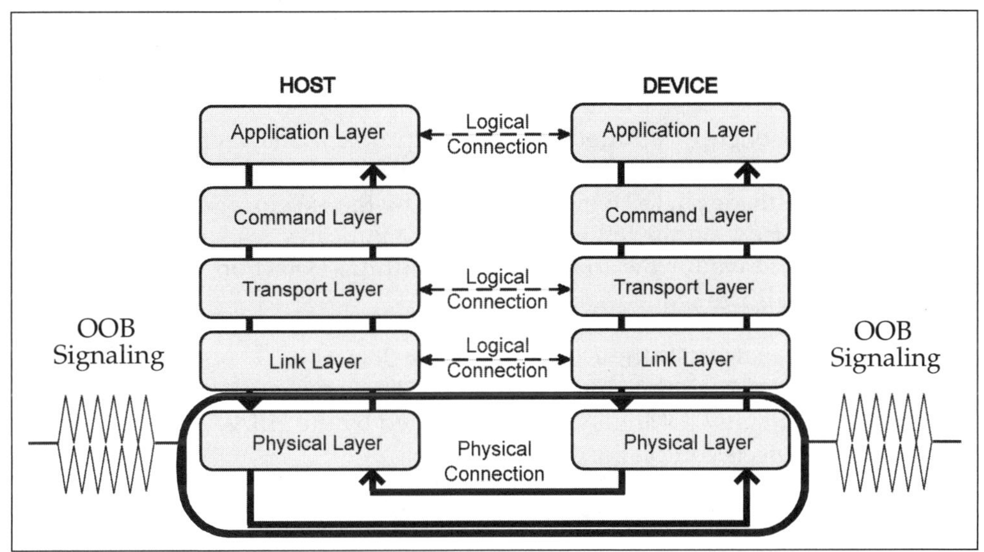

Establishing Link Communications

After reset, the hardware in devices on both ends of a link automatically begins the process of detecting whether another device is present and at what speed the interface can run. This initialization takes place using OOB (out of band) signaling even before the devices are able to recognize dwords as information from the transmitter. OOB uses the same signal path as every other bit from the transmitter, meaning they are not side-band signals, but occurs before the link is trained. Following OOB signaling the link is trained or synchronized to the incoming bit streams. When link initialization is completed the target device delivers a FIS to the host to identify itself.

OOB Signaling

Like most serial bus implementations, the physical layer in SATA is also responsible for establishing link communications immediately following hardware reset. In SATA this process begins with OOB signaling. Figure 3-14 illustrates the OOB burst consisting of six bursts of differential signaling followed by specified periods of electrical idle prior to the next sequence of 6 bursts. Because this signaling occurs following hardware reset, the receivers at both ends of the link will not yet be synchronized to the incoming traffic stream. This means that the bursts will not be detected by the normal receive logic and are therefore Out Of Band relative to normal in-band signaling. Instead the OOB bursts and idle periods are detected via squelch detection logic. This OOB sequence detects the presence of a SATA device and is used in other circumstances such as recovery from link power management states.

The OOB sequence captured by a SATA protocol analyzer in Figure 3-15 on page 60 simply shows the analyzer detecting beginning and end of each OOB event. Note that each OOB event is named by the specification and listed on the trace. The arrow on the left side of the trace indicates whether the HBA (arrow to right) or Drive (arrow to left) is transmitting. Detection, of course, is at the opposite end. The sequence is as follows:

1. HBA signals COMRESET and the drive detects it
2. Drive detects completion of COMRESET
3. Drive signals COMINIT and it is detected by the HBA
4. HBA detects completion of COMINIT
5. HBA signals COMWAKE and it is detected by the drive
6. Drive detects completion of COMWAKE
7. Drive signals COMWAKE and the HBA detects it
8. HBA detects completion of COMWAKE and enters Link initialization
9. Drive enters Link initialization in response (step 9 not shown)

Figure 3-15: OOB Sequence From SATA Protocol Analyzer

		Link	Bus Condition
→	H1 787.946.666 (us)	5	COMRESET Detected
→	H1 789.333.333 (us)	6	COMRESET Completed
←	D1 791.066.666 (us)	7	COMINIT Detected
←	D1 792.426.666 (us)	8	COMINIT Completed
→	H1 793.760 (us)	9	COMWAKE Detected
→	H1 794.373.333 (us)	10	COMWAKE Completed
←	D1 795.360 (us)	11	COMWAKE Detected
←	D1 795.946.666 (us)	12	COMWAKE Completed

Link initialization

Following the OOB signaling sequence, transmitters at each end of the link transmit continuous streams of data designed to facilitate synchronization by the receivers. The first step in initialization is the receiver synchronizing to the incoming bit stream (sometimes called "establishing bit lock"). The second step is achieving alignment with the 10-bit encoded bytes being transmitted. The entire synchronization and alignment process is accomplished through the transmission and reception of continuos streams of ALIGN primitives. Note that during this process speed determination is also performed. Once the link is trained normal in-band communications begin. Chapter 18, on page 303, details the link initialization process.

Normal FIS Communications

After all the work has been done in the upper layers of the SATA interface to create a FIS for transmission, the Physical Layer is the final piece of logic that this packet will pass through. This layer resides hierarchically at the bottom of the SATA layered architecture and performs two general functions:

- Prepares data for transmission/reception — this first part represents the logic needed to prepare the data for transmission (e.g., serialization of data) or to recover it properly at the receiver (e.g., deserialization of data and clock recovery).
- Transmits/receives data — this second part consists of the high-speed electrical interface that comprises the differential transmitter, receiver, and transmission line.

Details of the physical layer operation are located in Chapter 19, on page 325.

SATA Command Protocol

The previous focus has been primarily on FIS transmission. This section introduces several examples of the SATA Command protocol; that is, the sequence of FISs exchanged during the execution of a given command. The examples all exemplify the most basic operation and successful completion. Chapter 11, on page 177 details all the SATA command protocols and variations.

Example Non-Data Command

SATA supports over 30 different non-data commands. However, all non-data commands use the same FIS sequence as illustrated in Figure 3-16 on page 62. As with all commands, host software must initialize the registers (by performing a series of IO write operations) as required for a given command and then issue the command by writing the specific command value into the command register. Recall that in SATA implementations only the shadow registers are accessed by system software. The normal command sequence is as follows:

1. The write to the command register causes the HBA to send the contents of the shadow registers to the drive via a Register FIS.
2. The drive updates its ATA registers with the Register FIS contents.
3. The drive parses the command and performs the requested operation.
4. The drive updates the ATA registers to report completion status and delivers their content to the HBA via a Register FIS.
5. The HBA updates the shadow register contents and generates an interrupt to notify system software of command completion.
6. System software reads successful command completion status from the shadow registers.

Figure 3-16: Non-Data Command Sequence

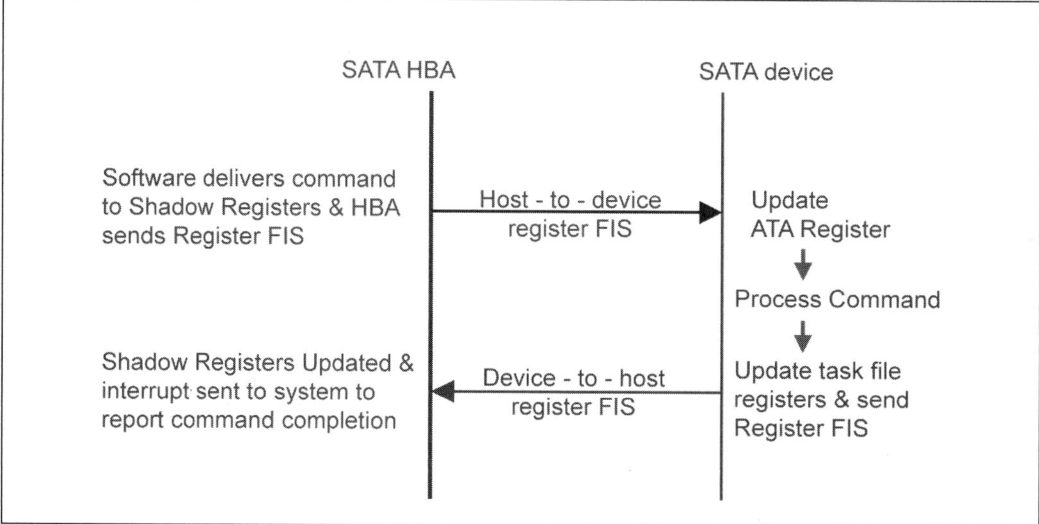

Example DMA Read Command

This example describes a typical DMA read command sequence involving a single data transfer between the drive and HBA. However, several data transfers may be required. Figure 3-17 illustrates a normal DMA Read command sequence. Once the shadow registers have been initialized to specify the start sector address, sector count, etc. the sequence is as follows:

1. A write to the command register causes the HBA to send the contents of the shadow registers to the drive via a Register FIS.
2. The drive updates its ATA registers with the Register FIS contents.
3. The drive parses the command and reads the requested data from disc.
4. Data is delivered to the HBA via a DATA FIS.
5. The HBA's DMA engine delivers the data to system memory.
6. The drive updates the ATA registers to report completion status and delivers their content to the HBA via a Register FIS.
7. The HBA updates the shadow register contents and generates an interrupt to notify system software of command completion.
8. System software reads successful command completion status from the shadow registers.

Figure 3-17: Sample DMA Data Read Command Sequence

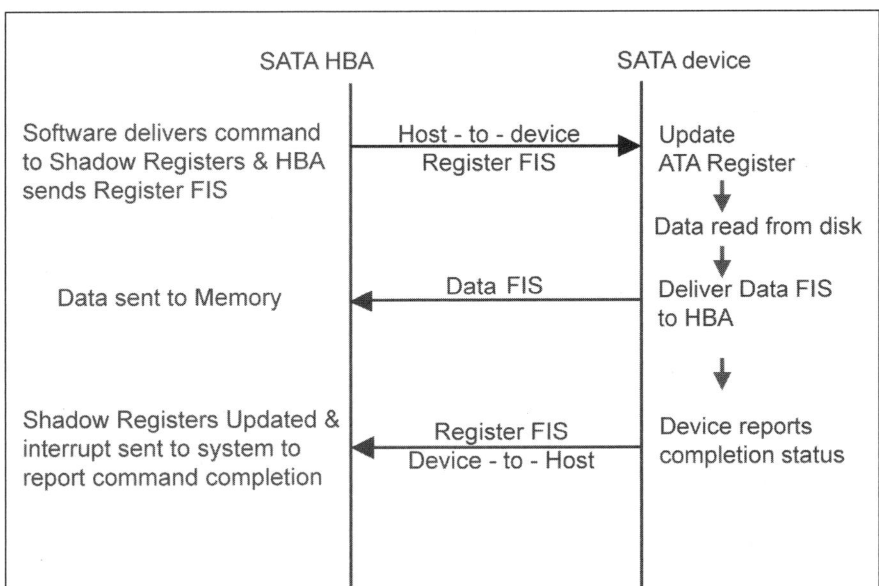

Example DMA Write Command

This example describes a typical DMA Write command sequence involving a single data transfer between the HBA and drive. Several data transfers may be required but a single transfer completes the command in this example. Figure 3-18 illustrates a normal DMA Write command sequence. Once the shadow registers have been initialized to specify the start sector address, sector count, etc. the sequence is as follows:

1. A write to the command register causes the HBA to send the contents of the shadow registers to the drive via a Register FIS.
2. The drive updates its ATA registers with the Register FIS contents.
3. The drive parses the command and seeks the disc's target sector.
4. When the drive is ready to receive the data it delivers a DMA Activate FIS to the HBA.
5. The DMA Activate FIS notifies the HBA's DMA engine to fetch the data.
6. Data is delivered to the drive via a DATA FIS and is written to disc.
7. The drive updates the ATA registers to report completion status and delivers their content to the HBA via a Register FIS.
8. The HBA updates the shadow register contents and generates an interrupt to notify system software of command completion.
9. System software reads successful command completion status from the shadow registers.

Figure 3-18: Sample DMA Write Command Sequence

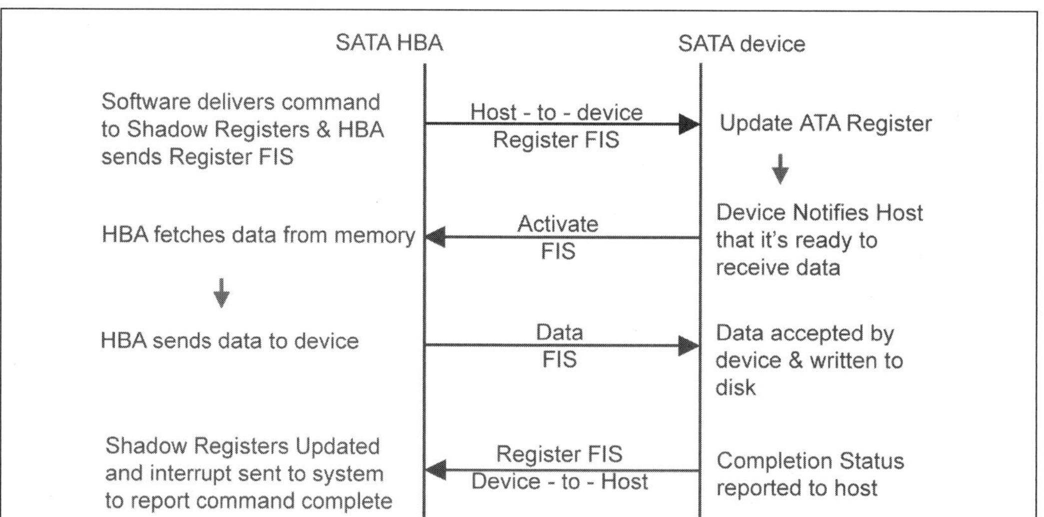

Major Features of SATA II

SATA II introduced many new features with a majority focusing on better support for SATA server-based solutions. The primary enhancements include:

- Native Command Queuing (NQC)
- Port Multipliers (PM)
- Port Selectors (PS)
- Enclosure services
- Enhanced Hot Plug support
- Doubling the serial transmission rate to 3.0Gb/s

Native Command Queuing

Support for command queuing was introduced in ATA 4 but never became a mainstream implementation for a variety of reasons. Amongst these reasons were two important issues:

1. Synchronous Disc IO Operations — software, by design, waited for each command to complete prior to issuing a subsequent command. This linear approach to processing commands was typical of IO operations because hardware was originally capable of processing only one command at a time. Consequently, without software support disc drive manufacturers were not quick to add the necessary hardware support.
2. The command queuing protocol in ATA was complex and inefficient.

A major effort to rewrite software to support asynchronous disc IO operations was started to support Native Command Queuing (NCQ) in SATA drives.

NCQ increases drive performance by enqueuing up to 32 commands within the drive and processing these commands in an out-of-order (asynchronous) fashion to reduce overall access latency. Figure 3-19 on page 66 illustrates the principles of NCQ. Note that example A depicts a drive reading a file that requires 4 sequential commands to complete the read. Using sequential command processing, 4.25 revolutions of the disc are required to read the entire file. Example B illustrates conceptually how NCQ can shorten the overall latency needed to execute the same commands. The drive performs the commands out of sequence such that only 2.25 revolution of the disk are required to read the file; thereby, significantly reducing access time. See Chapter 14, entitled "Native Command Queuing," on page 235 for details.

Figure 3-19: Principles of NCQ

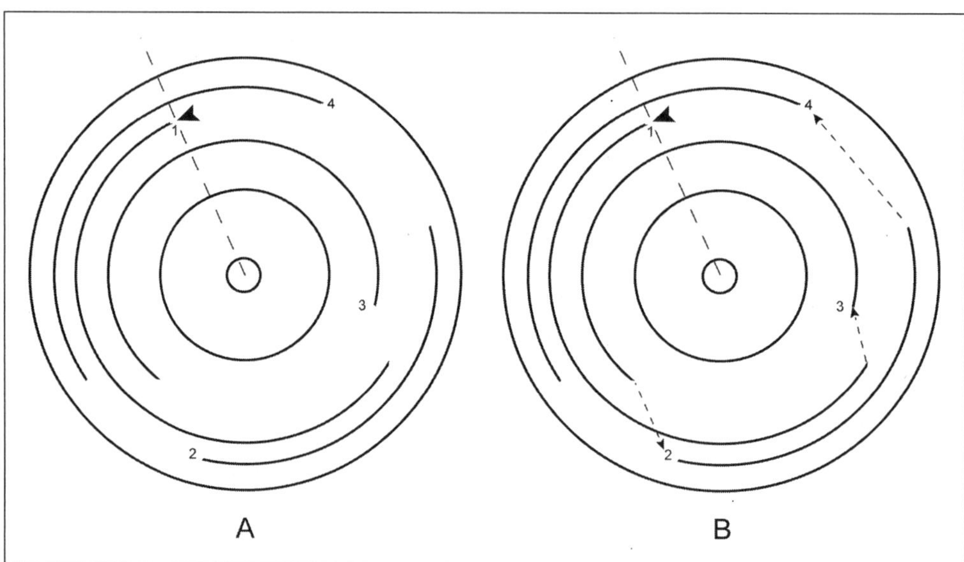

Port Multipliers

A given HBA may not support sufficient numbers of drivers for large drive rack implementations. Port Multipliers connect to a single HBA port and provide support for up to 15 additional ports. See Figure 3-20 on page 67. Each of the additional 15 ports must include the SATA SCRs to permit control of the individual links and to report status associated with link activity.

Figure 3-20: Port Multipliers Expand the Number of Ports for Server Applications

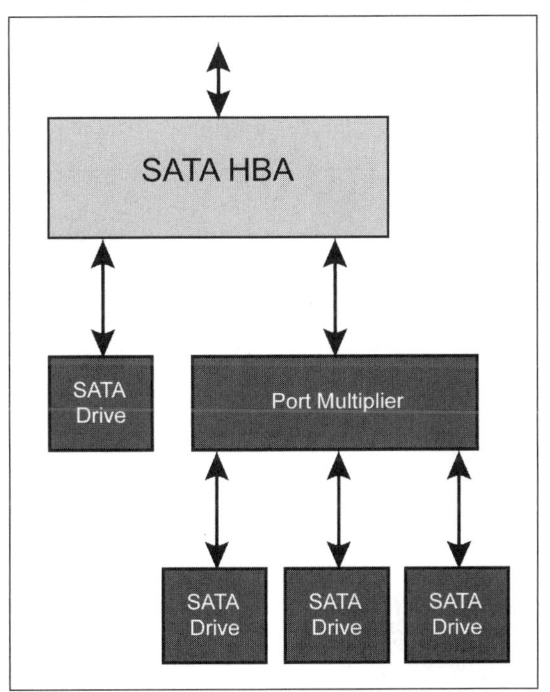

Port Selectors

In server implementations where hardware redundancy is important, the port selector feature provides a failover mechanism. Figure 3-21 illustrates an example implementation where redundant HBAs both have access to the SATA drives. The specification defines two possible methods for switching the input to the port selector:

1. A sideband signal can be implemented that selects the active input.
2. A special OOB protocol sequence can be delivered by the active HBA to force the port receiving the OOB switching sequence to become the active input.

Figure 3-21: Port Selectors Provide Redundancy

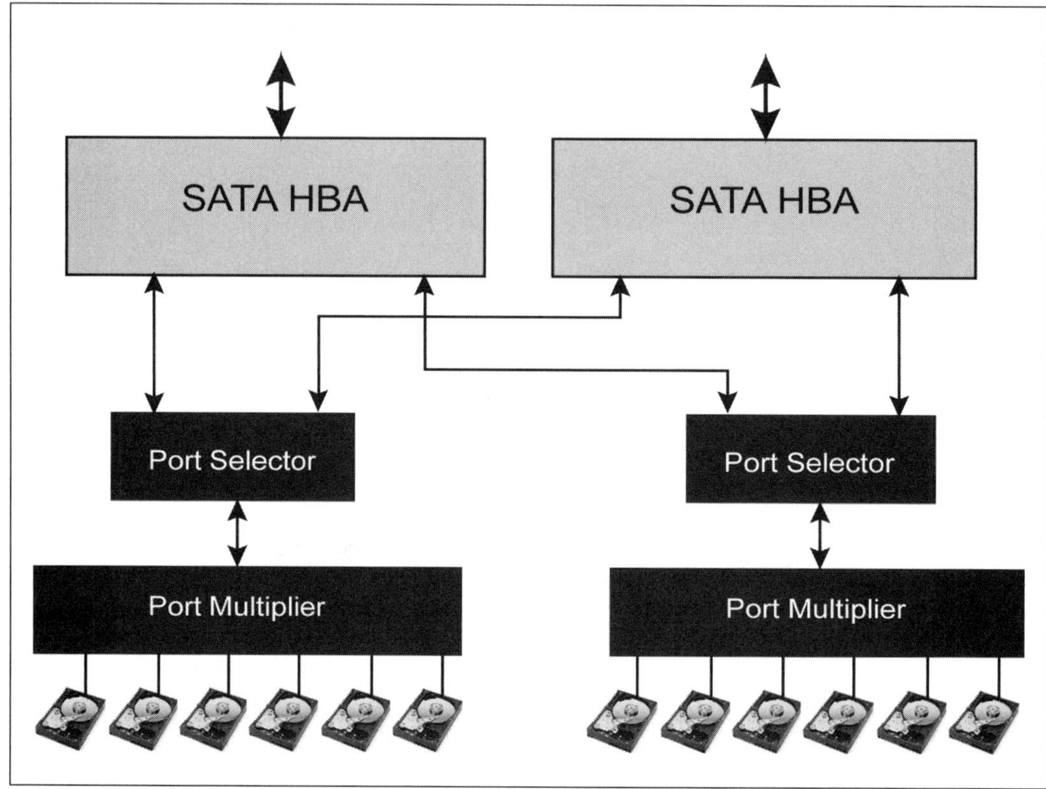

Enclosure Services

Large cabinets (enclosures) that house large numbers of drives require special hardware and software to monitor and control environmental conditions such as temperature, fan speeds, drive activity, power, etc. Existing standards have been developed in the SCSI environment to manage these enclosure services. The SATA II specification defines support for two standards:

1. SAF-TE — SCSI Attached Fault-Tolerant Enclosure
2. SES — SCSI Enclosure Services

Chapter 17, on page 295 introduces the SATA elements that support enclosure management.

Hot Plug Support

Another important feature in Server environments is the ability to remove and replace drives without having to bring down an entire server. SATA connectors were designed from the very beginning with long pins (for ground contact) and shorter pins for the interface signals. SATA II adds additional support by defining changes to the physical layer state machines to accommodate detection of drive insertion and removal. This along with hot-plug connectors makes it easier to implement Hot Plug solutions.

Higher Transmission Rate

SATA I defines a maximum transmission rate of 1.5Gb/s that appears to be more than sufficient given the speeds at which drives can read from or write to disc. However, in the wake of port multipliers where a single HBA port interface has up to 15 drives connected, higher transfer rates become more critical, particularly when Native Command Queuing is also employed.

The AHCI Programming Interface

The discussion to this point has focused on the legacy registers as the means to send commands to the HBA via a series of IO writes. Interestingly the SATA I specification discusses only the legacy interface, probably to emphasize ATA legacy software compatibility. This section describes another specified method of command delivery that does not involve the legacy registers. This solution is called the Advanced Host Controller Interface (AHCI). This programming interface is in widespread use in many PC chipsets. HBAs based on this interface use data structures in memory where the legacy registers are virtualized. The AHCI approach provides many advantages over the legacy task file programming interface that include support for:

- memory mapped HBA registers for better processor performance
- up to 32 ports
- 64-bit addressing
- integrated Serial ATA registers
- First-Party DMA
- Native Command Queuing
- Hot Plug
- Port Multipliers
- Staggered drive spin-up

Figure 3-22 illustrates the major elements of the AHCI implementation. As mentioned previously, the AHCI does not contain the IO-mapped legacy registers. Instead, virtual registers are in essence implemented in software data structures located in main DRAM. The register contents are actually provided in the form of a Register FIS that is ready to be forwarded from memory to the SATA drives. The data structure in DRAM containing these Register FISes that are pending execution is provided via the command list. The command list includes up to 32 entries and each one provides the information needed to fetch a Register FIS.

The FISes returned from the drive during command execution are forwarded directly to another data structure called the Received FIS structure. Specific offsets within the buffer guides software to fetch and evaluate the command results.

Figure 3-22: Primary AHCI Elements

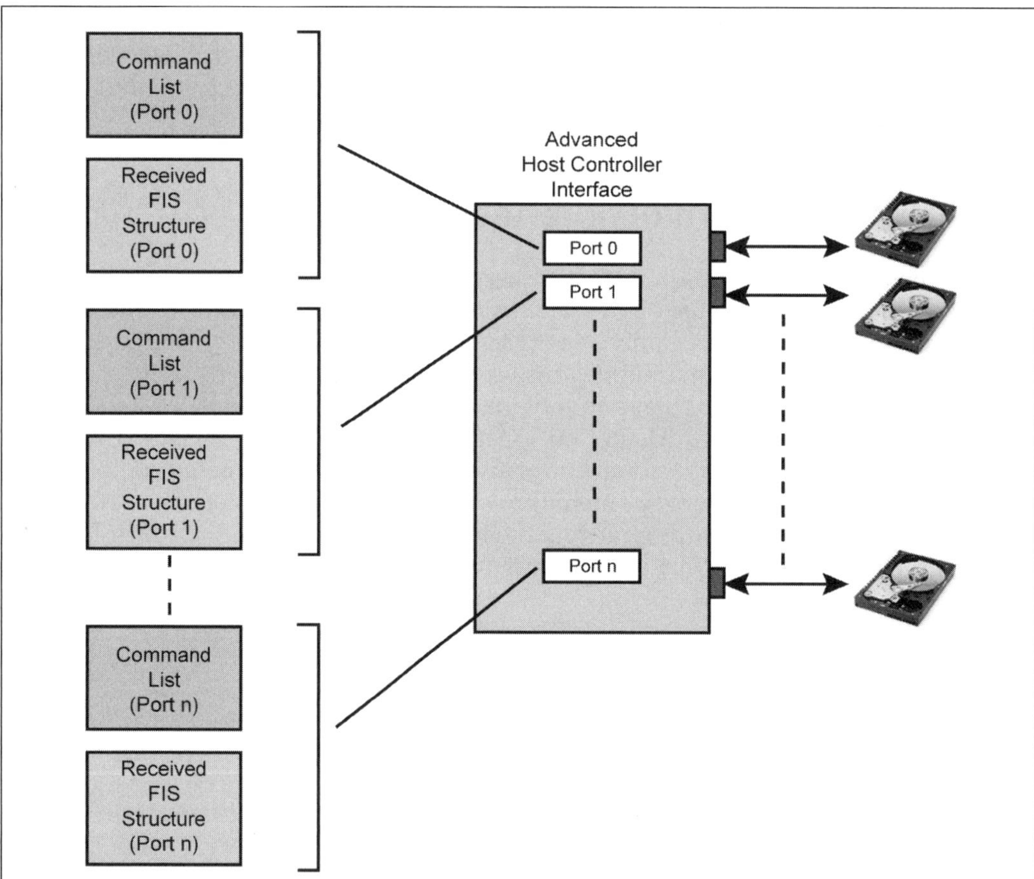

4 Introduction to FIS Transfers

Previous Chapter

The previous chapter provided a conceptual understanding of the operation of the SATA interface and transmission protocol. This included the basics of how SATA communication is handled and the primary functions of each layer defined by the specification. How SATA maintains software compatibility with parallel ATA was also covered in this chapter, along with the new features introduced by the SATA 2.0 extension.

This Chapter

Communications across the SATA interface consists primarily of transferring Frame Information Structures (FISes). A FIS may deliver shadow or ATA register contents, data, control information, etc. This chapter introduces the reader to the basics of the FIS transmission protocol. Subsequent chapters detail the protocol further and discuss variations due to flow control requirements, errors, and related issues.

The Next Chapter

The next chapter is provided primarily for reference purposes. It includes details associated with each of the Frame Information Structures, including definition of all fields within each FIS.

General

Whether a FIS originates at the HBA or a SATA device, the transmission protocol is the same. Figure 4-1 on page 72 illustrates the SATA interface layers in greater detail, showing both the transmit and receive sides. The following discussion describes the actions taken by each layer in the process of sending, receiving and reporting FIS transmission status. The following example describes a FIS being sent by the HBA as a result of software having issued a command using legacy methods (i.e., multiple IO writes to the HBA shadow registers).

Figure 4-1: FIS Transmission and SATA Layers

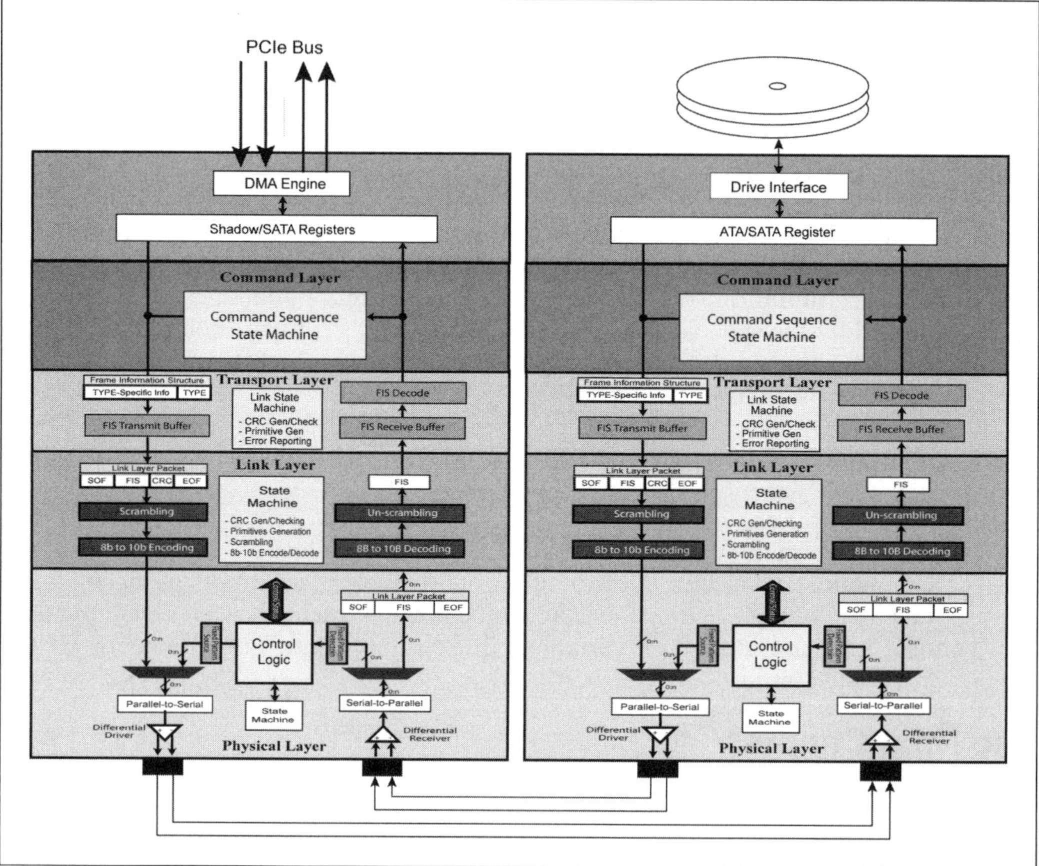

FIS Transfers

This section focuses on the transmission of a FIS between the HBA and a SATA drive, and the role that each layer plays in the FIS transfer protocol. The example used for explaining these actions results from host software having issued a Read DMA command. Note that the functions performed by the SATA layers are essentially the same irrespective of whether the HBA or Drive is transmitting the FIS.

Application Layer (HBA)

Host software issues commands to the HBA by performing a series of IO writes required to setup and issue a command. In a SATA HBA these writes target the shadow registers. The actual DMA Read command is issued when host software writes the DMA Read command code to the command register. The SATA specification requires the same behaviors as the Parallel ATA implementations as follows:

- When software writes to the shadow Command register, the HBA must set the BSY status bit within 400ns of the Command register write.
- When BSY (or DRQ) is set software is not permitted to write other shadow registers, including; Features, Sector Count, LBA Low, LBA Middle, LBA High, or Device registers.

The Command register write triggers the delivery of the entire shadow register contents to the Transport layer.

Transport Layer (HBA)

Once software has issued the command (a DMA read in this example), the Transport layer obtains the contents of the shadow register. See Figure 4-2 on page 74. The transport layer has several responsibilities associated with delivering the Register FIS as follows:

- Create a compliant FIS
- Notify Link layer of FIS pending delivery
- Notify link of flow control requirements during transmission

Figure 4-2 on page 74 also shows the presence of a transmit buffer that is intentionally small to reduce the cost of the SATA interface.

Figure 4-2: Transport Layer

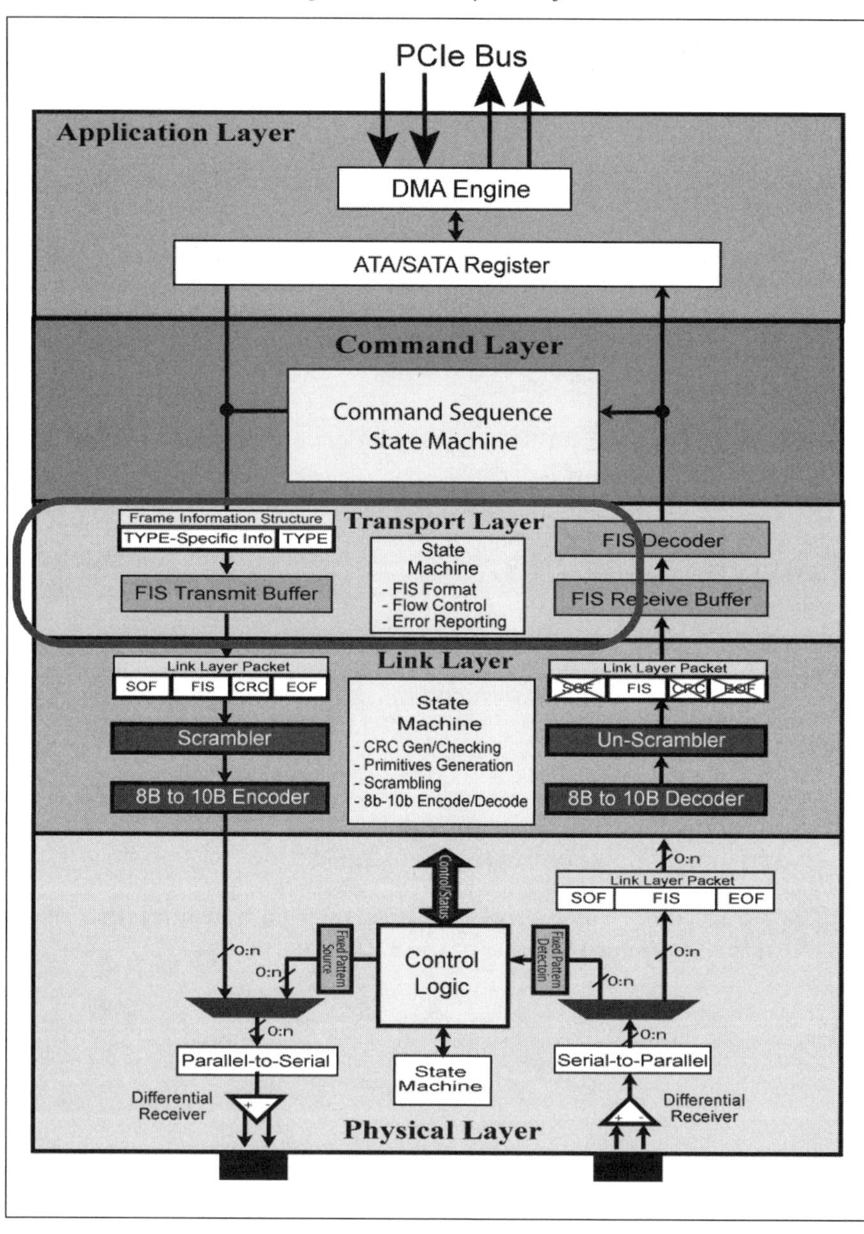

Frame Information Structures

SATA uses 12 types of Frame Information Structures to support the sizable number of commands defined by ATA and extended by SATA. Each FIS contains an ID value that identifies the particular FIS being transferred. Table 4-1 lists all of the SATA FISs defined through the 2.0 version of the specification.

Table 4-1: FIS Types

FIS Name	FIS ID
Host to Device Register	27h
Device to Host Register	34h
Set Device Bits	A1h
PIO Setup	5Fh
DMA Activate	39h
First Party DMA Setup	41h
Data	46h
BIST Activate	58h

Note that several of the FIS types are used for more than one purpose. For example, the Set Device Bits FIS is used by SATA drives to modify certain bits within the HBA's Shadow registers, and it's also used for event notification. FIS content and format is described in detail in Chapter 5, entitled "FIS Types and Formats," on page 85.

FIS Ready for Transfer

Upon receiving the FIS transfer request, the Link layer creates a "Transfer Ready" (X_RDY) primitive and forwards it to the physical layer for transmission to the drive. The drive detects the X_RDY primitive and if it's ready to receive a FIS, it returns a "Receive Ready" (R_RDY) primitive to the HBA. Note that these primitives are signaled continuously until it is time to send a different primitive.

Flow Control During FIS Transmission

The Transport layer transmission buffer is much smaller than the maximum payload size of a Data FIS, which is 8KB. Note that flow control can only occur during Data FIS transmission. During DMA Write commands, the contents of the Transport layer data buffer may be emptied faster than data can be delivered to the buffer. If the buffer approaches a dry condition, the Transport layer requests the Link layer to send a HOLD primitive, thereby notifying the receiver that FIS transmission has temporarily been suspended. Details regarding the Flow Control protocol can be found in Chapter 8, on page 133.

Link Layer (Transmit)

The Link layer performs most of the FIS transfer protocol using primitives that provide control and status information during FIS transmission. As can been seen in Figure 4-3 on page 77, the Link layer performs a series of actions to support the FIS transfer protocol and to prepare the FIS for transmission across the link. This includes:

- FIS delivery notification
- CRC generation
- Framing each FIS with start and end primitives
- Scrambling
- 8-to-10bit encoding

Figure 4-3 on page 77 illustrates the Link layer's position in the layered hierarchy and highlights its primary functions.

Figure 4-3: Link Layer

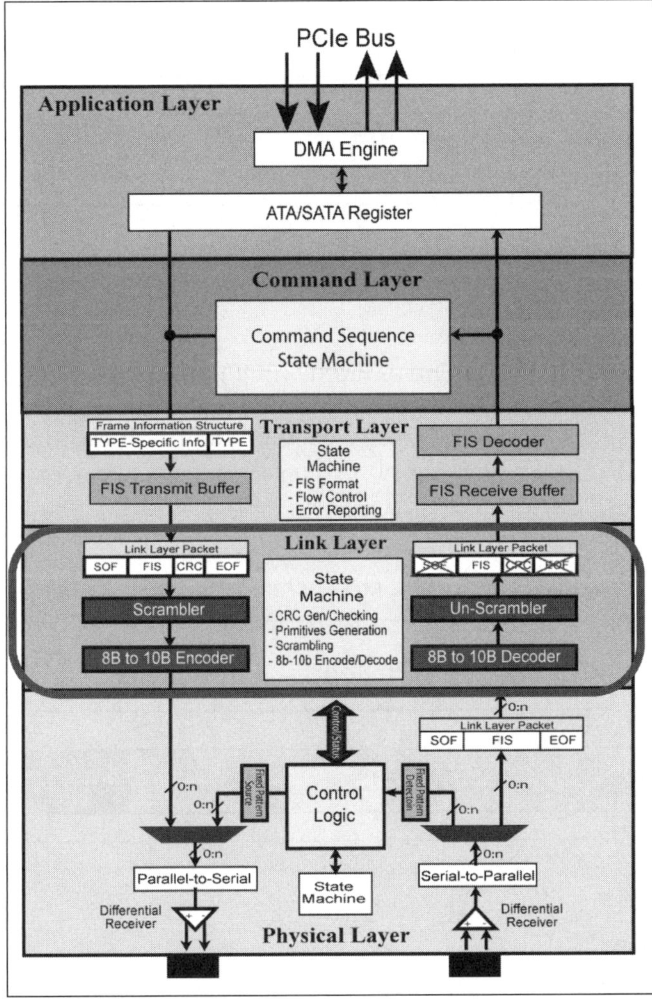

CRC Generation

The Link layer calculates a CRC value for the entire FIS contents and places it at the end of the FIS. (See Figure 4-4 on page 78.) The 32-bit CRC is designed to detect two bit errors within 10-bit value up to a maximum payload size 2064 DWs (including CRC). The maximum FIS payload size currently defined is 2049 DWs.

Figure 4-4: CRC Covers the Entire FIS Contents

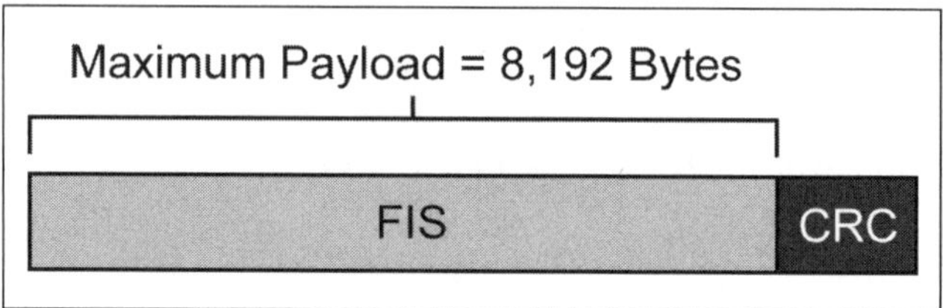

Framing the FIS

Start of Frame (SOF) and End of Frame (EOF) primitives are added to the beginning and end of each FIS. This framing allows the receiver to recognize each FIS that is delivered. The terminology used to identify the entire packet including SOF, FIS, CRC and EOF is simply "frame."

Figure 4-5: Example Primitives - Start of Frame and End of Frame (SOF/EOF)

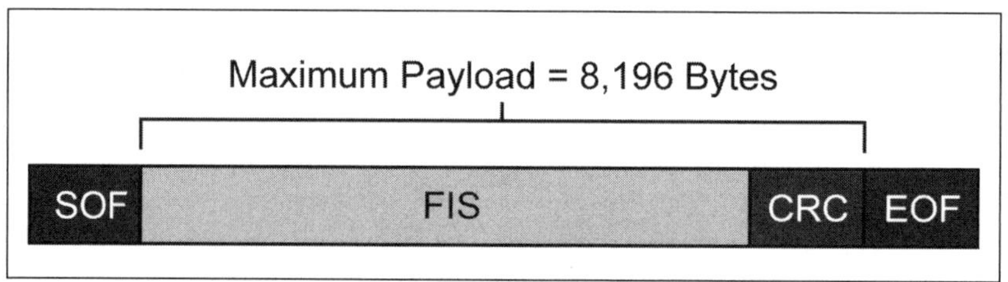

Scrambler

The Scrambler uses an algorithm to pseudo-randomly scramble the FIS. Scrambling eliminates repetitive patterns in the bit stream that can result in concentrations of energy at discrete frequencies, which leads to significant EMI noise generation. Scrambling spreads energy over a wide frequency range, thereby minimizing the average EMI noise generated. Note that none of the primitives including SOF and EOF are scrambled.

Perform 8b-to-10b encoding

Like most of today's high-speed serial buses, SATA uses the 8- to 10-bit (8b/10b) encoding scheme. This encoding permits the transmit clock frequency to be encoded into the data stream. This is accomplished through the encoding scheme where each byte of the FIS is converted from its 8-bit pattern to a 10-bit symbol. The 8b/10b Encoder creates sufficient numbers of 1-to-0 and 0-to-1 transitions in the bit stream that the receiver can synchronize to the transmit clock via the receivers Phase Lock Loop (PLL).

In this approach the receiver establishes synchronization to the transmitted bit stream immediately following device reset. Once synchronization is achieved data transmission continues uninterrupted. The bus generally does not go back to an electrical idle state, but if it does (typically due to power management) re-synchronization is required before FIS transmission can continue.

Immediately following FIS transmission, the Link layer adds the "Wait For Terminate" (WFTM) primitive. The WFTM primitive is transmitted until confirmation is received from the drive indicating whether the FIS was received without error. This confirmation is made via the "Receive OK" (R_OK) primitive.

Physical Layer (Transmit)

When the Link layer has delivered the FIS to the physical layer for transmission, two operations are performed:

- Parallel to Serial Conversion of the primitives and the FIS
- Differential Transmission of the serial stream

FIS Transmission

The differential transmitter runs at a clock rate of either 1.5 or 3.0 GHz depending on the SATA version (generation) and the capabilities of the device at the opposite end of the link. Figure 4-6 on page 80 illustrates the serial link and associated physical layers.

Figure 4-6: SATA Physical Link

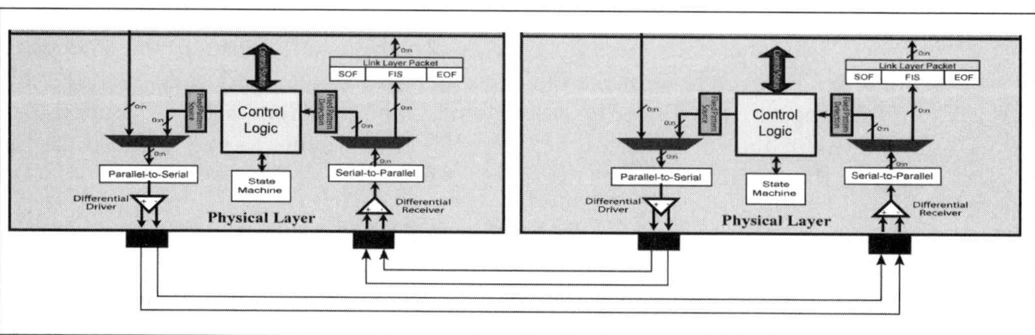

Physical Layer (Receive)

When the physical layer receives a primitive or FIS it performs three primary functions:

- Differential Reception and detection of primitives/FISs
- Parallel to Serial Conversion of the primitives/FISs
- Elastic buffer management to prevent overflow or underflow

Link Layer (Receive)

During FIS reception the Link layer performs the following operations:

- Arbitration
- Decodes start and end primitives to detect beginning and end of each FIS
- Sends Receive In Progress (R_IP) primitive when FIS is detected
- 8-to-10bit decoding
- Un-scrambling
- FIS CRC checking
- Reporting error to Transport layer
- Forwards FIS to Transport layer for decode

Figure 4-7 on page 81 illustrates the primary functions associated with the Link layer.

Figure 4-7: Primary Link Layer Receive Functions

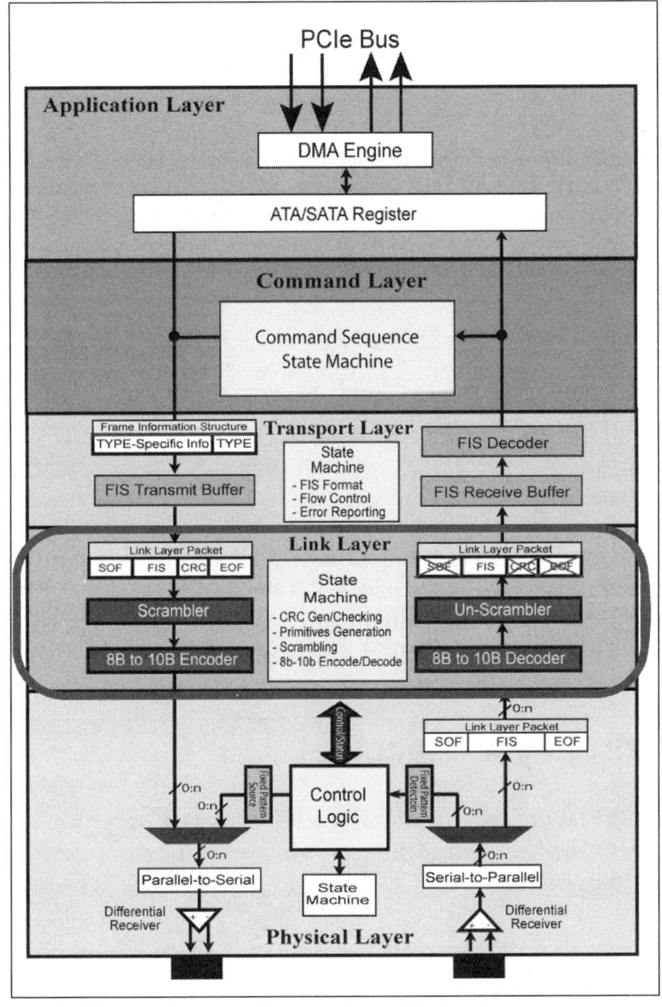

Arbitration

Prior to FIS reception the receiver will generally be receiving consecutive SYNC primitives indicating logical idle. At the same time, the transmitting side of this device will generally be transmitting SYNC primitives. When the receiving device detects the X_RDY (transmit ready) primitives from the remote device, it acknowledges the request by transmitting R_RDY (receive ready) primitives in reply.

8b-to-10b Decoding

All information received is decoded to convert it back to its original byte format. The decoder output also includes errors that may be detected.

Un-Scrambling

The Link layer performs the exact same operation on the receive data that was performed during transmission. That is, any primitives received are ignored by the scrambler, while the incoming FIS is unscrambled.

Detecting the FIS

The Link layer detects the Start of Frame (SOF) and End of Frame (EOP) primitives to identify presence of the FIS. SOF detection results in delivery of the Receive In Progress (R_IP) primitive to the FIS transmitter. EOP indicates end of the FIS and that CRC can be checked.

CRC Check

The Link layer checks the CRC value for the entire FIS contents. A good CRC results in the Link layer returning a R_OK primitive to the FIS transmitter. Bad Cracks are reported to the transmitter via the R_ERR (receive error) primitive and the transport layer is notified of the error.

Transport Layer (Receive)

The Transport layer receives and decodes the FIS. Contents of the FIS are passed to the upper layers for handling. Notification of errors detected in the FIS are also passed upstream.

Command and Application Layers (Receive)

Either the command or Application layer will handle the incoming FIS depending on its type and the command being performed.

Part Two

FIS Transmission Protocols

5 FIS Types and Formats

Previous Chapter

Communications across the SATA interface consists primarily of transferring Frame Information Structures (FISs). A FIS may deliver shadow or ATA register contents, data, control information, etc. The previous chapter introduces the reader to the basics of the FIS transmission protocol. Subsequent chapters detail the protocol further and discuss variations due to flow control requirements, errors, and related issues.

This Chapter

This chapter is provided primarily for reference purposes. It includes details associated with each of the frame information structures.

The Next Chapter

The link transfer protocol is implemented primarily within the link layer of both the transmitter and receiver. This chapter discusses the individual steps taken by the transport and link layers in transferring a FIS.

General

A variety of characteristics can be associated with each FIS these include:

- Each FIS includes an 8-bit ID value that identifies its type
- FIS size is always multiples of 4 bytes
- Direction of a given FIS may be HBA to Drive, Drive to HBA, or both
- Some FISs have alternate formats that are variations of their standard definition, which are determined by bit fields within the FIS
- Minimum FIS size is 4 bytes
- Maximum FIS size is 8196 bytes

Table 5-1 on page 86 summarizes all the FIS types, including their IDs, size, direction, and generation in which they were introduced.

Table 5-1: FIS Types and Characteristics

FIS Type	ID	Direction	Size	Generation
Register FIS	27h	HBA to Device	5 DWs	Gen 1
Register FIS	34h	Device to HBA	5 DWs	Gen 1
Set Device Bits with Active field with Event Notification field	A1h	Device to HBA	2 DWs	Gen 1 Gen 2 Gen 2
PIO Setup	5Fh	Device to HBA	5 DWs	Gen 1
DMA Activate	39h	Device to HBA	1 DWs	Gen 1
First Party DMA Setup with Auto Activation	41h	Bidirectional	7 DWs	Gen 1 Gen 2
Data	46h	Bidirectional	2049 DWs	Gen 1
BIST Activate	58h	Bidirectional	3 DWs	Gen 1

Register FIS - Host to Device

A Register FIS sent to a SATA device always contains the contents of the HBA's shadow registers. Two specific events trigger the HBA to send a Register FIS:

1. A write to the Shadow Command Register
2. A write to the Shadow Control Register

Figure 5-1 on page 87 depicts the shadow register set and highlights the Command and Control registers. The Register FIS contents are a reflection of the values previously written to the shadow register by host software.

Figure 5-1: Shadow Register Definition on Writes (Primary Interface)

Cmd Reg	Writes	Notes
Address	7 0	
01F0	Data	16-bit accesses
01F1	Feature	Two 8-bit accesses
01F2	Sector Count	Two 8-bit accesses
01F3	LBA Low (31:24 then 7:0)	Two 8–bit accesses
01F4	LBA Middle (39:32 then 15:8)	Two 8–bit accesses
01F5	LBA High (47:40 then 23:16)	Two 8–bit accesses
01F6	Device	8-bit access only
01F7	Command	8-bit access only
Ctrl Reg		
03F6	Device Control	8-bit access only

Figure 5-2 on page 88 depicts the contents and format of the Register FIS resulting from a write to the shadow command or control register. Note that the specification defines the fields within the shadow registers using the cylinder, head, sector terminology. Table 5-2 on page 88 describes the contents of each field and specifies the corresponding LBA addresses, where applicable.

Figure 5-2: Register FIS - Host to Device

	+3 (bits 7–0)	+2 (bits 7–0)	+1 (bits 7–0)	+0 (bits 7–0)
DW 0	Features	Command	C | R | R | Reserved	FIS Type (27h)
DW 1	Dev/Head	Cyl High	Cyl Low	Sector Number
DW 2	Features (exp)	Cyl High (exp)	Cyl Low (exp)	Sec Num (exp)
DW 3	Control	Reserved (0)	Sec Count (exp)	Sector Count
DW 4	Reserved (0)	Reserved (0)	Reserved (0)	Reserved (0)

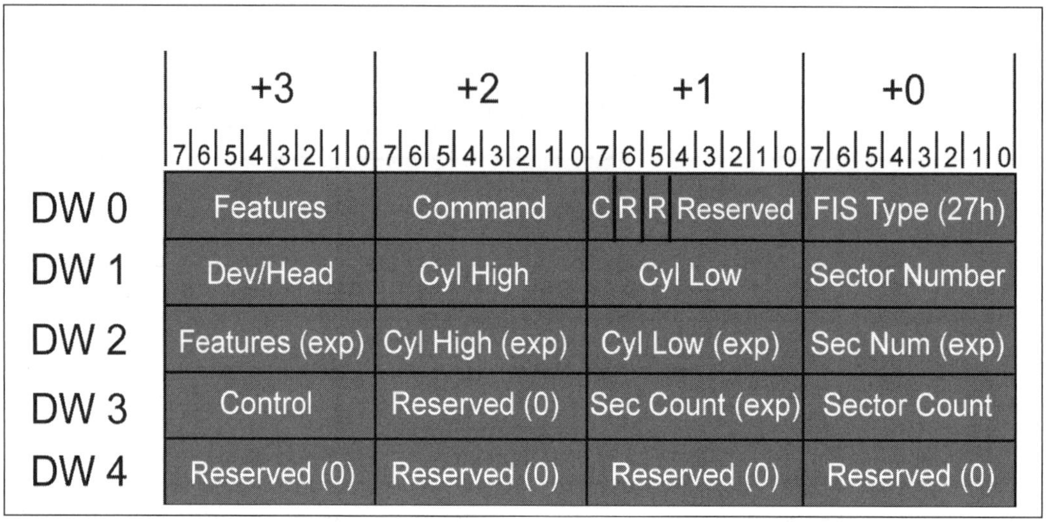

Table 5-2: Register FIS - Host to Device Fields and Descriptions

Field Name	Description
FIS Type	This field contains the ID (27h) of the Register - Host to Device FIS.
C	The "C" bit field (DW 0, offset +1) specifies which event caused the Register FIS delivery. 0 = write to Control register 1 = write to Command register
Command	Contains contents of the shadow Command register that when written causes a Register FIS to be sent to the SATA Device, and the "C" bit to be set.
Features	Contents of the shadow Feature register
Features (expanded)	Contents of the upper 8 bits of the shadow Feature register when using 48-bit addressing.

Table 5-2: Register FIS - Host to Device Fields and Descriptions

Field Name	Description
Sector Number	Contents of the shadow Sector number, or LBA 7:0
Sector Number (expanded)	Contents of the upper 8-bits of the expanded Sector Number value (LBA 15:8) when using 48-bit addressing.
Cylinder Low	Contents of the least significant 8 bits of the Cylinder number register, or LBA 23:16.
Cylinder Low (expanded)	Contents of the most significant 8 bits of the Cylinder number, or LBA 31:24 when using 48-bit addressing.
Cylinder High	Contents of the least significant 8 bits of the Cylinder number, or LBA 39:32
Cylinder High (expanded)	Contents of the most significant 8 bits of the Cylinder High number, or LBA 47:40 when using 48-bit addressing.
Device/Head	This field contains two values: - Bit 4 = the Device Number used to select drive 0 or drive 1 - Bits 3:0 = Head number when software uses the legacy addressing (Cylinder, Head, Sector).
Sector Count	This byte field specifies the number of contiguous sectors to be accessed from the start address on disc using bits 7:0
Sector Count Expanded	This byte field contains the upper bit 15:8 of the sector count when using 48-bit addressing.
Control	Contents of the Control register that when written cause a Register FIS to be sent to the SATA Device and result in the "C" bit to be cleared.
Reserved	The reserved fields all contain zeros.

Register FIS - Device to Host

In SATA, software does not have direct access to the ATA registers located within the drive. When the drive executes a command and updates status information within the ATA registers, the status information is not visible to host software until the shadow registers are updated. Therefore it is necessary for the drive to read it's ATA registers and deliver their contents to the HBA via a Register FIS. Figure 5-3 illustrates the contents of the ATA registers when read. Figure 5-4 on page 91 illustrates the Register FIS - Device to Host format. This FIS is typically sent to the host upon completion of a given command.

Figure 5-3: Contents of ATA Register when Read

Cmd Reg	Reads	Notes
Address	**7 0**	
01F0	Data	16-bit accesses
01F1	Error	8-bit access
01F2	Sector Count	8-bit access
01F3	LBA Low (7:0)	8-bit access
01F4	LBA Middle (15:8)	8-bit access
01F5	LBA High (23:16)	8-bit access
01F6	Device	8-bit access
01F7	Status	8-bit access
Ctrl Reg		
03F6	Alternate Status	8-bit access

Figure 5-4: Register - Device to Host FIS Content and Format

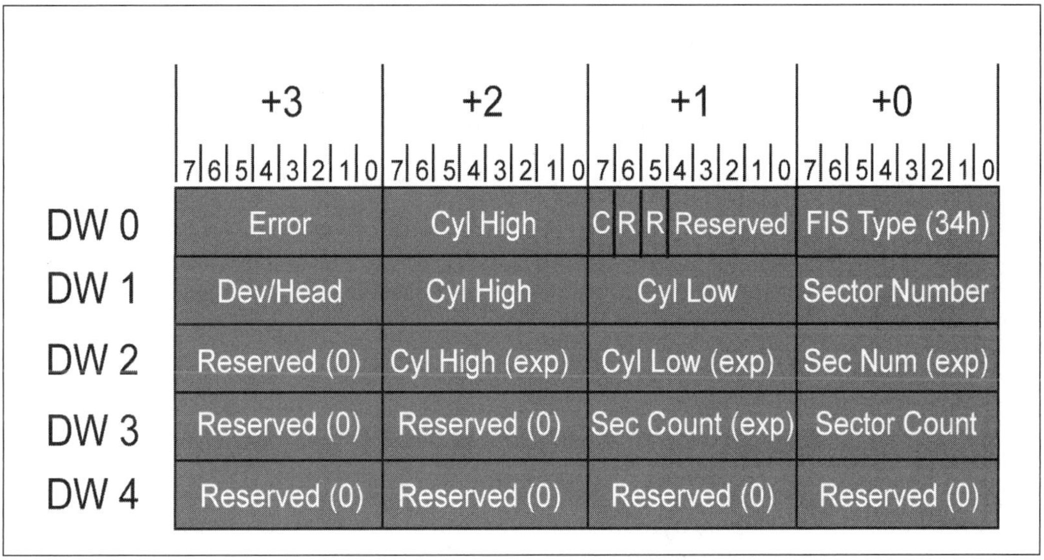

	+3	+2	+1	+0
	7 6 5 4 3 2 1 0	7 6 5 4 3 2 1 0	7 6 5 4 3 2 1 0	7 6 5 4 3 2 1 0
DW 0	Error	Cyl High	C R R Reserved	FIS Type (34h)
DW 1	Dev/Head	Cyl High	Cyl Low	Sector Number
DW 2	Reserved (0)	Cyl High (exp)	Cyl Low (exp)	Sec Num (exp)
DW 3	Reserved (0)	Reserved (0)	Sec Count (exp)	Sector Count
DW 4	Reserved (0)	Reserved (0)	Reserved (0)	Reserved (0)

Table 5-3 on page 91 describes each of the fields in the read Register FIS.

Table 5-3: Field Names and Descriptions of the Register FIS - Device to Host

Field Name	Description
FIS Type	This field contains the ID (27h) of the Register - Host to Device FIS.
C	The state of the "C" bit is returned when read
Status	Contents of the SATA device's status register
Error	Contents of the error register
Sector Number	Contents of the shadow Sector number, or LBA 7:0
Sector Number (expanded)	Contents of the upper 8-bits of the expanded Sector Number value (LBA 15:8) when using 48-bit addressing.

Table 5-3: Field Names and Descriptions of the Register FIS - Device to Host

Field Name	Description
Cylinder Low	Contents of the least significant 8 bits of the Cylinder number register, or LBA 23:16.
Cylinder Low (expanded)	Contents of the most significant 8 bits of the Cylinder number, or LBA 31:24 when using 48-bit addressing.
Cylinder High	Contents of the least significant 8 bits of the Cylinder number, or LBA 39:32
Cylinder High (expanded)	Contents of the most significant 8 bits of the Cylinder High number, or LBA 47:40 when using 48-bit addressing.
Device/Head	This field contains two values: - Bit 4 = the Device Number used to select drive 0 or drive 1 - Bits 3:0 = Head number when software uses the legacy addressing (Cylinder, Head, Sector).
Sector Count	This byte field specifies the number of contiguous sectors to be accessed from the start address on disc using bits 7:0
Sector Count Expanded	This byte field contains the upper bit 15:8 of the sector count when using 48-bit addressing.
Reserved	The reserved fields all contain zeros.

Set Device Bits FIS

This FIS is delivered from a SATA device to the Host when certain commands are being executed, including:

- Queued DMA Read
- Queued DMA Write
- First Party DMA Read
- First Party DMA Write

This FIS is merely 8 bytes in size and permits certain status bits within the shadow registers to be modified without sending to the host an entire 20 byte Register FIS. The format of the Set Device Bits FIS is shown in Figure 5-5 on page 93.

Figure 5-5: Format of Standard Set Device Bits FIS

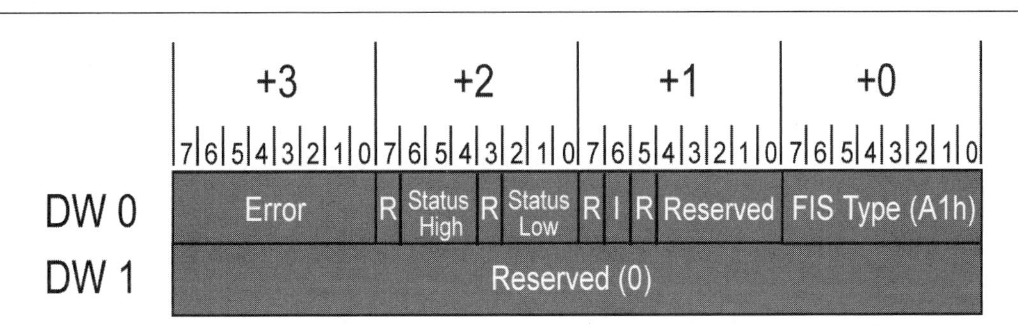

Two shadow registers are updated by the Set Device Bits FIS:

- Status Register (except bits 3 and 7)
- Error Register

The bits within DW0 offset +2 correspond to bits of the status register that will be modified by this FIS. Figure 5-6 illustrates the Status Register bits and shows that DRQ (bit 3) and BSY (bit 7) are reserved and not modified by the Set Device Bits FIS. Page See "Status Register" on page 26 for definitions of each bit field within the Status register.

Figure 5-6: Six Status Register Bits Modified by Set Device Bits FIS

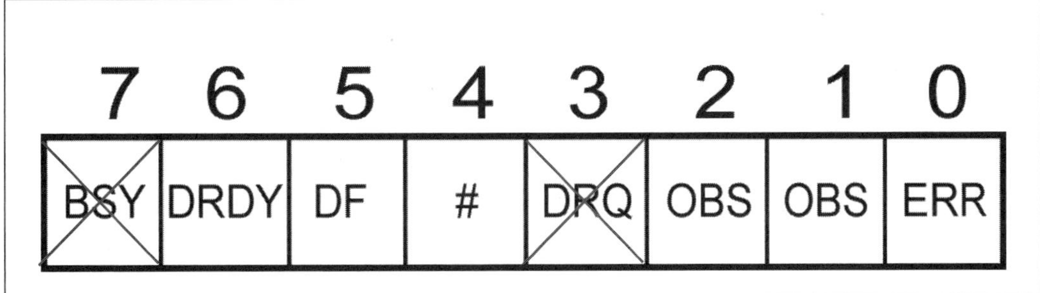

Set Device Bits with Active Field

Figure 5-7 pictures the Set Device Bits FIS with the 32-bit SATA Active (SActive) field in DW1. Bits within the SActive field, when set, will clear the corresponding bits in the HBA's SActive register. These SActive register bits are related to the Native Command Queuing (NCQ) protocols and indicate which commands are currently outstanding. See Chapter 14, on page 235 for details regarding NCQ and the use of the SActive field. The values in the Status and Error register fields in DW0 must also be valid.

Figure 5-7: Format of Set Device Bits FIS with Active Field

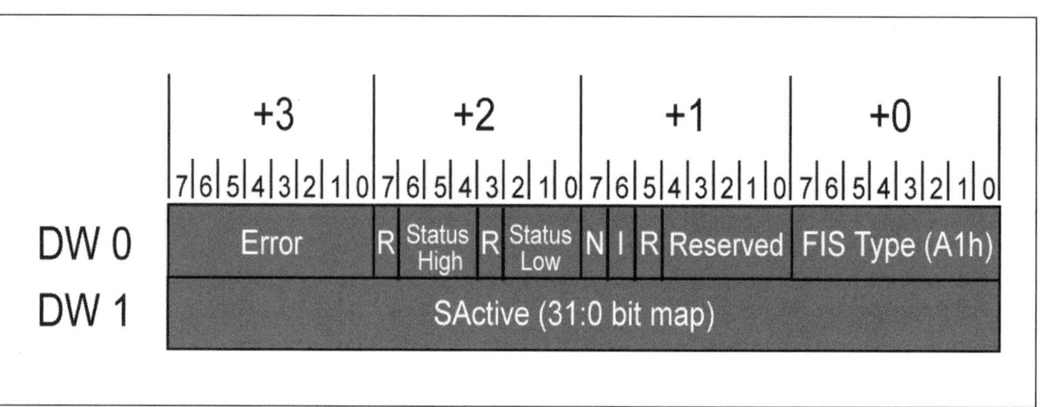

Set Device Bits with Event Notification

The Set Device Bits FIS is also used for Asynchronous Event Notification. Figure 5-8 on page 95 highlights the "N" bit within DW0, which is reserved unless Asynchronous Event Notification is supported by hardware and enabled by software. The values in the Status and Error register fields in DW0 must remain valid. See also the section entitled "Asynchronous Event Notification" on page 380.

Figure 5-8: Format of Set Device Bits with Event Notification

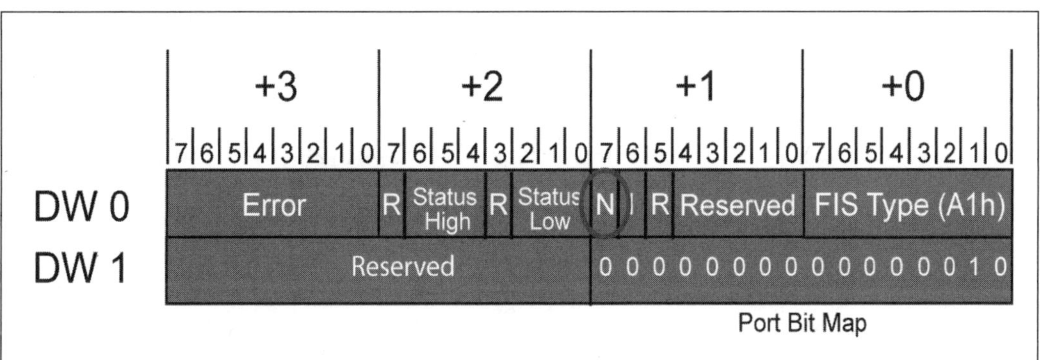

PIO Setup FIS

This FIS is delivered from a SATA device during execution of any Programmed IO (PIO) command prior to the transfer of data. The PIO Setup FIS provides the necessary information for the HBA to handle the data transfer efficiently and to report the correct status information.

Figure 5-9 on page 96 defines the content and shows the format of the PIO Setup FIS. The contents reflect that of the SATA device's ATA registers but also provides two additional pieces of information:

- End Status (E_Status) — End Status contains the valid status following Data transfer to/from the host. This is supplied in addition to the Status field contents that report beginning status.
- Transfer Count — This count indicates the amount of data to be transferred in the subsequent Data FIS.

See "PIO Commands" on page 187 for details regarding use of the PIO Setup FIS during PIO reads and writes.

Figure 5-9: Format and Content of PIO Setup FIS

	+3 (bits 7–0)	+2 (bits 7–0)	+1 (bits 7–0)	+0 (bits 7–0)
DW 0	Error	Status	R | I | D | Reserved	FIS Type (5Fh)
DW 1	Dev/Head	Cyl High	Cyl Low	Sector Number
DW 2	Reserved (0)	Cyl High (exp)	Cyl Low (exp)	Sec Num (exp)
DW 3	E_Status	Reserved (0)	Sec Count (exp)	Sector Count
DW 4	Reserved (0)		Transfer Count	

DMA Setup FIS

The DMA Setup FIS is defined as a bi-directional FIS that allows either the Host or Device to setup a DMA transfer.

Figure 5-10: Format of the DMA Setup FIS

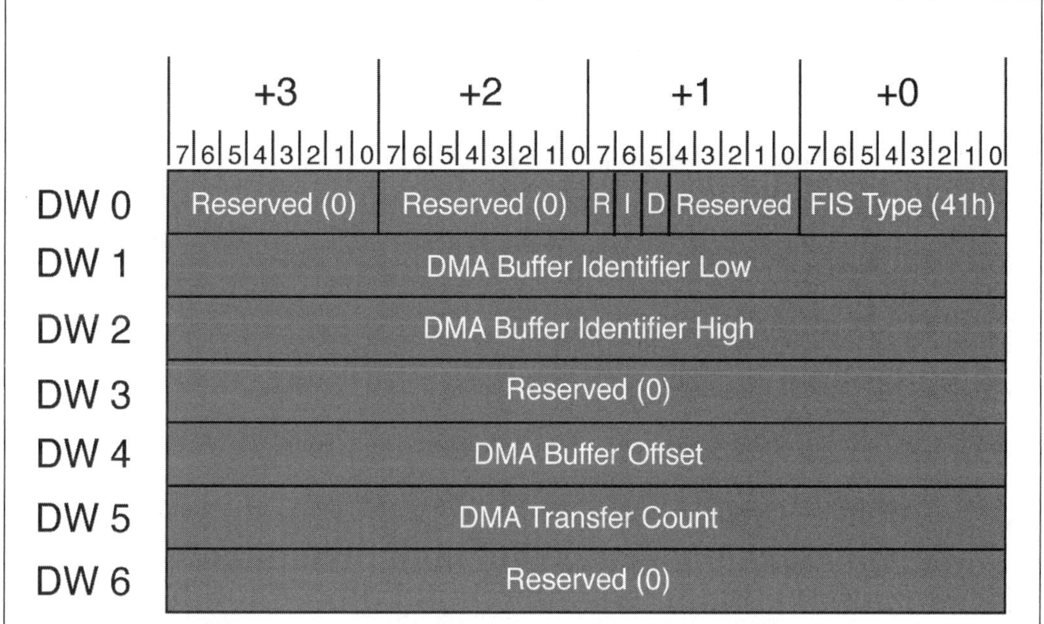

First Party DMA Setup

The second generation of SATA defines a different version of the DMA Setup to support Native Command Queuing. Using this technique, the drive can read data from or write data to disc out of order to reduce overall drive latency. Consequently, the drive must issues the DMA Setup FIS to the HBA to specify which command and the memory buffer offset that must be accessed to store or retrieve data it is currently transferring.

Figure 5-11 on page 98 illustrates the changes in content and format to the DMA Setup FIS. Note that a Tag field has been added to identify the command associated with the data transfer, the memory buffer offset, and amount of data to be transferred with the following Data FIS. See Chapter 14, on page 235, for details regarding NCQ and First Party DMA protocol.

Figure 5-11: Format of DMA Setup FIS for First Party DMA Operations

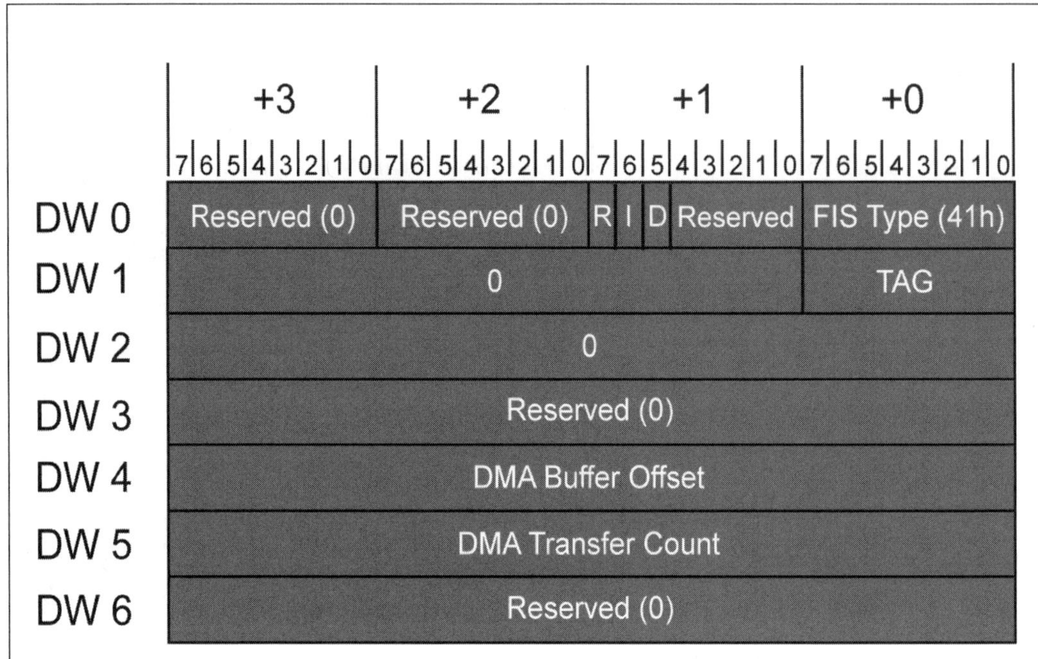

DMA Setup with Auto Activate

An optional bit called Auto Active may be supported by some drives to improve the efficiency of the First Party DMA write protocol. Figure 5-12 on page 99 shows the addition of the "A" (Auto Activate) bit that when set notifies the HBA that the drive is ready to receive the data. The normal protocol during a First Party DMA write command sequence is for the drive to send the DMA Setup FIS followed by a DMA Activate FIS (See Figure 5-13 on page 99). The DMA Activate FIS explicitly notifies the HBA that it's ready to receive the data. The DMA Activate FIS can be eliminated if the drive supports the auto activation feature within the DMA Setup.

Figure 5-12: Auto Activate Feature of the DMA Setup FIS

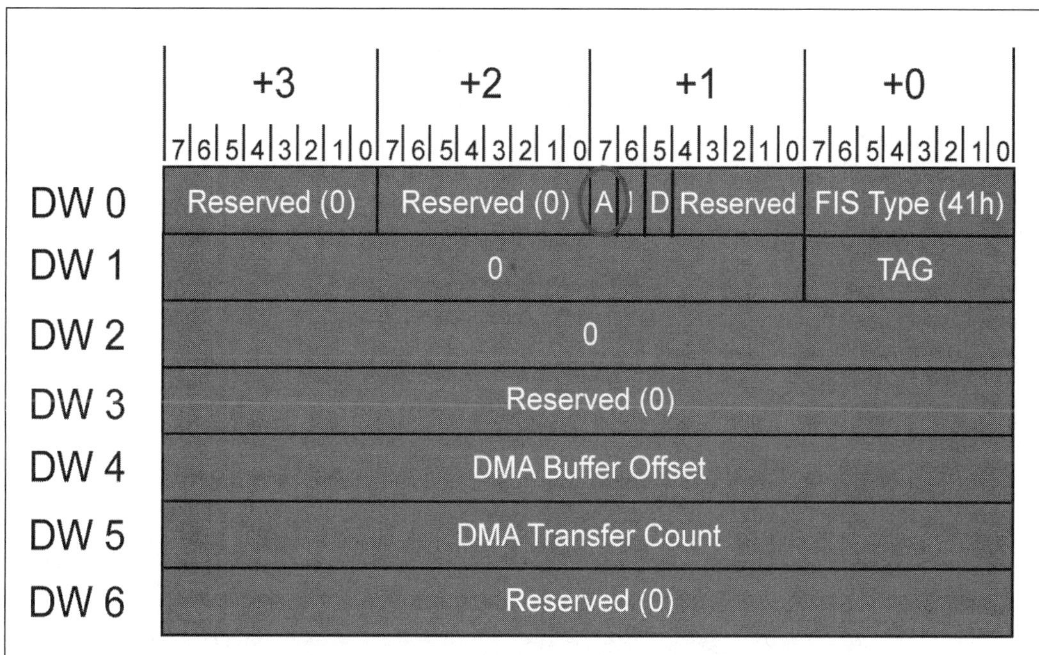

DMA Activate FIS

Drive's use the DMA Active FIS during DMA write operations to notify the HBA that it is ready to receive the DMA write data. This FIS consists of a single DWord and all bits other than the DMA Activate ID are reserved as shown in Figure 5-13 on page 99.

Figure 5-13: Format of the DMA Activate FIS

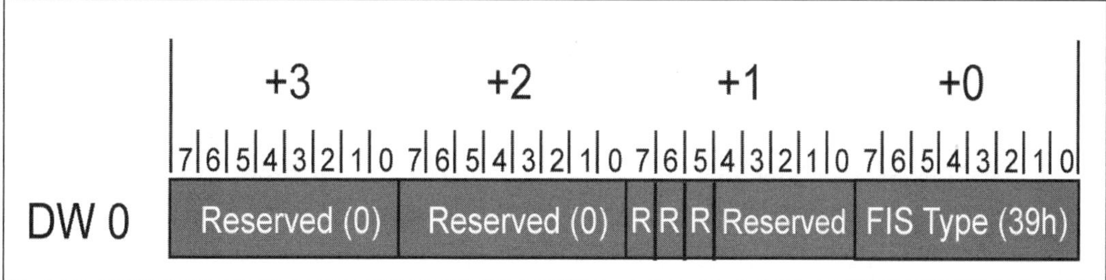

DATA FIS

A DATA FIS carries the data payload between the HBA and the Drive. The maximum payload size is limited to 2048 DWs (8,192 bytes), while the smallest payload size is 4 DWs. See Figure 5-14 on page 100. Note that the size of the Data FIS payload must always be multiples of 4 bytes. If the actual payload size is not a multiple of 4 bytes, the payload must be padded with zeros.

Figure 5-14: Format of the DATA FIS

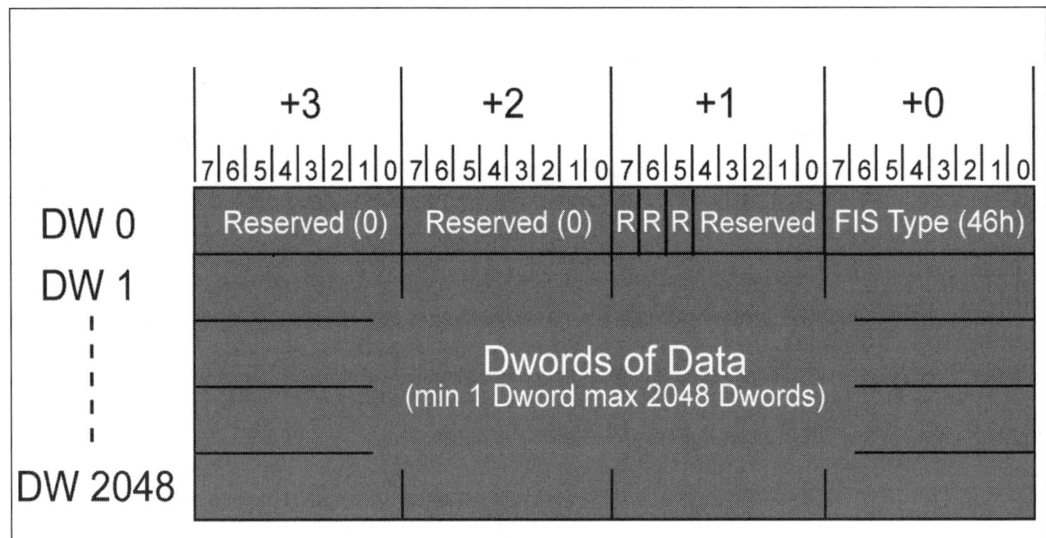

BIST Activate FIS

This BIST (Built In Self Test) Activate FIS is intended for verification and diagnostic purposes. See Figure 5-15 on page 101. The pattern definition bits are used to place the receiving device into a particular test mode. These modes include:

- Silicon loopback modes
- Bypass scrambling
- Compliance test pattern generation
- Vendor-specific tests

See Chapter 23, on page 393 for complete information regarding BIST capabilities.

Figure 5-15: BIST FIS Content and Format

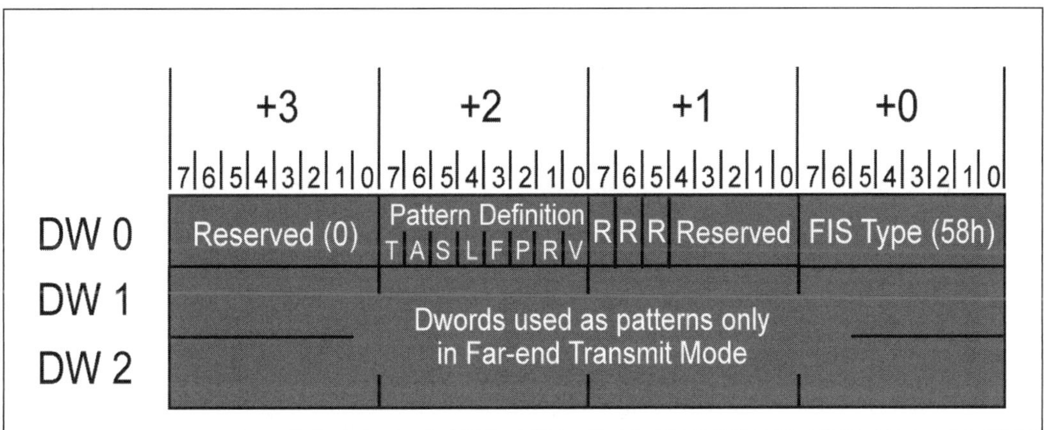

6 Transport and Link Protocols

Previous Chapter

The previous chapter is primarily for reference purposes. It includes details associated with each of the frame information structures, including definition of all fields within each FIS.

This Chapter

The link transfer protocol is implemented primarily within the link layer of both the transmitter and receiver. This chapter discusses the individual steps taken by the transport and link layers in transferring a FIS.

The Next Chapter

When a FIS is transferred across the SATA link transmission errors are typically detected and reported back to the transmitting device. Upon detection of the transmission error, the Transport layer is notified to the failure. Having retained a copy of the failed FIS, the Transport layer re-transmits the FIS. The next chapter discusses the mechanisms and conditions under which a FIS retry is permitted.

Overview

FIS delivery is most often triggered by software initiating a particular command. Each command consists of a sequence of frame information structures that are exchanged between the HBA and the drive. In some cases the frame information structure originates at the Application layer, while in other cases the frame information structure is determined at the command layer. As has been stated previously, regardless of the origin of a frame information structure the transfer protocol used for the delivery of each FIS is essentially the same.

The transport and link layers work together to create and control the delivery of each FIS. The Transport layer creates and stores each FIS in a transmit buffer and notifies the link that FIS delivery is pending. The Link layer manages most of the transmission protocol through delivery and reception of primitives. Figure 6-1 details the steps performed by the transport and link layers associated with the transmission and reception of each FIS.

Figure 6-1: Transport- and Link-Layer Elements Involved in FIS Transfers

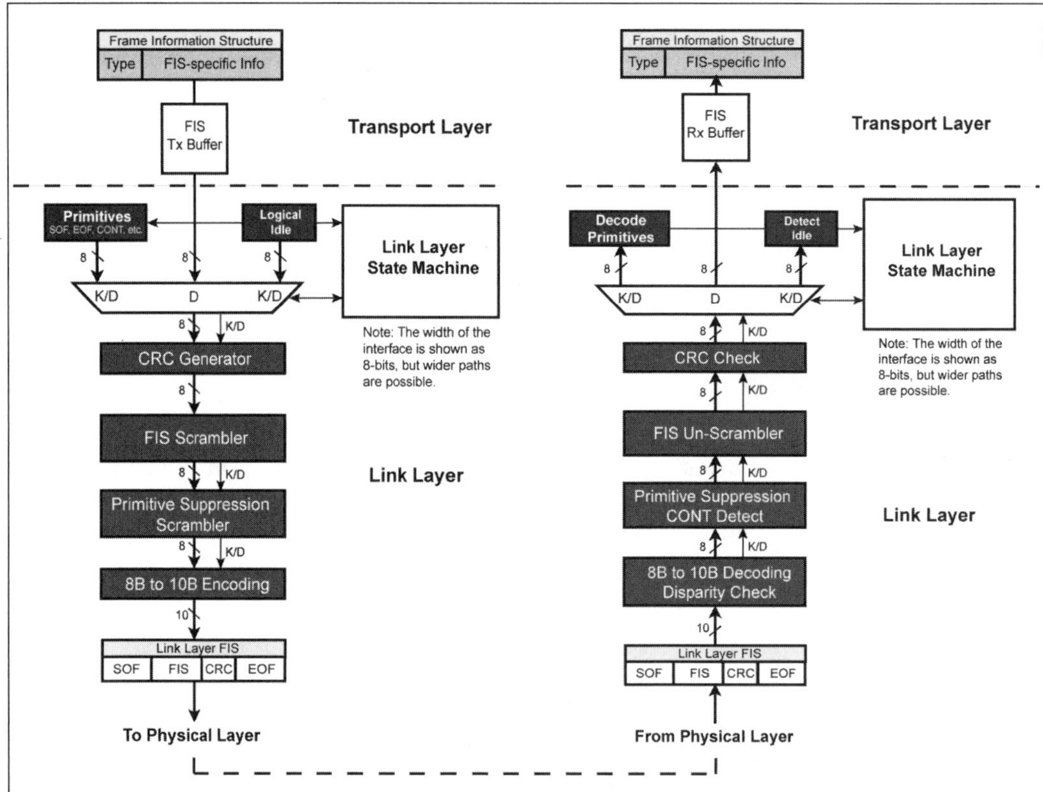

The descriptions in the following sections presume that the FIS transfer occurs successfully. Subsequent chapters detail protocol variations such as FIS transmission retries and flow control.

FIS Transmission

Figure 6-2 on page 106 illustrates the primary elements associated with preparing the FIS for transmission and managing the protocol. The link layer manages event sequences associated with the delivery of each frame information structure. These event sequences involve the generation and reception of primitives, along with preparing each FIS for delivery across the link. This process involves several steps:

- Link Transfer Request/Arbitration
- FIS Transfer (Transport layer to Link layer)
- CRC generation
- Framing each FIS with start and end of frame primitives
- FIS scrambling
- Primitive suppression scrambling
- 8- to 10-bit encoding

Figure 6-2: Major Transport- and Link-Layer Elements Associated with FIS transmission

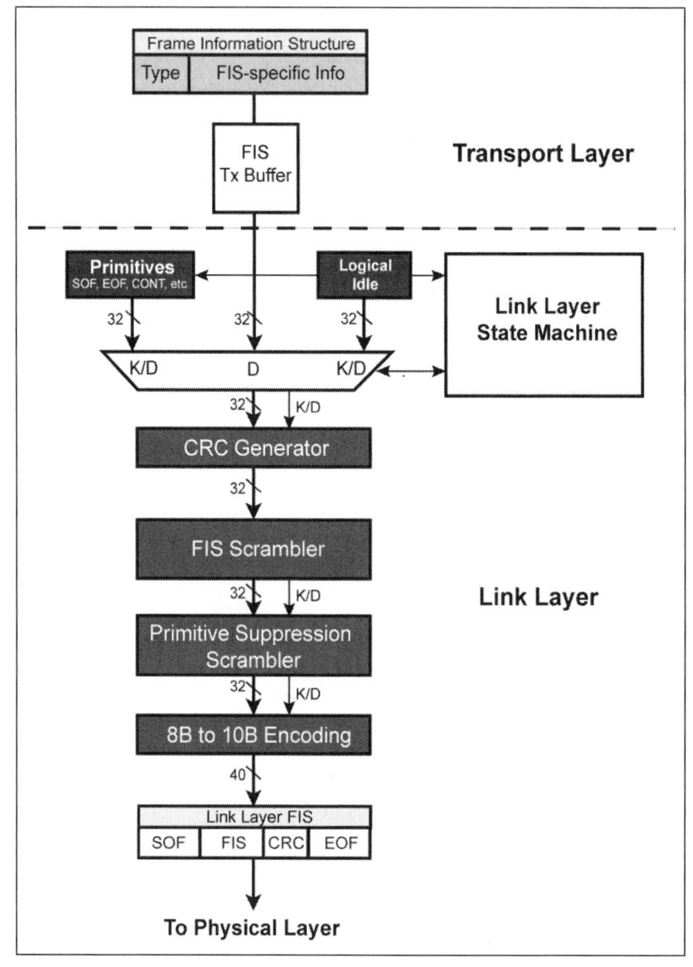

Primitive Generation - FIS Transmitter

Primitives originate in the link layer and provide control and status information during FIS transmission and for functions such as link power management. Figure 6-3 on page 107 is a general block diagram that depicts the source of primitives. The primitives like all of the information delivered across the serial link is encoded via the 8-to-10-bit encoder. (See "8b/10b Encoding" on page 116.)

Figure 6-3: Primitive Generation within the Link Layer

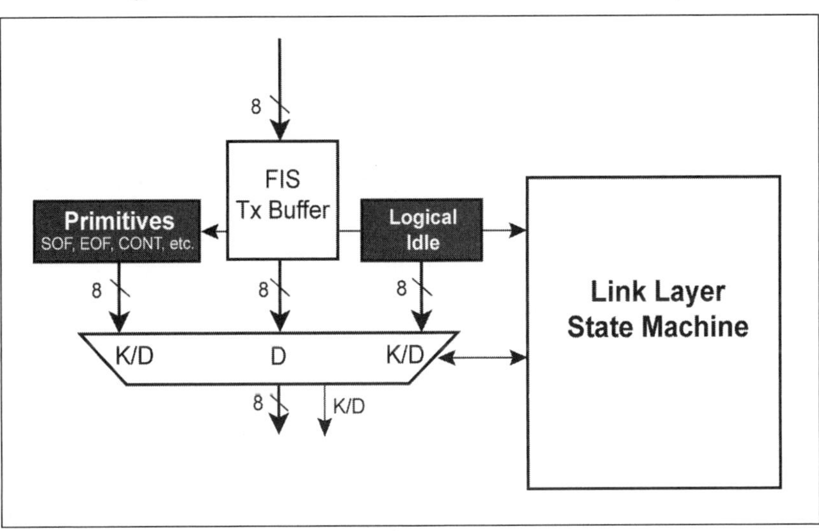

Primitives comprise a 10-bit control value followed by 3 consecutive data values. Other architectures use the terminology "ordered set" for this type of sequence. In SATA, once a SATA link is initialized via OOB signaling, it constantly carries primitives and occasionally frame information structures. Figure 6-4 shows the 10-bit encoded values and format of the Sync primitive. The Sync primitive, which is sent repeatedly, indicates an idle condition on the SATA interface and in most implementations is the most prevalent primitive.

Figure 6-4: Content and Format of Sync Primitive

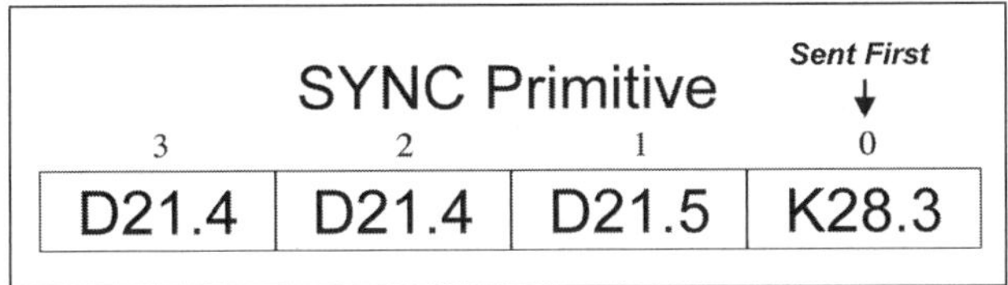

Table 6 - 1 on page 108 lists the primitives that the FIS transmitter sends and describes the purpose of each. Table 6 - 2 on page 119 describes the primitives that are transmitted by a device that is receiving a FIS. Each primitive is discussed in context to FIS transmission in the following sections. For a complete list of primitives along with the values please see Table 23-6 on page 403.

Table 6 - 1: Primitives Generated by FIS Transmitter

Primitive	Name	
SYNC	Synchronization	Used to indicate a logical bus idle condition
X_RDY	Transmitter Ready	Host or Device ready to transmit FIS
SOF	Start of Frame	Beginning of frame data payload and CRC to follow
EOF	End of Frame	EOF marks the end of a frame and that the previous non-primitive Dword is the frame's CRC
WTRM	Wait for Frame Termination	Following the EOP, which indicates FIS delivery is complete, the transmitter sends a WTRM primitive while awaiting reception of the status primitive from receiver.
CONT	Continue	The CONT primitive is used to support primitive suppression mechanism.

FIS Transmission Buffer

The primary function of the Transport layer is to create a valid or compliant FIS structure, store it in a transmission buffer, and notify the link layer that FIS transmission is pending. The size of this buffer must be large enough to store all of the frame information structures except the data FIS. The largest non-data FIS is 7 DWs (28 bytes). An entire non-data FIS is delivered from the transmit buffer to the link layer for delivery across the link. Note that a copy of the FIS is kept within the buffer until successful reception is reported by the receiver. This permits retransmission of the FIS in the event of a failed transfer. Chapter 7, on page 125 details the FIS Retry protocol.

FIS Arbitration

When the link layer receives notification from the transport layer that a FIS is ready for delivery, it generates and sends a Transmit Ready (X_RDY) primitive to the receiver. When the receiver detects X_RDY it returns a Receive Ready primitive to indicate it's prepared to receive the FIS.

A problem can occur when both the HBA and the SATA device each attempt to send a FIS at the same time. Such occurrences should be rare because command processing involves a defined sequence where delivery of a FIS from Device A typically triggers a FIS be returned from Device B. One example of the conflict can occur when the HBA needs to send a command to a drive and the drive needs to notify the host of an asynchronous. This results in both devices sending the X_RDY to the other. Figure 6-5 on page 109 A, illustrates this condition and lists the actual 10-bit values comprising the X_RDY primitives. The HBA must resolve the conflict by relinquishing its bid for link ownership by returning R_RDY as shown in Figure 6-5 B.

Figure 6-5: Arbitration Problem and Solution

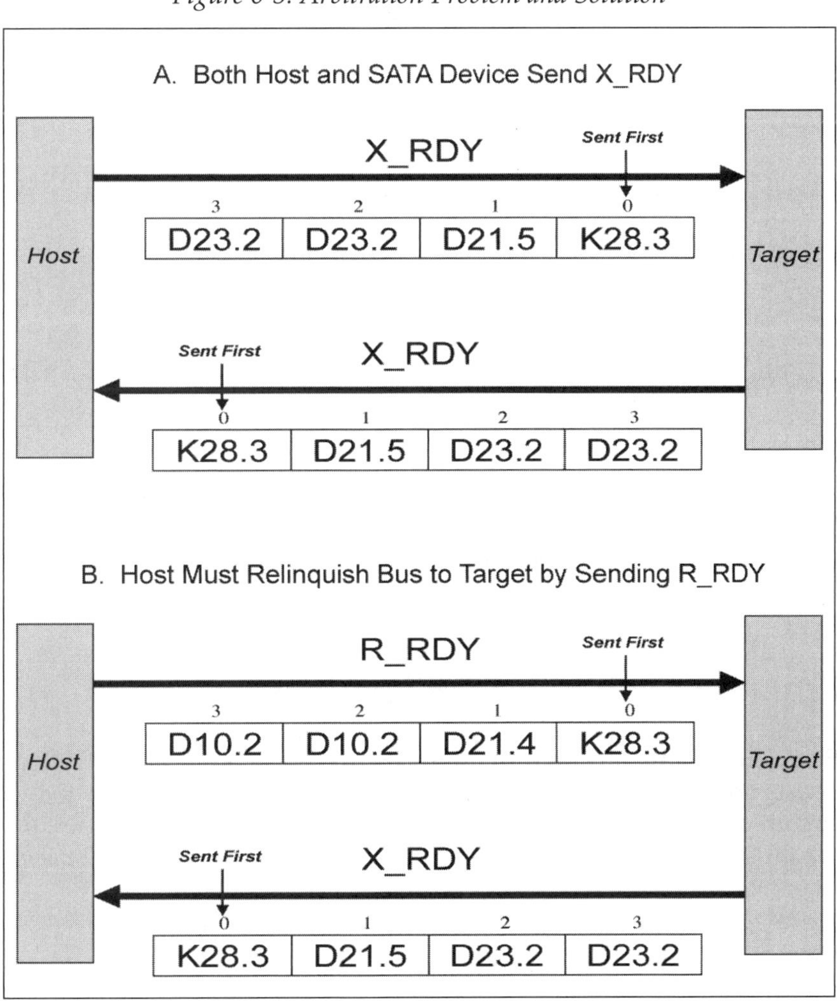

CRC Generation

The Link layer must generate a 32-bit CRC and append it to the end of each FIS. Note that the specification states that the maximum amount of data between the Start of Frame and End of Frame primitives must not exceed 2064 DWs. Figure Figure 6-6 pictures the Maximum payload supported along with the CRC generator polynomial. This Payload limit is specified to reflect the largest data block that can be supported by the 32-bit CRC and still accurately detect the required errors. The actual maximum-sized FIS currently defined is a DATA FIS containing a 4028 DWs of data plus 1 DWord of overhead.

Figure 6-6: Largest Payload Size Support by CRC

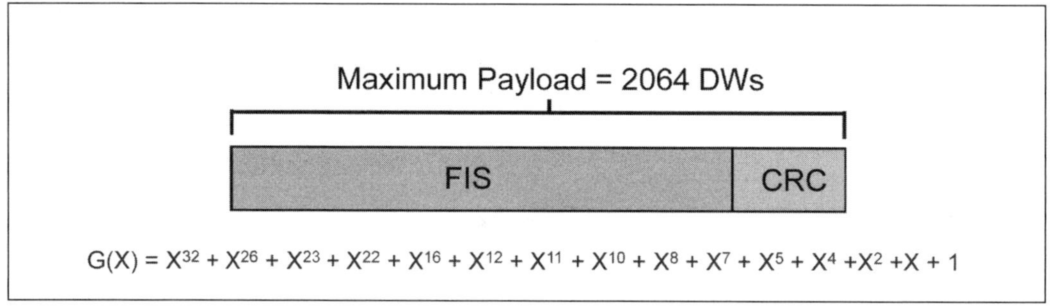

The CRC value is always calculated on DWord quantities; thus, data payloads that are not multiples of 4 bytes must be padded with zeros to create a DWord aligned quantity.

Framing Each FIS (SOF and EOF)

Each FIS is framed by Start of Frame (SOF) and End of Frame (EOF) primitives. These primitives allow the receiver to identify each FIS from the continuing stream of information constantly being sent across the link. Figure 6-7 on page 111 illustrates the SOF and EOF primitive and lists the contents of each.

Figure 6-7: Placement and Format of the SOF and EOF Primitives

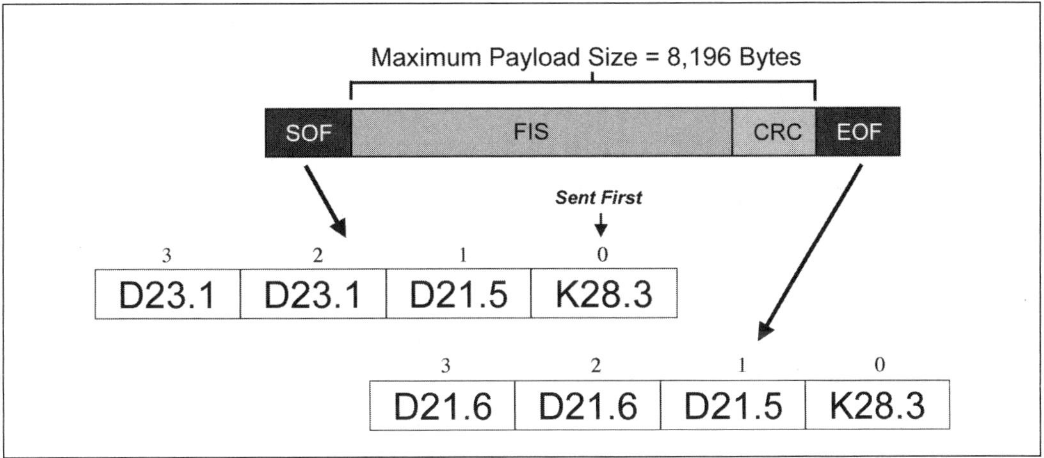

The FIS is delivered by the link layer upon detecting the R_RDY primitive from the receiver.

FIS Scrambling

FIS scrambling reduces EMI by spreading noise over a much broader frequency spectrum. That is, the repeated patterns of the information being sent across the link results in concentrations of energy at the frequency of the pattern repetition. Scrambling creates pseudo-random FIS data thus reducing EMI. All data between SOF and EOF including the CRC is scrambled. The algorithm used for scrambling each FIS is expressed as a polynomial and also described by the operation of a linear feedback shift register (LFSR). Figure 6-8 on page 112 depicts both.

As implied by its name, the FIS scrambling pattern is applied only to the FIS (data) but not to primitives. During delivery of a primitive the scrambler must not be advanced. Note also that in some cases primitives may be inserted within the FIS itself. This can occur during flow control and during clock compensation. Primitives are not subject to scrambling because the data patterns that define each primitive must be detected by the physical layer (i.e., prior to unscrambling).

Figure 6-8: The Scrambling Algorithm and LFSR implementation Model

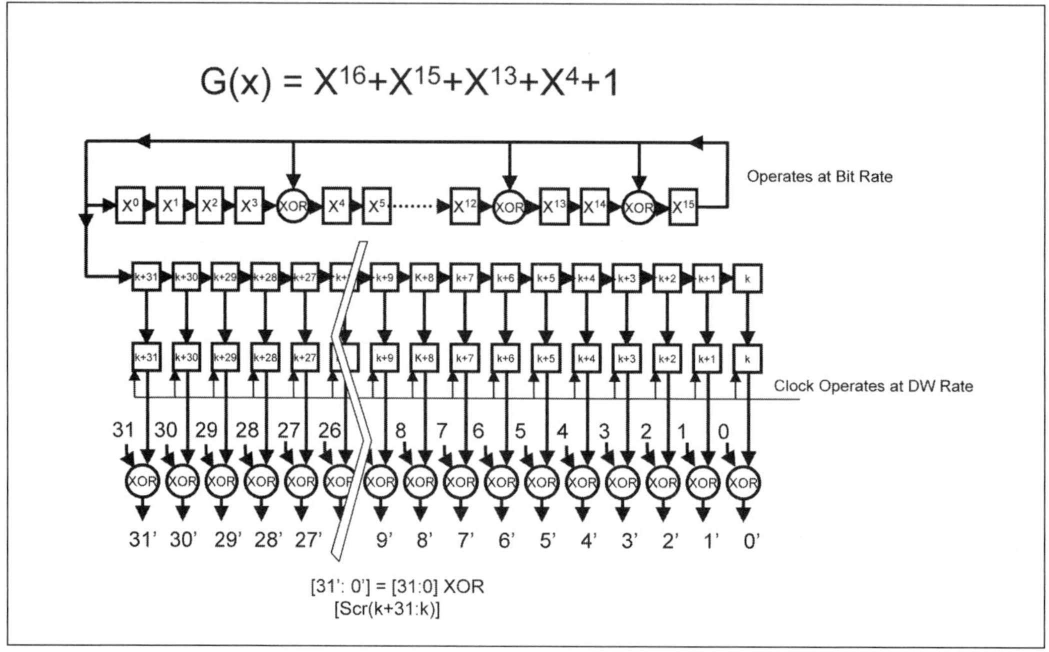

The scrambler implementation represented in Figure 6-8 requires clocking the LFSR at the bit rate (1.5 or 3.0 Gb/s) and the 32-bits of scrambled data would be output at the DWord rate (37.5MHz or 75MHz). The scrambler is reset to a value of all ones (FFFFh) when a SOF primitive arrives at the scrambler. This means that the scrambler is reset at the beginning of each FIS. Consequently, the maximum number of 32-bit scrambling patterns that the scrambler would ever produce is equivalent to the maximum FIS size in DWs (2064). These scrambling patterns could be generated and stored in a ROM for output at the DWord clock rate. Note that the specification does not specify any particular implementation.

Note that the scrambler width in Figure 6-8 illustrates a width of 32 bits (1 DWord); whereas, Figure 6-2 on page 106 depicts an 8-bit interface. The specification allows parallel widths of 8-, 16-, or 32-bits.

Repeated Primitive Suppression

The scrambling mechanism discussed in the previous section solves a potential EMI problem due to repeated patterns during FIS delivery. Primitives are not scrambled because the primitive's unique patterns could not otherwise be detected prior to the unscrambling stage within the receiver's link layer. However, when continuous strings of primitives are sent across the link, the repeated patterns can also cause EMI. Figure 6-9 exemplifies a slice of bus time and activity where primitives are being sent repeatedly. This diagram shows a column view of the information being simultaneously delivered from Host to Device and from Device to Host. Each row represents delivery of a single primitive (1 DWord), which is equivalent to 40 bit times (26.64ns for gen 1 and 13.32ns for gen 2).

Figure 6-9: Repeated Primitives

Host	Device
X_RDY	SYNC
X_RDY	SYNC
X_RDY	SYNC
X_RDY	SYNC
X_RDY	SYNC
X_RDY	SYNC
X_RDY	R_RDY
X_RDY	R_RDY
SOF	R_RDY
FIS Data	R_RDY

CONT Primitive

To suppress the repeated primitives and reduce the EMI problem, SATA uses a Continue (CONT) primitive to suppress long strings of repeated primitives. The specification requires that after repeating a given primitive once, that a CONT primitive can be delivered followed by pseudo-random data created by a second scrambler.

Consider the example in Figure 6-10. The illustration on the left illustrates primitives being repeated continuously and the right side illustrates the same sequence as it would appear with primitive suppression. Following the CONT primitive the "XXXX" values represent pseudo-random data generated by the repeated primitive suppression scrambler. CONT is an indication that the previous primitives are presumed to continue until another primitive is sent. The receiver simply discards the "XXXX" values following the CONT, while waiting for the next primitive.

Figure 6-10: CONT Primitive Used to Eliminate Repeated Primitives

Host	Device
X_RDY	SYNC
X_RDY	SYNC
X_RDY	SYNC
X_RDY	SYNC
X_RDY	SYNC
X_RDY	SYNC
X_RDY	R_RDY
X_RDY	R_RDY
SOF	R_RDY
FIS Data	R_RDY

No Primitive Suppression

Host	Device
X_RDY	XXXX
X_RDY	XXXX
CONT	XXXX
XXXX	XXXX
XXXX	XXXX
XXXX	XXXX
XXXX	R_RDY
XXXX	R_RDY
SOF	CONT
FIS Data	XXXX

With Primitive Suppression

Some primitives such as SOF, EOF, and CONT are never repeated and some repeated primitives are restricted in their use. The following list defines the primitives that are subject to repeated primitive suppression.

- HOLD
- HOLDA
- PMREQ_P
- PMREQ_S
- R_ERR
- R_IP
- R_OK
- R_RDY
- SYNC
- WTRM
- XRDY

Repeated Primitive Scrambler

The DWord output of the repeated primitive scrambler is represented by "XXXX." The repeated primitive scrambler uses the same algorithm as the FIS scrambler. The scrambler does not need to exclusively OR any information with the scrambler output as shown in Figure 6-11. Nor does this scrambler need to be reset periodically. Finally, none of the data generated by this primitive suppression scrambler affects the operation of the FIS scrambler.

Figure 6-11: Primitive Suppression Scrambling Algorithm and Implementation

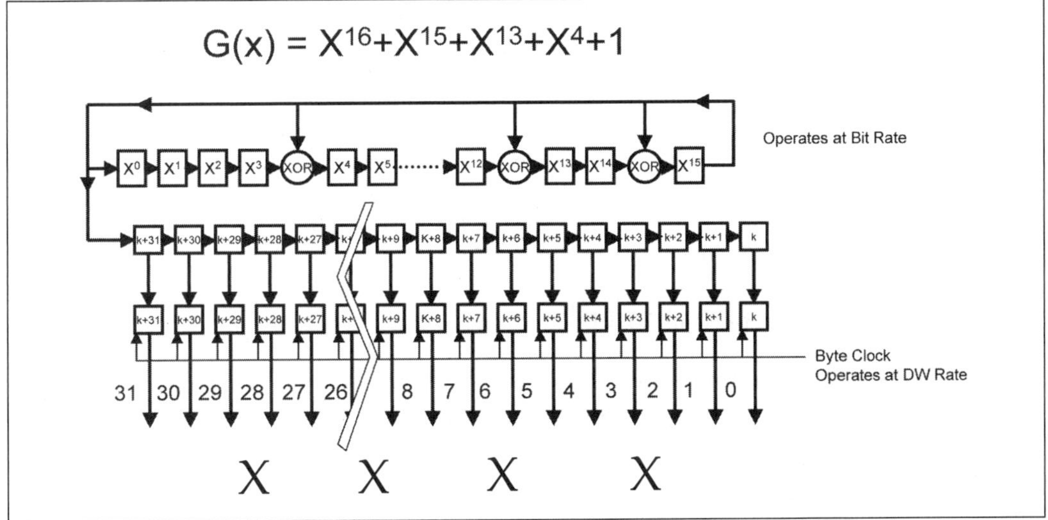

8b/10b Encoding

General

Like the vast majority of high-speed serial bus implementations, SATA encodes all data using the 8-bit to 10-bit (8b/10b) encoding scheme. Because many readers may already be familiar with 8b/10b encoding, this section describes the characteristics of only the SATA version. Those not familiar with 8b/10b encoding may want to review the Tutorial included in Appendix A, entitled "8b/10b Encoding Tutorial," on page 409.

Purpose of Encoding a Character Stream

One of the major goals of 8b/10b encoding is to embed a clock into the serial bit stream before transmission across the link. This eliminates the need for a high frequency 1.5/3.0 GHz clock signal on the link that would generate significant EMI noise.

The 8b to 10b Conversion

Every byte to be transmitted across the link is converted to a 10-bit value, called an encoded character. Figure 6-12 on page 117 illustrates the look-up table associated with the encoder. As the two tables suggest, two types of information are encoded:

- Data bytes — consisting of every byte within every FIS, the attached CRC, the last 3 bytes of each primitive, and all data output from the repeated primitive scrambler. The data lookup table must support the 256 possible input values.
- Control bytes— consisting of the first byte of each primitive. Note that only 2 control characters are used by SATA.

Current Running Disparity

The 8b/10b encoding scheme also provides a mechanism for detecting transmission error based on the concept of disparity. Each encoded character has disparity associated with it. That is, whether the 10-bit value has:

- 5 zeros and 5 ones - neutral disparity
- 6 zeros and 4 ones - negative disparity
- 4 zeros and 6 ones - positive disparity

Each entry within the lookup table has two possible value outputs depending on the disparity of the last non-neutral value delivered. This results in the current running disparity (CRD) toggling between negative and positive, with neutral values having no impact on CRD. Based on this pattern the 8b/10b decoder can detect most transmission errors.

Figure 6-12: 8b/10b Encoding

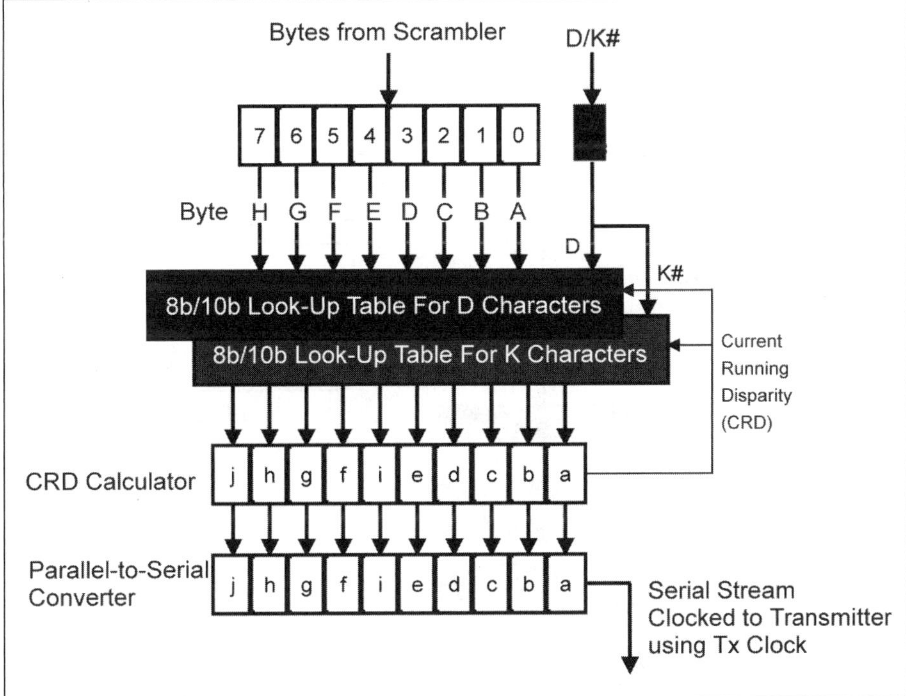

FIS Reception

Having discussed the transmission of a FIS in detail, discussion of the reception is much easier given that it's primarily an inverse set of operations with respect to transmission. Figure 6-13 on page 118 highlights processes and steps involved in FIS reception. These include:

- 8b/10b Decode and Error Detection
- Receiving Suppressed Primitives
- Unscrambling
- Primitive Decoding

- CRC Checking and Error Reporting
- Passing FIS to Transport layer receive Buffer
- FIS Decoding

Figure 6-13: Major Elements Involved in FIS reception

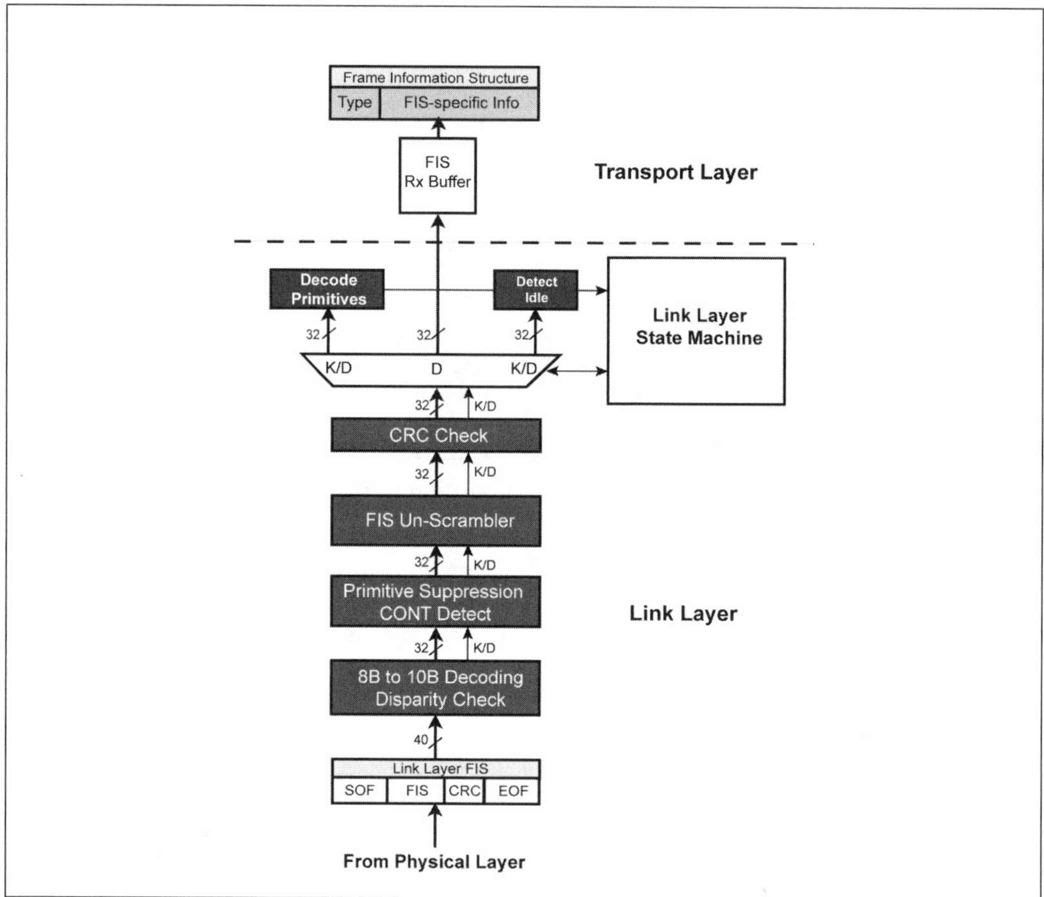

Primitive Generation - FIS Receiver

During arbitration and FIS reception the receiver must respond by returning primitives to the FIS transmitter. The primitives sent by the receiver in association with receiving a FIS are listed in Table 6 - 2 on page 119.

Table 6 - 2: Primitives Sent by FIS Receiver

Primitive	Name	
SYNC	Synchronization	Used to indicate a logical bus idle condition
R_RDY	Receiver Ready	Host or Device ready to receive FIS
R_IP	Reception in progress	Host or device is receiving the FIS
R_OK	Reception OK	No error detected during FIS reception
R_ERR	Reception Error	Error(s) detected during FIS reception
CONT	Continue	The CONT primitive allows long strings of repeated primitives to be eliminated. The CONT primitive implies that the previously received primitive be repeated as long as another primitive is not received.

8b/10b Decode

Information from the physical layer is passed to the link layer where the 8b/10b decoding takes place. Two functions are involved — the decoding and the disparity error check. Appendix A details the decoding process and disparity error checking.

The 8b/10b Decoder uses two lookup tables (the D and K tables) to convert the 10-bit value stream back into bytes. Each value is submitted to both lookup tables but only one of the tables will find a match for the value. The state of the D/K# signal indicates that the received value is a:

- Data (D) value — a match for the received value is located in the D table. D/K# is driven High.
- Control (K) value — a match for the received value is located in the K table. D/K# is driven Low.

Error Detection

The two types of errors detected are:

- Code violation errors (i.e., a 10-bit symbol could not be decoded into a valid 8-bit Data or Control value)
- Disparity errors.

When an error is detected it is reported to the higher layers where status bits are set and decisions are made regarding error recovery. In addition if an error is detected during FIS reception the receiver returns the receiver error (R_ERR) primitive to the FIS transmitter after the FIS has been received.

See Appendix A, entitled "8b/10b Encoding Tutorial," on page 409 for details regarding 8b/10 decoding.

Figure 6-14: 8b/10b Decoding Elements

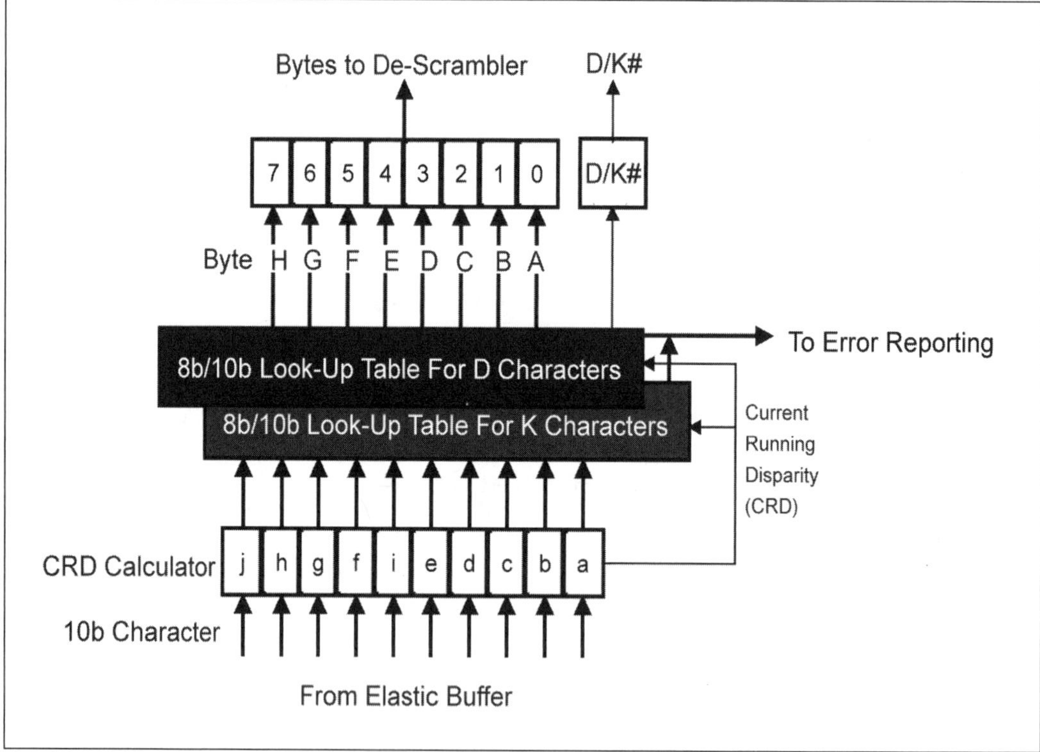

Primitive Suppression Detection

When the receiver detects a CONT primitive it must presume that the primitive received just prior to the CONT primitive is considered to be continuing until another primitive is detected. All data received between the CONT primitive and the next valid primitive are discarded.

FIS Unscrambling

The FIS Unscrambler must maintain synchronization with the scrambler. This is achieved by ensuring that the Linear Feedback Shift Register is preset to all ones with each SOF. This ensures that the scrambler and unscrambler produce the same scrambling value for each byte of the FIS, thereby allowing the original data to be recovered by exclusively ORing the same scrambling value with the scrambled data.

Detecting FIS

The link layer decodes the primitives as they are forwarded to the upper portion of the link layer. Once the receiver has sent the R_RDY primitive it awaits the arrival of the FIS. When the SOF primitive is decoded the link layer returns the Receive In Progress (R_IP) primitive to the FIS transmitter.

CRC Check

CRC is checked to validate the FIS before it's forwarded to the Transport layer for decoding. If an error is detected, the R_ERR primitive is returned to the transmitter and the error is forwarded to the upper layers for updating SATA Error register and to notify software if required.

FIS Decode

Once the frame is validated the link layer forwards it to the Transport layer where the frame is decoded. The Transport layer forwards the data payload to the command and application layers for processing.

Summary of FIS Transfer Protocol

The preceding sections detailed the steps taken during FIS transmission and reception. This section summarizes the link traffic starting with the FIS transmission request to the receiver reporting final transfer status. Figure 6-15 on page 123 defines these steps using 3 segments as follows:

1. FIS transmission begins with the X_RDY primitive being sent by the transmitter. X_RDY is signaled continuously.
2. The receiver having detected a transfer request returns the R_RDY primitive.
3. Upon detecting R_RDY on its back-bus, the transmitter starts delivery of the frame by transmitting the SOF primitive followed by the FIS and CRC.
4. The receiver upon detecting SOF indicates it is receiving the frame by sending the R_IP primitive.
5. Completion of frame delivery is signaled via the EOF primitive followed immediately by WTRM (wait for terminate).
6. The receiver completes reception of the frame verifies successful delivery and reports status via the R_OK primitive.

Once the transmitter detects R_OK it delivers the SYNC primitive to return the bus to logical idle, and in response to detecting SYNC from the transmitter the receiver sends SYNC also returning it's transmitting side to idle.

It may not be obvious from the example in Figure 6-15 that neither the frame transmitter or receiver stop sending information. Figure 6-16 on page 124 illustrates a successful frame transfer using the column view of bus traffic at the 1.5Gb/s transmission rate. Each row equates to one DWord or 4 value times (26.64ns) and lists the content of the link in both directions. Note that the delayed responses are due to propagations delays associated with the reception and transmission of the information. For example, the time between X_RDY being sent by the host and R_RDY being send by the drive is 12 DWord times.

Figure 6-15: FIS Transfer Protocol Sequence

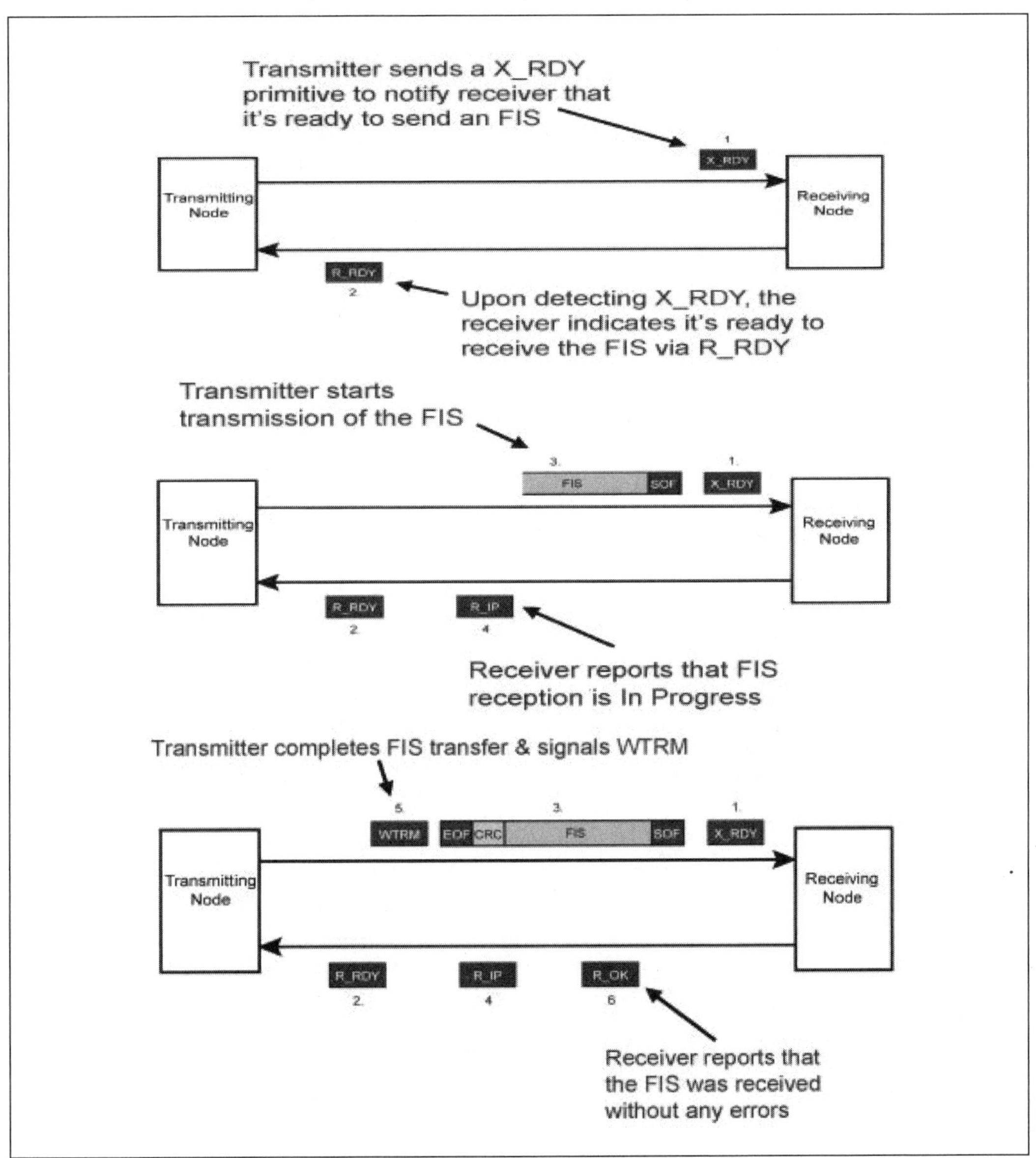

Figure 6-16: Column View of Successful FIS Transfer

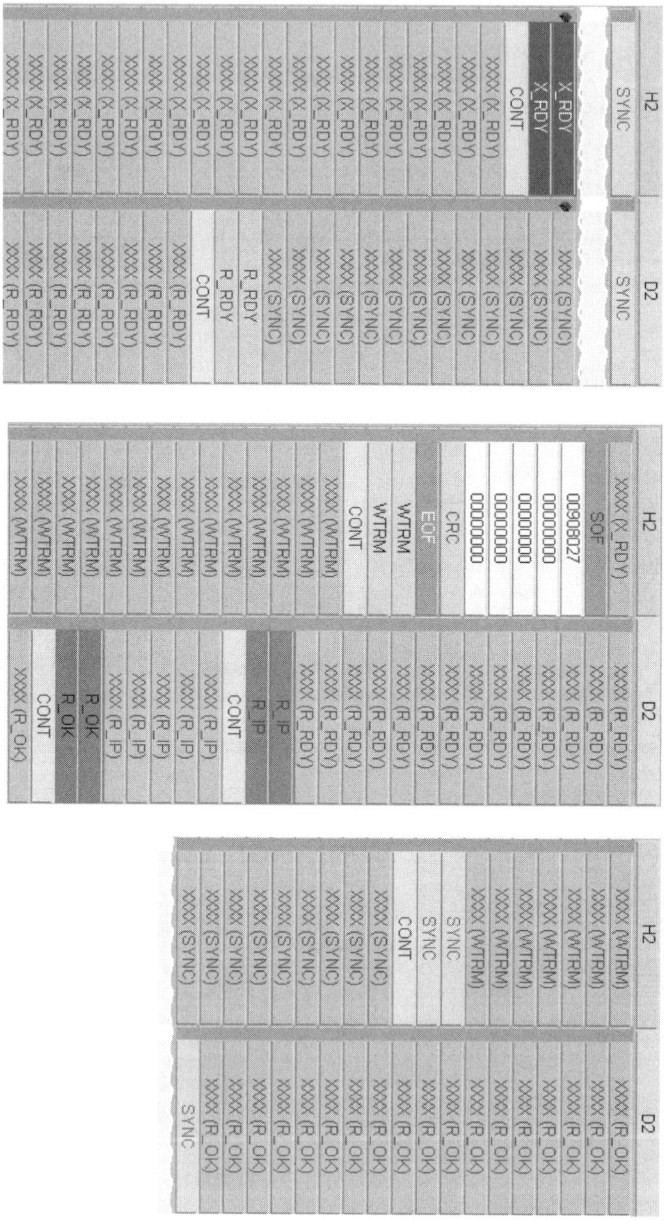

7 FIS Retry

Previous Chapter

The link transfer protocol is implemented primarily within the link layer of both the transmitter and receiver. The previous chapter discussed the individual steps taken by the transport and link layers in transferring a FIS.

This Chapter

When a FIS is transferred across the SATA link, transmission errors are typically detected and reported back to the transmitting device. Upon detection of the transmission error, the Transport layer is notified of the failure. Having retained a copy of the failed FIS, the Transport layer re-transmits the FIS. This chapter discusses the mechanisms and conditions under which a FIS retry is permitted.

The Next Chapter

When performing large data transfers the transmit and receive buffers within the transport layers may either overflow or underflow without some flow control mechanism. The next chapter describes the flow control mechanisms and protocols.

General

In many instances a FIS transmission error can be recovered without notification of software by simply re-sending (e.g., retrying) the FIS. This retry mechanism is managed by the Transport layer and requires the use of buffers that can retain a copy of the FIS after having sent it. Note that retry can be performed by either the HBA or drive.

Which FISes Can be Retried?

A FIS is eligible for retry only if it can be stored in its entirety within the replay buffer. Table 7-1 on page 126 lists each FIS type and its size. The Data FIS is by far the largest with a maximum size of 2049 DWs (8196 bytes). Note that the total size includes only the header and its payload because CRC, SOF and EOF are added by the link layer. The other FIS types have sizes no larger than 7DWs (28 bytes). Due to cost considerations the Transport layer's transmission buffer is not required to store an entire Data FIS, thereby eliminating the Data FIS from the retry protocol. This permits a 28 byte transmission buffer to support FIS retry for all other FIS types, except the BIST type, which is typically used during testing and diagnostics operations.

Without a buffer sufficient to store the maximum-sized data FIS, retry cannot be supported. Transmission of a data FIS results in a change in the host bus adapter's internal state, either through the DMA controller changing its state or through a change in the remaining PIO repetition count, data transmission FIS's shall not be retried.

Table 7-1: FIS Type, Size and Retry Eligibility

FIS Type	Size	Retry?
Data	2049 DWs	No
First Party DMA Setup	7 DWs	Yes
Register FIS	5 DWs	Yes
PIO Setup	5 DWs	Yes
BIST Activate	3 DWs	No
Set Device Bits	2 DWs	Yes
DMA Activate	1 DWs	Yes

Retry Protocol Overview

The retry protocol if implemented is triggered by an R_ERR handshake primitive being returned from the receiving device. Figure 7-1 on page 127 illustrates either an HBA or drive receiving an R_ERR primitive indicating that the FIS was received with some type of error condition. In this example the contents of the FIS remains in the Transport layer's transmit buffer so it can be retried. The specification does not limit the number of retries that can be attempted. If the FIS re-transmission fails repeatedly, host software will ultimately time-out, which results typically in the link interface being reset.

Figure 7-1: FIS Retry on Transmission Error

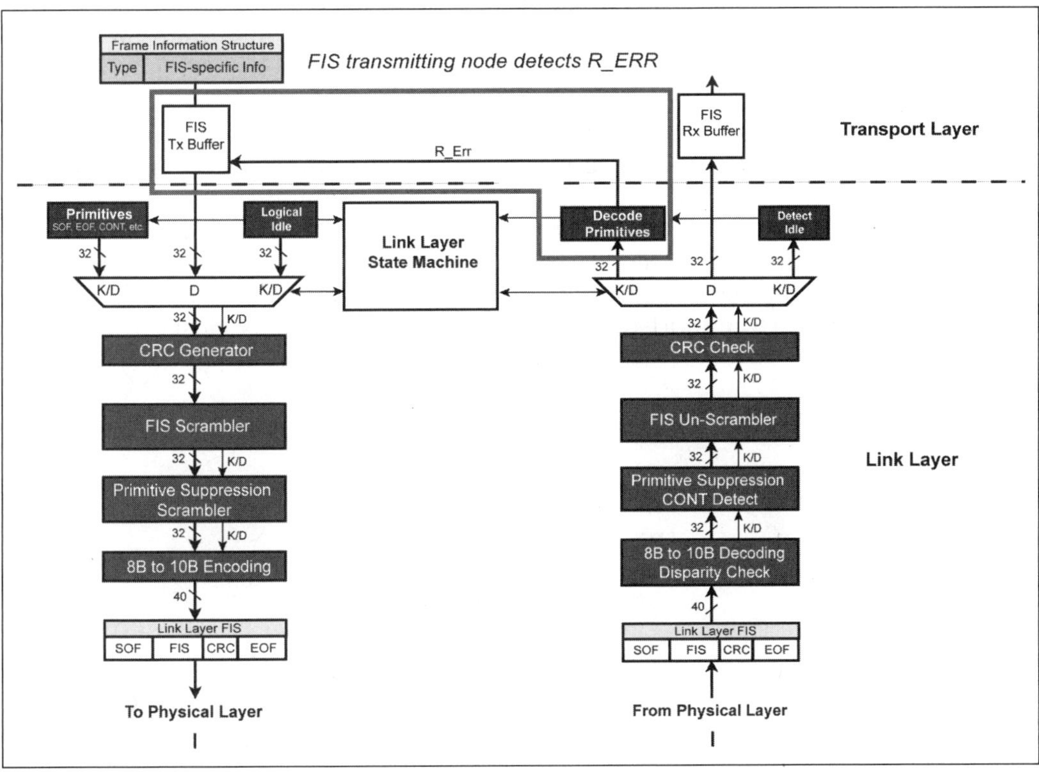

What Errors Result in Retry Attempts?

In general, errors that are transient in nature are those that qualify for and are likely to be recovered via the retry protocol. For example, errors may be due to transmission problems such as noise or due to power glitches, etc. Such errors are typically detected within the link layer and forwarded to the Transport layer for handling. Other FIS errors may be detected within the Transport layer itself.

Figure 7-2 on page 129 illustrates the Transport and Link layers and the FIS error detection and reporting features. Several error detection mechanisms are used (e.g., disparity and CRC checks) and two error reporting mechanisms are employed:

1. Delivery of R_ERR back to the transmitting node (Both HBA and drive)
2. Notifying upper layers to set the appropriate bits in the HBA's SATA Error Register (when the HBA receives an R_ERR primitive from the drive or when the HBA detects an error when receiving a Frame)

Whether the HBA or the drive transmits a frame, transmission errors are detected by the receiving node and reported back to the transmitter. If the corresponding retry is successful, no further action is required and the recovered error is reported in the HBAs SError register as noted above. However, some types of error are not allowed to attempt retry. In these cases no R_ERR is returned and the fatal error is reported by sending SYNC primitives. This forces the command to be aborted, which is ultimately detected by Host software via a timeout.

Figure 7-2: FIS Receiver Error Detection and Reporting

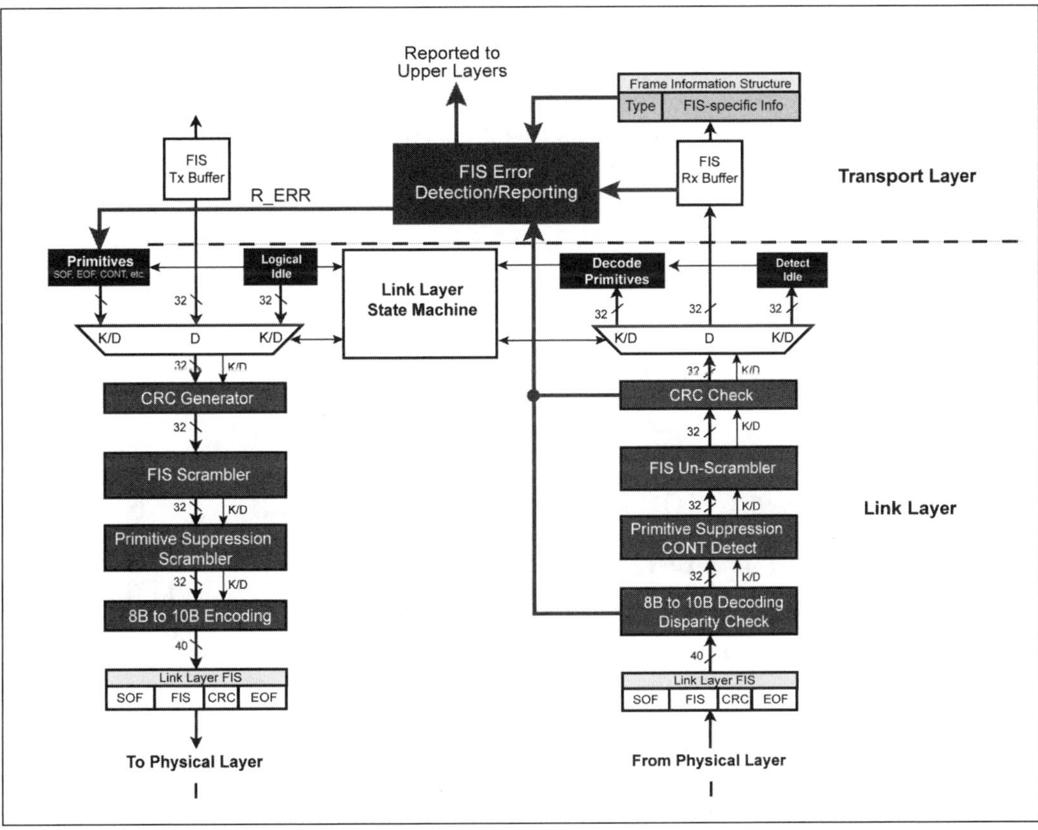

Transmission Errors — Detected by Link Layer

The link layer detects two error types both of which are typically due to link transmission errors:

- CRC Errors
- Disparity Errors

These errors are reported to the Transport layer, which is required to return an R_ERR primitive to the FIS transmitting node. In addition the HBA's Transport layer causes the appropriate bit(s) in the SATA Error register to be updated as indicated in Figure 7-2 (whether acting as transmitting or receiving node). In each case the error is typically transient and can be solved with retry, and are generally reported in the Error field of the SATA Error register as referenced in Figure 7-3.

When the HBA detects an error on an incoming frame, it returns the R_ERR primitive to the drive and awaits the retry. If the retry is successful, it sets the "I" bit within the SError register (see Figure 7-3). The other case involves the HBA transmitting a FIS and detecting an R_ERR failure. This may trigger a retry that upon success (i.e., host receives R_OK during retry) the host would also set the "I" bit.

Figure 7-3: Error Reporting for Data Integrity Error Solved with Retry

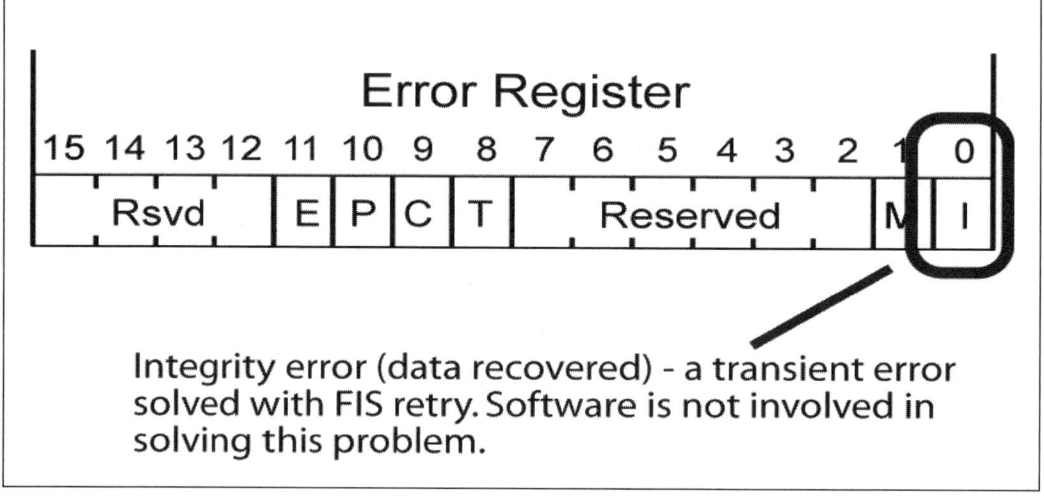

Other FIS errors — Detected by Transport Layer

The Transport layer also checks for a variety of errors that can be categorized as follows:

- **Internal Transport Errors** — these errors are detected within the Transport layer and may include buffer overflow errors etc.
- **Frame Errors** — these errors occur when a problem exists with the frame itself, such as a malformed header. Some of these errors may be considered transient and others may be persistent.
- **FIS Transmission Protocol Errors** — when the FIS transmission protocol is

violated, such as events occurring out of order, or when the data payload size disagrees with the requested size, no transient failure would typically have caused the condition. Consequently, these errors are never retried and not discussed further in this chapter.

Internal Transport Layer Errors

Internal Transport layer errors may either be handled by simply reporting the error to the upper layers (e.g., to update the SError register) or reporting the error to the FIS transmitter via R_ERR. The action taken depends upon the severity of the error; that is, whether the error is persistent (report to upper layers) or transient (send R_ERR). The SATA specification cites one specific internal error condition that requires R_ERR be returned as described below:

If the node receiving a FIS overflows the transport receive buffer the receiver is required to return the R_ERR primitive.

All other internal Transport layer errors are handled as required by the specification based on their severity.

FIS Errors

Technically, Transport layer FIS errors include errors reported from the link layers. Other forms of FIS error detected by the Transport layer must be handled as expected.

Transient FIS Errors — FIS errors expected to be transient are reported via R_ERR. Such errors are likely to result in one or more FIS retries. If the error is persistent, retries will be performed repeatedly until software times out, ultimately resulting in a reset.

Persistent FIS Errors — FIS errors considered to be persistent are reported to the upper layers. These errors are typically detected when the FIS is decoded and are often due to a malformed packet or illegal FIS type.

The Retry State Machine

The retry protocol is specified by the FIS Transfer state machine illustrated in Figure 7-4 on page 132. As discussed in the previous section only non-data FISs can be retried as indicated by the state machine diagram.

Figure 7-4: FIS Transport State Machine Diagram

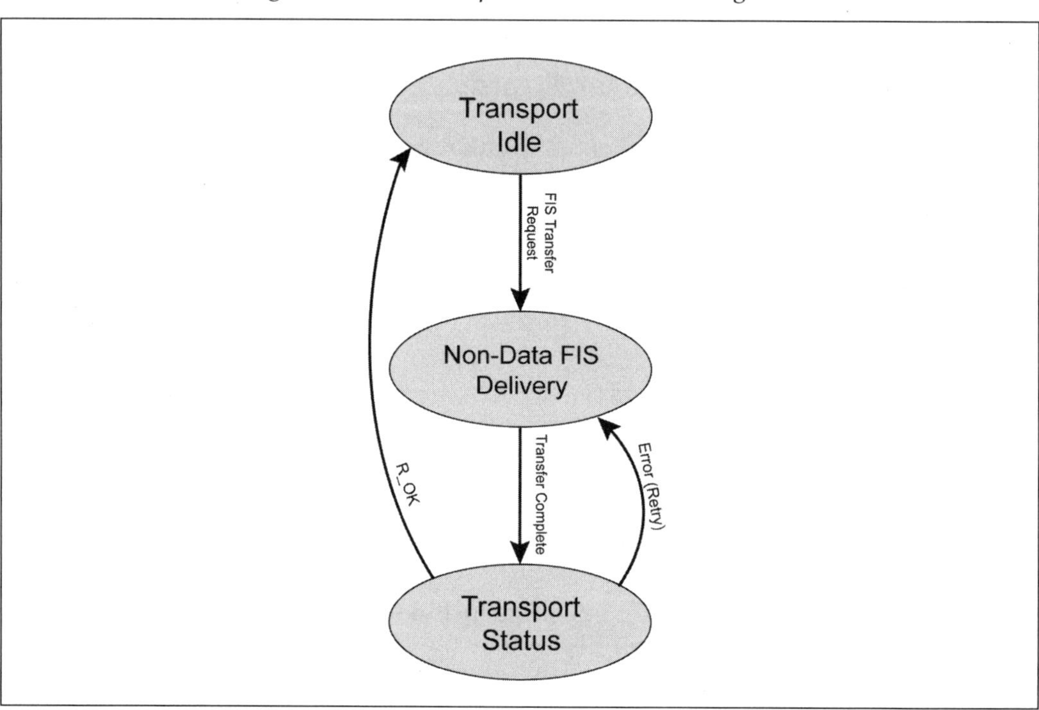

8 Data Flow Control

Previous Chapter

The previous chapter discussed the mechanisms and conditions under which a FIS retry is permitted. When a FIS is transferred across the SATA link, transmission errors are typically detected and reported back to the transmitting device. Upon detection of the transmission error, the Transport layer is notified of the failure. Having retained a copy of the failed FIS, the Transport layer re-transmits the FIS.

This Chapter

When performing large data transfers the transmit and receive buffers within the transport layers may either overflow or underflow without some flow control mechanism. This chapter details the mechanism defined for managing flow control for two circumstances. The first condition is when the node transmitting a data FIS is starved for data to send. This buffer dry condition triggers the flow control protocol for the FIS transmitter. The second condition occurs when the receiving node is unable to empty its buffer as quickly as its being filled. The resulting buffer full condition trigger the flow control mechanism from the receiving side.

The Next Chapter

This portion of the book focuses on FIS protocol and correspondingly this discussion of physical layer focuses on the functions related to FIS transmission and reception. Part 5 of this book details the physical layer's role in reset, initialization, Hot Plug, and electrical details.

Overview

One of the major design goals of the SATA implementation is to keep drive design costs low. To this end, the buffers used in the SATA interface are intentionally kept small. As discussed in the previous chapter, transmit and receive buffers within the SATA Transport layer are sized just large enough to support transaction retries of the largest non-data FIS (28 bytes), which is much smaller than the maximum data FIS size (8196 bytes). Consequently, flow control is needed only for data FISs. Figure 8-1 on page 135 illustrates the Transport layer transmit and receive buffers, along with essential link layer elements involved in flow control. Figure 8-1 A illustrates a the buffer nearly dry condition that can occur at the transmit buffer and Figure 8-1 B depicts a receive buffer nearly full condition.

The additional buffers shown below the Transport layer buffers are located in the Link layer. These buffers are typically only one or two DWs in size and are used for handling link-specific delays such as the insertion of primitives into a FIS.

The SATA flow control mechanism prevents Transport layer buffer underruns and overruns. The mechanism uses two primitives to support the protocol:

- HOLD — indicates the need to pause FIS delivery
- HOLDA — hold acknowledge verifies the FIS pause

Flow control can be implemented by either the FIS transmitter or receiver. Both cases are discussed in the following sections.

Flow Control by Transmitter

When a node transmits a Data FIS the data may be supplied to the Transport layer at a slow rate than data being delivered from the Transport layer to the node on the opposite end of the link. This condition can cause a potential buffer underrun. For example, during DMA write operations one or more Data FISs are used to deliver data from the HBA to the drive. The data must be fetched from memory by the HBA's DMA engine, which may be required to gather the data from multiple 4KB pages in memory. When the DMA engine delivers the initial 4KB data block the HBA may start transmission of a Data FIS with a payload size of 8KBs. Delays in gaining access to memory can occur as the DMA engine attempts to fetch the next page. This could result in a buffer underrun condition, if the flow control mechanism were not present.

Figure 8-1: Essential Flow Control Elements

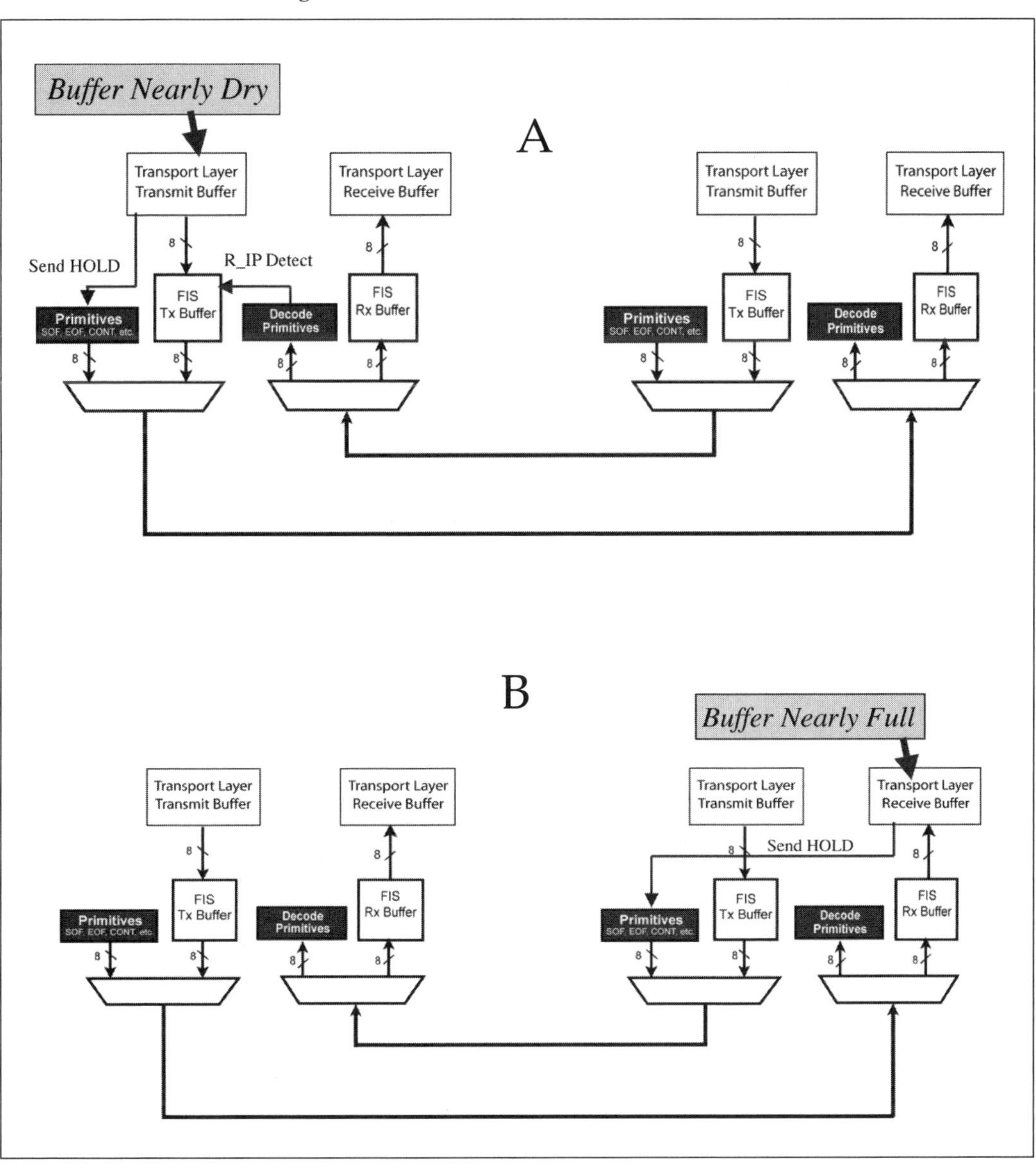

Flow Control Protocol (Transmitter Initiated)

This example discusses the protocol used to avoid an underrun at the transmit buffer. The example also presume that primitive suppression scrambling is being used by the transmitting node.

Dry Condition Results in HOLD

Figure 8-2 A on page 137 illustrates a condition in which the Transport layer transmit buffer has reached a nearly dry condition. The Data FIS transfer begins normally with the receiving node detecting the FIS and returning the receive in progress (R_IP) primitive. When the transmitting node reaches a nearly dry buffer condition is sends a HOLD primitive is to notify the receive that data is being temporarily stopped. The HOLD primitive is delivered continuously until it's time to resume the data transfer. Although not shown in Figure 8-2 A, the example presumes that the HOLD primitive is delivered twice followed by a continue (CONT) primitive to avoid repeated primitives that would contribute to EMI.

Receiver Acknowledges HOLD

The receiver continues to receive the data until it detects the HOLD primitive. The receiver responds to HOLD by returning a Hold Acknowledgement (HOLDA) primitive to the transmitting node as presented in Figure 8-2 B on page 137. Also notice that the information being sent across the link following HOLD is shown as "XXXX" to represent the pseudo-random data associated with primitive suppression scrambling. The receiver may also implement primitive suppression when delivering continuous HOLDA primitives.

Figure 8-2: Data FIS Transmission Temporarily on Hold and Acknowledged

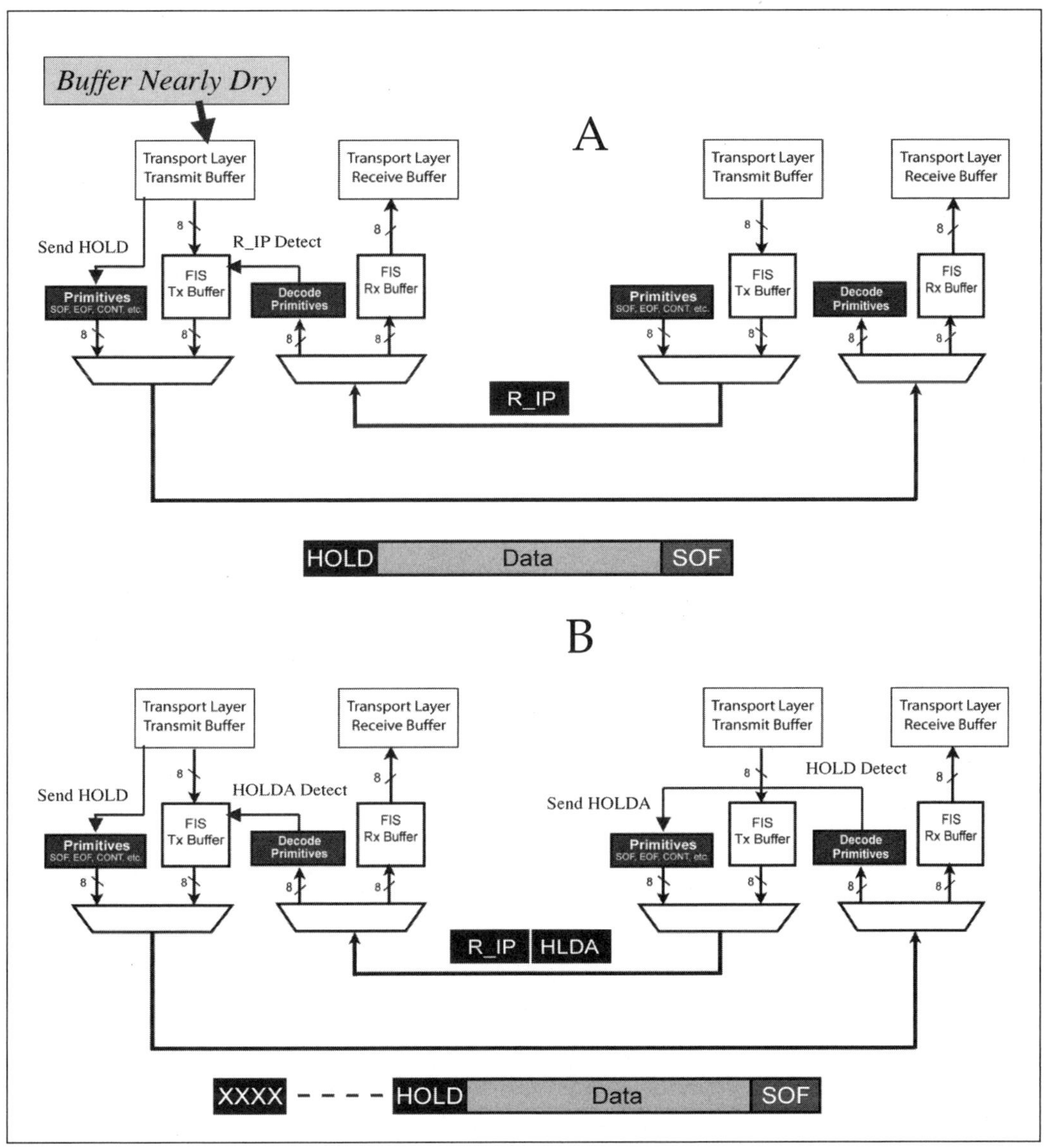

Buffer Nearly Full and Hold Released

Once the Transport layer's transmit buffer is nearly full, the HOLD primitive can be discontinued and data transfer can resume. See Figure 8-4 A on page 139. In the absence of primitive suppression, the transmitting node would have sent continuous HOLD primitives until it was ready to resume the data transfer. The receiver would detect that data that immediately follows the HOLD primitive. However, in this example pseudo-random data (XXXX) has replaced the HOLD primitive and the receiver cannot recognize the resumption of FIS data from the scrambled data. To solve the problem the transmitter must deliver a valid HOLD primitive just prior to continuing the FIS transfer.

Receiver Detects Data and Releases HOLDA

Figure 8-4 B illustrates the receipt of data and release of HOLDA. When the receiver detect the continuation of the Data FIS it release HOLDA. Whether or not HOLDA was delivered using primitive suppression scrambling does not matter in this case because another primitive will be delivered following HOLDA. The receiver merely continues by sending receive in progress (R_IP), which will be detected by the transmitter.

Protocol Example

Figure 8-3 presents a column view of a flow control sequence from a captured FIS transfer during execution of a read command from a slow CD-ROM drive.

Figure 8-3: Transmit Flow Control Example - CD-ROM Drive Asserting HOLD

H2	D2
XXXX (R_RDY)	XXXX (X_RDY)
XXXX (R_RDY)	XXXX (X_RDY)
XXXX (R_RDY)	SOF
XXXX (R_RDY)	00000046
XXXX (R_RDY)	HOLD
XXXX (R_RDY)	HOLD
XXXX (R_RDY)	CONT
XXXX (R_RDY)	XXXX (HOLD)
XXXX (R_RDY)	XXXX (HOLD)
XXXX (R_RDY)	XXXX (HOLD)
XXXX (R_RDY)	XXXX (HOLD)
XXXX (R_RDY)	XXXX (HOLD)
XXXX (R_RDY)	HOLD
XXXX (R_RDY)	32008005
R_IP	HOLD
R_IP	HOLD
HOLDA	CONT

Figure 8-4: Hold Released and Data Transfer Resumed

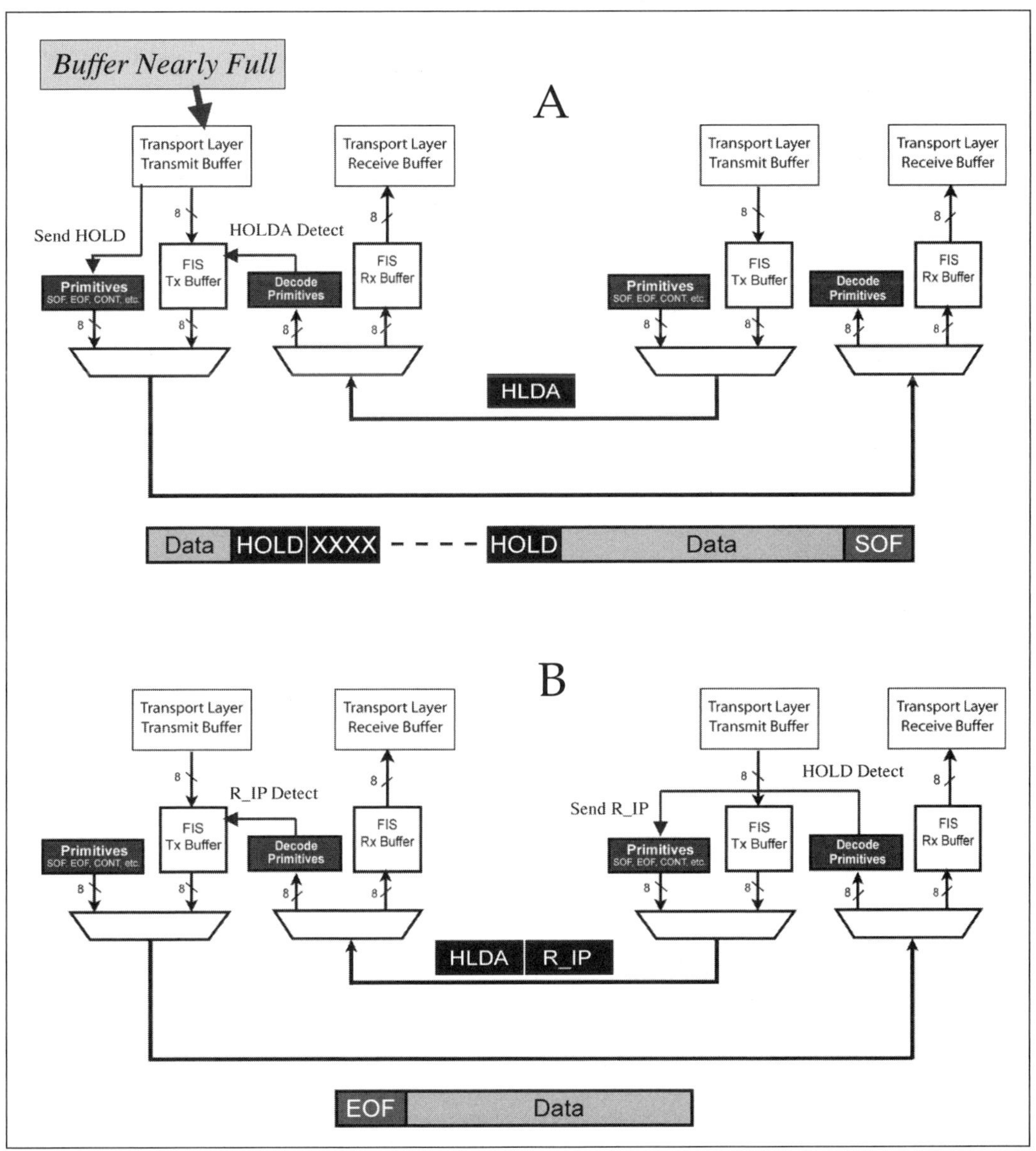

Flow Control by Receiver

The receiver buffer would overflow if the rate at which data is being send across the link exceeds the ability of the device to move data to internal cache or to disc.

Flow Control Protocol (Receiver Initiated)

This example discusses the protocol used to avoid an overrun at the receive buffer. The example also presumes that primitive suppression scrambling is being used by the transmitting node.

Buffer Nearly Full Results in HOLD

Figure 8-5 A on page 141 depicts the receive buffer nearing a full condition and in response the receiving node sends a HOLD primitive to the transmitting node; thereby requesting data transmission be stopped. However, note that data continues until the transmitter receives and decodes the HOLD primitive. Consequently, the receiver must know the maximum amount of data it will continue to receive once it has sent HOLD. See "Flow Control Protocol (Receiver Initiated)" on page 140 for details regarding timing associated with receiver initiated flow control.

Transmitter Recognizes HOLD request and Returns HOLDA

Refer to Figure 8-5 B. The transmitter continues to source data until it receives the HOLD request. Immediately following the termination of data delivery the HOLDA primitive is transmitted to the receiver notifying it that data transfer has stopped.

Figure 8-5: Receive Buffer Nearly Full, Asserts Hold and Transmitter Stops Data Transmission

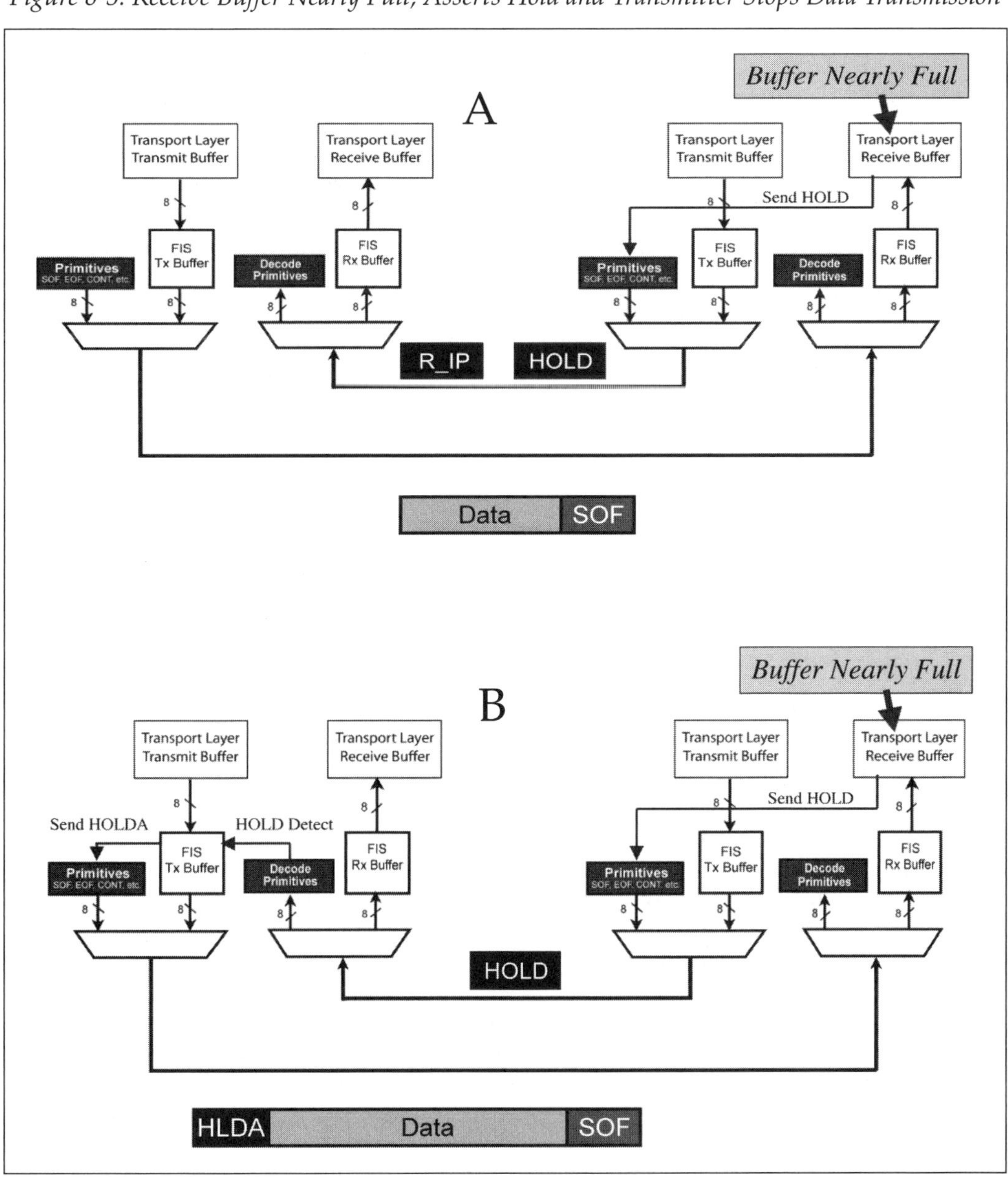

Receive Buffer Nears Empty and HOLD Released

When the receiver has nearly emptied its transport receive buffer, it releases HOLD by resuming the repeated transmission of R_IP primitives, as depicted in Figure 8-6 A on page 143. Whether or not HOLD is followed by scrambled primitive suppression data, R_IP will terminate HOLD and notify the transmitting node that it can resume data delivery.

Transmitting Node Resumes Data Transfer

R_IP notifies the transmitter to continue the data transfer. Figure 8-6 B, illustrates HOLDA being followed with scrambled data. This requires that the transmitter send HOLDA primitives immediately before resuming the data transfer. Without doing so the receiving node would be unable to detect that the data transfer has resumed.

HOLD/HOLDA Propagation Delay

Due to propagation delays, a receiver that initiates HOLD because its receive buffer is nearly full must have sufficient buffer space remaining to accept the additional data that will continue to arrive before the transmitter actually stops the data. The components of this delays are summarized below (also see Figure 8-7 on page 144):

1. **Receiving Node HOLD Transmission Delay** — time between HOLD primitive transmission request and HOLD having been delivered to the link.
2. **Link Propagation Delay** — time required to transmit HOLD primitive across a 5 meter cable.
3. **Transmitting Node HOLD Reception Delay** — time required to receive and decode HOLD primitive and request data be stopped.
4. **Transmitting Node HOLDA Transmission Delay** — time from HOLDA primitive transmission request until HOLDA is delivered to the link.
5. **Link Propagation Delay** — time required to transmit HOLDA primitive across a 1 meter cable.
6. **Receiving Node HOLDA Reception Delay** — time required for HOLDA to propagate through the receive logic to the Transport layer, indicating that data has stopped.

Figure 8-6: Receiver Releases Hold and Transmitter Continues Data Transfer

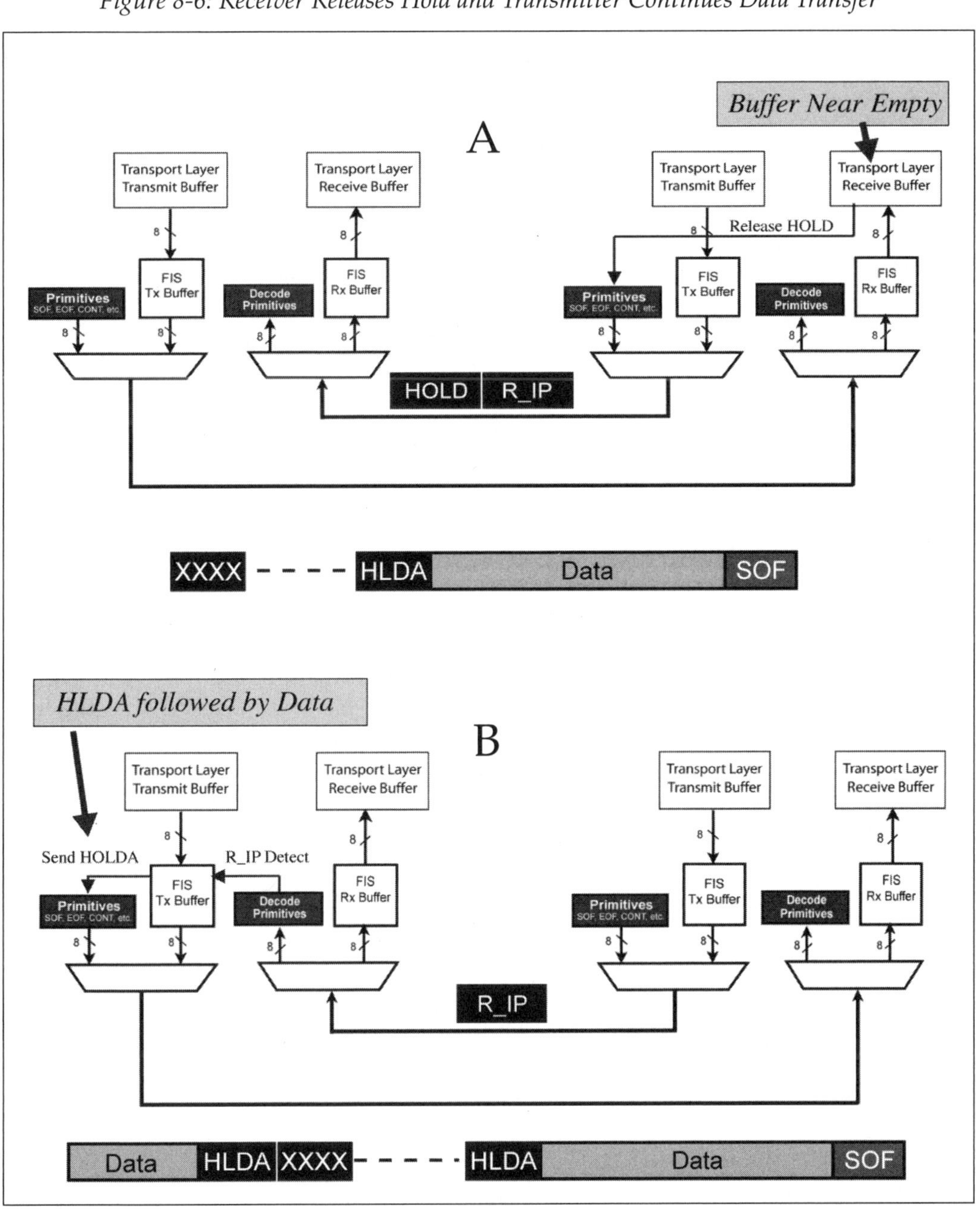

Figure 8-7: HOLD to HOLDA Delay

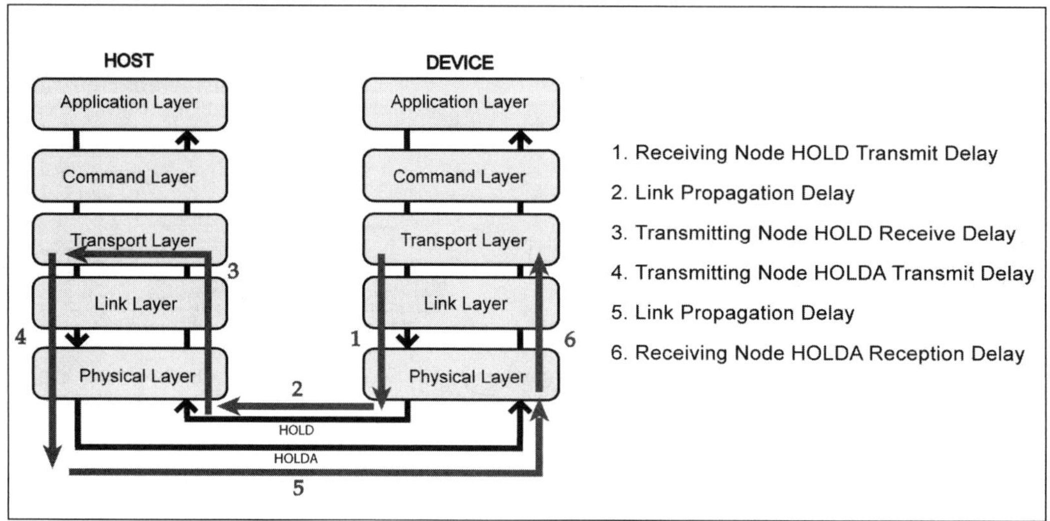

Receiving Node HOLD Transmission Delay

When the receiving node nears a buffer full condition it transmits HOLD to notify the transmitting node to pause data delivery. Figure 8-8 shows the HOLD primitive request and the various stages within the link and physical layers it must traverse until the entire HOLD primitive has been clocked onto the link. During this delay data continues to be delivered by the transmitting node. The designer has specific knowledge of this delay and must account for it in buffer sizing and buffer threshold trigger points that determine when to request HOLD transmission

Figure 8-8: Internal HOLD Transmission Delay

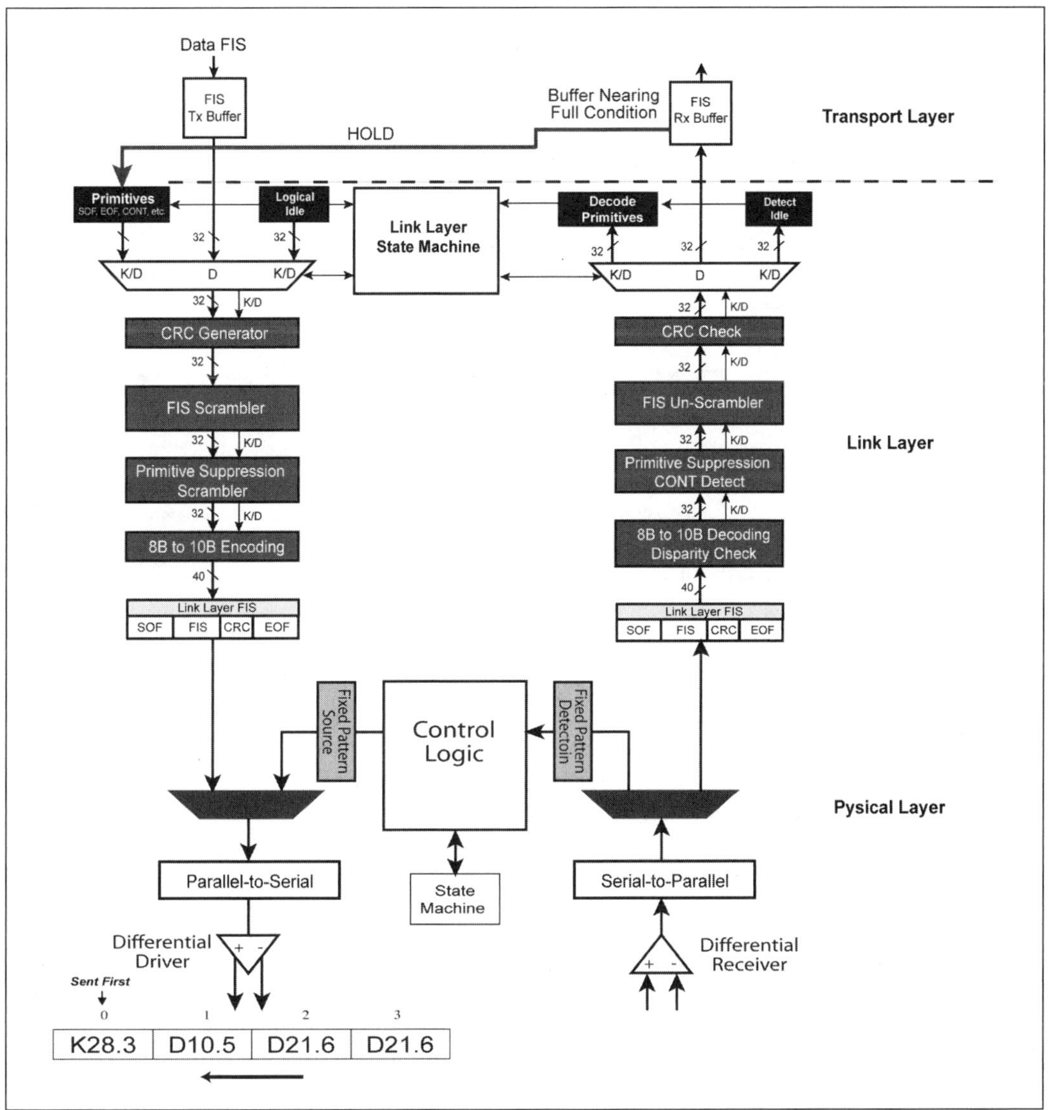

HOLD to HOLDA Round Trip Delay

The round trip time between HOLD being placed on the link and HOLDA to be returned is specified to be no more than 20 DWords. Figure 8-9 on page 146 illustrates this round trip delay. The receiving node must ensure that is has at least 20 DWords of addition buffer space in addition to the internal delay.

Figure 8-9: Total Delay Between HOLD Being Transmitted and HOLDA Being Returned

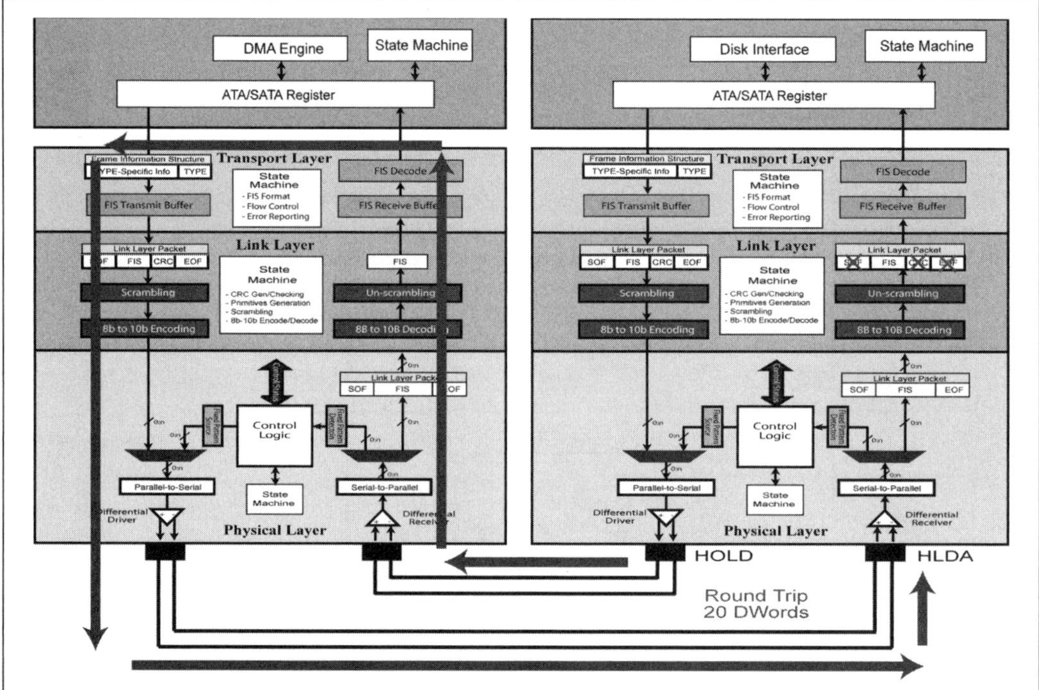

The largest portion of the HOLD to HOLDA round trip delay is within the transmitting node. The specification discounts the importance of the actual link delay because with a five meter cable the propagation delay is less than one-half of a double word. The other sources of the round trip delay are described in Table 8-1 on page 147 and illustrated in Figure 8-10 on page 148.

Table 8-1: Sources of HOLD to HOLDA Delay

Delay	Source of Delay
1 DW	Incoming HOLD primitive converted from Serial to Parallel form.
1 DW	Packet decoded from 10 bits to 8 bits
1 DW	Primitive passes through Unscrambling stage even though it is not scrambled.
3 DWs	Clock Synchronization (Rcv/Link State Mach)
1 DW	Primitive Rcv Notification
1 DW	HOLD Primitive Decoded
1 DW	Transmit Buffer Notified
1 DW	Transmit Buffer Stops Data
1 DW	HOLDA Request
1 DW	HOLDA Inserted
1 DW	Scrambling
1 DW	8b/10b Encoding
1 DW	Sync to Xmit Clock
1 DW	Serialize HOLDA
2 DW	Transmit HOLDA Primitive

Figure 8-10: Stages Involved in HOLD to HOLDA Delay

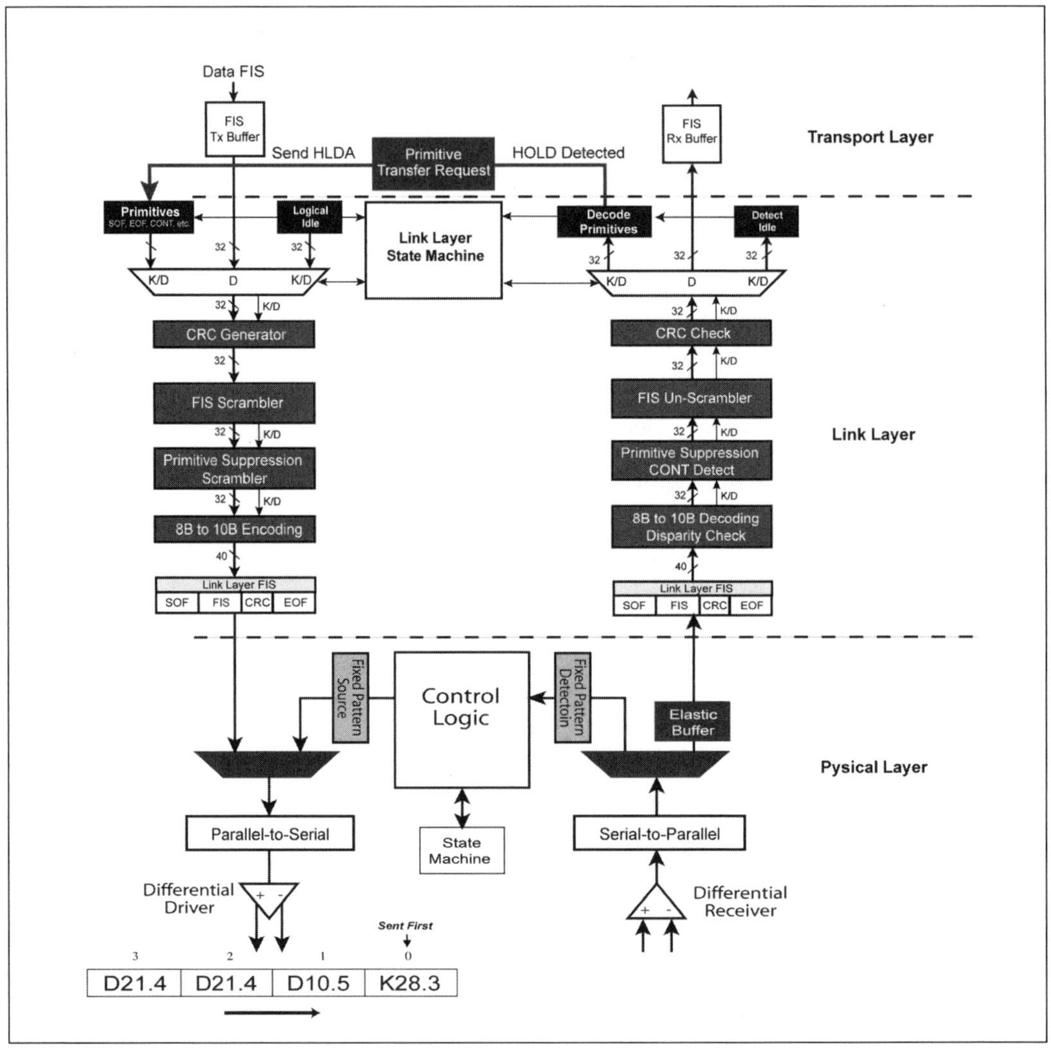

Receiver Initiated Hold Example

This capture is from an example in which a DMA Write Operation is targeting a hard drive. Notice that the device initiates HOLD primitives indicating that the receive buffer is nearing a full condition. In this example, the HOLDA is observed back on the wire after 13 DWord times, well within the maximum HOLD/HOLDA delay. The drive notifies the HBA that it's ready to accept data again by asserting the HOLD primitive followed by R_IP primitives.

Figure 8-11: Example DMA Write with Receiver Issuing HOLD

H1	D1
00000000	HOLD
00000000	HOLD
00000000	CONT
00000000	XXXX
00000000	XXXX
00000000	XXXX
00000000	XXXX
00000000	XXXX
00000000	XXXX
00000000	XXXX
00000000	XXXX
00000000	XXXX
HOLDA	XXXX
HOLDA	XXXX
CONT	XXXX
XXXX	XXXX
XXXX	XXXX
XXXX	XXXX
XXXX	XXXX
XXXX	XXXX
XXXX	XXXX
XXXX	XXXX
XXXX	XXXX
XXXX	XXXX
XXXX	XXXX
XXXX	XXXX
XXXX	XXXX
XXXX	XXXX
XXXX	XXXX
XXXX	XXXX
XXXX	XXXX
XXXX	XXXX
XXXX	XXXX
XXXX	XXXX
XXXX	XXXX
XXXX	HOLD
XXXX	R_IP
XXXX	R_IP
XXXX	CONT
XXXX	XXXX

9 Physical Layer Functions

Previous Chapter

When performing large data transfers the transmit and receive buffers within the transport layers may either overflow or underflow without some flow control mechanism. The previous chapter detailed the mechanism and protocols defined for managing the flow control.

This Chapter

This portion of the book focuses on FIS protocol and correspondingly this discussion of physical layer focuses on the functions related to FIS transmission and reception. Part 5 of this book details the physical layer's role in reset, initialization, Hot Plug, and electrical details.

The Next Chapter

The discussions thus far have focused on the FIS transfer protocols and for the most part has presumed that the transfers occur without error. The next chapter discusses the error detection mechanisms, describes the sources of these errors, and specifies the methods used to handle and report them.

Introduction

Functions associated with the physical layer during FIS transmission and reception are illustrated in Figure 9-1 on page 152 and include the following activities:

FIS Transmission

- Parallel to serial conversion
- Differential transmission at 1.5 or 3.0Gb/s
- Align primitive insertion for clock compensation
- Spread-spectrum clocking optional

FIS Reception

- Differential reception
- Data Extraction
- Serial to parallel conversion
- Align primitive decoding
- Elasticity buffer

Figure 9-1: Functional Block Diagram — Physical Layer

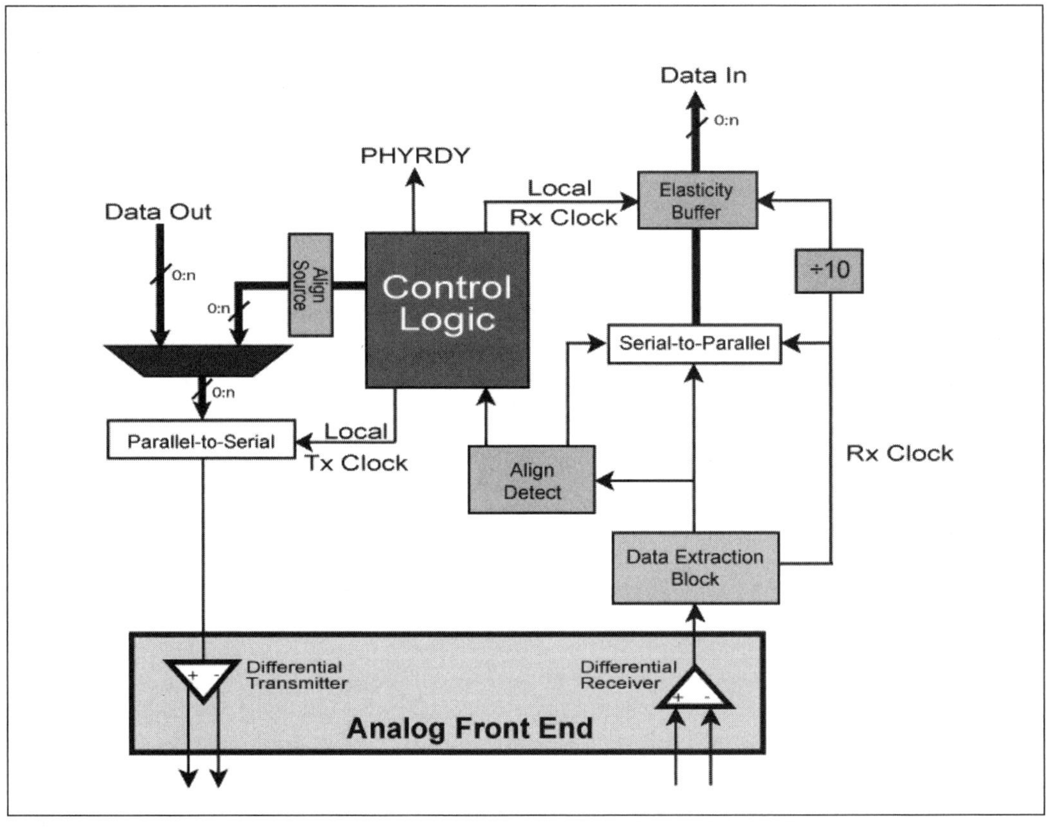

Differential Transmitter/Receiver

Figure 9-2 provides a schematic view of the transmitter, receiver and link characteristics. Notice that the optional AC-coupling capacitors are implemented on many drives to allow different common mode voltages at the drive and HBA. The differential impedance of the link is nominally 100 ohms and the terminations provide impedance matching to reduce reflections.

Figure 9-2: Link Electrical Interface

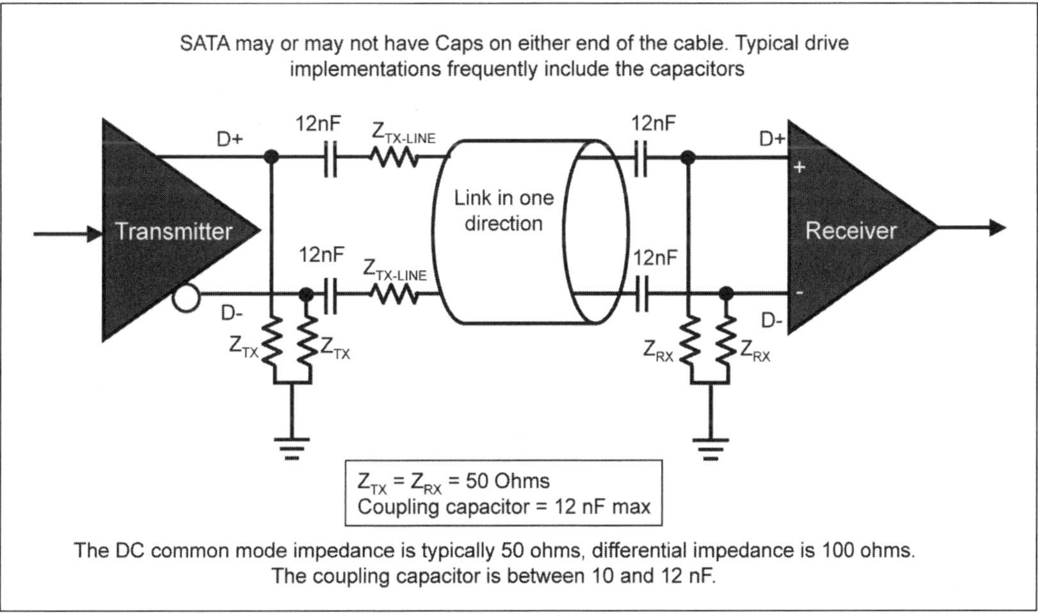

Transmitter Characteristics

The peak-to-peak transmit voltage is specified as 400-600mV for Gen 1 drives and hosts and 400-700mV for Gen 2 drives and hosts. However, the transmission voltage required depends on the signaling environment, specified as:

- Internal connections (i) — internal or inside-the-box connections (e.g., internal to PC)
- Medium length (m) — longer cables and short backplane environments
- External Cabled (x) — very long external cables and long backplane applications

The minimum and maximum transmit voltages for the m and x applications change due to increased signal attenuation. Figure 9-1 lists the specified m and x voltages. These voltage specifications are required by the host side and may require additional interface circuitry between the host and drive, but no change is required for the drive itself. Otherwise, different drives would be required for different signaling applications. Similarly, receiver sensitivity is modified to account for these signaling applications (Table 9-2). See Chapter 19, entitled "Physical Layer," on page 325 for addition electrical information.

Table 9-1: Minimum/Maximum Transmit Voltages

Application	Gen 1	Gen2
Internal (i)	400 - 600mV	400-700mV
Medium (m)	500-600mV	500-700mV
External (x)	800-1600mV	800-1600mV

Receiver Characteristics

The differential receivers have an input sensitivity specified inTable 9-2 based on the different signaling applications described previously.

Table 9-2: Minimum/Maximum Receive Voltages

Application	Gen 1	Gen2
Internal (i)	325 - 600mV	275 - 750mV
Medium (m)	240 - 600mV	240 - 750mV
External (x)	275 - 1600mV	275 - 1600mV

Clock Management

The physical layer is responsible for a variety of clock-related functions:

- Local clock generation
- Local clock division and distribution
- Receive clock recovery for data extraction
- Clock compensation management
- Spread-Spectrum Clocking (SSC) - optional

Local Clock Frequency

The local clock in the host and target is generated within the physical layer. This clock is used as the reference clock for transmitting data (at the Gen 1 or Gen 2 rate) and for clocking receive data out of the elasticity buffer. Figure 9-3 illustrates a clock distribution implementation. In this example, the parallel data path between the upper layers and the physical layer is 40-bits wide; thereby reducing the clock frequency by a factor of 40.

Figure 9-3: Example Clock Implementation

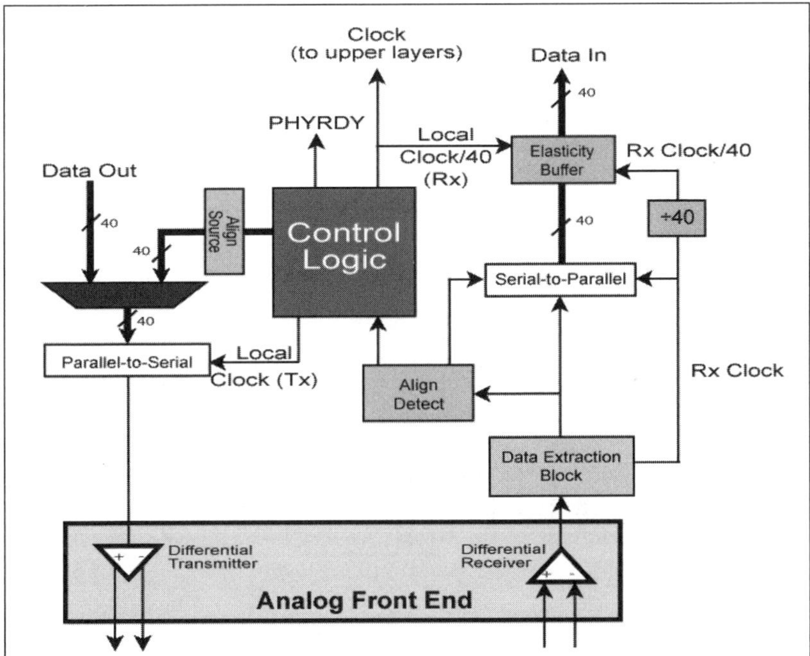

Clock Accuracy

The clock used by SATA HBAs and drives must be accurate within +350/-350ppm, yielding a total variance of 700ppm. These parameters apply to both the Gen 1 and Gen 2 frequencies.

Spread-Spectrum Clocking

Optionally, spread-spectrum clocking (SSC) may also be employed in mobile and desktop environments where the PC is essentially another household appliance that can interfere with other appliances. The specification allows the clock to vary in frequency over time between the nominal bit rate of 1.5 or 3.0Gb/s down to -5000 ppm. The modulation rate of frequency change is specified at 30-33 kHz. SSC reduces EMI by spreading the frequency over a much broader range.

SATA Devices must be designed to tolerate SSC transmissions which results in frequency variance that is specified as +350/-5350ppm.

Data Extraction

Data extraction involves the receive circuitry synchronizing to the income bit stream and accurately detecting the incoming NRZ data. Data extraction comprises a PLL or other means to extract the receive clock from the incoming bit stream. The discussion of the "Receive Block" on page 330 provides detailed examples. Figure 9-4 illustrates the relationship between the recovered receive clock and the incoming data. The recovered clock is used to sample the state of the NRZ data during each bit time.

Figure 9-4: Receive Clock and Data Extraction

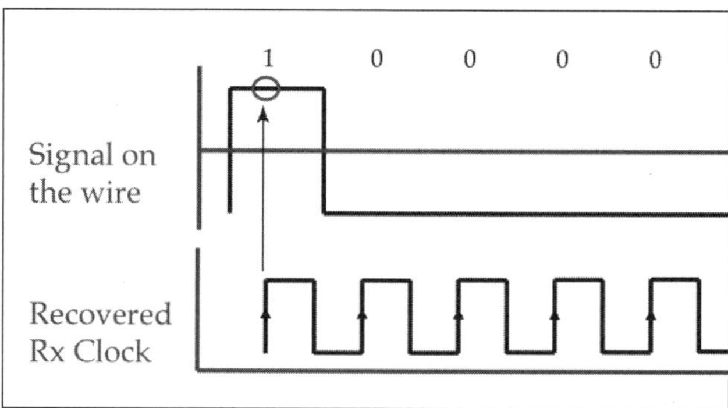

Double Word (DWord) Detection

Once the receiver is synchronized and detecting bits, it must detect the DWord boundaries. This detection is done during initialization based on the unique patterns associated with the 10-bit Comma (COM) control value. This comma value is the first DWord of every align primitive. Figure 9-5 illustrates the unique COM pattern.

Figure 9-5: Double Word Boundary Detection

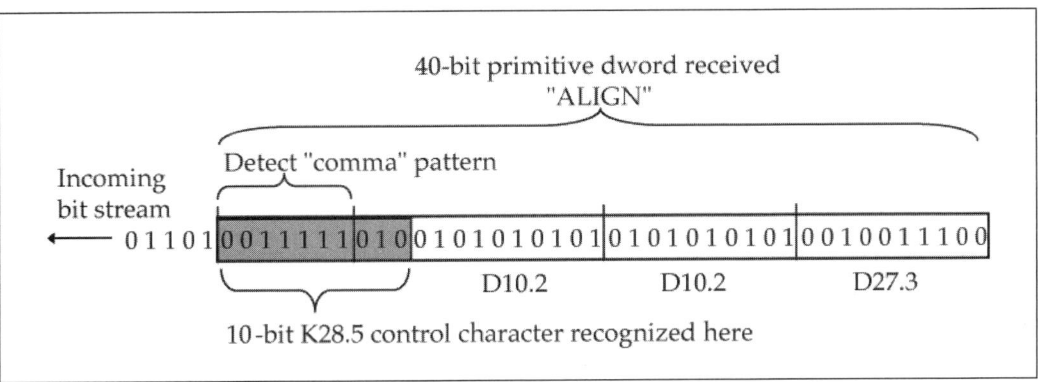

Clock Compensation

The recovered receive clock has the same frequency as the clock used to transmit the incoming information and may be different from the local clock by up to 700ppm. Consequently, an elastic buffer is implemented to manage this variance. The recovery receive clock is used to clock data into the buffer and the local clock is used to transfer data from the buffer. The buffer depth must be sufficient to absorb the possible overrun or underrun condition.

The elastic buffer management is accomplished via back-to-back align primitives that are injected into the bit stream at regular intervals. A 256 DWord counter within the transmit side of the link layer triggers the delivery of 2 align primitives. Note that the align primitives are included in the 256 DWord count. Elastic buffer management detects these align primitives and either adds or removes a primitive to compensate for the clock variance. See the section entitled "Clock Compensation" on page 335 for details.

10 Error Detection and Handling

Previous Chapter

Because this portion of the book focuses on FIS protocol the previous chapter focussed on the physical layer functions related to FIS transmission and reception. Part 5 of this book details the physical layer's role in reset, initialization, Hot Plug, and electrical details.

This Chapter

The discussions thus far have focused on the FIS transfer protocols and for the most part has presumed that the transfers occur without error. The next chapter discusses the error detection mechanisms, describes the sources of these errors, and specifies the methods used to handle and report them.

The Next Chapter

Much of the discussion prior to the next chapter has focused on the delivery of individual Frame Information Structures. Next, the discussion turns to the various categories of commands that each require the exchange of a particular sequence of Frame Information Structures. It is the responsibility of the command layers to manage this sequencing.

Scope of SATA Error Checking

The SATA environment supports ATA error checking as well as SATA-specific error checking. This capability can be segmented into the following categories:

- Commands failing to complete properly — reported in the ATA completion status and error registers
- FIS transfer Protocol Errors — reported in the SATA-specific error register
- SATA Link Transfer Errors — reported in the SATA-specific error register
- HBA Errors — reported in the SATA-specific error register and/or in IO bus-specific registers (e.g., in PCI configuration status registers)

Figure 10-1 on page 160 illustrates the location of the status and error registers that system software accesses to detect errors. The specific registers that contain error-related information include the ATA status and error registers located within the Shadow registers, along with the SStatus and SError registers. Note that in the AHCI implementation, the contents of the ATA registers are located in main memory instead of the HBA.

Figure 10-1: Location of Shadow (ATA) and SATA-Specific Register Blocks

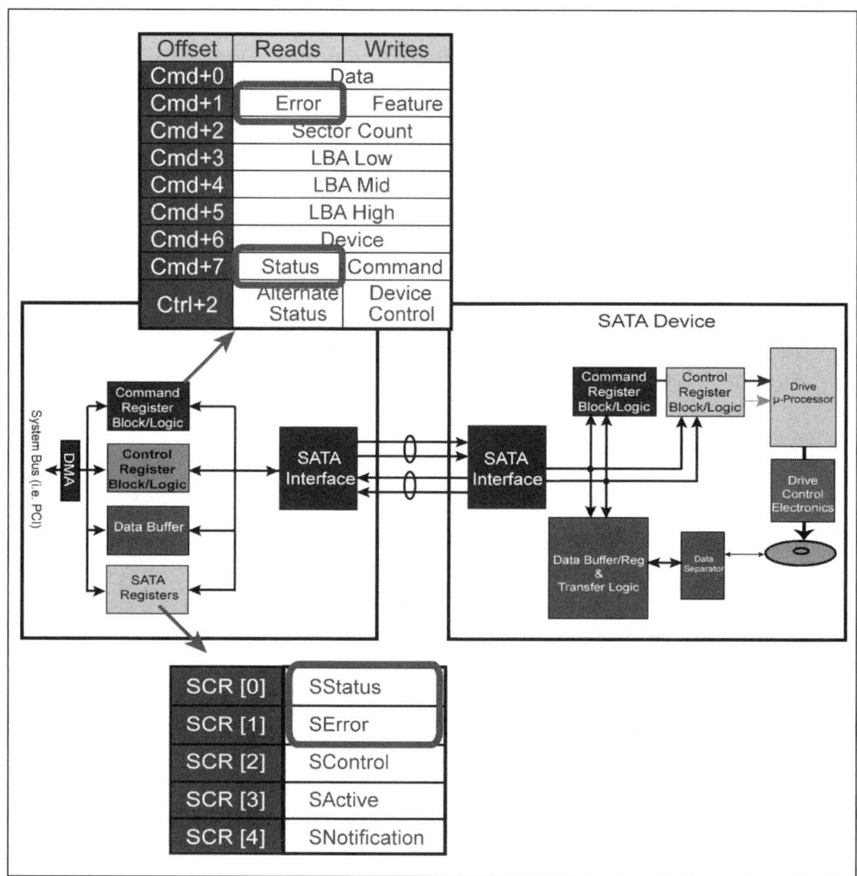

Error Reporting — HBA Versus SATA Drives

The error reporting capabilities of the SATA drives and HBA are quite different. All of the status and error registers are located within the HBA, giving software the ability to detect that an error has occurred and in some cases determine the type of error, along with its severity. Drives can also detect errors but must forward notification of the error to the HBA for reporting to software. Two primary mechanisms are available for drives to communicate errors to the host:

1. Drives update the ATA Status and Error registers during command execution and forward the results to the HBA via the Register FIS - Device to Host.
2. Drives report FIS transmission errors via the FIS transfer protocol handshake (R_ERR). In this case, the HBA has no visibility regarding the nature of the error.

Many SATA errors can only be reflected in the HBA's SStatus and SError registers. These same errors may be detectable within the drives but no mechanism is available to report the exact nature of these errors as is done by the HBA.

Error Reporting and Handling Mechanisms

SATA errors are generally detected and forwarded to upper layers where status and error registers may be updated and where the method of error handling is determined. Figure 10-2 on page 162 illustrates the hierarchical error detection and handling approach defined by the specification. On the left side of the diagram the type of information passed between the layers is highlighted, and the right side lists the types of error checks made at each layer.

Figure 10-2: SATA Error Detection and Reporting Methodology

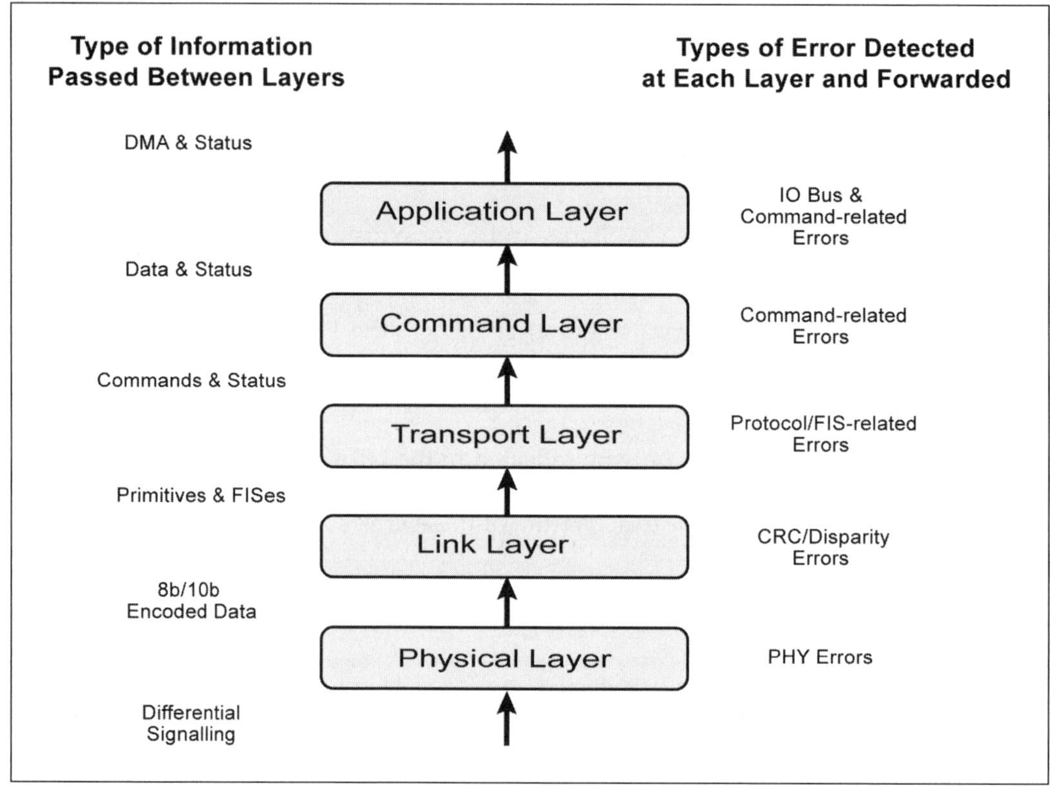

The actions taken at each layer depend, in part, on the type and severity of the error. The specification identifies four actions or responses that can be taken:

- Freeze — indicates that no action is taken because of a severe error condition that is unrecoverable. In these circumstances, software will time-out because the command being performed did not complete. A reset is typically required to clear the error.
- Abort — indicates that the error conditions is presumed to be persistent and the associated command has failed. Persistent errors are typically forwarded to the Application layer to inform host software of the failed command.

- Retry — indicates that the error condition is expected to be transient, such as a CRC or disparity error. Such errors must have no adverse affect on the state of the SATA system; therefore, the failed transfer is generally retried. Errors detected at the Transport layer or below may be retried under hardware control (non-data frames only); whereas, errors detected above the Transport layer must rely on software to initiate the retry.
- Track/ignore — indicates a recoverable error conditions that is not critical and therefore can be ignored or tracked by software. Such errors include those that have been successfully retried by the Transport layer hardware. Even though these errors have been corrected by hardware, they typically affect performance adversely and may also indicate a component that is pending failure.

ATA Compatible Registers

When a drive executes a command it reports completion status within the ATA Status register. If a command fails to complete successfully, the Status register reflects the failure and the Error register identifies the nature of the error as described below.

ATA Status Register

Figure 10-3 depicts the contents of the ATA Status register. Note that for error reporting purposes, only the Error bit (ERR) is relevant. When set, ERR indicates the command failed due to some type of error condition and that the Error register contains additional information regarding the failure. Note that if the Status register Error bit is not set, then the contents of the Error register are invalid.

Figure 10-3: ATA Status Register Indicates if an Error Has Occurred

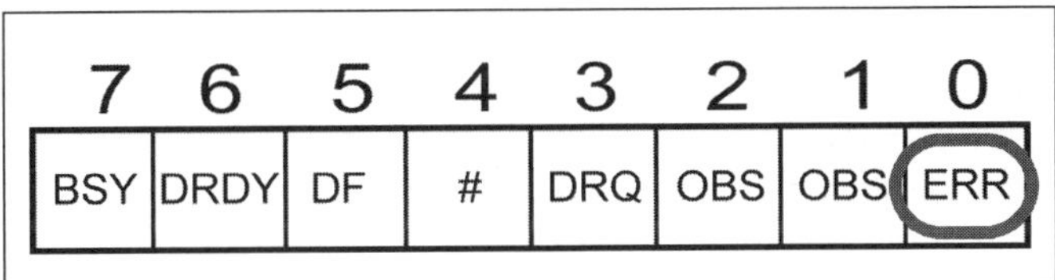

ATA Error Register

Many of the Error register bit fields are command specific, with only the Abort field defined as a standard source of command failure. Some commands use nearly all of the bit fields to specific the nature of the failure, while others name only support the Abort field. The Read DMA command is an example command that can report a specific cause of the error (Figure 10-4 on page 164).

Figure 10-4: Error Register Definition of Read DMA Command

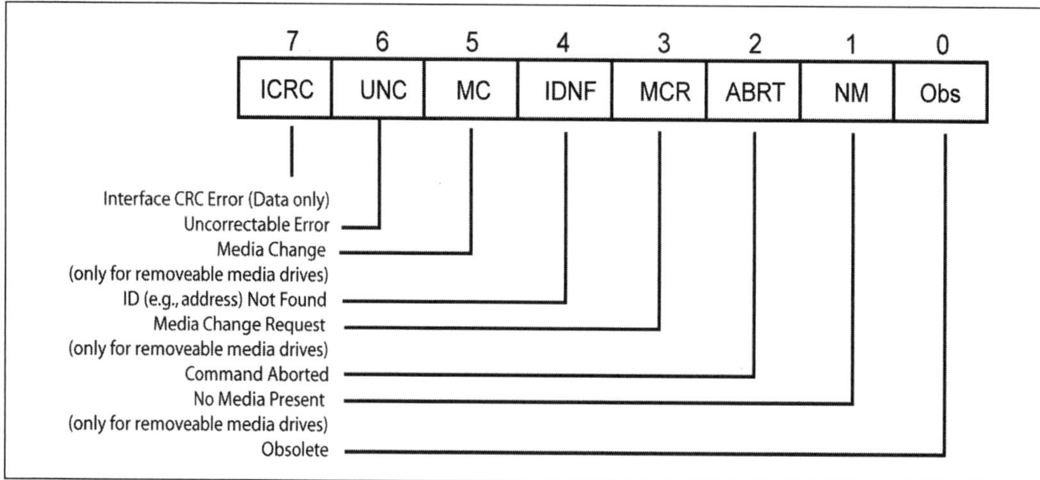

SATA-Specific Error Related Registers

SATA-specific registers provide considerable granularity regarding the type and severity of errors that are detected, including status information regarding the state of the link.

SATA Status (SStatus) Register

The SStatus register provides information regarding link status. Figure 10-5 on page 165 highlights the fields within the SStatus register where link status is reported. Note that two error conditions may exist:

- Device not present — occurs if the drive cable is pulled out or other failure resulting in the device no longer being recognized during normal operation
- Device detected by PHY is not communicating — the drive is detected but communications have been lost

Figure 10-5: Contents and Format of the SStatus Register

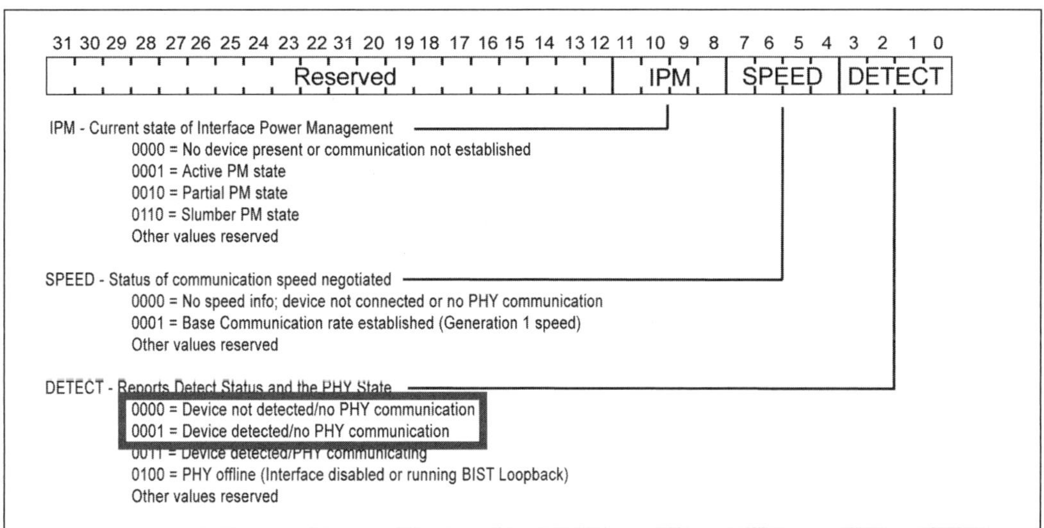

SATA Error (SError) Register

The error register is segmented into two primary fields as illustrated in Figure 10-6. The Error field provides information intended to assist run-time software determine the severity of the error condition so that corrective action can be taken. The Diagnostic field provides detailed information about the specific nature of the error.

Figure 10-6: The Error and Diagnostic Fields within the SError Register

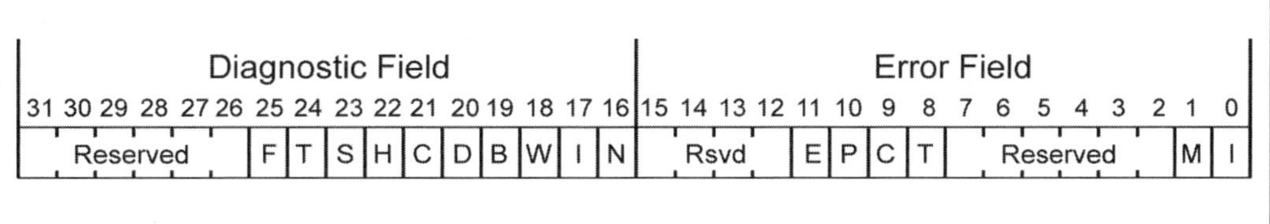

The Error Field. The focus of the error field is to provide software with the information needed to determine the best error recovery approach. Depending on the nature of the error actions may range from doing nothing (error condition was corrected by SATA hardware) to resetting the SATA interface. Figure 10-7 on page 166 lists and describes each of the Error bit fields.

Figure 10-7: Format and Content of the Error Field within the SError Register

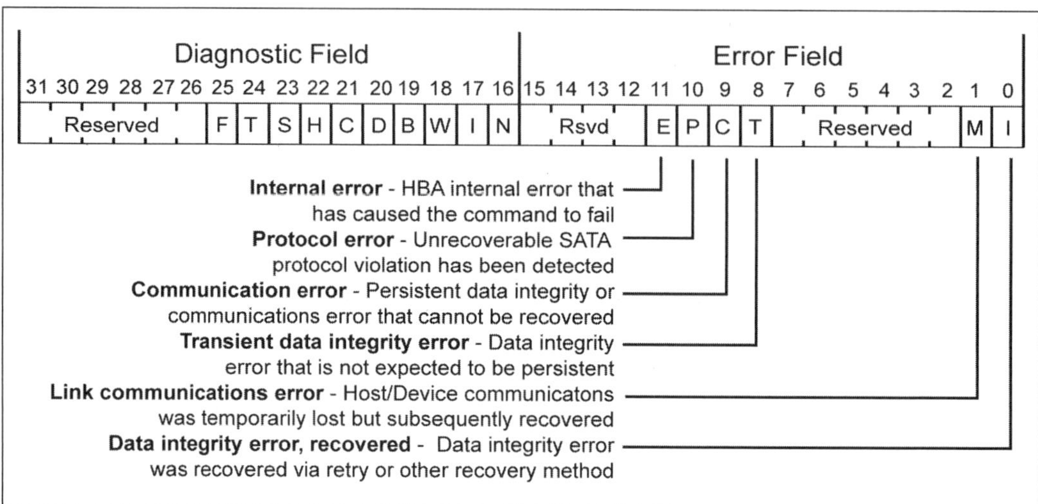

The Diagnostic Field. The intent of the diagnostic field is to provide granularity regarding the specific nature of a failure. As illustrated in Figure 10-8 on page 166 the source of the error can be generally pin-pointed to a particular layer and in some cases a particular error within the layer.

Figure 10-8: Format and Content of the Diagnostic Field within the SError Register

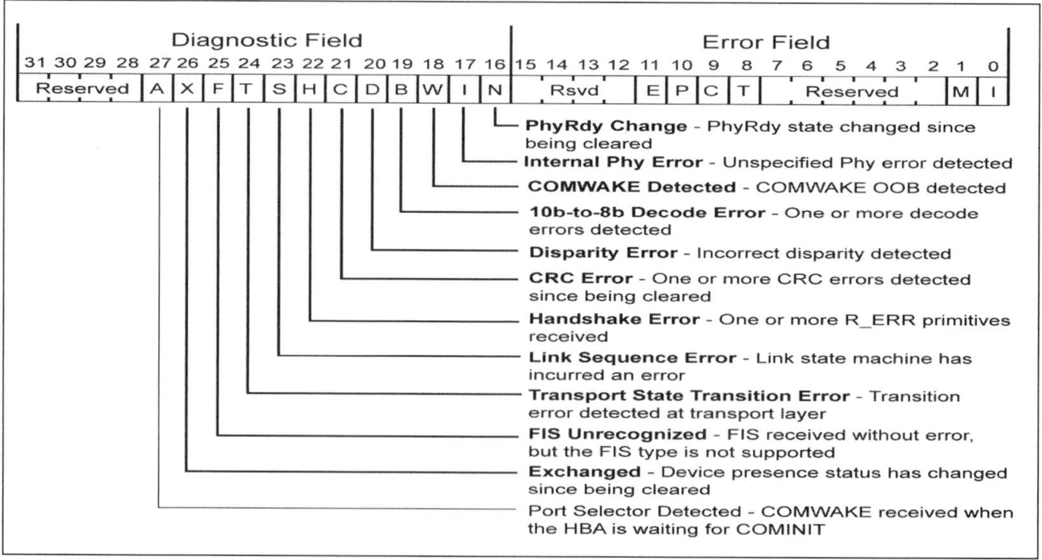

Error Detection and Recovery Mechanisms

SATA error detection mechanisms are certainly more robust than the parallel ATA implementations, but are limited when contrasted with other high-speed serial bus implementations. The limitations may be related to two important SATA design goals.

- Maintaining backward compatibility with the legacy software was a critical design goal as discussed previously. Because legacy software only has knowledge of the parallel ATA, some error detection and reporting capabilities are of little use.
- Perhaps the most important design goal that kept SATA's error detection and reporting capabilities modest is maintaining low cost drives.

CRC Checks

Successful transfer of each FIS across the SATA link is verified with a Cyclic Redundancy Check (CRC). These checks make it possible to support hardware retries of most failed FIS transfers; thereby improving link reliability.

CRC generation is performed only on DWord quantities and covers only the FIS. Any FIS not ending on an aligned DWord boundary must be padded with zeros to complete the DWord size. The 32-bit CRC generator polynomial is:

G(X) = X32 + X26 + X23 + X22 + X16 + X12 + X11 + X10 + X8 + X7 + X5 + X4 +X2 +X + 1

An initial seed value of 52325032h is applied before starting the CRC calculation.

At the receiving side the CRC check is made upon detection of the End of Frame (EOF) primitive. The 32-bits preceding the EOF primitive always represent the CRC value.

Disparity Error Checks

The 8b/10b encoding mechanism includes the ability to detect 8b/10b coding errors. This is accomplished via disparity error checking during 8b/10b decoding within the link layer. Details regarding disparity errors can be found in Chapter Appendix A, entitled "8b/10b Encoding Tutorial," on page 409. A disparity error results in a failed frame transfer and triggers the same behavior as CRC errors.

Time-outs

Commands issued by host software may fail due to a variety of error conditions, including but not limited to the follow list:

- Failure of the host system to deliver a valid command to the HBA.
- Internal HBA errors
- SATA transmission errors
- Internal drive errors

Any of these errors can lead to a command failing execution. Depending on the failure mode, interrupts may be generated to report command failure, while in other instances command execution may stall command execution, resulting in a host software time-out. The command may simply be requeued by software or if the error is persistent more complex recovery may be required, such as resetting the link.

Layer-Specific Errors and Actions

The following sections describe the various SATA errors that may be detected at each layer and how they are reported.

Physical Layer Errors

The physical layer can encounter a variety of errors, but many of these errors are not individually reported. Every instance of a PHY error is reported simply as a generic PHY error. The specification categorizes PHY error into three groups:

- No device present
- OOB signaling sequence errors
- Phy internal error

No Device Present Error

This error condition is caused by a physical disconnect between the HBA and drive. The standard mechanism for detecting a device is present involves the out-of-band (OOB) signaling following reset. When the drive-initiated OOB signaling is detected by the HBA (detection of COMINIT), the HBA indicates device present in the SStatus register (Figure 10-5 on page 165). When communications fail the HBA attempts to re-establish communications by initiating the OOB sequence. If no response is returned from the drive, the device is presumed to no longer be present, which is reflected in the SStatus register.

OOB Signaling Errors

A failure of the OOB signaling sequence prevents the HBA and drive to establish communications. Figure 10-9 on page 169 illustrates the exchange of OOB signal bursts that define the signaling events and the sequence in which the events are exchanged. If the OOB sequence fails to complete, link initialization will not complete and the PHY will remain in the non-communicating state. The only timing requirement specified for initialization is that the drive must detect device presence within 10ms after power-on reset is complete. Otherwise the OOB sequence will continuously to be attempted. OOB Errors are reflected in the SStatus register as a result of the PHY remaining in the non-communicating state. Refer to "OOB (Out of Band) Signaling" on page 307 for additional detail regarding the OOB Sequence.

Figure 10-9: The OOB Sequence Following Power-On Reset

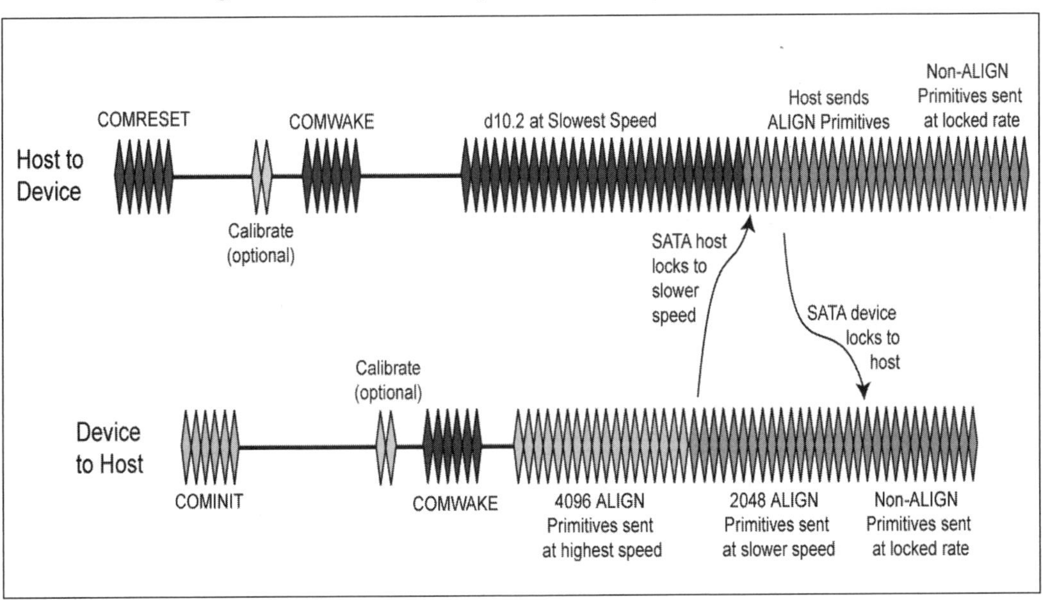

PHY Internal Errors

PHY internal errors generally result in loss of link communications.

PHY errors consist of items such as:

- Elasticity Buffer overflow or underflow
- PLL tracking errors
- Clock variance errors
- Electrical error conditions

Internal PHY errors are reflected in both the Error and Diagnostic fields or the SError register and potentially in the SStatus register in the event that the failure is not recoverable. Figure 10-10 on page 170 depicts the Diagnostic field of the SError register and identifies the "I" bit in the Diagnostic field that indicates a PHY internal error has been detected. Similarly, the SStatus register (Figure 10-11 on page 171) reports PHY-related errors indicating whether the link is still communicating or not.

Additional error reporting capability can be implemented such as, adding device-specific error registers that provide more granularity to identify a specify type of PHY error.

Figure 10-10: Physical Layer Internal Error Reported in the SError Register

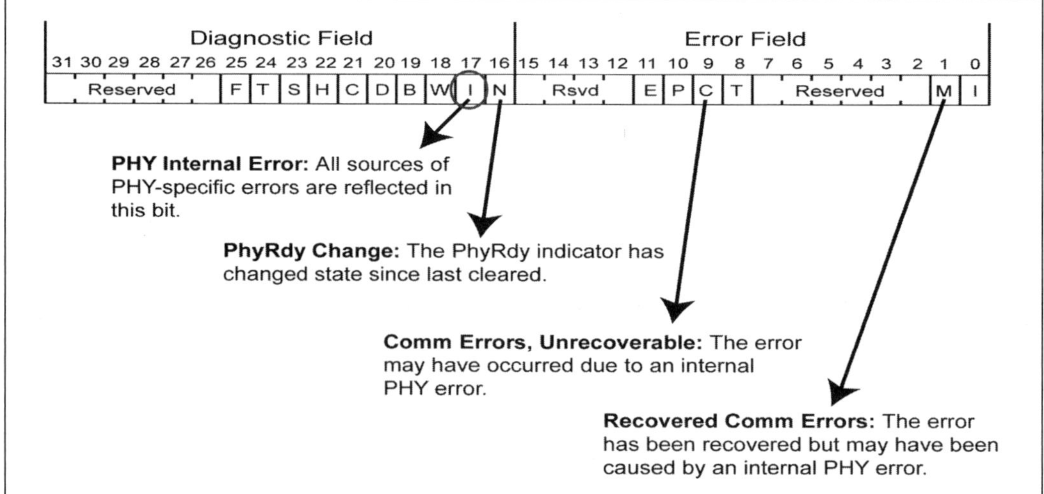

Figure 10-11: Physical Layer Error Reported in the SStatus Register

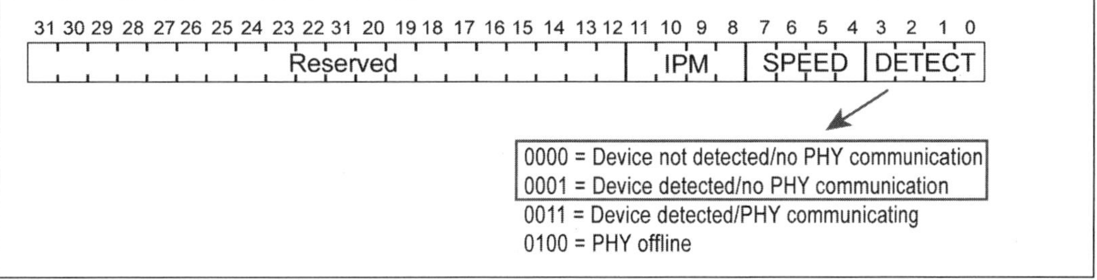

Link Layer Errors

The primary error checking performed by the link layer verifies that the frames and primitives have been transmitted successfully across the differential signals and into the link layer of the receiver. Link errors are perhaps more likely to be recoverable than most other errors because they typically occur as a result of random events. Sources of Link layer errors include:

- 8b/10b encoding and decoding errors
  - Disparity Errors
  - 10b/8b decoding errors
- CRC errors

8b/10b Encoding and Decoding Errors

The 8b/10b encoding and decoding mechanism provides error checking to detect coding errors. Coding errors are generally detected via disparity error checks. These checks apply to all information sent across the link, including frames and primitives. See Appendix A for a detailed description of encoding and disparity error checking. When a disparity or 10b-to-8b decoding error is detected by the HBA during reception several bits may be set within the SError register as illustrated and described in Figure 10-12.

Figure 10-12: Disparity Error Reporting

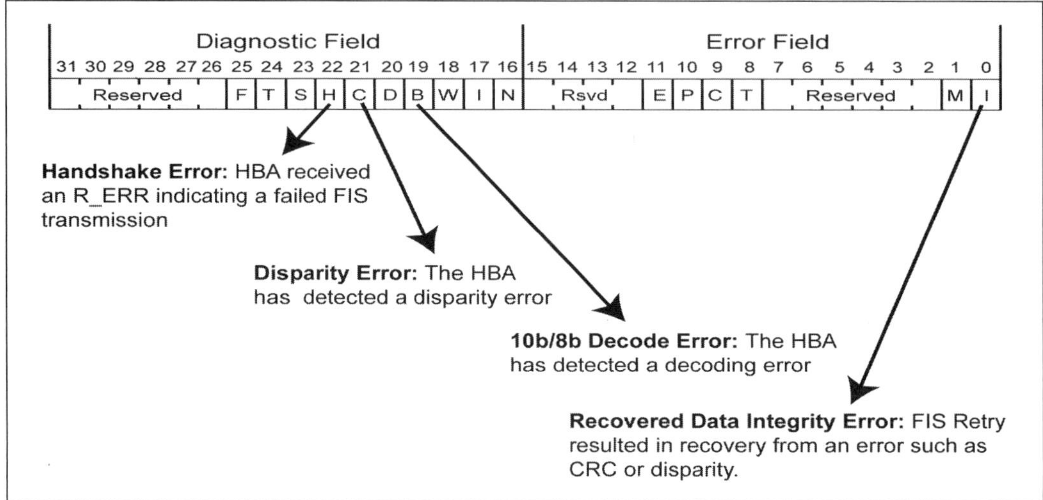

Disparity Errors within FISes. When disparity errors are detected during the reception of a FIS, the Transport layer is notified. The Transport layer returns the R_ERR primitive to the FIS transmitter to report the failed tranmission. If the FIS is eligible for retry, the Transport layer automatically re-transmits the FIS as described in Chapter 7, entitled "FIS Retry," on page 125.

Disparity Errors within Primitives. Disparity errors detected in conjunction with primitives are reported to the Transport layer and the primitive is discarded. Because primitives are typically repeated a subsequent primitive may supersede the primitive that failed transmission. In other cases, a failed primitive may result in a FIS transmission failing, which would be reported via R_ERR. Ultimately, the result of a disparity error condition depends on the particular conditions in which the failure has occurred and whether the error was detected by the HBA or the drive.

CRC Errors

The CRC value is automatically generated and checked within the link layer of the HBA and drives. When the link layer detects a CRC error within a FIS it is required to report the error condition to the Transport layer for handling. In turn, the Transport layer is required to report the error by returning an R_ERR to the FIS transmitter. Upon detecting R_ERR, the Transport layer will retry the transmission, except in the case of a Data FIS.

Note that the actions taken to report and handle a CRC error are generally the same as disparity error reporting, because both conditions are likely due to a transient condition. Figure 10-9 illustrates the error-related bits set when a CRC error is detected and R_ERR is returned to the transmitter.

Figure 10-13: CRC Error Reporting

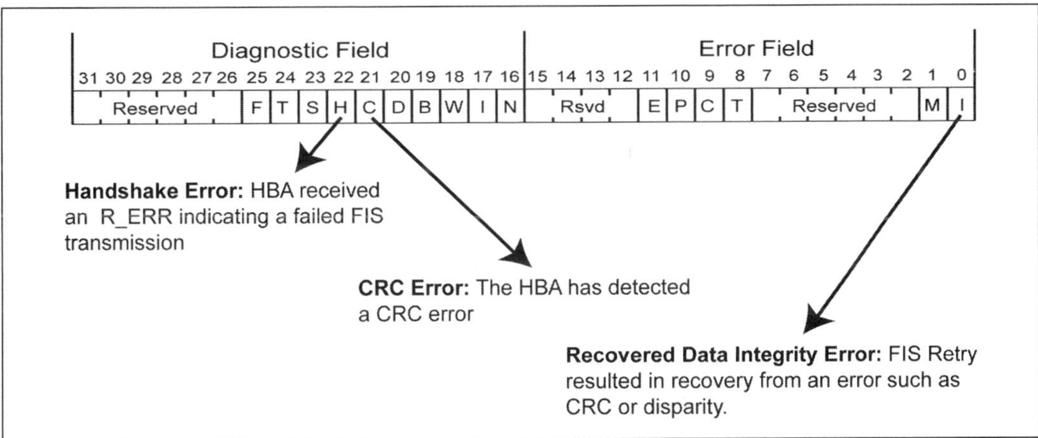

ATA Error Status. Later versions of ATA provide CRC error checking on data transfers. Consequently, a CRC error detected during Data FIS transfer to the drive will be reported in the ATA Status register within the drive. ATA status is reported to the HBA via Device-to-Host FIS. The Status register will have the ERR bit set and the BSY and DRQ bits will be cleared. The Error register will have the ABRT bit set.

Link Sequence Errors

The Link layer state machine defines many states and associated transitions. A link sequence error is reported due to illegal transitions, which implies events have occurred out of sequence. Sequence errors are reported by sending SYNC primitives, causing FIS transmission to be aborted. Link state transitions associated with normal FIS delivery are discussed in Chapter 6, entitled "Transport and Link Protocols," on page 103. State transitions associated with entry into and exit from the low-power states are discussed in Chapter 22, entitled "Link Power Management," on page 383. Finally, state transitions associated with flow control are discussed in Chapter 8, entitled "Data Flow Control," on page 133.

Transport Layer Errors

The Transport layer is responsible for reporting errors to the FIS transmitter by initiating delivery of the R_ERR primitive. Sources of error reported by the link layer include:

- Error detected in the lower layers of the SATA interface (link and PHY)
- Frame errors
- State Transition errors
- Internal Transport layer errors

Transport layer errors are generally handled via retries. When the R_ERR primitive is received by the transmitting node, it will retransmit the failed frame. Depending on whether the error condition is transient or persistent the retried transmission may also fail, triggering another R_ERR and subsequent retry. No retry limit or time-out is defined by the specification, so the retries will continue until host software times out. In this case, host software will typically requeue the command.

Frame Errors

Frame errors are categorized as a failure to correctly receive and identify an incoming frame. This includes detecting a disparity or CRC error that has been reported by the Link layer, frames with an invalid TYPE field, and malformed frames (e.g., frames of incorrect length or other recognized formatting problems).

Transport State Transition/Protocol Errors

Transport layer state transition errors generally result from violations in the specified SATA protocol defined by the state machine definitions in the specification. Note that the Diagnostic field within the SError register defines a bit (T) that is set when the HBA Transport layer detects a State Transition error.

Internal Transport Layer Errors

Internal errors are generally handled by reporting the failed transaction by returning R_ERR to the transmitting node. For example, a receive buffer overflow within the Transport layer requires the receiver to sent R_ERR to the transmitting node. A Transport layer overflow condition at the transmitter requires the frame to be invalidated by forcing a bad CRC value to the receiver can detect the failed frame.

Part Three

Command and Control Protocols

11 The Command Protocol

Previous Chapter

The discussions to this point have focused on the FIS transfer protocols and for the most part have presumed that the transfers occur without error. The previous chapter discussed the error detection mechanisms, described the sources of these errors, and specified the methods used to handle and report them.

This Chapter

Much of the discussion prior to the last chapter focused on the delivery of individual Frame Information Structures. The discussion now turns to the various categories of commands, each of which require the exchange of a particular sequence of Frame Information Structures. It is the responsibility of the command layer to manage this sequencing.

The Next Chapter

The next chapter discusses the functions associated with the ATA Control register. Writing to the Device Control register forces the HBA to send a Register FIS to the device. The particular bits written force the drive to take the specified action. Each of the Control register functions is discussed in detail.

Overview

This chapter focuses on the protocols associated with executing commands in the SATA environment. Most of the commands implemented are commands supported by the Parallel ATA implementations. However, new commands have been added to support new features available only in the SATA environment.

Figure 11-1 illustrates the Command layer within the hierarchy of SATA interface layers. When host software issues the command to the HBA it forwards the command to the drive where it is decoded and passed to the Application layer within the drive. The command layer state machine knows the sequence of FISes that must be exchanged to complete the command successfully. Similarly, the Command layer within the HBA also knows the FISes to expect and return for a given command.

Figure 11-1: Command Layer in Hierarchy

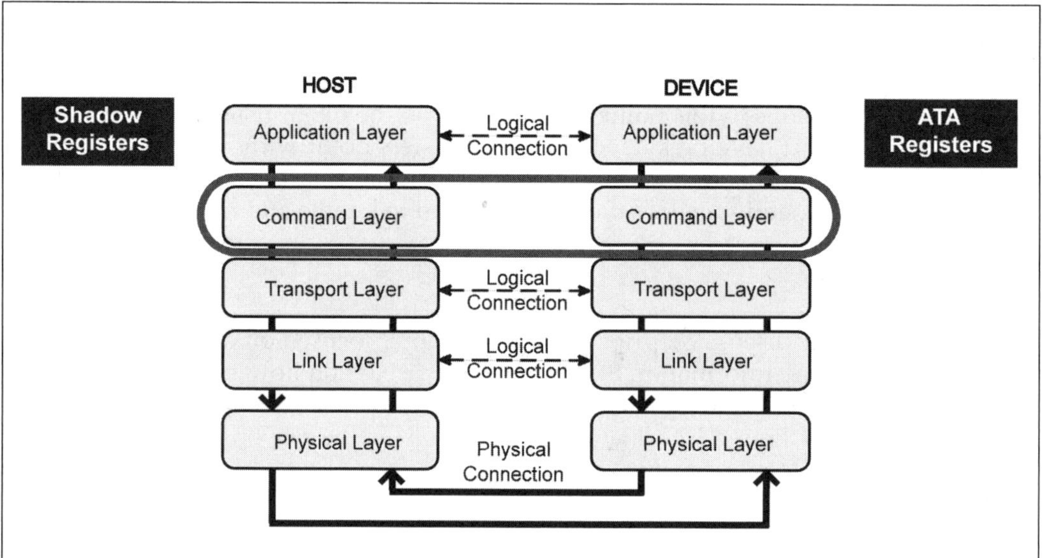

Command Types

Twelve different categories of command are defined by the specification. Commands are grouped by category because all commands within a given category have behaviors in common that allow them to use the same command protocol. That is, the sequence of FISes exchanged and the actions taken in the process of executing and completing the command is the same. Table 11-1 on page 179 lists the 12 command categories and identifies the number of commands supported by each.

Table 11-1: Command Protocol Types

Command Category	Number of Commands
Command Not Implemented	NA
Non-Data	34
PIO Data-In	13
PIO Data-Out	14
DMA-In	2
DMA-Out	2
DMA-In Queued	2
DMA-Out Queued	2
Packet (ATAPI)	1
Service	1
Device Reset	1
Execute Device Diagnostics	1

Command Delivery

Every command sequence begins with a register FIS used to delivered the command to the drive. Once a command is received and recognized, the command protocol is established within the drive. The steps involved in this process are detailed below.

Command Transport to Disc Drive

The state diagram in Figure 11-2 on page 180 shows the delivery of a Register Host to Device FIS to the drive. Initially the host Transport layer is idled because is has not received a FIS transfer request from the Application layer. When a command value is written to the shadow register the HBA transitions to the "Host Command FIS" state, triggering FIS delivery to the drive. During transmission the FIS transfer protocol is followed and the FIS is generally received without error and R_OK is returned to the HBA. Note that violations of the transfer protocol that are detected by the HBA can force the link back to the idle state as illustrated in Figure 11-2. Once the FIS is received, the drive performs various checks (disparity, CRC, etc.) to verify that the FIS is valid. Errors are reported via R_ERR and the FIS is retried.

Figure 11-2: State Diagram for Register FIS delivery to the Disc Drive

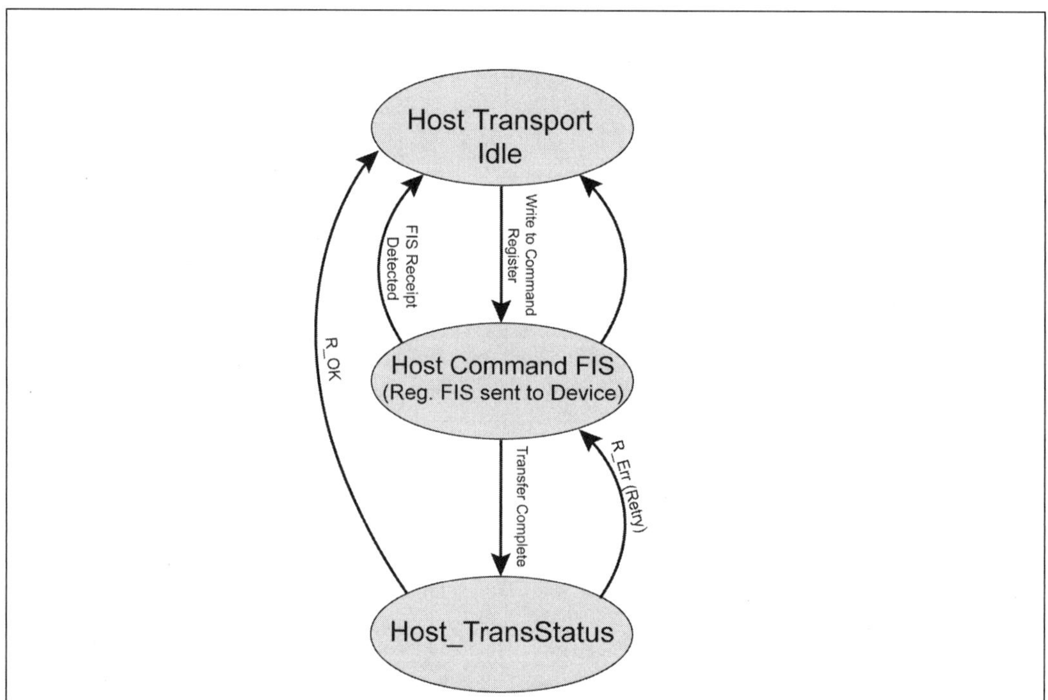

Command Reception

The state diagram in Figure 11-3 on page 181 illustrates the required actions associated with Register FIS reception by a disc drive. When the incoming FIS is detected by the Link layer it is forwarded to the Transport layer. The first byte received by the Transport layer is the FIS type field, which is checked and determined to be a Register FIS and the drive transitions to the "Dev_RegFIS" (Device Register FIS) state. Two transitions are possible while the drive is in this state:

- If during reception an illegal transition error occurs, the device sends SYNC primitives to the HBA; thereby transitioning its transmit side to logical idle.
- Once the FIS has been completely received with no illegal transitions, the drive transitions to the "Device Transfer Status" state.

In the Dev_TransStatus state, the Transport layer, having received and checked for errors returns either R_OK or R_ERR. Presuming the status is OK and that its type is a Register FIS, the Transport layer knows that the contents of the FIS must be forwarded to the Application layer, where the ATA registers are loaded with the new command and its associated parameters.

Figure 11-3: Receive States for Register Host-to-Device FIS Reception

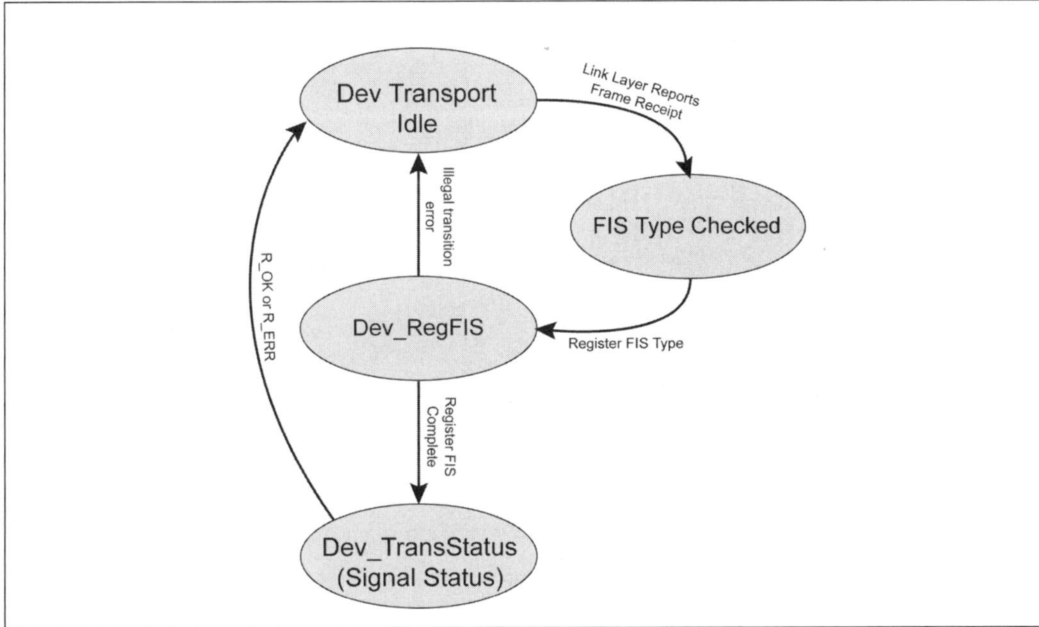

Recognizing and Decoding the Command

Once the FIS type is known to be a Register FIS its contents are delivered to the disc drive's ATA registers. Because software triggers the delivery of a Register FIS to the drive, there must be some way to determine which action triggered the Register FIS delivery:

- write to the command register
- write to the control register

The Register Host-to-Device FIS contains a field that specifies whether a write to the Command or Control register has triggered FIS delivery. Figure 11-4 on page 182 highlights the "C" bit that reports a "0" if a write to the Control register triggered the Register FIS and a "1" if a Command register write has trigger FIS delivery.

Figure 11-4: C-bit within Register Host-to-Device FIS Reports Reason For FIS Delivery

	+3	+2	+1	+0
	7 6 5 4 3 2 1 0	7 6 5 4 3 2 1 0	7 6 5 4 3 2 1 0	7 6 5 4 3 2 1 0
DW 0	Features	Command	C R R Reserved	FIS Type (27h)
DW 1	Device	LBA High	LBA Middle	LBA Low
DW 2	Features (exp)	LBA High (exp)	LBA Mid (exp)	LBA Low (exp)
DW 3	Control	Reserved (0)	Sec Count (exp)	Sector Count
DW 4	Reserved (0)	Reserved (0)	Reserved (0)	Reserved (0)

Once the command is decoded, as shown in Figure 11-5 on page 183, processing can begin. Also, the command layer now knows which one of twelve command types is being performed and the corresponding command protocol is selected.

Figure 11-5: Command Layer Identifies Protocol

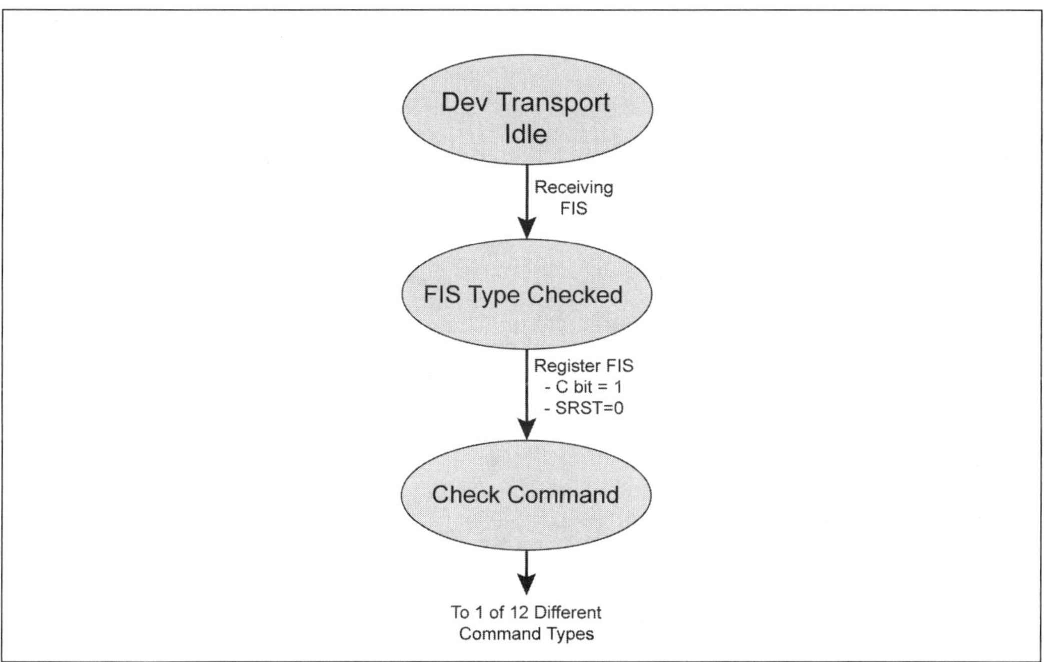

Command Not Implemented

One of the twelve command types that must be handled, is the case where the command detected is not supported by the drive. The required actions are illustrated in the state diagram in Figure 11-6 on page 184. The actions required include:

- setting the error bit in the ATA Status register
- setting the abort bit in the ATA Error register
- returning a Register Device-to-Host FIS

Figure 11-6: State Diagram for Command No Implemented

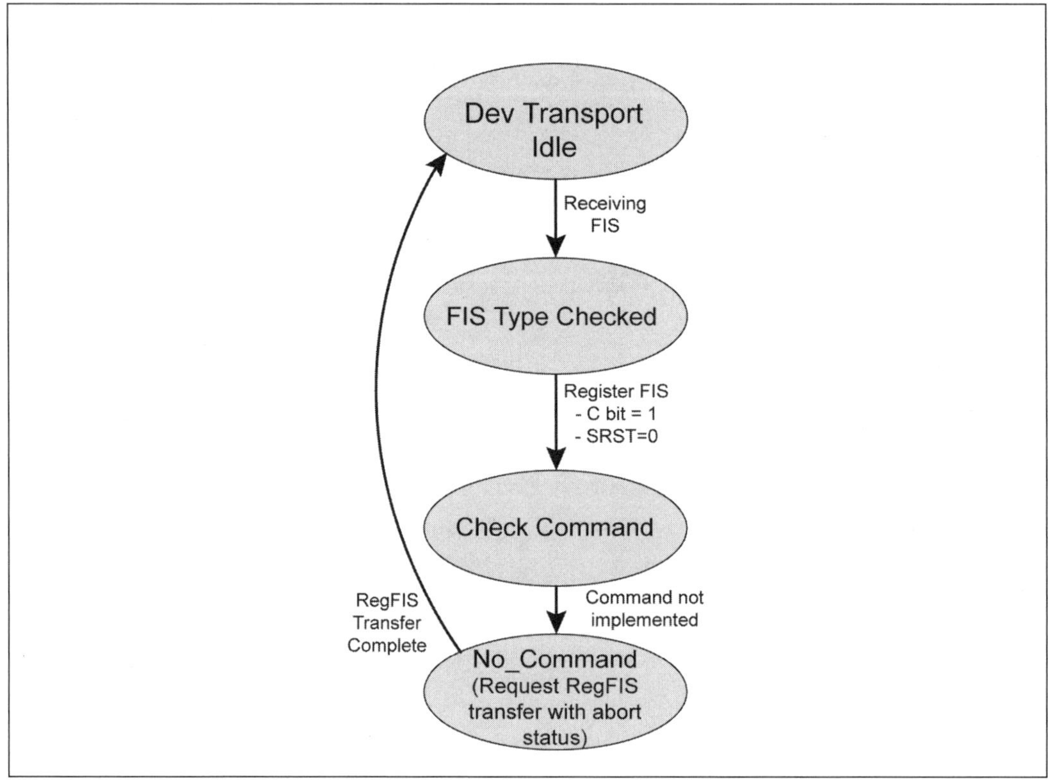

Non-Data Commands

A large category of commands do not involve the movement of data to or from the drive, thus, no DATA FIS is used during in the command protocol. This results in a very simple command sequence as illustrated in Figure 11-7 on page 185. Notice the sequence consists of the exchange of Register FISes between the HBA and drive. Table 11-2 on page 185 lists the collection of commands that use the Non-Data command protocol, along with the command code and whether the command is Optional, Mandatory or Not allowed for ATA and ATAPI commands. Note that the first entry under that ATA command column is listed as "F" indicating that the command is only mandatory for "Flash Drives."

Figure 11-7: Non-Data Command Sequence

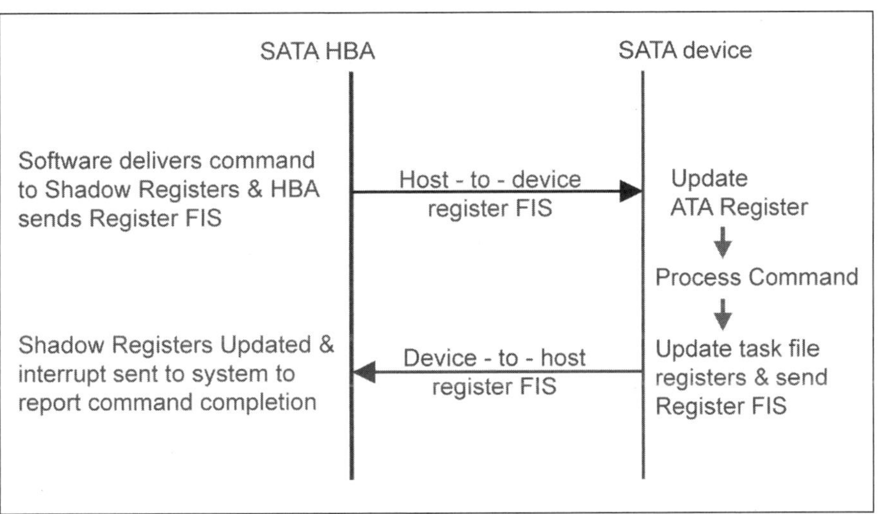

Table 11-2: Non-Data Commands

Command	Code	ATA Command	ATAPI Command
CFA Erase Sectors	C0h	F	N
CFA Request Extended Error	03h	O	N
Check Media Card Type	D1	O	N
Check Power Mode	E5h	M	M
Configure Stream	51h	O	O
Device Configuration Freeze Lock	B1h	O	O
Device Configuration Restore	B1h	O	O
Flush Cache	E7	M	O
Flush Cache Ext	EAh	O	N
Get Media Status	DAh	O	O
Idle	E3h	M	O
Idle Immediate	E1h	M	M

Table 11-2: Non-Data Commands

Media Eject	EDh	O	N
Media Lock	DEh	O	N
Media Unlock	DFh	O	N
NOP	00h	O	M
Read Native Max Address	F8h	O	O
Read Native Max Address Ext	27h	O	N
Read Verify Sector(s)	40h	M	N
Read Verify Sector(s) Ext	42h	O	N
Security Erase Prepare	F3h	O	O
Security Freeze Lock	F5h	O	O
Set Features	EFh	M	M
Set Max	F9h	O	O
Set Max Address Ext	37h	O	N
Set Multiple Mode	C6h	M	N
Sleep	E6h	M	M
Smart Disable Operations	B0h	O	N
Smart Enable/Disable Autosave	B0h	O	N
Smart Enable Operations	B0h	O	N
Smart Execute Off-Line Immediate	B0h	O	N
Smart Return Status	B0h	O	N
Standby	E2h	M	O
Standby Immediate	E0h	M	M

F = Mandatory for Flash Drives
M = Mandatory
N = Not Allowed
O = Optional

Figure 11-8: SATA Drive Non-Data Command Received State Diagram

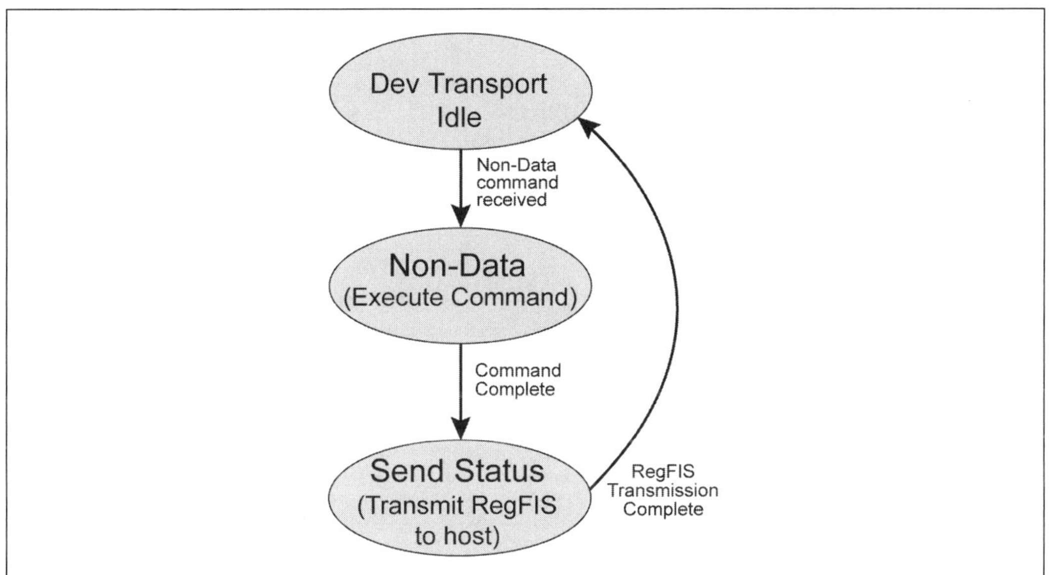

PIO Commands

Programmed IO (PIO) Commands are those in which the CPU explicitly executes the code necessary to move data between memory and the ATA 16-bit Data register. For example, a read sector command would result in two bytes of data being moved at a time until 512 bytes (one sector) have been moved. This of course means that 256 Data register reads must be performed to complete the transfer. Note that the disc drive triggers the 512 byte transfer by sending an interrupt to notify software that data is ready to be read. If the sector count associated with the Read Sector command is set to four, then the sequence just described would be performed four times to satisfy the transfer count.

The PIO command protocol has two primary variations based on direction of data movement:

- PIO Data-In — data movement from disc drive to memory
- PIO Data-Out — data movement from memory to the disc drive

The following two sections discuss the PIO Data-Out and PIO Data-In commands

PIO Data-In Commands

Table 11-3 lists the commands that use the PIO Data-In protocol. These commands are typically used during the system boot sequence and typically not be used once the OS loads the run-time device drivers.

Table 11-3: PIO Data-In Commands

Command	Code	ATA Command	ATAPI Command
CFA Translate Sector	87h	O	N
Device Configuration Identify	B1h	O	O
Identify Device	ECh	M	M
Identify Packet Device	A1h	N	M
Read Buffer	E4h	O	N
Read Log Ext	2Fh	O	O
Read Multiple	C4h	M	N
Read Multiple Ext	29h	O	N
Read Sector(s)	EDh	M	M
Read Sector(s) Ext	DEh	O	N
Read Stream Ext	2Bh	O	N
Smart Read Data	B0h	O	N
Smart Read Log	B0h	O	N
M = Mandatory N = Not Allowed O = Optional			

Parallel ATA PIO Data-In Review

Prior to discussing the SATA PIO Data-In protocol, a brief review of the ATA protocol may help in understanding the related SATA version of the protocol. Below is a brief summary of Parallel ATA protocol for a Read Sector command.

1. The BSY and DRQ status bits are cleared (0) permitting host software to initialize and issue the command directly to the ATA registers (task file) within the disc drive. When the command is written the drive sets the BSY bit to notify software that the task file should not be updated.
2. The drive decodes the command and reads the entire first target sector from disc.
3. The first two bytes of data read from disc are transferred to the task file's Data register, making data available for host software to fetch.
4. The drive clears the BSY bit, sets the DRQ bit, and generates an interrupt to notify software that status has changed.
5. Host software reads status and detects BSY cleared and DRQ set, indicating that data is ready to be read from the Data register.
6. Host software continuously reads the contents of the Data register until an entire sector (512 bytes) has been read.
7. If the transfer count is satisfied, the drive will clear the DRQ and BSY bits to notify the host that the transfer is complete.
8. If the transfer count is not yet satisfied, the drive will set the BSY bit. Software is expected to read status to determine if the command has completed. When the drive is ready to transfer the next sector, it repeats the process beginning at step 3.

The command protocol differs depending on the type of PIO Data-In command being performed. Most PIO commands transfer information in 512 byte blocks, resulting in an interrupt for each transfer. However, some commands transfer multiple sectors at a time. For example, in a Read Multiple command an interrupt is generated once for each set of sectors to be transferred. The number of sectors to be transferred in each set is initialized via a Set Multiple Mode command.

SATA PIO Data-In Command Protocol Overview

Figure 11-9 illustrates the command protocol performed during a PIO Data-In operation, in which a single sector (512 bytes) is transferred. The steps involved are enumerated below:

1. The BSY status bit is cleared, permitting software to initialize the task file.
2. Software writes the PIO Data-In command, thereby triggering the delivery

SATA PIO Data-In Command Protocol Overview

Figure 11-9 illustrates the command protocol performed during a PIO Data-In operation, in which a single sector (512 bytes) is transferred. The steps involved are enumerated below:

1. The BSY status bit is cleared, permitting software to initialize the task file.
2. Software writes the PIO Data-In command, thereby triggering the delivery of the Register FIS that transports the task file contents to the drive.
3. The disc drive receives the Register FIS and decodes the command which establishes the PIO Data-In command protocol within the drive.
4. The drive reads the target sector from the disc.
5. Knowing the result of the read, the drive updates status information (BSY=0 and DRQ=1) and reports that data is ready for delivery via the PIO Setup FIS. This FIS conveys the contents of the task file, including initial status and end status and sets the "I" (Interrupt) bit. See figure Figure 5-9 on page 96 to review the PIO Setup FIS contents.
6. The HBA receives the PIO Setup FIS and confirms that the direction of the transfer is consistent with the PIO Data-In command originally initiated by software. The HBA stores the contents of the PIO Setup FIS and awaits the delivery of data.
7. The drive delivers data via a Data FIS.
8. The HBA receives the data into a local buffer and places the first 2 bytes into the shadow Data register and updates the remaining shadow registers with the contents of the PIO Setup FIS, including Initial status. The "I" bit within the PIO Setup FIS notifies the HBA to send an interrupt request. Note that end status is temporarily stored for later use (see step 10).
9. Software reads status (BSY=0 and DRQ=1) indicating that data is ready to be read. Software continues to read data until the entire contents of the Data FIS have been transferred.
10. After all the data is transferred, the shadow registers are updated with end status (BSY=0 & DRQ=0).
11. Host software reads completion status and the command is retired. Note that no interrupt is generated after the command has been completed. Software is expected to check status to determine completion results.

When the sector count of a command involves transferring more that one block of data, the end status supplied by the drive would be set to BSY=1 and DRQ=0; thereby, indicating that one or more additional block transfers are pending for this command. The drive will send another PIO Setup FIS and the process is repeated until all sectors have been transferred.

Figure 11-9: PIO Data In Command Protocol Overview

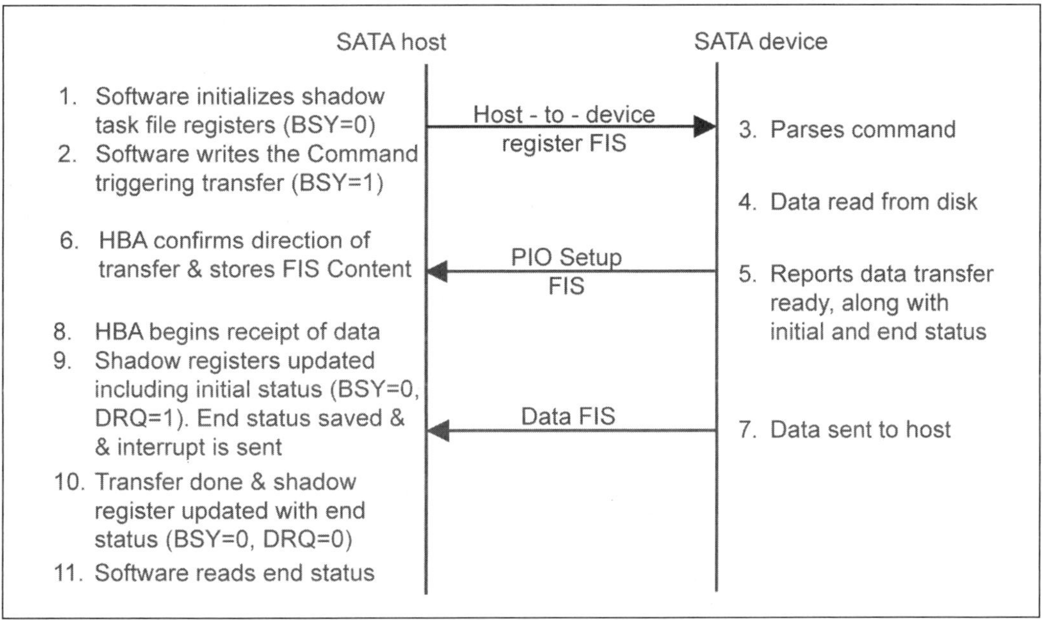

SATA Device PIO Data-In Command Protocol

The state diagram in Figure 11-10 on page 192 illustrates the command protocol used by a device during a PIO Data-In operation. Two additional conditions are added and described that were not included in the previous overview:

- Multiple Data FIS transfers due to a large sector count
- Error conditions that cause the command to abort

PIO_IN State. The state machine is entered when a Register FIS is received that contains a PIO-In command. This causes the device to prepare the first data block for transfer. When the drive has acquired the requested data block from the disc, it transitions to the Send PIO Setup state.

Send PIO Setup State. The drive must notify the HBA that data is ready for delivery via a PIO Setup FIS. In preparation the contents of the task file is loaded into the PIO Setup FIS, and further includes two separate Status register values; initial status and end status. Initial status indicates that data is ready to be read (BSY=0 and DRQ=1). End status indicates the status after the current data block is transferred (BSY=1 and DRQ=0) if additional data blocks are pending transfer for this command, or BSY=0 and DRQ=0 when the current transfer completes the sector count. Additionally, the Interrupt (I) bit must also be set, causing the HBA to generate an interrupt to notify software that data is ready to transfer.

Transmit Data State. The data is delivered to the HBA via a Data FIS. The HBA upon receiving the data moves the first 2 bytes of data to the task file Data register and the contents of the PIO Setup FIS are loaded into the HBA's task file registers, including initial status. Once the entire data block is read by host software, either the command terminates and the device transitions to the Device Transport Idle state, or if one or more data blocks are pending transfer a transition is made back to the Send PIO Setup state. If errors occur that cause the command to be aborted the transition is to the Error state.

Error State. When the device detects an error, it reports the error to the HBA via a Device to Host Register FIS.

Figure 11-10: State Diagram of Device's PIO Data-In Command Protocol Behavior

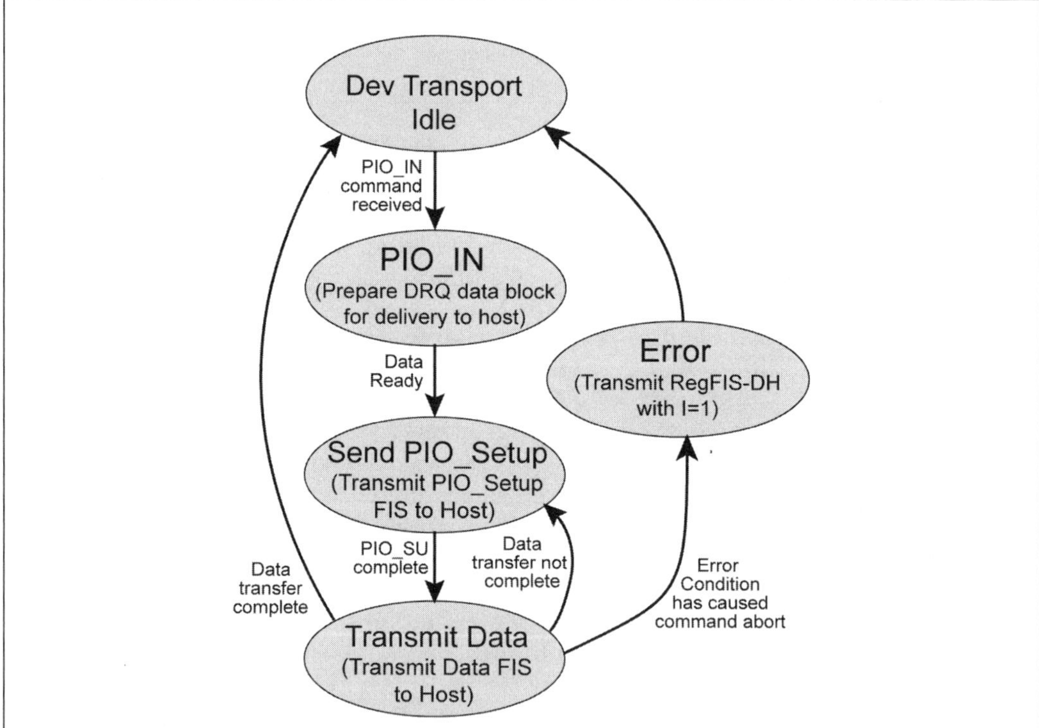

HBA PIO Data-In Command Protocol

During PIO Data-In commands, the HBA must serve data to host software and manage status updates provided by the drive. The HBA protocol is specified by the state machine diagram in Figure 11-11. After the HBA delivers the PIO Data-In command via a Register FIS, it returns to the Host Transport Idle state and awaits receipt of the PIO Setup FIS.

PIO Setup FIS Received. The HBA detects in incoming PIO Setup FIS from the drive as illustrated in Figure 11-11, entry point 1). The HBA checks the FIS type and verifies the direction (D) specified in the PIO Setup FIS is "IN" or D=1. The HBA also saves the contents of the FIS for use when the Data arrives and transitions back to the Host Transport Idle state.

Data FIS Received. Next, an incoming Data FIS is detected by the HBA (entry point 2). The HBA verifies that the Data FIS was preceded by a PIO Setup FIS and transitions to the Host_PIOITrans1 state (PIO In Transport state 1). In this state, the HBA waits for the data to arrive into the receive FIFO.

When data arrives the HBA transitions to the Host_PIOITrans2 state. During this transition the HBA updates the shadow registers with the saved contents of the PIO Setup FIS. This includes initial status (BSY=0 and DRQ=1) and because the interrupt pending bit (I=1) is set the HBA sends an interrupt request to notify software that status has changed.

Host software, having been called via the interrupt, checks status and determines that data is ready to be read. During Host_PIOITrans2 state, software performs back-to-back reads to fetch the contents of the Data FIS from the shadow Data register 2 bytes at a time. When the transfer is complete the HBA transitions to the Host_PIOEnd state where the end status value is loaded into the shadow Status register.

If during the data transfers an illegal transition occurs or if host software sends a Reset to the Control register, the HBA transitions to the idle state. If other forms of unrecoverable error (such as a Data FIS CRC error) are detected, the command is aborted and the HBA transitions to the Host_PIOEnd state where the final status and errors are reported.

Figure 11-11: State Diagram Defining Host Actions During PIO Data-In Commands

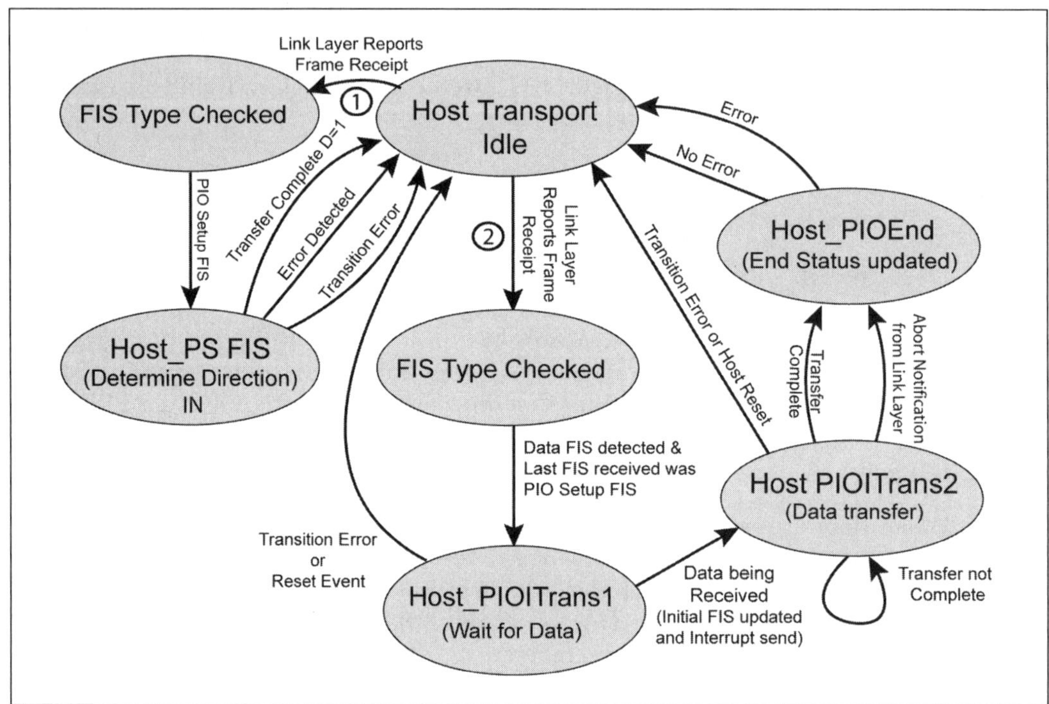

PIO Data Out Commands

Table 11-4 lists the commands that use the PIO Data-Out protocol. Like the Data-In command, these commands are typically used during the system boot sequence and generally not be used once the OS loads the run-time device drivers.

Table 11-4: PIO Data Out Commands

Command	Code	ATA Command	ATAPI Command
CFA Write Multiple Without Erase	CDh	O	N
CFA Write Sectors Without Erase	38h	O	N
Device Configuration Set	B1h	O	O
Download Microcode	92h	O	N
Security Disable Password	F6h	O	O
Security Erase Unit	F4h	O	O
Security Set Password	F1h	O	O
Security Unlock	F2h	O	O
Smart Write Log	B0h	O	N
Write Buffer	E8h	O	N
Write Log Ext	3Fh	O	O
Write Multiple	C5h	M	N
Write Multiple Ext	39h	O	N
Write Multiple FUA Ext	CEh	O	N
Write Sector(s)	30h	M	N
Write Sector(s) Ext	34h	O	N
Write Stream Ext	38h	O	N
M = Mandatory N = Not Allowed O = Optional			

Parallel ATA PIO Data-Out Review

Prior to discussing the SATA PIO Data-Out protocol, a brief review of the parallel ATA protocol may help in understanding the related SATA version of the protocol. Below is a brief summary of Parallel ATA protocol for a write Sector command.

1. The BSY & DRQ status bits are cleared (0) permitting host software to initialize and issue the command directly to the ATA registers (task file) within the disc drive. When the command is written the drive sets the BSY bit to notify software that the task file should not be updated.
2. The drive decodes the command and prepares to write a sector to disc.
3. The drive clears the BSY bit, sets the DRQ bit, indicating the disc drive is ready to receive data. During PIO Data-Out operations no interrupt is generated by the drive to notify the host that the drive is ready to receive the first sector. The presumption is that the drive will be ready to receive data from the host almost instantaneously after the command is delivered. Consequently, software may simply write the data knowing the drive will be ready long before the data arrives. Note that during multi-sector commands (sector count greater than one) that while no interrupt is sent prior to the first sector transfer, interrupts are sent prior to all subsequent sector transfers.
4. Host software continuously writes the sector contents to the task file Data register 2 bytes at a time until an entire sector (512 bytes) has been delivered.
5. If the transfer count is satisfied, the drive will clear the DRQ and BSY bits to notify the host that the transfer is complete.
6. If the transfer count is not yet satisfied, the drive will set the BSY bit to indicate that one or more sectors are pending delivery. Software is expected to read status to determine if the command has completed successfully. When the drive is ready to transfer the next sector, it repeats the process beginning at step 3, with the exception that an interrupt is also sent by the drive during step 3.

The command protocol differs depending on the type of PIO Data-Out command being performed. Most PIO Data-Out commands transfer information in 512 byte blocks, resulting in an interrupt for each sector transferred, except the first sector. However, some commands transfer multiple sectors at a time. For example, in a Write Multiple command an interrupt is generated once for each block of sectors to be transferred. The number of sectors to be transferred in each block is initialized via a Set Multiple Mode command.

SATA PIO Data-Out Command Protocol Overview

Figure 11-12 illustrates the SATA PIO Data-Out command protocol associated with a PIO Write Sector command, with a sector count of one. Each step in the process is described below.

1. The BSY status bit is cleared, permitting software to initialize the task file.
2. Software writes the PIO Data-Out command, thereby triggering the delivery of the Register FIS that transports the task file contents to the drive.
3. The disc drive receives the Register FIS and decodes the command which establishes the PIO Data-Out command protocol within the drive.
4. The drive prepares to write the target sector to the disc.
5. The drive sets BSY=0 and DRQ=1 indicating that it's ready to receive data. The drive then delivers the contents of the task file to the HBA via a PIO Setup FIS. Because I=0 no interrupt will be sent by the HBA.
6. The HBA receives the PIO Setup FIS and confirms that the direction of the transfer is consistent with the PIO Data-Out command originally initiated by software.
7. The HBA loads the contents of the PIO Setup FIS into the shadow registers, including initial status.
8. Host software delivers data two bytes at a time to the task file's Data registers. When the entire sector has been delivered it is sent to the drive via a Data FIS.
9. The drive receives the data into a local buffer and writes the data to disc. Because in this example a single sector is being stored to disc, end status is updated (BSY=0 and DRQ=0).
10. The drive reports completion status to the HBA via a Register FIS.
11. The HBA receives the Register FIS and updates the shadow registers.
12. Host software reads completion status and the command is retired. Note that no interrupt is generated after the command has been completed. Software is expected to check status to determine completion results.

When the sector count of a command involves transferring more that one block of data, the end status supplied by the drive would be set to BSY=1 and DRQ=0; thereby, indicating that one or more additional block transfers are pending for this command. The drive will send another PIO Setup FIS (this time with I=1) causing the HBA to generate and interrupt, and the process is repeated until all sectors have been transferred.

Figure 11-12: PIO Data-Out Command Protocol Overview

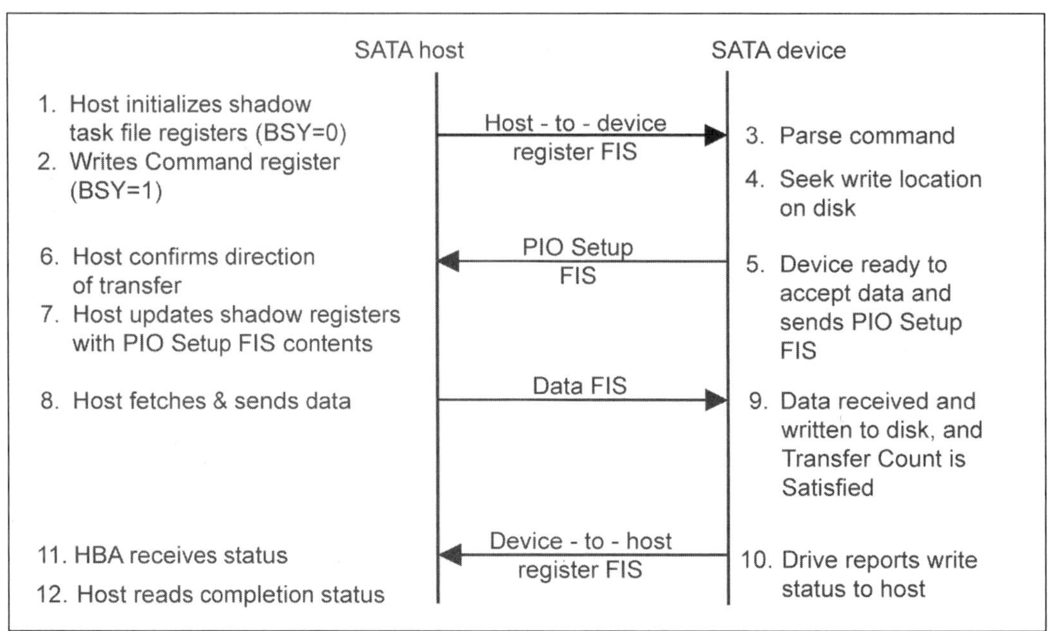

SATA Device PIO Data-Out Command Protocol

The state diagram in Figure 11-10 on page 192 illustrates the command protocol used by a device during a PIO Data-Out operation. Two additional conditions are added and described in the protocol that were not included in the previous overview:

- Multiple Data FIS transfers due to a large sector count
- Error conditions that cause the command to abort

The state machine is entered when the device receives a Register FIS that contains a PIO-Out command.

Figure 11-13: State Diagram of Device's PIO Data-Out Command Protocol Behavior

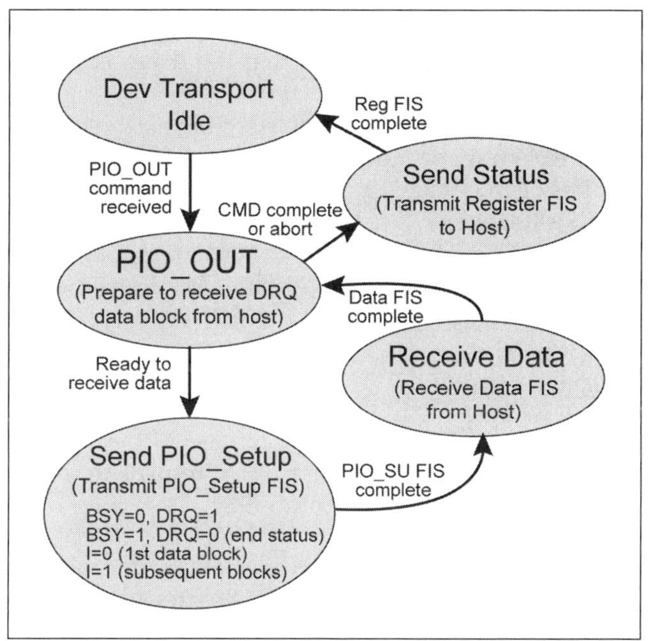

PIO_Out State. The state machine is entered when a Register FIS is received that contains a PIO-Out command. This causes the device to prepare for receiving the first block of data and the drive transitions to the Send PIO Setup state.

Send PIO Setup State. The drive notifies the HBA that it is ready to receive data via a PIO Setup FIS. In preparation for delivering the PIO Setup, the contents of the task file are loaded into the FIS, which includes two separate Status register values; initial status and end status. Initial status indicates that data is ready to be read (BSY=0 and DRQ=1). End status indicates whether, after the current transfer, additional data blocks will be pending transfer for this command (BSY=1 and DRQ=0), or if the current transfer completes the sector count (BSY=0 and DRQ=0). Additionally, the Interrupt (I) bit must be cleared (0) on the first data block transfer and must be set (1) for all subsequent data block transfers for this command.

Receive Data State. After the HBA has accumulated the data written by host software, it delivers the data to the drive via a Data FIS. The drive receives the Data FIS and checks for errors. Once the data is received and written to disc, the drive transitions back to the PIO Out state.

PIO Out State. Three possible conditions can occur that cause transition from the PIO Out state:

- The Sector Count has not been achieved, causing the delivery of another PIO Setup FIS to notify the HBA that the drive is ready for the next data block transfer.
- The Sector Count has been completed, causing the drive to send a Register FIS to the HBA to report good completion status and with I=1.
- An error has been detected by the drive causing the command to abort and delivery of a Register FIS to the HBA to report bad completion status, also with I=1.

HBA PIO Data-Out Command Protocol

During PIO Data-Out commands, the HBA delivers data to the drive and manages status updates provided by the drive. The HBA protocol is specified by the state machine diagram in Figure 11-14 on page 201. After the HBA delivers the PIO Data-Out command via a Register FIS, it returns to the Host Transport Idle state and awaits receipt of the PIO Setup FIS.

PIO Setup FIS Received. The HBA detects the incoming PIO Setup FIS from the drive as illustrated in Figure 11-14, entry point 1. The HBA checks the FIS type and verifies the direction bit in the PIO Setup FIS is Out (D=0). The HBA then transitions to the Host PIO Out Transport 1 state (Host_PIOOTrans1). The HBA updates the contents of the task file with the PIO Setup FIS contents, and uses initial status in the process. Also I=0 during the first data block transfer so no interrupt is generated. During the second and all subsequent data block transfers I=1, causing the HBA to send an interrupt to notify software to send data. The HBA then transitions to the Host Transport Idle state.

Data Received from Host. As illustrated in Figure 11-14, entry point 2, the HBA exits idle and enters the Host_PIOOTrans2 state when the PIO Setup FIS was the last FIS received and host software has written to the shadow Data register. In this state the HBA continues to accumulate data into its local transmit FIFO and starts sending the data via a Data FIS. When the Data FIS completes the HBA transitions to the Host PIO End state, where the HBA awaits the Register FIS from the drive. A transition to the Host PIO End state can also occur due to errors reported by the link layer that causes the command to abort.

Register FIS Received. When the Register FIS is received from the drive, end status is updated by loading the Register FIS contents into the shadow registers. The I bit is also set, causing the HBA to send an interrupt to tell software to read completion status, either good or bad.

Figure 11-14: Host PIO Data-Out Command Protocol

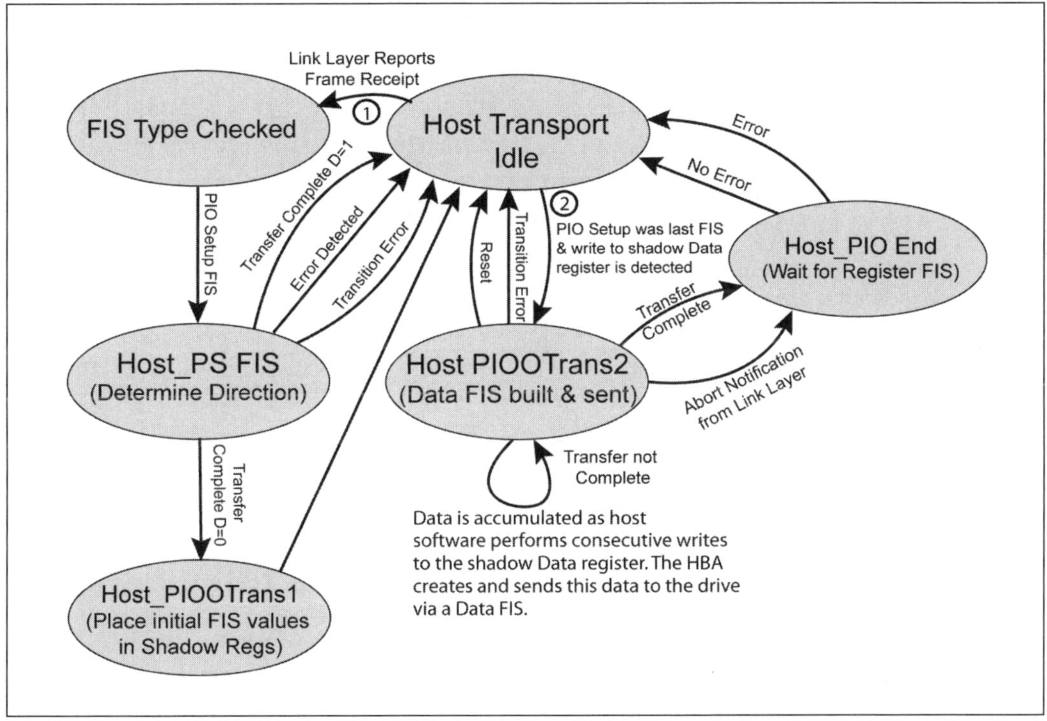

DMA Commands

DMA commands come in several types that each have different command protocols:

- DMA-In Commands
- DMA-Out Commands
- DMA-In Queued Commands
- DMA-Out Queued Commands
- First Party DMA Read Commands
- First Party DMA Write Commands

The following sections describe the protocols associated with these commands.

DMA-In Protocol

Table 11-5 lists the three commands that use the DMA-In command protocol. This protocol is relatively simple, in contrast with the PIO Commands. Figure 11-15 on page 203 provides an overview of the protocol.

Table 11-5: Commands that use the DMA-In Command Protocol

Command	Code	ATA Command	ATAPI Command
Read DMA	C8h	M	N
Read DMA Extended	25h	O	N
Read Stream DMA Ext	2Ah	O	N
M = Mandatory N = Not Allowed O = Optional			

The steps involved is performing the DMA-In Command protocol are enumerated below:

1. Software initializes the DMA engine associated with the HBA. This initialization involves specifying the memory buffer locations (e.g., pages) in memory where the data to be read from disc will be stored. This series of pages is referred to as a scatter list.
2. Host software initializes the shadow task file registers (BSY=0)
3. Host software writes the DMA-In command to the shadow Command register, causing BSY to be set and triggering delivery of a Register FIS.
4. The drive receives the Register FIS and checks and decodes the command.
5. The target sector or sectors are read from the drive and placed into local memory.
6. Next, the drive delivers data via a Data FIS. More than one Data FIS transfer may be required depending on the sector count. Recall that a single Data FIS carries up to 16 standard sectors (16 x 512 bytes). The Data FISes are delivered consecutively until all of the requested data has been delivered.
7. The HBA receives the data and verifies there are no errors.
8. As the data arrives it is stored in a local HBA memory buffer and then moved to host memory by the DMA controller. Flow control may be asserted if data is delivered by the drive faster than it can be sent by the DMA controller.

9. After the drive has transferred all of the requested data, it updates completion status (BSY=0 and DRQ=0) and sends the task file contents to the HBA via a Register FIS. The Register FIS must also have the Interrupt Pending bit (I) set.
10. The HBA updates the shadow registers with the contents of the Register FIS.
11. The HBA then generates an interrupt to call host software, which reads completion status and retires the command.

Figure 11-15: DMA Read Command Protocol Overview

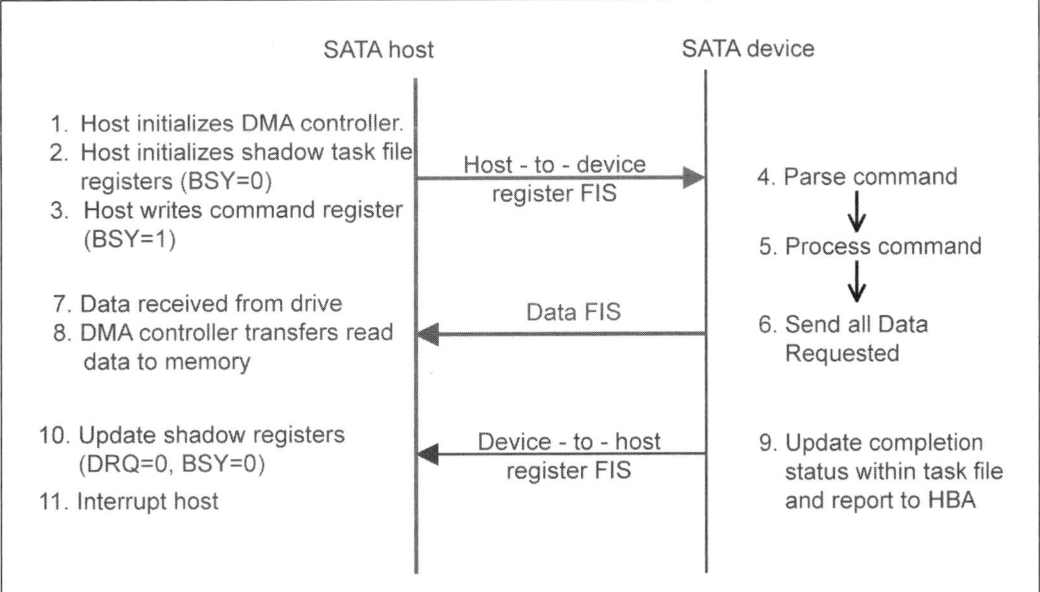

Device DMA-In Command Protocol

Figure 11-16 on page 204 illustrates the state transitions and actions taken by a device when performing a DMA-In operation. The process of course begins with the reception of the DMA-In command via a Register FIS. During command processing the device transitions to the DMA_IN state, during which time the requested data blocks are read from the drive and prepared for transmission to the host. When the Data FIS is ready to be sent, the device transitions to the Send Data state. Once the Data FIS has been successfully delivered, the device transitions back to the DMA_IN state. If more sectors are to be transferred, then another Data FIS is prepared for delivery to the host. However, when the sector count has been fulfilled, the drive transitions to the Send Status state. In this state the drive updates completion status, reads the task file and sends the information to the host via Register FIS.

Figure 11-16: State Transitions During DMA-In Command Protocol

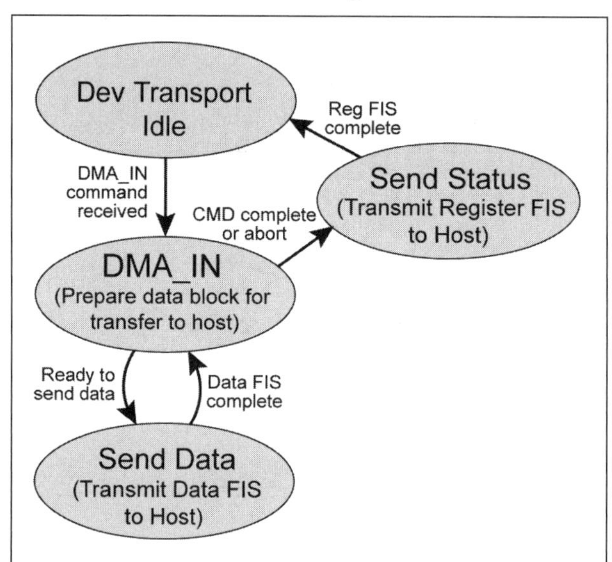

Host DMA-In Command Protocol

The actions taken by the host when performing a DMA-In command are illustrated in Figure 11-17 on page 205. Once the host has sent a command to the drive, it awaits the return of a FIS from the device. In this case an incoming Data FIS is detected first.

Data FIS Detected. The HBA transitions to the DMA-IN Transport (Host_DMAITrans) state when it recognizes that a Data FIS has been received and that the previously received FIS was not a PIOSetup. In this state, the HBA receives a single Data FIS, during which time, the DMA controller within the HBA begins transferring data to host memory. Once the Data FIS has been received, the HBA transitions to the Host_DMAEnd state where the results of the DMA transfer are detected. Presuming there is no error condition, the Host awaits the next FIS from the device. If an error is detected the command may complete with bad completion status reported or it may be aborted.

If the DMA sector count is not complete, another Data FIS will be received and the process is repeated. If the DMA transfer has completed, then the next FIS will be a Register FIS.

Register FIS Detected. The Register FIS contains the contents of the Device's task file, which reports the completion status from the Device's perspective. The HBA must first verify that the Register FIS has been received without and errors. If so, the shadow registers are updated with the Register FIS contents. If an error is detected the Register FIS is discarded. Depending on the nature of the error, the Register FIS is either retried or the command is aborted.

Figure 11-17: State Diagram for Host DMA-In Command Protocol

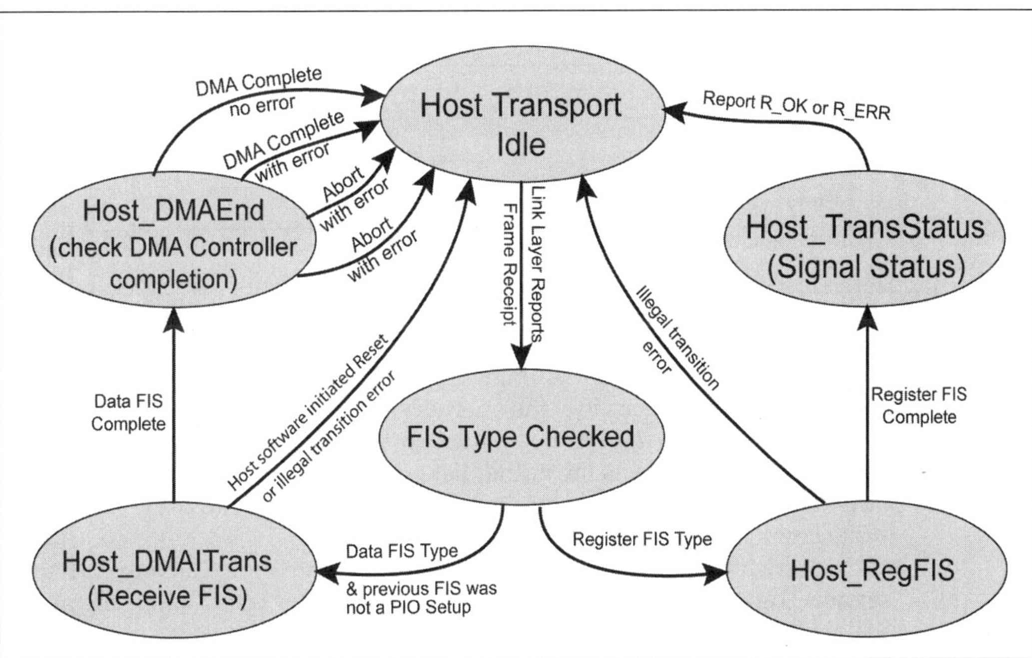

Write DMA

Four commands use the Write DMA protocol as listed in Table 11-6 on page 206.

Table 11-6: Command that use the Write DMA Command Protocol

Command	Code	ATA Command	ATAPI Command
Write DMA	CAh	M	N
Write DMA Extended	35h	O	N
Write DMA FUA	3Dh	O	N
Write Stream DMA Ext	3Ah	O	N
M = Mandatory N = Not Allowed O = Optional			

Figure 11-18 on page 207 overviews the sequence of events associated with the Write DMA command protocol. The primary actions are enumerated below:

1. Software initializes the DMA engine associated with the HBA. This initialization involves specifying the memory buffer locations (e.g., pages) in memory where the data to be written to the drive will be fetched. This is commonly referred to as the gather list.
2. BSY=0 permitting host software to initialize the shadow task file for a DMA Write command.
3. Next, software issues one of the DMA Write commands, causing BSY to be set and triggering the HBA to send the contents of the shadow register to the drive via a Register FIS.
4. The drive receives the Register FIS and decodes the Write DMA command; thereby, establishing the command protocol.
5. Next, the drive notifies the HBA (via a DMA Activate FIS) that it's ready to receive data.
6. The DMA Activate notifies the HBA to activate the DMA controller to fetch the requested data from memory.
7. Once data arrives at the HBA a Data FIS is delivered to the Drive.

8. The drive receives the data FIS, verifies it is error free. Note that drives normally default to Write Caching enabled, meaning they will send ending status to a Write command once the data is in their buffer. If a Read command comes in immediately after, it will preempt the Write command for access to the media. The write to media will be performed in the background unless a cache flush is needed to free buffer space for a new Read or Write command. Also there can be data from several Write commands queued for writeback. If more data is to be transferred, another DMA Activate FIS must be delivered for each Data FIS needed for completing the sector count. Steps 6-9 are repeated until transfer is complete.
9. When the sector count has been completed, the drive updates the task file with completion status (BSY=0 and DRQ=0) and delivers the task file to the HBA via a Register FIS.
10. The HBA receives the Register FIS, verifies successful delivery, updates the shadow registers, and sends an interrupt to call software.

Figure 11-18: Overview of the Write DMA Command Protocol

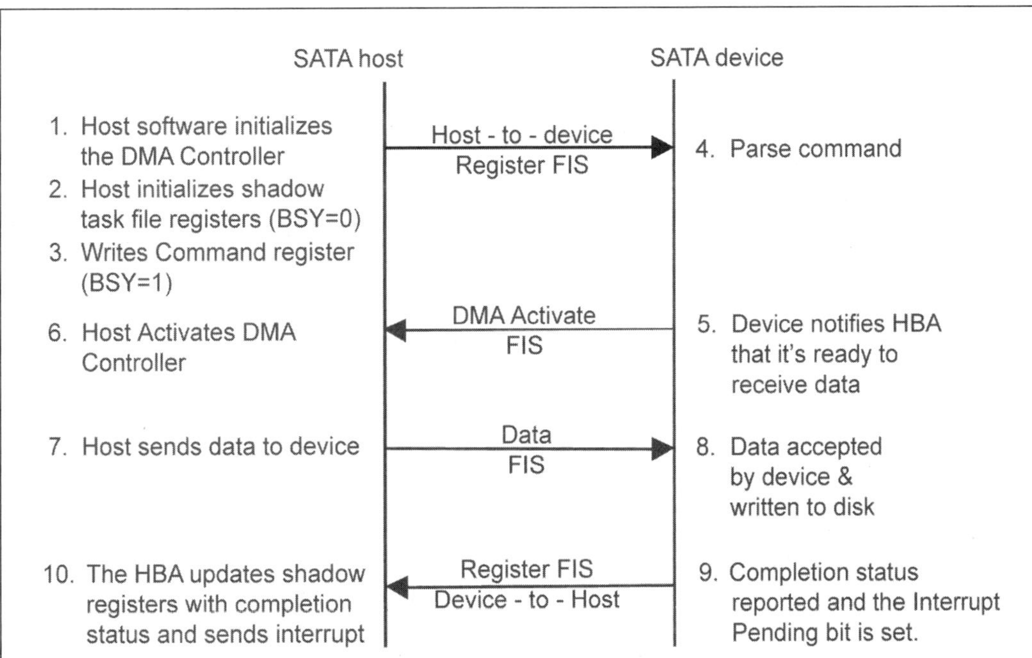

Device's Write DMA Protocol

Refer to Figure 11-19 on page 208 during the following discussion. The device recognizes a DMA-Out command type when it decodes the command and transitions to the DMA_OUT state. In this state the drive prepares to receive data. Once prepared, the drive transitions to the Send DMA_Activate state, during which time the DMA Activate FIS is delivered to the HBA. When the device receives confirmation that the DMA Activate FIS was received by the HBA, it transitions to the Receive_Data state where it awaits the return of data from the HBA. After an entire Data FIS is received, the drive transitions back to the DMA_Out state where several conditions are checked:

1. The sector count has not completed — this requires the drive to send another DMA Activate FIS to request more data from the HBA. This process is repeated until all the data requested has been received.
2. The sector count has completed — this causes the drive to transition to the Send Status state to report completion status to the HBA.
3. An error has occurred that cannot be recovered by hardware — this also causes the drive to send bad completion status to the HBA.

During the Send Status state the drive updates completion status within the task file and delivers its contents to the HBA via a Register FIS. When the FIS is successfully received by the HBA, the drive returns to logical idle and awaits the next command.

Figure 11-19: Device State Transitions During Execution of a DMA Out Command

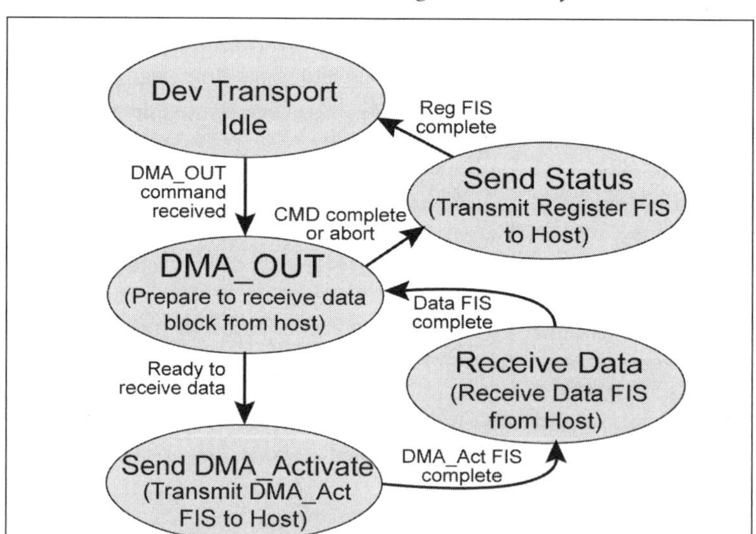

Host's Write DMA Command Protocol

Figure 11-20 on page 209 illustrates the HBA delivering the Register FIS to the drive. Once the HBA gets confirmation that the FIS has been successfully received by the drive, it returns to the logical idle state and waits for the response from the drive. The host depends on the drive's response to recognize which command protocol to use. Entry point 2, in Figure 11-20 indicates receipt of a DMA Activate FIS and the DMA_Out protocol being established within the HBA. Upon receiving the DMA Activate FIS, the HBA transitions to the Host_DMAOutTrans1 state until the DMA Controller is initialized. If it is already initialized, the HBA moves to the Host_DMAOutTrans2 state, during which time data is fetched from memory and forwarded to the drive. Upon completion of the data transfer either more data is pending delivery or the transfer count has completed. The HBA transitions to the Host_DMAEnd state. During this state possible error conditions are checked and the DMA controller is deactivated before transitioning to idle. It is also possible that the DMA operation has been terminated by host software, in which case, the current Data frame is truncated and the command ends.

Figure 11-20: Host States, DMA-Out Command Protocol

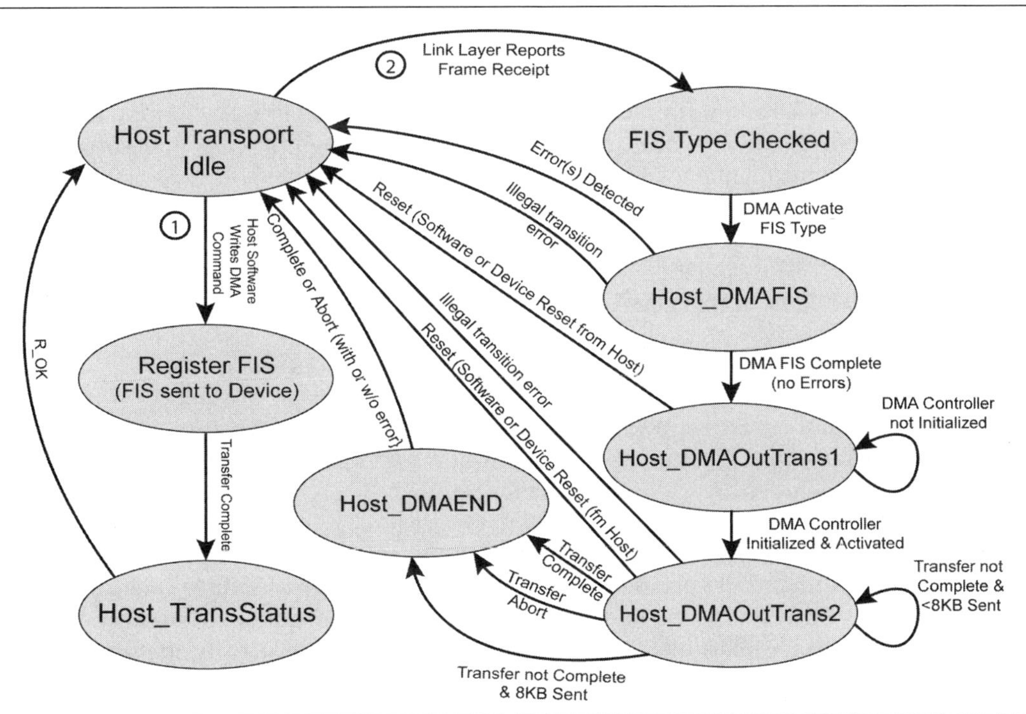

If the sector count is not completed, another DMA Activate FIS will be received and the process described above is repeated. Upon completion of the sector count or due to errors resulting in a command being aborted, completion status will be sent by the SATA drive via a Register FIS. Note that reception of the Register FIS is not shown in Figure 11-20.

DMA Queued Commands

The DMA Queued Commands never gained wide acceptance. In addition, a review of the SATAI and SATAII drives reveals that most (if not all) do not support the DMA Queued commands. Instead they support standard DMA and Native Command Queuing. Consequently, the author has chosen to provide only an overview of the command protocol.

DMA Queued Command Concepts

A primary requirement of queued operations is that the drive must notify software that it is ready to receive another command. This is the mechanism referred to as a bus release in the parallel ATA environment. The bus release is accomplished via a combination of hardware and software. First, software knows whether a drive supports the overlap feature via the Identify Device command that returns device capability information. Software may choose to enable this feature within the drive. Once overlap is enabled and upon receiving a command, the drive can release the bus by setting and clear the appropriate bit fields within the ATA Status register. Subsequently, software will poll the device to see if it has released the bus. If so, a subsequent command can be issued. Software continues to poll the drive to determine when a command completes. The specific SATA protocol used to perform these operations are described later in this DMA Queued Commands section.

Register Definition for Queued Commands

The Shadow Feature and Sector Count registers change definition when a queued command is initialized. To support service requests, the shadow Status register includes an additional service bit.

Queued Command Initialization. When software initializes a Queued DMA command, it specifies a Tag value that uniquely identifies each command that has been enqueued within the drive command queue. This 5-bit value is placed into the shadow Sector Count register and consequently, the sector count value is moved to the Features register. See Figure 11-21 on page 211.

The shadow Sector register bit fields are defined as follows:

- C/D — defines whether a command (ATAPI) or data is being delivered
- I/O — indicates the direction of data transfer; 0 = In and 1 = Out
- REL — indicates the drive is releasing the bus

Figure 11-21: Register Definition - Queued DMA Commands

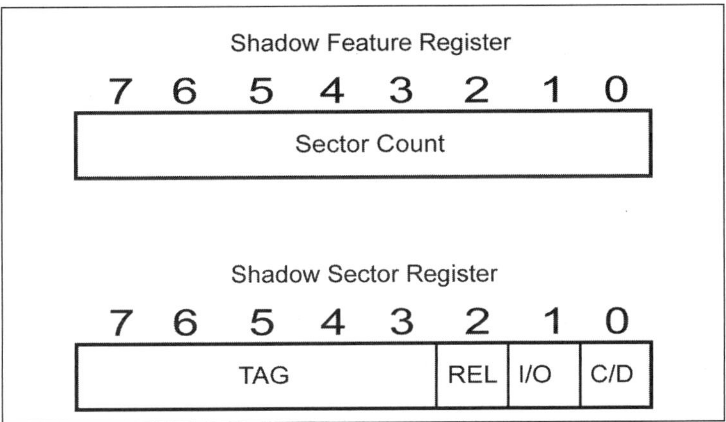

Service Request. During command execution, if a bus release is performed, it is necessary for the drive to notify software that data is ready for transfer. This is accomplished by the drive setting the SERV (service) bit illustrated in Figure 11-22. The drive reports this status change to the HBA via a Register FIS and software polls the shadow Status register to detect the service request.

Figure 11-22: Status Register with Service Bit

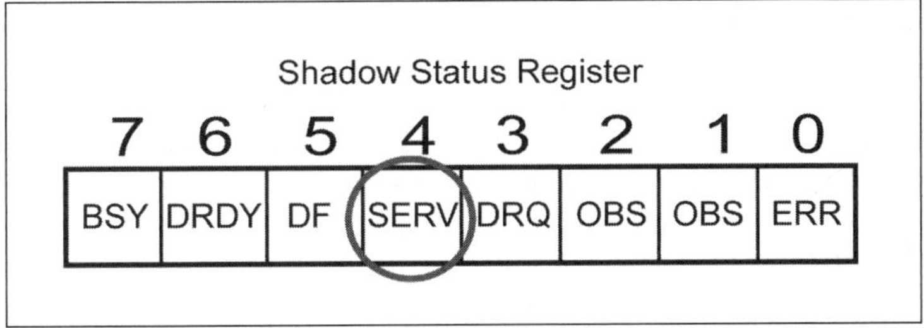

DMA-In Queued Command Protocol Overview

The two commands use the DMA-In Queued command protocol as listed in Table 11-7.

Table 11-7: Commands That Use the DMA-In Command Protocol

Command	Code	ATA Command	ATAPI Command
Read DMA Queued	C7h	M	N
Read DMA Queued Ext	26h	O	N

Figure 11-23 on page 213 provides an overview of the command protocol. Each step is described below:

1. Because the BSY and DRQ bits are both cleared software has write access to the registers and initializes them for the DMA-In Queued command.
2. Next, software writes the command code for the DMA-In Queued command to be performed. This causes the BSY bit to be set, and the contents of the shadow registers are delivered to the drive via a Register FIS.
3. The drive receives the Register FIS updates its ATA registers and parses the DMA-In Queued command.
4. The drive begins execution of the command and also releases the bus by clearing the BSY and DRQ bits and setting the REL bit in the Sector Count register. The register contents are delivered to the HBA via a Register FIS.
5. The HBA updates the shadow registers and host software eventually polls the shadow registers and detects the bus release. Software can now issue another queued command to the drive. Note that the illustration deals only with the completion of the first command and does not show the other activity that results from addition commands being queued and executed.
6. Once the drive is ready to send the requested data, it sets the SERV in the Status register. Also BSY and DRQ must be cleared. The drive then delivers the status change information to the HBA via a Set Device Bits FIS. Note that the interrupt request bit may also be set.
7. The HBA updates the shadow Status register and sends and interrupt if the "I" bit is set in the FIS, otherwise software will poll the status register and detect the service request.
8. In response to the service request host software issues a Service command to the HBA shadow registers and sends a Register FIS to the drive.
9. Upon detecting the service command, the drive recognizes the host is ready

to receive the data.

10. The drive may simply deliver the data if the last Register FIS sent to the HBA contained the Tag value of the device requesting service. Otherwise, the drive must send a Register FIS back to the drive to report the Tag of the command currently requesting service. Figure 11-23 illustrates the Tag being delivered.
11. Upon receiving the Register FIS the host sets up the DMA engine for the command that is ready to send data.
12. After sending the Tag value to the HBA, the Drive starts delivery of data. One or more Data FIS frames may be required to transfer the data block requested. The Data FIS has a maximum payload of 8KB.
13. The HBA receives the data and the DMA engine transfers it to memory.
14. Once the entire data block is delivered, the drive updates completion status and sends it to the HBA via a Register FIS with the Interrupt Pending (I) bit set.
15. The HBA updates the shadow registers and sends an interrupt to notify sofware.

Figure 11-23: Overview of the Queued DMA-In Command Protocol

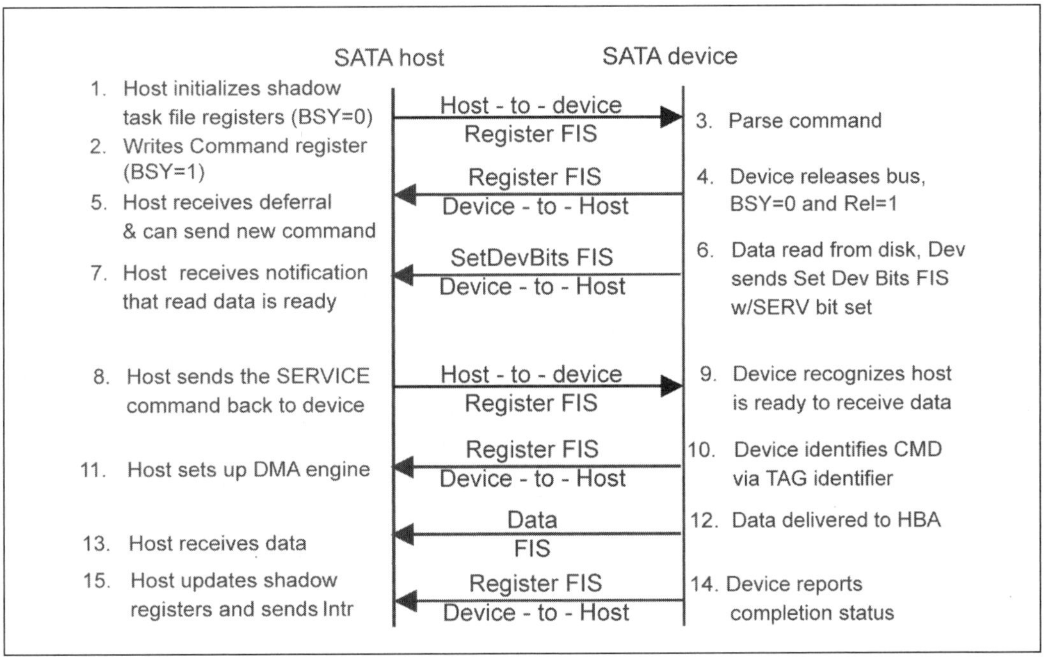

DMA-Out Queued Command Protocol Overview

The DMA-Out command protocol includes a DMA Activate FIS sent by the drive to identify the command and establish the host command protocol. Otherwise the Queued DMA-Out protocol is very similar to the Queued DMA-In protocol discussed previously. The three commands listed in Table 11-8 use this protocol.

Table 11-8: DMA-Out Queued Commands

Command	Code	ATA Command	ATAPI Command
Write DMA Queued	CCh	O	N
Write DMA Queued Ext	36h	O	N
Write DMA Queued FUA (Force Unit Access) Ext	3Eh	O	N
M = Mandatory N = Not Allowed O = Optional			

Figure 11-24 on page 216 presents an overview of the DMA-Out command protocol and each is enumerated below. The example presumes that the commands are completed in order.

1. Because the BSY and DRQ bits are both cleared software has write access to the shadow registers and initializes them for the DMA-Out Queued command.
2. Next, software writes the command code for the DMA-Out Queued command to be performed. This causes the BSY bit to be set, and the contents of the shadow registers are delivered to the drive via a Register FIS.
3. The drive receives the Register FIS, updates its ATA registers, and parses the DMA-Out Queued command.
4. The drive queues the command for execution and releases the bus by clearing the BSY and DRQ bits and setting the REL bit in the Sector Count register. The drive reads the register contents and delivers it to the HBA via a Register FIS.
5. The HBA updates the shadow registers and host software eventually polls the shadow registers and detects the bus release. This frees software to issue another queued command to the drive. Note that the diagram deals only

with the completion of the first command and does not show the other activity resulting from addition commands being queued and executed.

6. Host software issues the Service command to notify the drive that its ready to continue with the oldest outstanding command.
7. Upon receipt of the Service command, the drive recognizes that the host is ready to continue command execution and deliver data.
8. The drive sends a DMA Activate FIS to the HBA, requesting data delivery.
9. In response, the HBA activates the DMA controller that in turn starts to fetch the data.
10. Upon receiving data, the HBA starts delivery of the Data FIS to the drive, during which time flow control may be used by the HBA if the DMA controller cannot continue to deliver data in order to keep up with Data FIS transmission.
11. The drive receives the Data FIS, but in this case the sector count has not completed.
12. The drive requests more data by sending another DMA Activate FIS.
13. The HBA receives the DMA Activate and the DMA controller fetches the next block of data.
14. Upon receiving data the HBA sends the Data FIS to the drive.
15. The drive receives the data and recognizes that the sector count is complete.
16. The drive updates completion status and sends it to the HBA via a Register FIS with Interrupts Pending.
17. The HBA updates the shadow registers and sends an interrupt to notify sofware.

Figure 11-24: Overview of the DMA-Out Queued Command Protocol

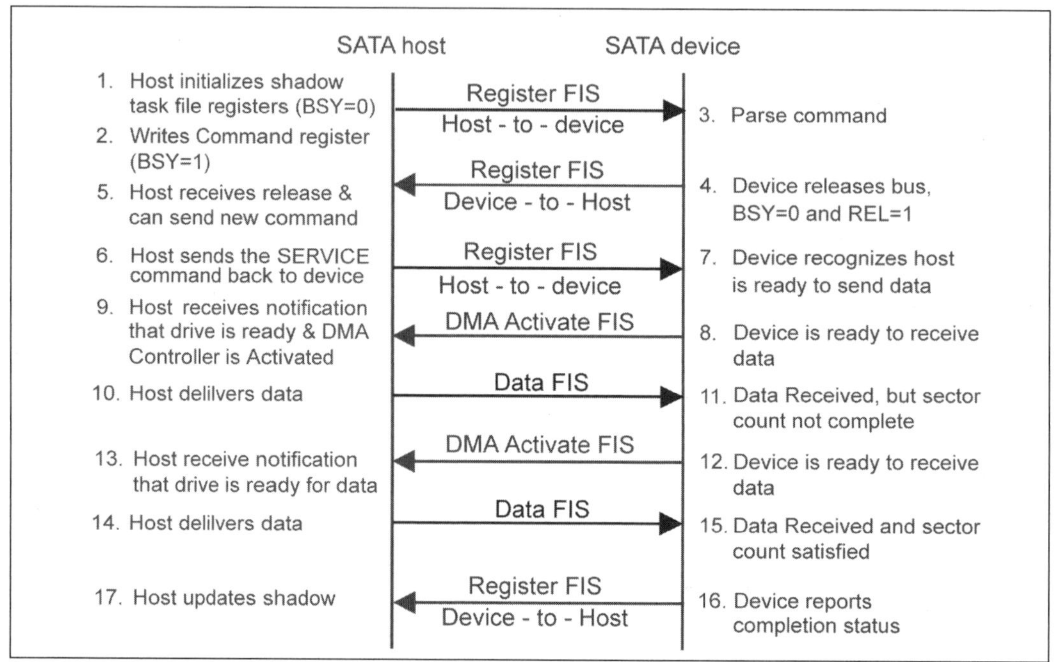

First Party DMA Commands

The First Party DMA Command is used in conjunction with Native Command Queuing (NCQ). NCQ and the First Party DMA protocol is discussed in Chapter 14, entitled "Native Command Queuing," on page 235.

Packet Command Protocol

The packet protocol is used in conjunction with the ATA Packet Interface (ATAPI). Recall that ATAPI devices use SCSI commands that are encapsulated within the Data FIS of a Packet command. In this respect, the delivery of the command uses the initial portion of the PIO-Out command.

Figure 11-25 on page 217 illustrates the packet command delivery. The process of course begins with the HBA delivering a Packet command to the ATAPI device. The device responds by delivering a PIO Setup FIS to the HBA, which then awaits delivery of the data (in this case, a SCSI command) and returns a Data FIS to the ATAPI device.

Next, the device decodes the command to determine which command protocol will be used to complete the command. Once the protocol is established, the actions taken are the same as those defined for the standard command protocol.

For example, if the command is a read from drive media using DMA protocol, then host software would already have initialized the DMA controller. The drive would simply read data from drive media and deliver a Data FIS to the host. The HBA would recognize the Data FIS and know the DMA controller was initialized. The DMA controller would then send data to memory. Once all the data requested in the command are transferred then completion status is returned to the HBA via a Register FIS.

Figure 11-25: Packet Command Delivery

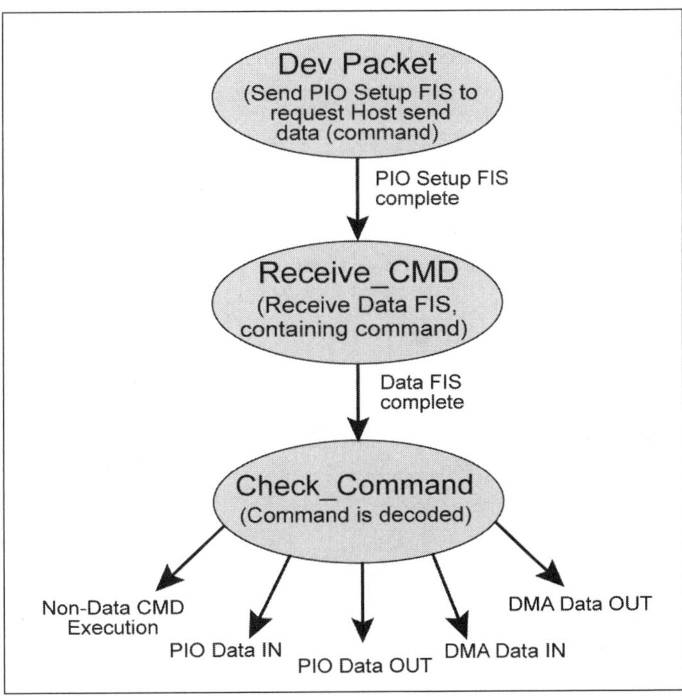

Device Reset Command Protocol

The Reset command is generally delivered only to ATAPI devices. The Control register initiated Soft Reset (SRST) targets all device, including those that use the ATAPI. The motivation for the Device Reset command was to support the overlap feature when an ATA and ATAPI device are attached to the same cable. The perceived need for the Reset command was to provide a way to reset the ATAPI device without affecting the hard drive (as would happen with SRST).

The Reset command protocol is illustrated in Figure 11-26. When the Reset command is received, the device stops all activity and then performs internal diagnostics. Upon completion of the diagnostics, good status is returned via a Register FIS. Interestingly, no option is presented for reporting bad status. The specification states that good status is always returned when internal diagnostics successfully completes. Consequently, successful completion of the Reset command (receipt of good status) does not imply that the drive diagnostic passed.

Figure 11-26: Device's Reset Command Protocol States

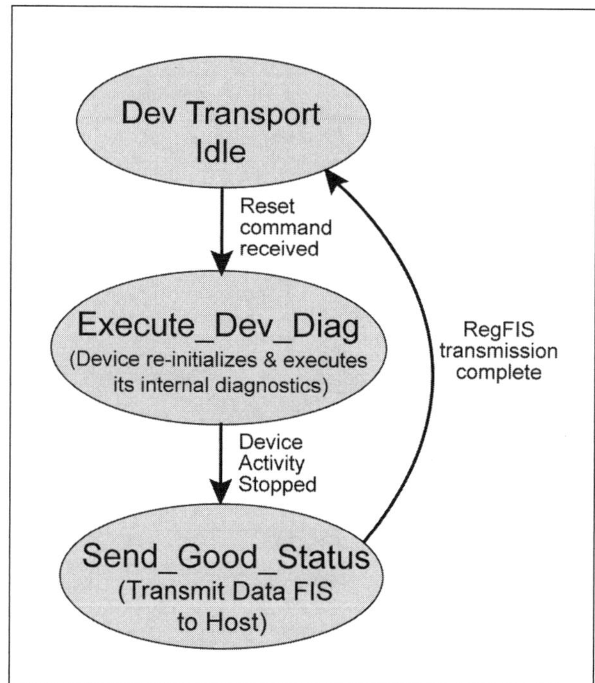

Execute Device Diagnostic

This command forces a device to perform internal diagnostics and to report the results back to the HBA. Figure 11-27 on page 219 illustrates the two possible responses following internal diagnostic having completed:

- Diagnostics have passed and Good Status is sent
- Diagnostics have failed and Bad Status is sent

Figure 11-27: Device's Diagnostic Command Protocol

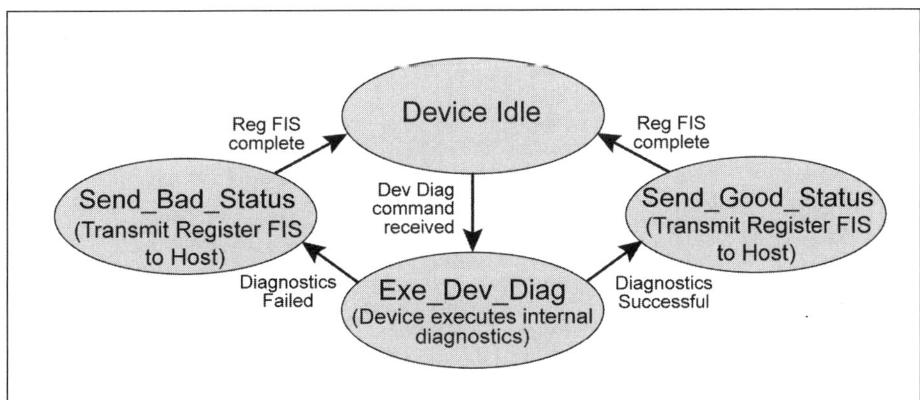

12 Control Protocol

Previous Chapter

Earlier portions of the book focussed on the delivery of individual Frame Information Structures. The last chapter discussed the various categories of command, each of which require the exchange of a particular sequence of Frame Information Structures. It is the responsibility of the command layer to manage this sequencing.

This Chapter

This chapter discusses the functions associated with the Device Control register. Writing to the Device Control register forces the HBA to send a Register FIS to the device. The particular bits written force the drive to take the specified action. Each of the Control register functions is discussed in detail.

The Next Chapter

The next chapter introduces the primary features added by the SATA II specification.

Write Control Protocol

When software writes to the shadow Control register, the Control register contents are copied to the Control field of a Register FIS and the FIS's "C" bit cleared. The contents last written to the Command Block registers are also copied to the FIS and the Register FIS is delivered to the drive. Figure 12-1 on page 222 illustrates the HBA protocol associated with a write to the shadow Control register. Prior to the Control register write operation, the HBA Transport layer is in the logical idle state. When the shadow control register is written by host software the HBA transitions to the Host Control FIS state. During this state the Register FIS is delivered to the device. Three possible conditions can occur:

1. If the Register FIS is transmitted without error, the HBA transitions to the Host_TransStatus state, where the HBA waits for the drive to report results of the transmission.

2. If an illegal transition is detected during transmission of the FIS, the HBA terminates the FIS transfer and returns to logical idle.
3. If the HBA detects reception of a FIS from the drive, it must also return to idle and respond to the incoming FIS.

Once FIS transmission is complete the HBA transitions to the Host_TransStatus state where it awaits the result of the transmission from the drive. In the event a transmission error is detected, the HBA will be notified via an R_Err primitive and the Register FIS will be retried. Upon successful receipt of the Register FIS, the drive updates its Control register with the new Control register values.

Figure 12-1: Host Control Protocol

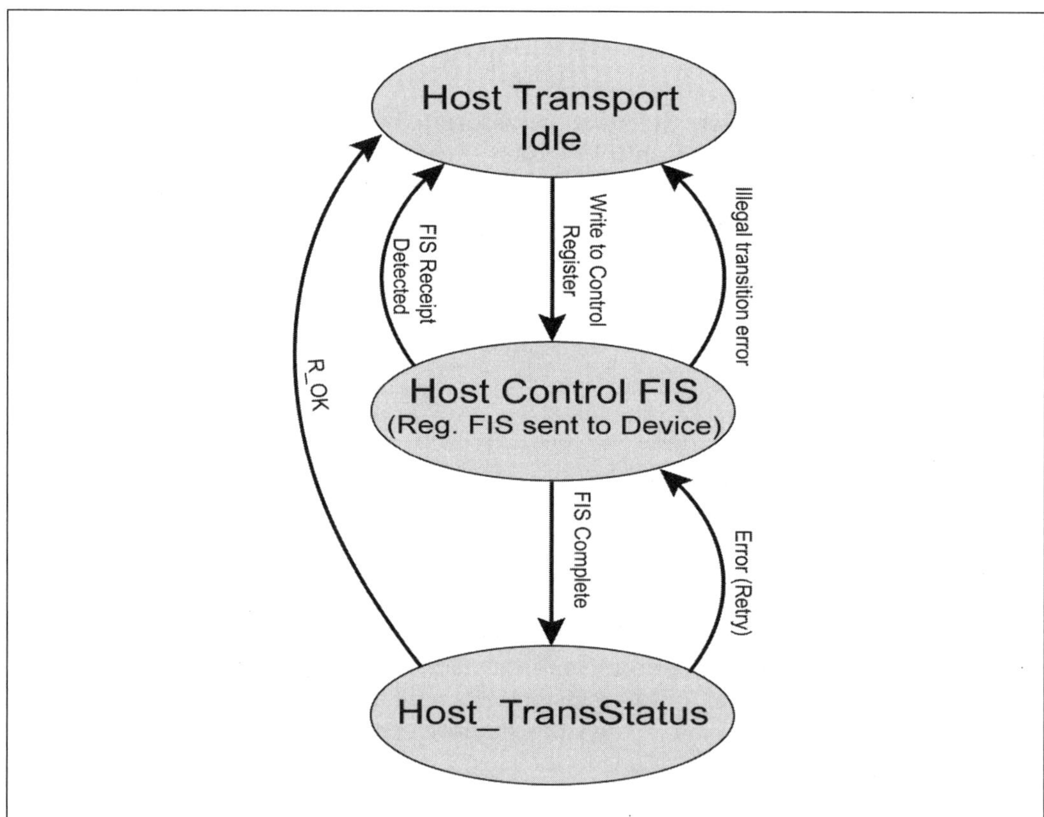

Device Control Register Functions

The Control register supports several functions defined below. Figure 12-2 on page 223 illustrates the Control register bit field designations.

- nIEN (Interrupt Enable, negative logic) when nIEN is cleared (0), interrupt request generation is enabled within the device, while setting the bit disables interrupt generation.
- SRST (Soft Reset) — Software sets this bit to reset the drive. Reset is asserted when the SRST bit is set (1) and is cleared when the SRST bit is cleared (0).
- HOB (High Order Byte) — Some register address support back-to-back byte-sized writes to the same address location to load additional values to support features such as 48-bit Logical Block Addressing. Setting the HOB bit enables software to read the previous written byte from the selected 8-bit register.

Figure 12-2: Control Register Contents

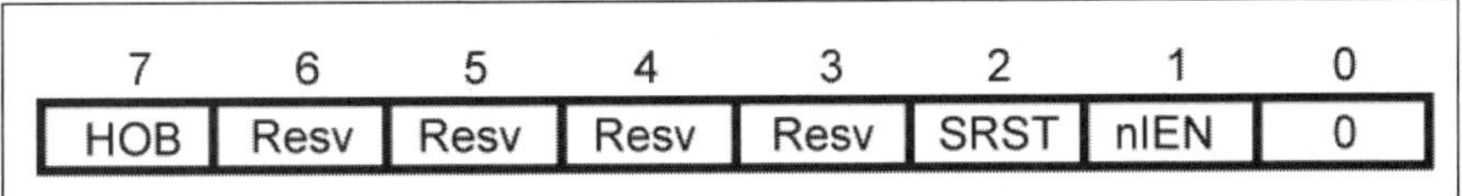

Interrupt Enable (nIEN) Control Protocol

The nIEN bit is implemented to provide legacy software support. Following reset the nIEN bit is cleared, resulting in interrupts being enabled. Software can disable interrupts by setting the nIEN bit. When software either sets or clears the nIEN bit, a Register FIS is delivered to the SATA drive; thereby, setting or clearing the nIEN bit within the drive's control register. Note, that any write to the shadow control register clears an interrupt pending condition within the HBA.

Also, unlike the PATA environment, the nIEN bit has no affect on a SATA drive's behavior. In the SATA environment the HBA actually signals interrupt requests and also handles the nIEN function.

Software Reset (SRST)

Software resets a SATA drive in legacy fashion by writing a one to the SRST bit within the shadow Control register. This of course causes the HBA to send a Register FIS (with "C" bit cleared) to the drive. Software must write a zero to the SRST bit to clear the reset.

An SRST affects only the SATA device and has no effect on the link (unlike a COMRESET). Also during a soft reset the SATA device performs internal diagnostics and once the SRST bit is cleared (followed be a Host-to-Device Register FIS) the drive returns a Register FIS to the HBA to report results of the drive's diagnostics. This SATA drive protocol is illustrated in Figure 12-4 and described below:

1. The HBA has delivered a Register FIS to the drive to notify it that software has set the SRST bit in the shadow Command register. The Device is currently sending logical idle when the drive receives the Register FIS.
2. The drive checks the FIS type and detects the C bit cleared and the SRST bit set; thereby, indicating that Software has issued a Reset.
3. During the Reset_Assert state, the drive re-initializes to its default state, starts internal diagnostics, and waits for software to clear the reset condition.
4. The drive receives the second Register FIS with the C bit clear and SRST bit cleared, causing transition to the Execute Diagnostic state. The drive waits for the diagnostics to complete (if not already done) and updates its ATA registers to report either good or bad status.
5. The drive sends a Register FIS to the HBA to report the results.

Figure 12-3 illustrates the contents of the ATA registers when reporting both good and bad status. When bad status is returned, the Error register contains a drive-specific error code (any value except 01h).

Figure 12-3: Soft Reset Status Values

Good Status

Register	Value
Sector Count	01h
Sector Number	01h
Cylinder Low	00h
Cylinder High	00h
Device/Head	00h
Error	01h
Status	00h-70h*
* Bits 4-6 are device specific	

Bad Status

Register	Value
Sector Count	01h
Sector Number	01h
Cylinder Low	00h
Cylinder High	00h
Device/Head	00h
Error	00h, 02h-27h
Status	00h-70h*
* Bits 4-6 are device specific	

Figure 12-4: SATA Drive Reset Protocol

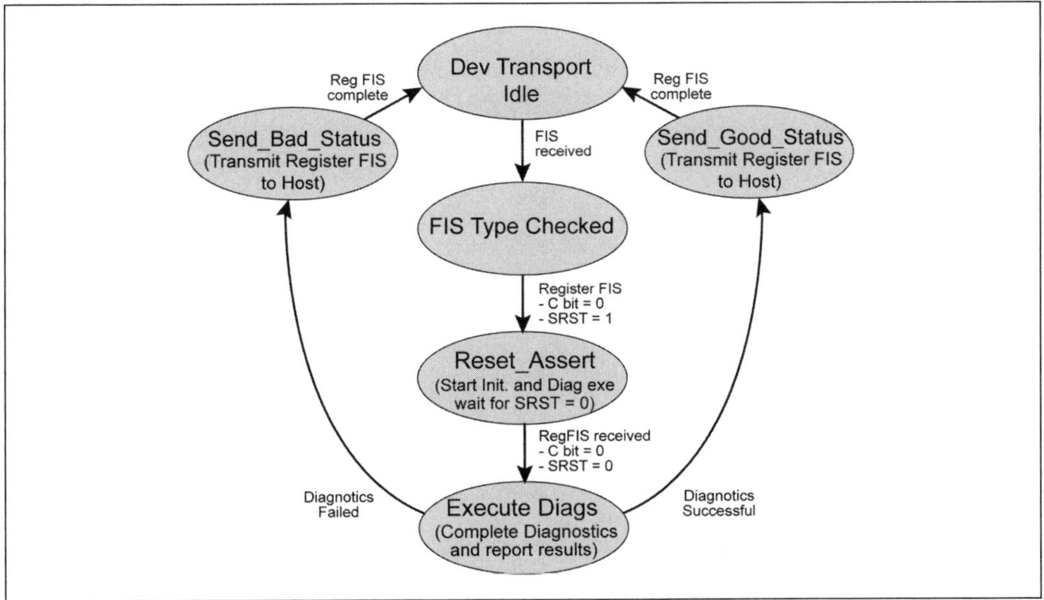

Part Four

SATA II

13 SATA II Features

Previous Chapter

The previous chapter discussed the functions associated with the Device Control register. Writing to the Device Control register forces the HBA to send a Register FIS to the device. The particular bits written force the drive to take the specified action. Each of the Control register functions is discussed in detail.

This Chapter

This chapter introduces the primary features added by the SATA II specification and describes the motivation for adding them.

The Next Chapter

The next chapter describes the concepts and mechanisms associated with Native Command Queuing (NCQ). This mechanism provides major performance improvements over mainstream ATA and SATA drives that use standard DMA Read and Write operations.

Overview

The SATA II implementation was introduced as an extension to the initial SATA specification. SATA II introduced many new features most of which are optional. The new features fall into several categories:

- Performance and Reliability Features — Higher transmission rates and support for Native Command Queuing are among the most important improvements added by SATA II.
- Server-specific Support — Many new SATA II features focused on making SATA more appealing for server applications. Most of the server-related enhancements focus more on the SATA infrastructure and less on the drives themselves.
- Fixes and Enhancements to SATA — A variety of fixes and miscellaneous features were added to SATA II; including, asynchronous event notification.

Another potentially important issue is that Serial Attached SCSI (SAS) connectors permit attachment of SATA drives, and supports the SATA protocol.

This chapter introduces the major features of the SATA II specification.

Performance and Reliability

Three notable features introduced with the SATA II specification improve performance and/or reliability over the previous versions:

- SATA Generation 2 transmission rates (3Gb/s)
- Native Command Queuing
- Asynchronous Signal Recovery

Generation 2 Transmission Rates

The generation 2 transmission rates of 3 Gb/s increased the maximum throughput of the SATA interface to 300 MB/s. The increased transmission speed is particularly important when multiple SATA drives share the same HBA link, which is characteristic of the SATA II Port Multiplier implementation. Chapter 19, on page 325 for details regarding the Gen II clock and signaling.

Native Command Queuing

Native Command Queuing (NCQ) can improve overall storage subsystem performance, and can also improve drive reliability and durability. NCQ enhances drive performance by executing queued commands out of order; thereby, reducing overall seek time. This process also results is less mechanical movement when compared with sequential execution of commands, thus reducing wear. See Chapter 14, entitled "Native Command Queuing," on page 235 for more information.

Asynchronous Signal Recovery

The Phy Layer state machine defined prior to SATA II did not include the ability to automatically attempt recovery when communication is lost between the Host and SATA device (i.e., no signals are received). This condition can occur for a variety of reasons including the signal connector being unplugged during normal operation and then replaced while power is still present.

SATA II Phys that support Asynchronous Signal Recovery will, upon detecting that link communications are down, automatically attempt to re-establish communication. These Phys use a variable named the RetryInterval that determines the rate at which signal recovery polling is attempted. See "Asynchronous Signal Recovery" on page 316.

Enhanced Support for Server Applications

A number of server-related features were introduced with the SATA II specification:

1. Port Multipliers that allow a single HBA port to support up to 15 drives
2. Port Selectors that provide dual-port functionality at the drives
3. Hot Docking support
4. Multilane Cables
5. Support for Enclosure Services and Management

Port Multipliers

Rather than having SATA drives connect directly to individual HBA ports, the port multiplier provides up to 15 additional ports to which SATA drives can be connected. This provides port fan-out capability needed in large rack mount implementations.

Figure 13-1 on page 232 illustrates the typical SATA drive connection to an HBA port, along with the Port Multiplier approach. Obviously, the HBA can only communicate with one drive at a time, thus overall performance may be affected with the Port Multiplier approach, but provides access to huge amounts of storage at much lower costs when compared to SCSI and Fibre Drive implementations. Additional information regarding the Port Multiplier implementation can be found in Chapter 15, on page 257.

Figure 13-1: Port Multiplier Example

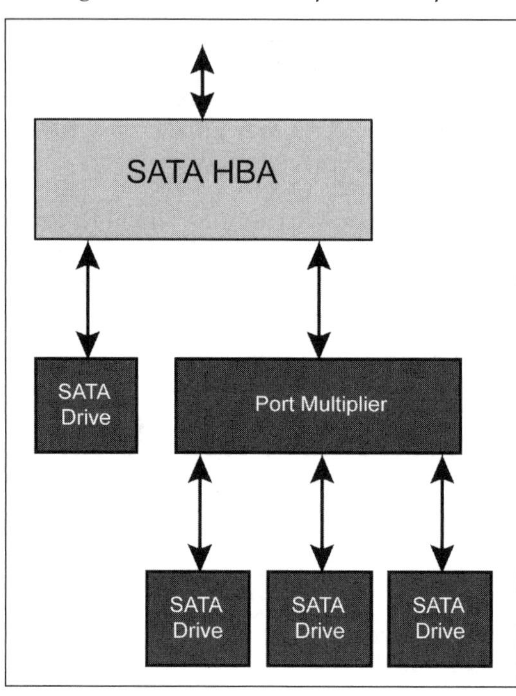

Port Selectors

The port selector feature provides a way for two HBAs to access a SATA drive. The goal of the port selector capability is to provide a fail-over mechanism to assist in the goal of "non-stop operation" for server implementations. Figure 13-2 on page 233 illustrates an example port selector implementation that includes the use of port multipliers.

Figure 13-2: Example Port Selector Implementation

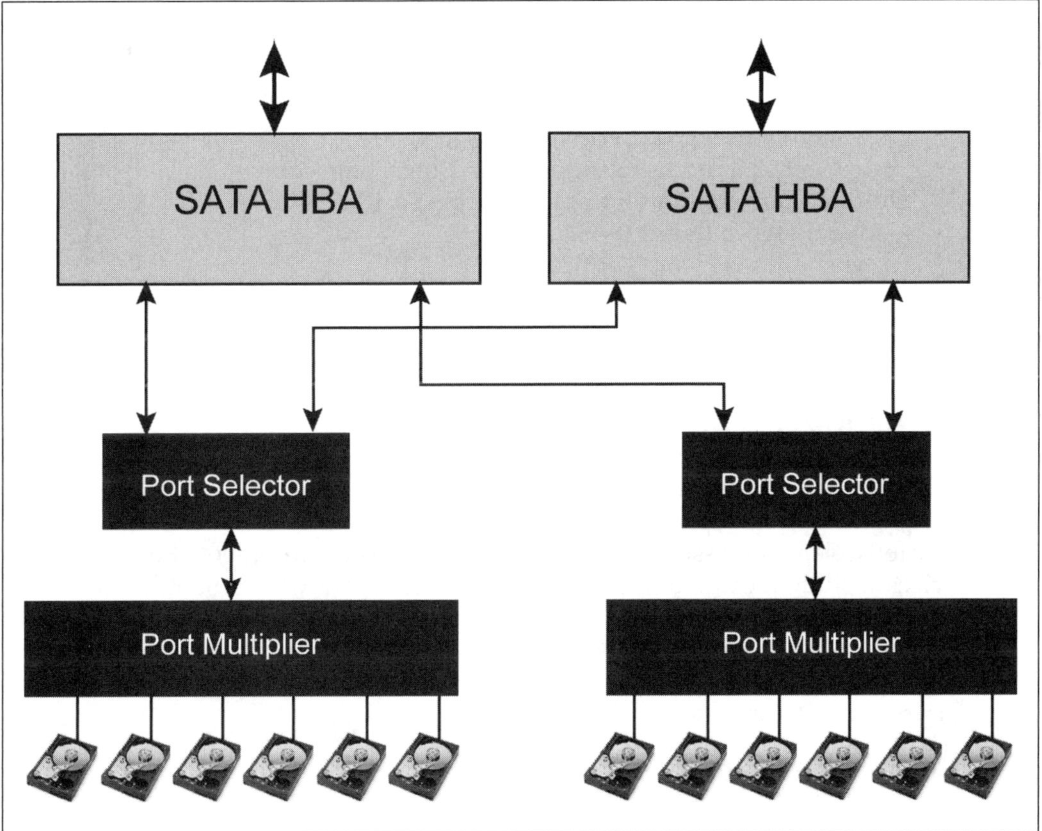

Multilane Cables

The SATA specification defines a variety of Multilane cables for both internal and external implementations. These cables are discussed in Chapter 20, on page 361.

Hot Plug

The ability to safely remove and replace a faulty drive is critical in server applications. The SATA specification defines several mechanisms that enable hot pluggable implementations, including:

- Asynchronous Signal Recovery (SATA II)
- Two Contact Lengths to support Hot Plug Connectors.
- In-rush Current Limiting Definition (SATA II)
- Drive Presence Detect (SATA II)
- Asynchronous Event Notification (SATA II)

These features are described in Chapter 21, on page 375.

Enclosure Services

Large rack-mounted (and other) storage enclosures associated with large server implementations typically implement services used to sense and manage the various elements associated with the enclosure environment. Enclosure Services include a command set used to communicate with a Storage Enclosure Processor (SEP) monitors controls enclosure elements such as fans, sensors, and LEDs. SATA II defines support for transporting enclosure service commands across SATA links. The specification supports two protocols enclosure services implementations:

- SES (SCSI Enclosure Services)
- SAF-TE (SCSI Attached Fault-Tolerant Enclosure)

Refer to Chapter 17, on page 295 for additional detail regarding SATA Enclosure Services support.

Reporting/Detecting Feature Support

The Identify Device data structures include new entries that define which new features are supported by a SATA drive. The location and definition of the new entries are described in the specific chapters that discuss these new features.

14 Native Command Queuing

Previous Chapter

The previous chapter introduced the primary features added by the SATA II specification.

This Chapter

This chapter describes the concepts and mechanisms associated with Native Command Queuing (NCQ). This mechanism provides major performance improvements over mainstream ATA drives that use standard DMA Read and Write operations.

The Next Chapter

Port Multipliers provide a fan-out capability, whereby up to 15 ports can be accessed via a single HBA port. This capability is useful in large rack mount implementations. The next chapter details the hardware and software required to support the Port Multiplier solution.

Overview

This section takes an evolutionary approach to describing the performance limitations associated with typical Parallel ATA drives and associated software. Next, the concept of command queuing is reviewed as a method of improving performance, and its limitations are explored. Finally, today's drives supporting Native Command Queuing can provide significant improvements in performance over the earlier approaches.

The Problem - Limited Performance

In the mainstream PC environment, software and most ATA drives were designed to execute one command at a time. That meant that once a drive completed a command, the drive remained idle for relatively long period of time before the next command was issued. Even if a drive had the ability to deliver data across the ATA bus at a rate of 66MB/s, that speed advantage was less significant due to the requirement that a given command must have completed before the next could be sent. This type of command processing is sometimes termed synchronous IO.

Queuing Helps

Once software supports asynchronous IO, it can issue (or queue) one or more subsequent commands prior to the current command completing. This ability reduces the time that a drive remains idle between commands. This capability is often referred to as software queuing. Note however, that software is still restricted to sending the next command to a standard ATA drive only after the previous command completes.

Even better performance is possible if the drive also supports Command Queuing. That is, some drives are designed to queue commands internally. This reduces even further the delays between completing one command and beginning the next. Command Queuing was first included in the ATA/ATAPI-4 specification, but mainstream software at the time did not support asynchronous IO. Consequently, few drives ever supported Command Queueing.

Native Command Queuing is Better

Today's drives based on SATA II typically support Native Command Queuing, or NCQ. This queuing technique is similar to that described in the previous section, except the commands enqueued within an NCQ drive can be completed out-of-order. Algorithms used by NCQ drives schedule the next command to perform based on the shortest time required to reach the associated target sector, rather than scheduling commands based on the order in which they were received. This can result in average seek times being reduced significantly; thereby, providing dramatic increases in a drive's performance. Some testing has reported that the performance of a 7200 rpm drive with NCQ is roughly equivalent to that of a standard 10k rpm drive.

Figure 14-1 on page 238 illustrates two disc layouts that depict the same sequence of four commands pending and the associated sectors to be read. Side A in Figure 14-1 illustrates the commands being performed sequentially, while side B illustrates the same commands being performed using the NCQ approach. In the examples, sequential accesses of the sectors start a point 1. Side A accesses might proceed as follows:

- Sector 1 sequence to start of Sector 2 sequence (approx. 1.34 revolutions)
- Sector 2 sequence to start of Sector 3 sequence (approx. 1.26 revolutions)
- Sector 3 sequence to start of Sector 4 sequence (approx. 1.22 revolutions)
- Sector 4 sequence to end (approx 0.45 revolutions)
- Total Revolutions = approx. 4.27

In contrast with NCQ the accesses might proceed are shown in Side B in Figure 14-1.

- Sector 1 sequence to start of Sector 3 sequence (approx. 0.60 revolutions)
- Sector 3 sequence to start of Sector 2 sequence (approx. 0.76 revolutions)
- Sector 2 sequence to start of Sector 4 sequence (approx. 0.46 revolutions)
- Sector 4 sequence to end (approx 0.45 revolutions)
- Total Revolutions = approx. 2.27

This simple example shows how the overall time required to perform the four commands can be significantly reduced when using NCQ. Another factor associated with this approach is that the amount of mechanical movement is also reduced, in terms not only of the number of rotations but also of the number of steps taken by the head as it moves between tracks (cylinders). This should also lead to better drive reliability.

The drive, the HBA, and software all must be designed to support NCQ. The following sections define the specific elements used in the SATA environment to support NCQ.

Figure 14-1: Sequential versus NCQ Example

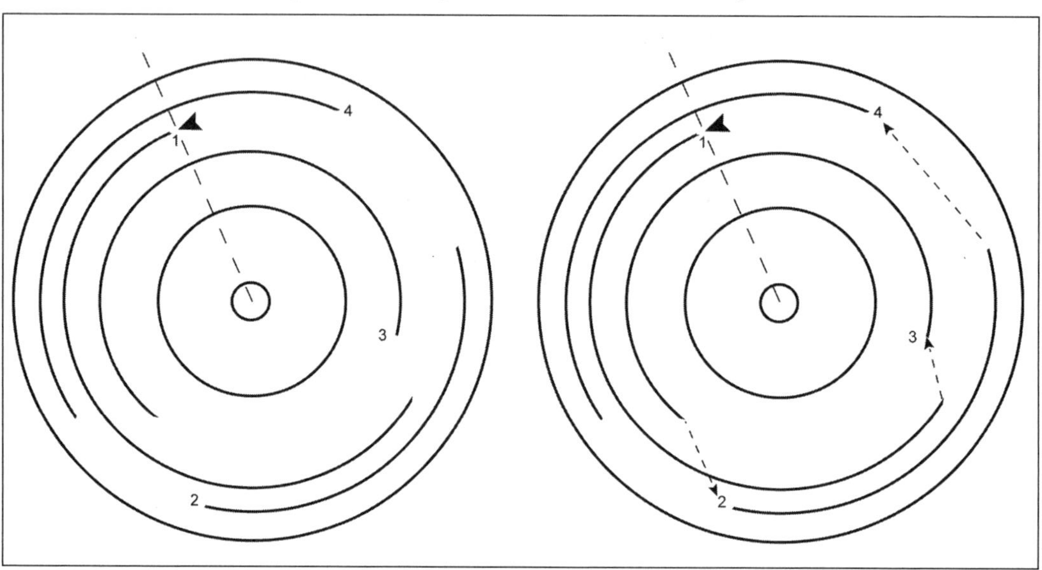

System Support Requirements

Three primary elements are included in the SATA protocols that support NCQ:

- First Party DMA — this mechanism provides an NCQ drive with the ability to select and initiate a DMA operation for any of the enqueued commands without involving host software. Because an NCQ drive re-orders command execution, when data is ready for transfer only the drive knows which command is being performed and therefore which locations in memory should be accessed. This is accomplished via the The First Party DMA Read and Write commands that include a tag value that associates each command with the scatter/gather list that software has prepared for the command.
- Race-Free Status Return — the First Party DMA protocol allows completion status to be sent to the host for whichever command happens to have completed. This mechanism does not require that a separate Register FIS be transmitted to the host in order for status to be communicated. Instead, a Set Device Bits FIS is used to communicate which command has completed, and in some cases, multiple completions can be reported with a single FIS.
- Interrupt Aggregation — The drive generally sends an interrupt each time it completes a command. This adds to overhead and overall system perfor-

mance suffers. However, the average number of interrupts per command can be fewer than one when using NCQ. This can happen when two queued commands complete is a short span of time, resulting in two interrupts being reported to the HBA. When the interrupt handler checks status it will detect that two interrupts have occurred and will handle both; thereby, reducing overhead.

A variety of new features are required to support Native Command Queuing (NCQ). This support includes:

- NCQ Drive Features
- New First Party DMA Read and Write Commands
- Queue Management Capability
- Command Tracking

NCQ Drive Support

As suggested earlier in this chapter, one of the major impediments to improving drive read and write performance is the latency experienced when seeking the next starting sector. The two primary components of this latency are:

- Seek Latency (Head Positioning) — the time it takes the actuator to move the head to the target track
- Rotational Latency — once the target track is reached, the disc must rotate to the starting sector position in the selected track.

NCQ drives implement complex algorithms to re-order command execution to determine the shortest overall access time. An NCQ drive attempts to reduce this latency by reordering the execution of a group of up to 32 pending commands. This process attempts not only minimizing seek time, and rotational latencies, but also considers the age of the pending commands. That is, it tracts the amount of time a command has spent in the queue. Note also that when new commands are placed on the queue, they are dynamically included in the ordering schedule.

Some drives may also support accessing portions of a contiguous sector block to reduce overall latency. This means that offsets associated with a given command block transfer must also be managed by the drive. For example, consider the following scenario where multiple FPDMA Read command are pending completion:

1. A command sector block transfer consisting of sector n through n+18 is pending.
2. The drive has just completed a block transfer, but the beginning of the next start sector is over one-half of a full disc rotation from the current head position.
3. The adjacent track contains the sector block mentioned in item 1, above so the drive, knowing that these sectors are to be read, steps to the adjacent track and reads sectors n+11 through n+18.
4. The otherwise waisted rotational time is used to read the back portion of the command pending in item 1.
5. When sectors n+10 through n+18 are delivered to the HBA, a 10 sector offset (5,120 Bytes) must be delivered to the HBA so the data is delivered to the appropriate buffer location.

Note that using non-zero offsets also requires support at the host side.

Software learns of a drive's capability to support NCQ, it's Command queue depth, and whether it supports non-zero offsets via the Device Identify Data, which is read by software during initialization. (See Table 14-1.) If the host also supports NCQ and its extended features, these features are enabled by software.

Table 14-1: Identify Data Indicating NCQ Features Supported

Word Offset	R/O	Description
0 - 74		**Defined in ATA/ATAPI-7**
75	Optional	**Queue Depth** 15-5 Reserved **4-0 Maximum queue depth-1**
76		**Serial ATA Capabilities** 15-11 Reserved 10 Phy event counters supported 9 Host-initiated link Power Management requests received **8 Native Command Queuing supported** 7-4 Reserved 3 Reserved for SATA 2 Supports Serial ATA Gen-2 signaling 1 Supports Serial ATA Gen-1 signaling 0 Reserved (0)
77		**Reserved for SATA**
78	Optional	**Serial ATA Features** 15-7 Reserved 6 Software settings preservation supported 5 Reserved 4 In-order data delivery supported 3 Drive initiates link power management requests 2 DMA Setup FIS Auto-Activate optimization supported **1 DMA Setup FIS non-zero buffer offsets supported** 0 Reserved (0)
79	Optional	**Serial ATA Features Enabled**

New Commands

SATA II added support for two new types of Queued commands:

- First Party DMA Read command
- First Party DMA Write command

NCQ operation with a SATA drive functions only when sequences of First Party DMA commands are used. When any other command type is received, out-of-order execution stops. Details regarding these commands is described in the following two sections.

One notable issue associated with FPDMA operations is that they are new commands specific to SATA implementations. This permits behaviors that do not follow the normal legacy behaviors. For example, a drive will always set the interrupt pending (I) bit within a FIS without regard to the state of its nIEN bit. However, the HBA must always honor the state of the nIEN bit within its Shadow Control register.

First Party DMA Read Command

The ATA register definition used when software issues a First Party DMA Read command is illustrated in Figure 14-2. This register content is delivered to the drive via a Register FIS. At the bottom of Figure 14-2 is the command value of 60h that defines the FPDMA Read command. The sector count field carries a 5-bit value supporting up to 32 commands that can be outstanding at one time. The sector count information is relocated to the Features and Features (exp) fields.

Figure 14-2: Register Contents for First Party DMA Read Command

Register	7	6	5	4	3	2	1	0
Features	Sector Count 7:0							
Features (exp)	Sector Count 15:8							
Sector Count	TAG					Reserved		
Sector Count (exp)	Reserved							
Sector Number	LBA 0:7							
Sector Number (exp)	LBA 31:24							
Cylinder Low	LBA 15:8							
Cylinder Low (exp)	LBA 39:32							
Cylinder High	LBA 23:16							
Cylinder High (exp)	LBA 47:40							
Device/Head	FUA	1	Res	0	Reserved			
Command	60h							

First Party DMA Write Command

The write version of the FPDMA command is illustrated in Figure 14-3. The command value is 61h but otherwise the format is the same as the FPDMA Read command. except bit 5 in the Device field is cleared (0).

Figure 14-3: Register Contents for FPDMA Write Command

Register	7	6	5	4	3	2	1	0
Features	Sector Count 7:0							
Features (exp)	Sector Count 15:8							
Sector Count	TAG					Reserved		
Sector Count (exp)	Reserved							
Sector Number	LBA 0:7							
Sector Number (exp)	LBA 31:24							
Cylinder Low	LBA 15:8							
Cylinder Low (exp)	LBA 39:32							
Cylinder High	LBA 23:16							
Cylinder High (exp)	LBA 47:40							
Device/Head	FUA	1	0	0	Reserved			
Command	61h							

Queue Management

Host software, the HBA, and DMA controller must support some form of command queue management. The specification does not define a specific implementation, but the AHCI controller definition embodies a queuing management solution that is described in this section.

The Software Command Queue

To perform command queuing software must support asynchronous IO; that is, the ability to issue multiple commands (up to the maximum of 32) prior to the current or previous commands being completed. In the AHCI implementation these commands are queued within a memory buffer called the Command List. The AHCI controller (HBA) has an internal register that points to the Command List buffer (illustrated in Figure 14-4 on page 243). Note also, that each port supported by the AHCI controller has its own DMA engine and associated command table. Figure 14-4 details Command List and Command Table content for only port 0, but software sets up the same data structures for each port interface.

During operation, the controller reads the contents of the command list entry; however, the entries within the command list do not actually contain a command. Instead, each command entry contains a memory pointer that directs the HBA to the Command Table, which does contain the command. The command is actually stored in the form of a Register FIS - Host to Device (containing a FPDMA command for NCQ) that is fetched by the AHCI controller and delivered to the drive.

Figure 14-4: Software Builds a Command Queue of up to 32 Entries

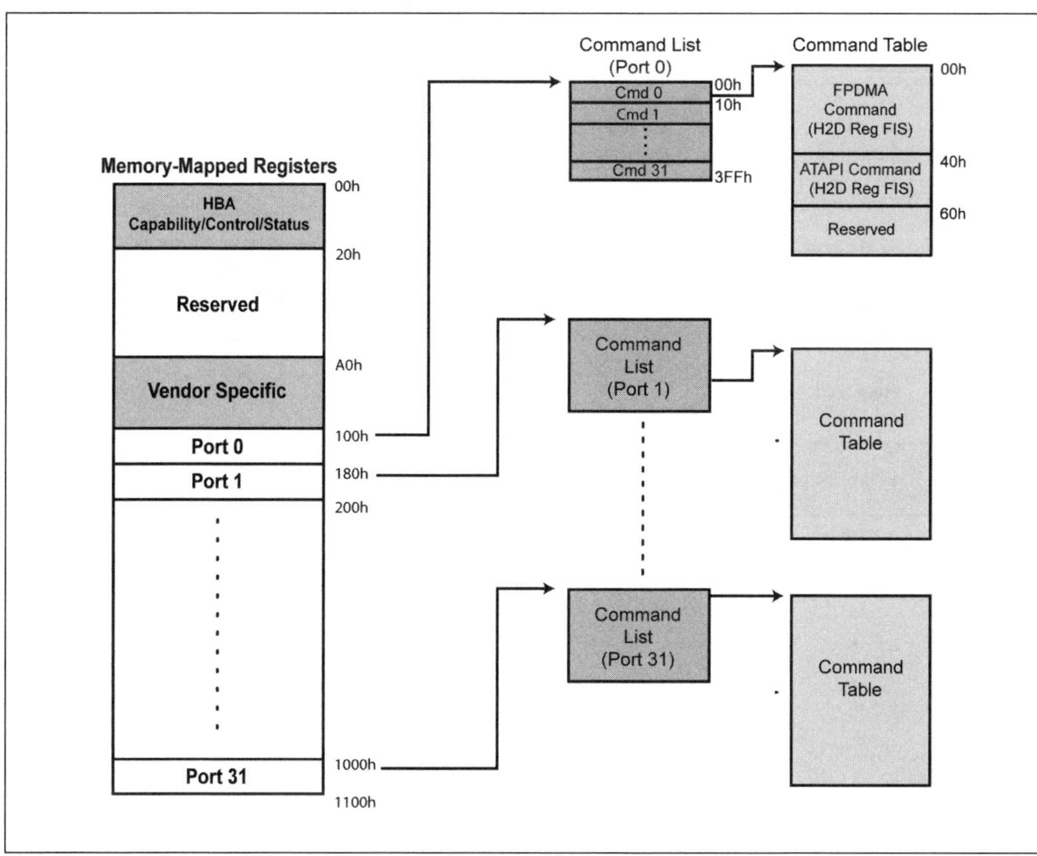

Programming the DMA Transfer

When software enqueues a command it must also set up the DMA transfers to/from main memory. This entails specifying whether the command is a read from or write to the disc, the size of the transfer, and the physical memory pages that must be accessed during the DMA operation. The scatter/gather lists determine the locations within physical memory where data is to be transferred. The scatter/gather lists are often referred to as Physical Region Descriptors (PRDs) because these lists point to physical regions (one or more pages) in memory that must be accessed to either store or retrieve data. In AHCI the PRDs are added as extensions of the Command Table (see Figure 14-5 on page 244). Each entry specifies a base address location and size (in bytes) of the physical memory buffer.

Figure 14-5: Each Command Has an Associated PRD

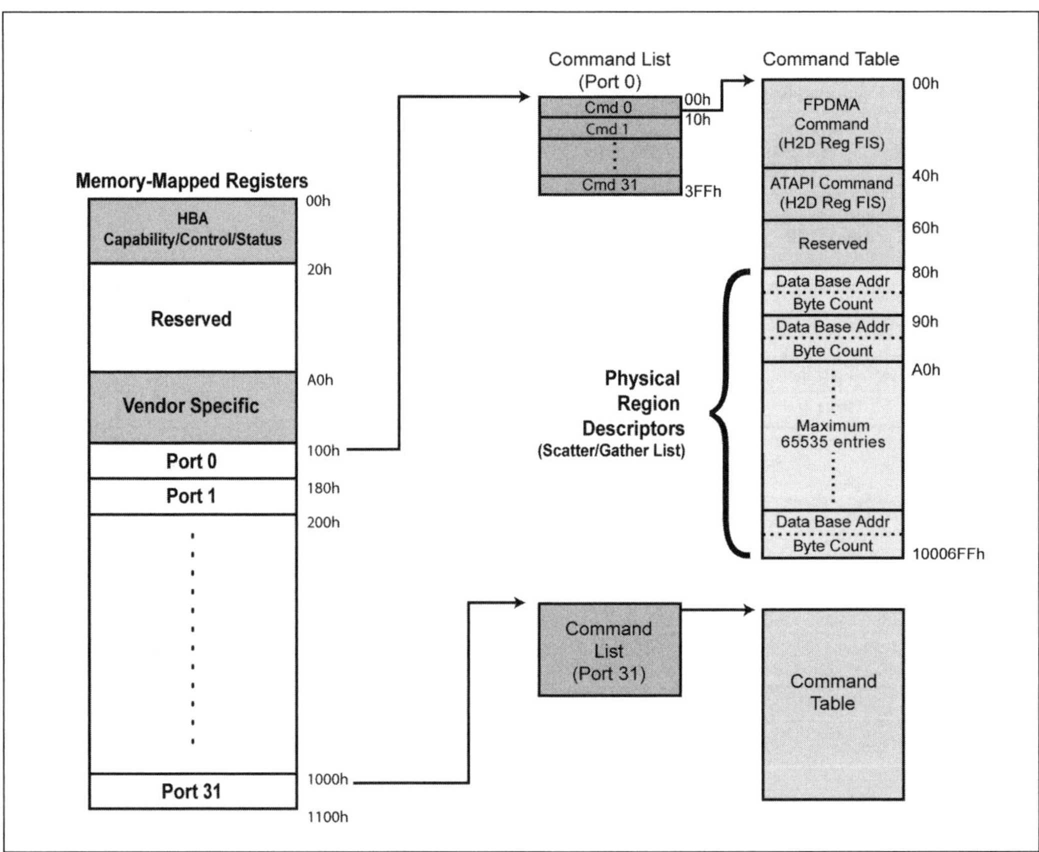

Tracking Pending Commands

Each of the 32 entries (0-31) within the command list is directly associated with the corresponding Tag value. When the HBA reads an entry from the Command List, the entry number is used to create the 32-bit tag value associated with this command. When the HBA fetches the FPDMA command from the Command Table, it places the tag value in the upper 5 bits of the Sector Count field as shown in Figure 14-2 on page 241 and Figure 14-3 on page 242. The drive internally enqueues up to 32 commands and processes them based on the concepts of command reordering. When the drive is ready to deliver or receive data associated with one of the outstanding commands, it notifies the HBA by delivering the tag for the current command via a DMA Setup FIS, shown in Figure 14-6. When all of the data associated with the command has been transferred, it is retired.

Figure 14-6: Format and Content Definition for DMA Setup FIS

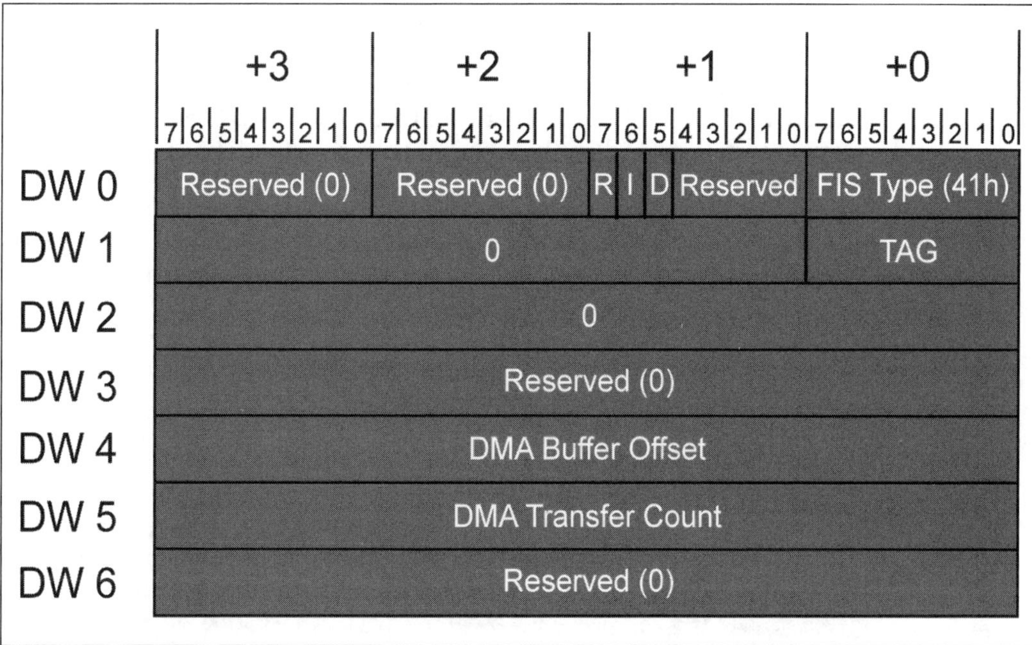

SATA Active Register

To track which commands have been issued to the drive and are current pending completion, the HBA implements a SATA-specific register called the SActive register. This register depicted in Figure 14-7 contains a bit-map of 32 bits, one for each possible tag value. As described previously, when the HBA assigns a tag to an FPDMA command that is being delivered to the drive, it also updates the corresponding bit field associated with the tag value.

Figure 14-7: Format of the SATA Active (SActive) Register

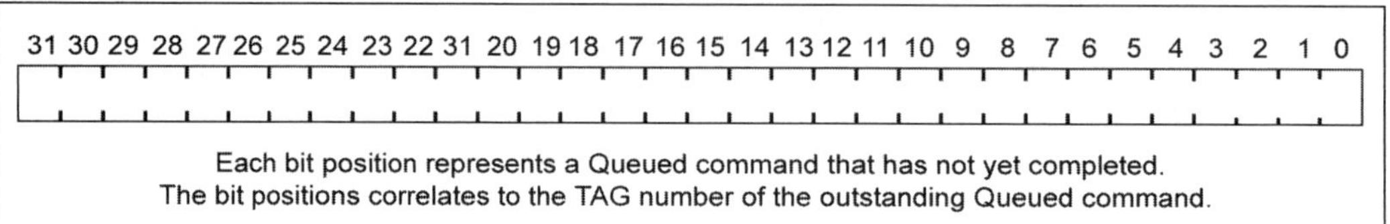

Set Device Bits FIS

When the drive completes the data block transfer associated with a given command, it delivers a Set Device Bits FIS to the HBA. This FIS updates completion status and also indicates which command has completed. The SATA II specification defined the second DWord of the Set Device Bits FIS (previously reserved) as the SActive field as illustrated in Figure 14-8 on page 246. The 32 bits SActive field of course corresponds directly to the SActive register definition.

When an NCQ drive sets completes one of the outstanding commands, it delivers a Set Device Bits FIS with the corresponding SActive field set to reflect the tag value of the command having just completed. Upon receiving the Set Device Bits FIS, the HBA updates the SActive register with the 32-bit SActive field from the FIS. A bit value of one clears the corresponding SActive bit and a value of zero has no effect. The Interrupt Pending (I) bit is also set, which causes the HBA to send an interrupt to notify software of the status change.

Figure 14-8: Format of Set Device Bits FIS with SActive Field

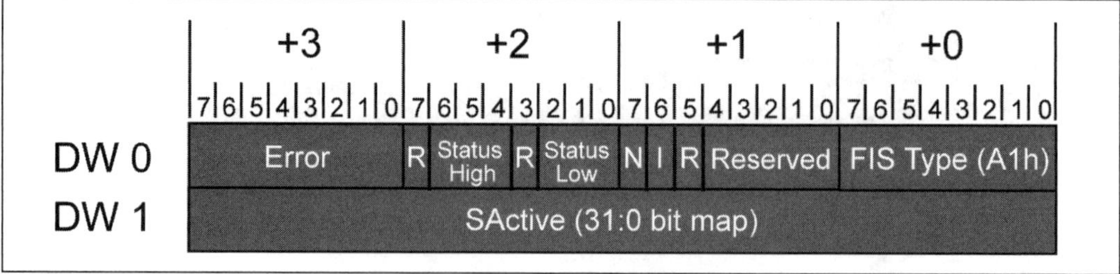

First Party DMA Command Protocol

SATA II defines the protocol associated with the FPDMA Read and Write commands. This new protocol is defined to support the mechanisms described previously in this chapter.

FPDMA Read Protocol Overview

The sequence of events associated with a First Party DMA Read command is illustrated in Figure 14-9 on page 248. This example assumes that software has already set up the DMA transfer. Note also that in this example a single Data FIS satisfies the sector count, and the command completes without any errors. Successful completion of the command is reported to the HBA by delivering the Tag number of the command via the Set Device Bits FIS.

The sequence of actions is enumerated below:

1. Software initializes the shadow registers and issues the First Party DMA Read command (60h). The HBA forwards the contents of the shadow registers to the Drive via the Register FIS and indicates the drive is busy (BSY=1).
2. The device parses the command and places it into the internal queue.
3. The device releases the bus to notify the host that the command has been enqueued and is pending completion. The release is performed by sending a Register FIS (with BSY=0 and REL=1) to the HBA.
4. The HBA updates the shadow registers and detects the release. Next, the HBA sets the SActive bit corresponding to the Tag number returned in the Register FIS. When software reads status it will detect the bus release and is free to send another queued command. Note that this example deals with a single command and does not show or describe other link activity related to other commands previously pending completion and/or being enqueued.
5. The drive notifies the HBA when it is ready to return data by delivering a DMA Setup FIS. The DMA Setup FIS contains the Tag number of the command being completed.
6. The HBA receives the DMA Setup FIS, updates the status and error registers, and associates the Tag value with the DMA setup for this command. The drive then awaits delivery of data from the drive.
7. After sending the DMA Setup FIS, the drive delivers a Data FIS to the HBA. In this example, the sector count is completed with a single Data FIS transmission.

8. The HBA receives the Data FIS and transfers the payload to memory using the DMA controller, previously set up for this command by software.
9. Next, the drive updates the following information:
    - o status and error registers, indicating no error conditions
    - o the corresponding Tag bit is set in the SActive field of the Set Device Bits FIS (the bit position corresponds to the Tag number of the command just completed)
    - o the interrupt pending bit is set in the Set Device Bits FIS

    The HBA then sends the Set Device Bits FIS to the HBA.
10. Upon receiving the Set Device Bits FIS, the HBA updates the status and error registers, clears the corresponding bit position within the SActive register, indicating the command is no longer pending completion, and generates an interrupt to notify software to check status.

Figure 14-9: Overview of FPDMA Read Command Protocol

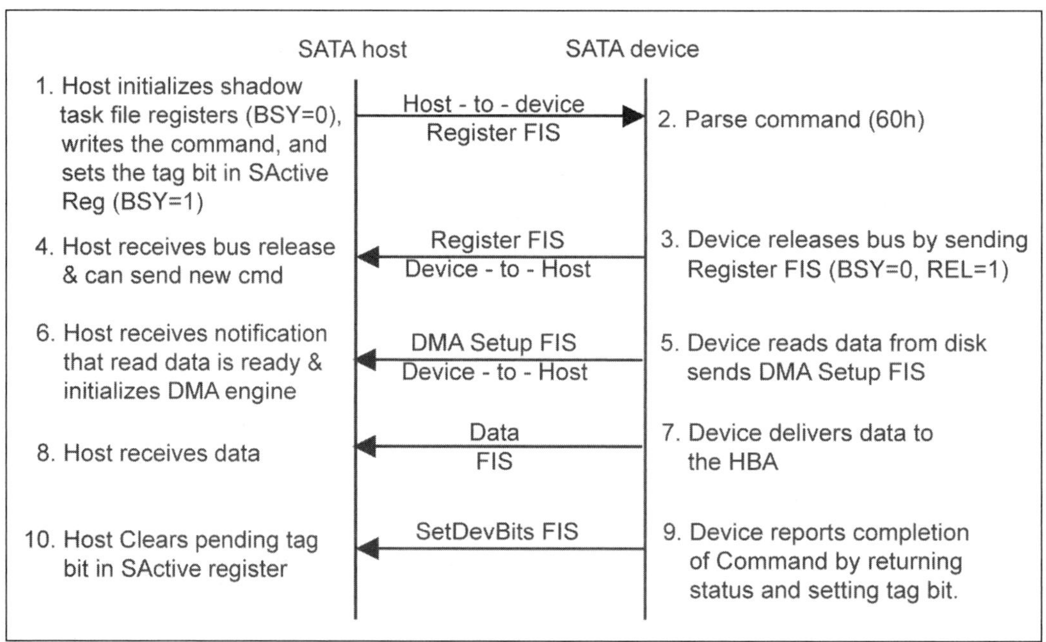

FPDMA Write Protocol Overview

Figure 14-10 on page 250 illustrates the command protocol for a standard FPDMA Write command. Like other Queued DMA commands, the bus must be released in order for a subsequent command to be issued by software. Also, the drive must send a DMA Setup FIS to notify the DMA engine which transfer is to be performed, and the drive must send a DMA Activate FIS to the HBA to notify it that it is ready to receive data. This example illustrates a command that requires a single Data FIS to satisfy the sector count. In addition, the command is retired via a Set Device Bits FIS, by using the Tag number of the command to indicate the command has completed. Each step in the sequence is enumerated below:

1. Software initializes the shadow registers and issues the First Party DMA Read command (61h). The HBA sends the contents of the shadow registers to the Drive via the Register FIS and indicates the drive is busy (BSY=1).
2. The device parses the command and places it into the drive's queue.
3. The device releases the bus to notify the host that the command has been enqueued and is pending completion. The release is performed by sending a Register FIS (with BSY=0 and REL=1) to the HBA.
4. The HBA updates the shadow registers and detects the release. Next, the HBA sets the SActive bit corresponding to the Tag number returned in the Register FIS. When software reads status it will detect the bus release and is free to send another queued command. Note that this example deals with a single command and does not show or describe other link activity related to other commands previously pending completion and/or being enqueued.
5. The drive notifies the HBA when it is ready to receive data by delivering a DMA Setup FIS. The DMA Setup FIS contains the Tag number of the command being performed currently.
6. The HBA receives the DMA Setup FIS, updates the status and error registers, and associates the Tag value with the DMA setup for this command. The HBA also initializes the DMA engine associated with the Tag.
7. After sending the DMA Setup FIS, the drive delivers the DMA Activate FIS to the HBA, thereby requesting the data be delivered.
8. The HBA receives the DMA Activate FIS and begins fetching data from memory.
9. The HBA delivers data to the drive as it is received from memory.
10. The drive receives the Data FIS and recognizes that the sector count is complete.

11. Next, the drive reports successful command completion be updating the following information and sending a Set Device Bits FIS:
    - o status and error registers, indicating no error conditions
    - o the corresponding Tag bit is set in the SActive field of the Set Device Bits FIS (the bit position corresponds to the Tag number of the command just completed)
    - o the interrupt pending bit is set in the Set Device Bits FIS
12. Upon receiving the Set Device Bits FIS, the HBA updates the status and error registers, clears the corresponding bit position within the SActive register, indicating the command is no longer pending completion, and generates an interrupt to notify software to check status.

Figure 14-10: First Party DMA Write Command Protocol

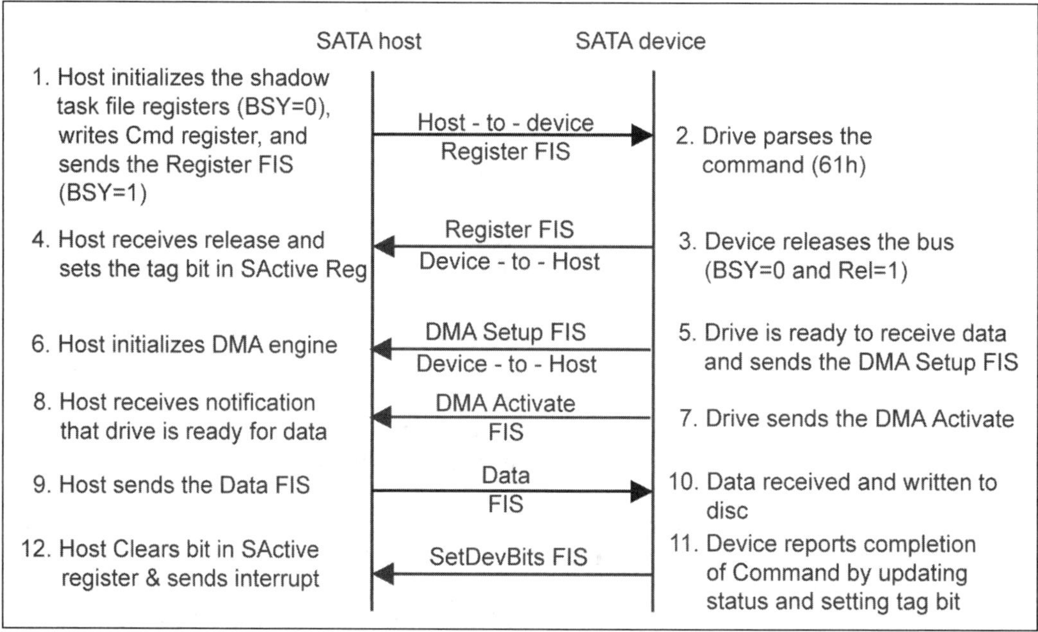

Auto-Activate Feature

The auto-activate feature improves the efficiency of the First Party DMA Write command protocol. Normal First Party DMA protocol requires the drive to deliver a DMA Setup FIS to the HBA to specify the command that is ready to be performed (via the Tag number). Next, the drive must send a DMA Activate FIS to request that data be sent. Auto-activate combines the DMA Activate function into the DMA Setup FIS; thereby, eliminating transmission of the first DMA Activate FIS. Figure 14-11 illustrates the addition of the "A" (Activate) bit within the DMA Setup FIS, which indicates to the HBA that DMA Activation is included within the DMA Setup FIS.

Figure 14-11: DMA Setup FIS with Auto-Activate Enabled

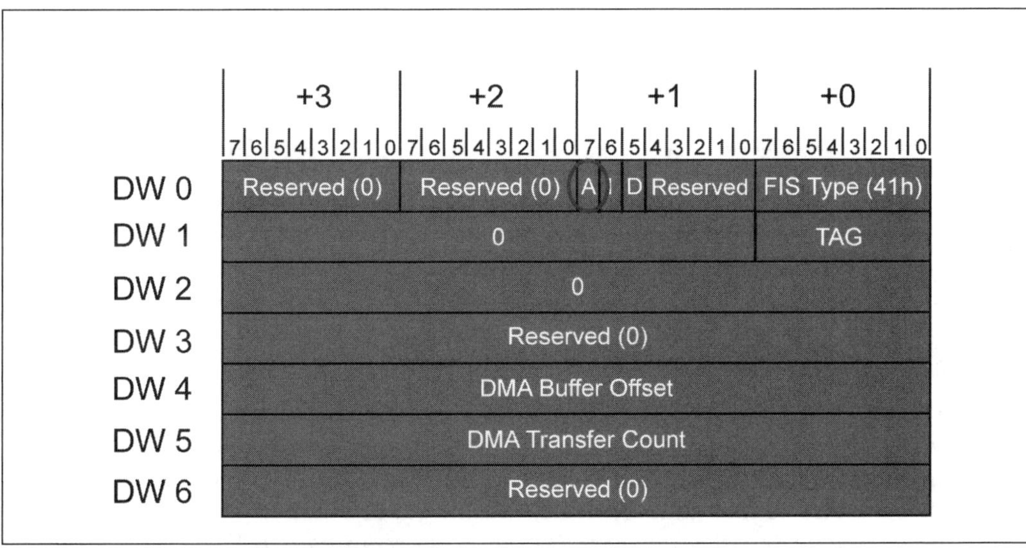

Auto-Activate with Single Data FIS

Figure 14-12 on page 252 further illustrates the FPDMA Write protocol when a single Data FIS completes the sector count. In this example, the DMA Setup FIS with activation enabled is followed by the Data FIS transmission to the drive.

Figure 14-12: FPDMA Write with One Data FIS Transfer

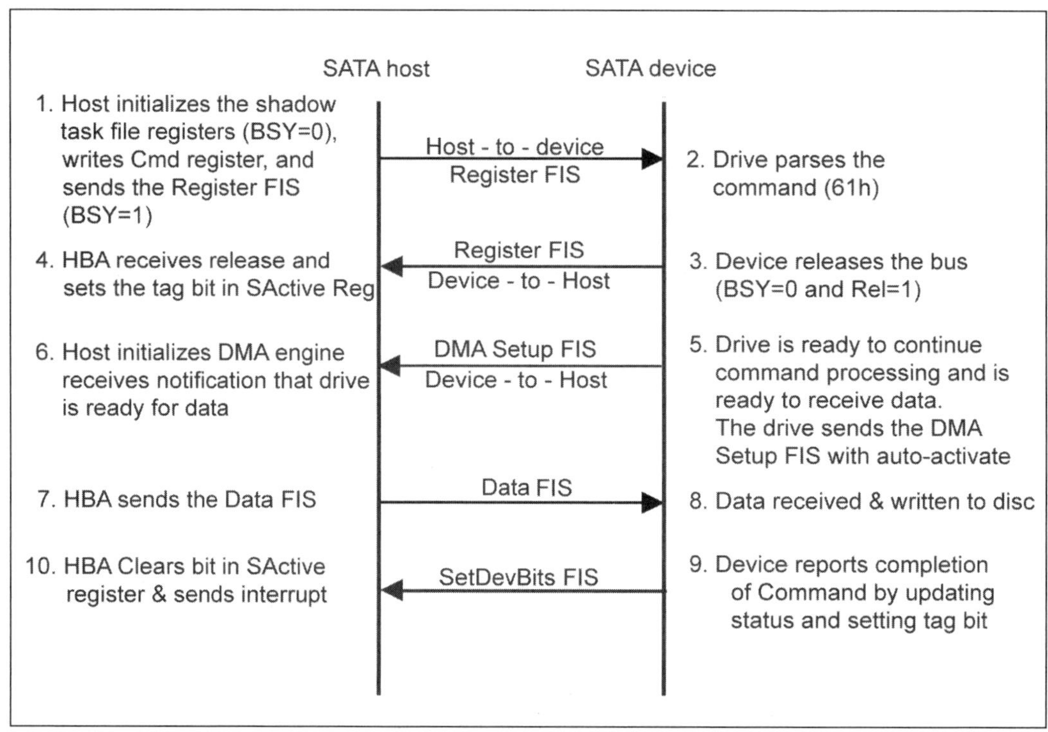

Auto-Activate with Multiple Data FISs

Figure 14-13 on page 253 illustrates the FPDMA Write protocol with auto-activation. As discussed previously the DMA Setup issued by the drive eliminates the need to send a DMA Activate FIS. The DMA Setup FIS in this example specifies a DMA context that represents a contiguous block of 32 sectors (512 bytes each), which satisfies the sector count. This requires two Data FIS packets be sent to the drive to complete the transfer. In such cases, a DMA Activate FIS must be delivered prior to sending a subsequent Data FIS.

If the DMA context changes when executing a command (e.g., a different physical memory page must be accessed), another DMA Setup FIS would be required and of course it could use the auto-activation feature to eliminate a DMA Activate FIS for the following Data transfer.

Figure 14-13: FPDMA Write with Two Data FIS Transfers from Contiguous Physical Memory Pages

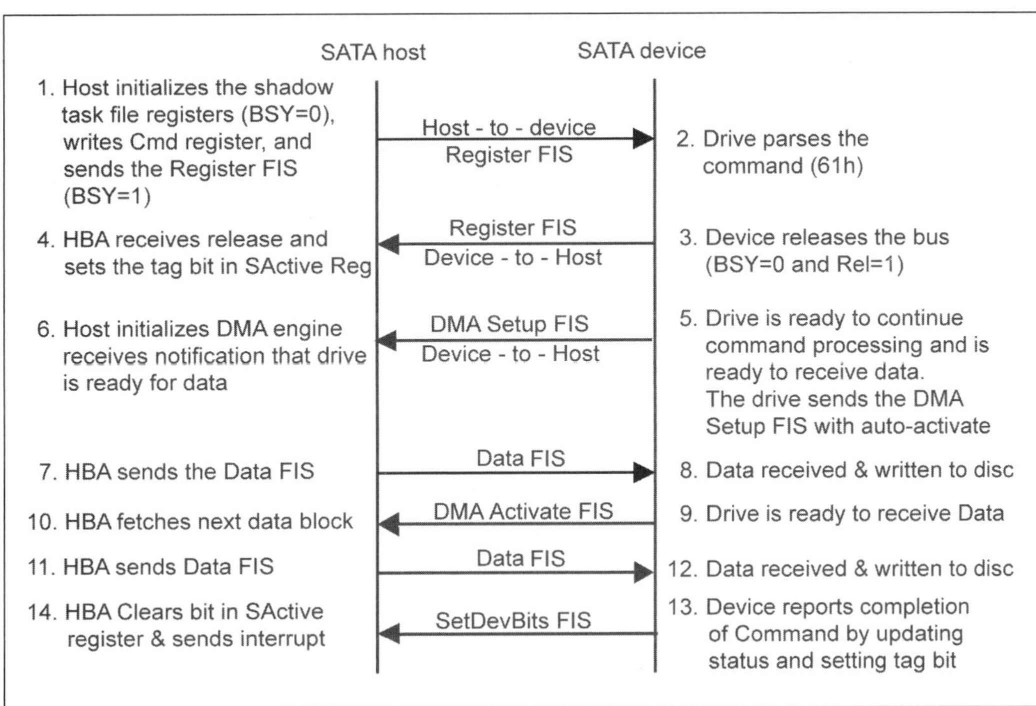

Detecting and Enabling Auto-Activation Support

The Identify Device data includes the auto-activation feature in bit 2 position of word offset 78. If this bit is set, the drive support auto activation optimization. Upon detecting this support, software can enable the feature via the Set Feature command. Once enabled, bit 2 of word offset 79 will be set in the Identify Device data. Refer to Figure 14-14 on page 254

Figure 14-14: Auto-Activation Capability Reported in Identify Device Data

Word Offset	R/O	Description
0 - 74		**Defined in ATA/ATAPI-7**
75	Optional	**Queue Depth** 15-5 Reserved 4-0 Maximum queue depth-1
76		**Serial ATA Capabilities** 15-11 Reserved 10 Phy event counters supported 9 Host-initiated link Power Management requests received 8 Native Command Queuing supported 7-4 Reserved 3 Reserved for SATA 2 Supports Serial ATA Gen-2 signaling 1 Supports Serial ATA Gen-1 signaling 0 Reserved (0)
77		**Reserved for SATA**
78	Optional	**Serial ATA Features** 15-7 Reserved 6 Software settings preservation supported 5 Reserved 4 In-order data delivery supported ~~3 Drive initiates link power management requests~~ 2 DMA Setup FIS Auto-Activate optimization supported ~~1 DMA Setup FIS non-zero buffer offsets supported~~ 0 Reserved (0)
79	Optional	**Serial ATA Features Enabled** 15-7 Reserved 6 Software settings preservation enabled 5 Reserved 4 In-order data delivery enabled ~~3 Drive initiates link power management requests~~ 2 DMA Setup FIS Auto-Activate optimization enabled ~~1 DMA Setup FIS non-zero buffer offsets enabled~~ 0 Reserved (0)
80-255		**Defined in ATA/ATAPI-7**

Supporting Non-Zero Offsets

Native Command Queuing also supports the possibility of accessing data associated with a command in an out-of-order fashion. Consider the FPDMA Read sequence exemplified in Figure 14-15 on page 255. The data to be read for each of the read commands pending execution are labeled one through four in the order they were enqueued within the drive. The arrow shows the starting head position. In this contrived example, the drive proceeds as follows:

1. Data for command 1 is read in its entirety and the DMA Setup is sent to the HBA to specify the command that is ready. The offset of the data buffer is zero because the data was read in order.
2. Next, the drive moves to an adjacent track and reads the back portion of command two's data. The DMA Setup is sent to the HBA to specify which command this data is associated with along with an offset that indicates the location within the memory buffer where the data must be written.
3. Once the drive completes reading the back end of command two's data it moves to read the end of command four's data. Once again a DMA Setup FIS must be send that includes the appropriate non-zero offset for storing command four's data within the DMA buffer.
4. After reading the end of command four's data, the drive proceeds to command three. All of the data is read in order so the DMA Setup FIS contains an offset of zero when writing into the DMA buffer.
5. This is followed by reading the first portion of command two's data and the first half of command four's data. Each of the DMA Setup FISes for these DMA operations include offsets of zero.

Figure 14-15: Example Execution of FPDMA Read Sequence with Non-Zero Offsets

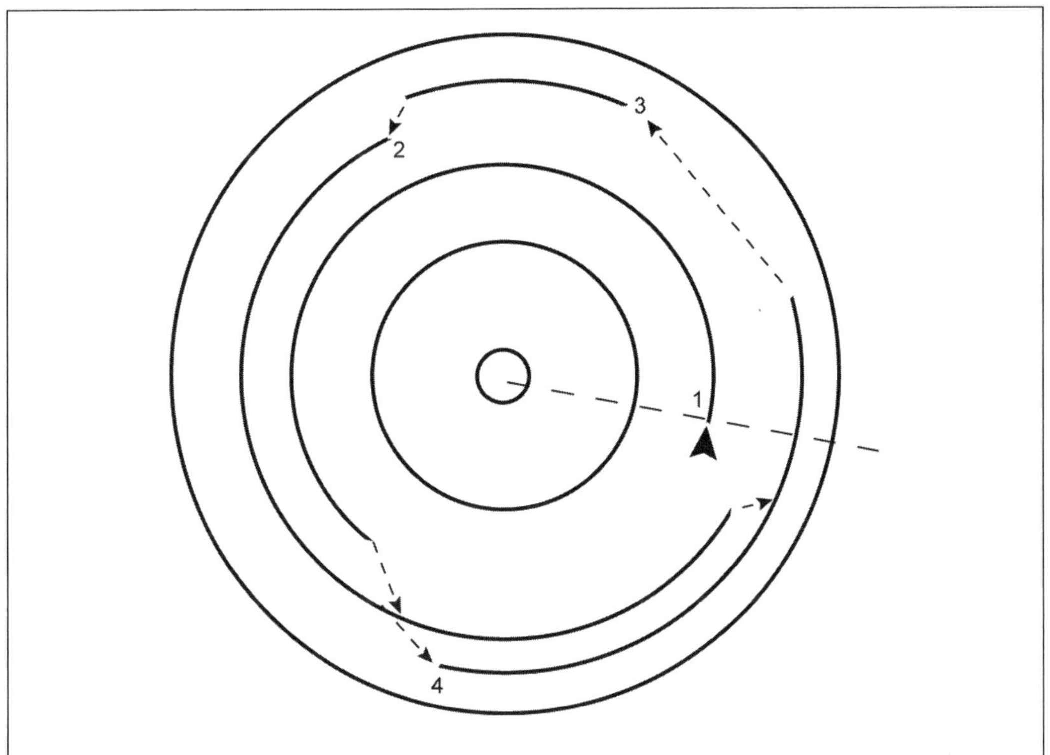

15 Port Multipliers

Previous Chapter

The previous chapter described the concepts and mechanisms associated with Native Command Queuing (NCQ). This mechanism provides major performance improvements over mainstream ATA drives that use standard DMA Read and Write operations.

This Chapter

Port Multipliers provide a fan-out capability, whereby up to 15 ports can be accessed via a single HBA port. This capability is useful in large rack mount implementations. This chapter details the hardware and software required to support the Port Multiplier solution.

The Next Chapter

A common goal of server implementations is non-stop operation. This typically includes some type of redundant capability that allows for failures to be managed without shutting down the entire system. Port Selectors provide access to SATA drives from two separate sources, thereby permitting a fail-over solution. The next chapter discusses the Port Selector implementation and associated protocols.

Overview

Because SATA drives are normally implemented with a point-to-point connection to a single HBA port, the cost and ease of implementing large drive installations is problematic. To mitigate this problem SATA II defined Port Multipliers that provide up to 15 additional ports to which SATA drives can be connected, called Device Ports. This provides the port fan-out capability needed in large rack mount implementations.

Figure 15-1 on page 258 illustrates the typical SATA drive connection to an HBA port, along with the Port Multiplier approach. Obviously, the HBA can only communicate with one drive at a time, thus overall performance may be affected with the Port Multiplier approach, but it provides access to huge amounts of storage at much lower costs when compared to SCSI and Fibre Drive implementations. Note also that Port Multipliers are not allowed to be cascaded.

Figure 15-1: The Port Multiplier Concept

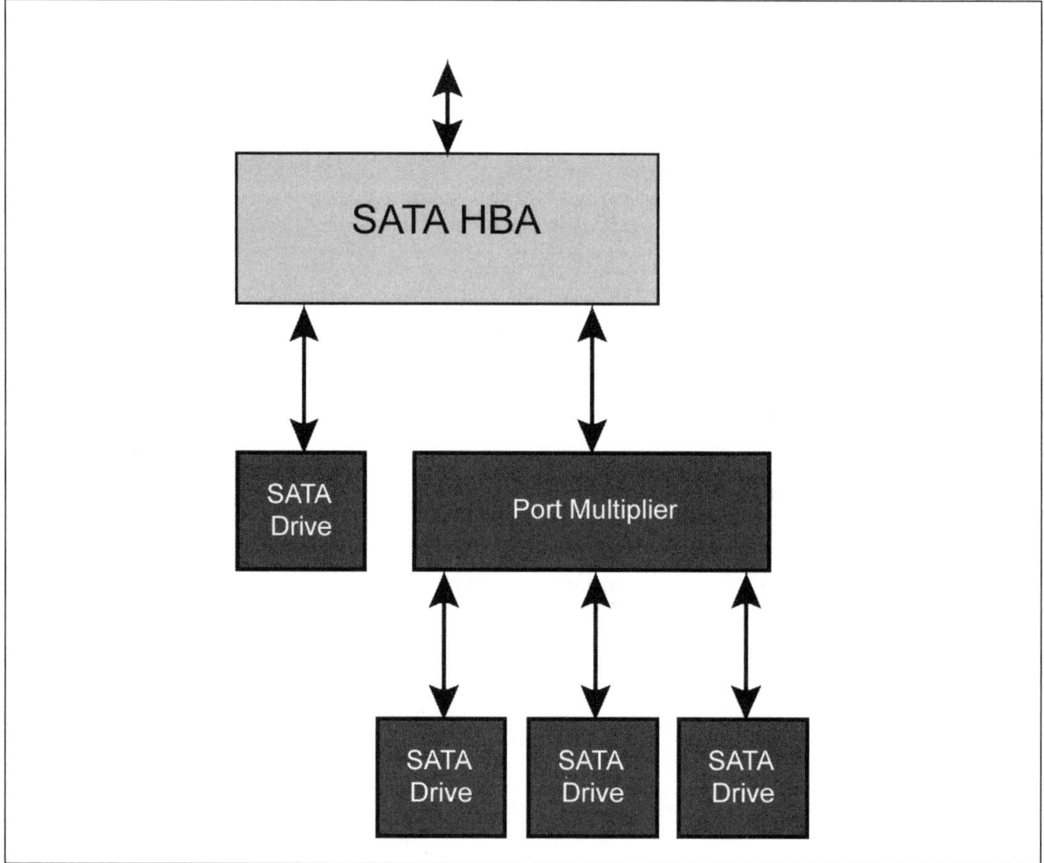

The Port Multiplier implementation does not require any modifications to the drives. However, host software must be able to assign port numbers to each FIS that is delivered so that it can be routed to the intended recipient. The FIS definition includes a Port Number field that was previously reserved. For example, Figure 15-2 on page 259 depicts a Register FIS, Host-to-Device with the Port Number field highlighted.

Figure 15-2: Port Number Added to Support Port Multiplier Routing

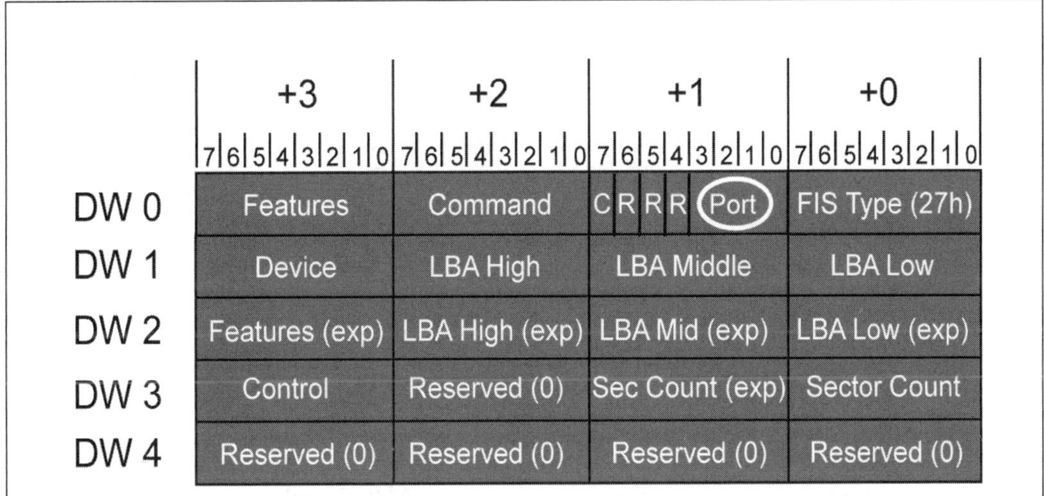

Port Multiplier Port Addresses

Some method was needed to direct frames sent from the HBA to the appropriate target drive. SATA uses a port numbering scheme to accomplish this routing. Software normally targets a specific drive by specifying an HBA port. When port multipliers are used drives must be targeted based on both an HBA port and Port Multiplier port. Two mechanisms can be used to assign port numbers that determine which drive is being targeted:

1. **Command-Based Switching** — This method of port number assignment is used when an HBA supports command queueing to one drive at a time. In this case, software assigns the PM port number via the Port Multiplier Port (PMP) field within the SControl register before writing the command. (See Figure 15-3 on page 260.) The HBA uses that PMP value to populate the Port field within the FIS. If a subsequent command targets a different drive, the PMP field must be updated with the new port number prior to issuing the next command. This approach is limiting in that when a Port Multiplier is used, only one drive at a time can be efficiently performing queued commands.

Figure 15-3: PMP Field within the SControl Register

31 30 29 28 27 26 25 24 23 22 31 20 19 18 17 16 15 14 13 12 11 10 9 8 7 6 5 4 3 2 1 0

Reserved	PMP	IPM	SPEED	DETECT

PMP - Port Multiplier Port (optional)
The Port Multiplier Port (PMP) field specifies the 4-bit value to be placed in the PM Port field of all transmitted FISs. PM software loads this value during initialization. The value by default (following Reset) is 0h.

2. **FIS-Based Switching** — This method provides dynamic context switching between ports. That is, the HBA supports the ability to handle consecutive commands, each of which can have different port numbers. In the case of AHCI, a port number field is associated with each entry of the command queue. When the queue is read by the AHCI controller it saves the Port number and than populates the Port field within the corresponding FIS.

Figure 15-4: PM Port Assignment within Command Queue in AHCI Implementations

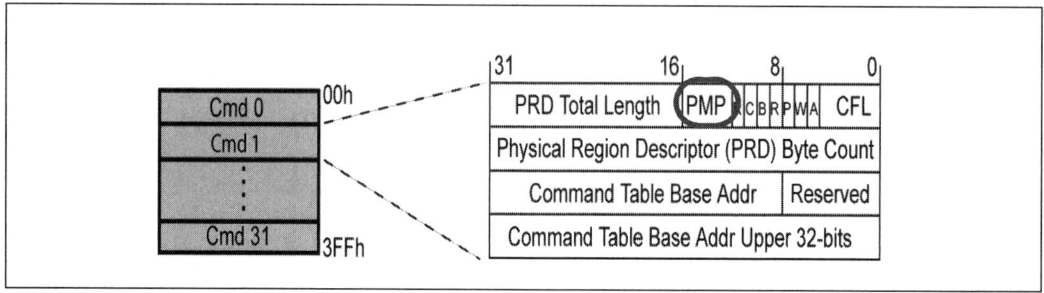

Frame Routing

Each frame that targets a PM port is routed as illustrated in Figure 15-5 on page 261. Note that a frame being sent from the HBA to a drive will have the target Port number specified. The PM routes the frame to the specified port but will remove the port number before forwarding the frame to the drive. When the drive returns a frame the port number field will initially be reserved, and the PM will assign a port number to identify which drive sent the frame.

Figure 15-5: Routing Frames to the Target Drive

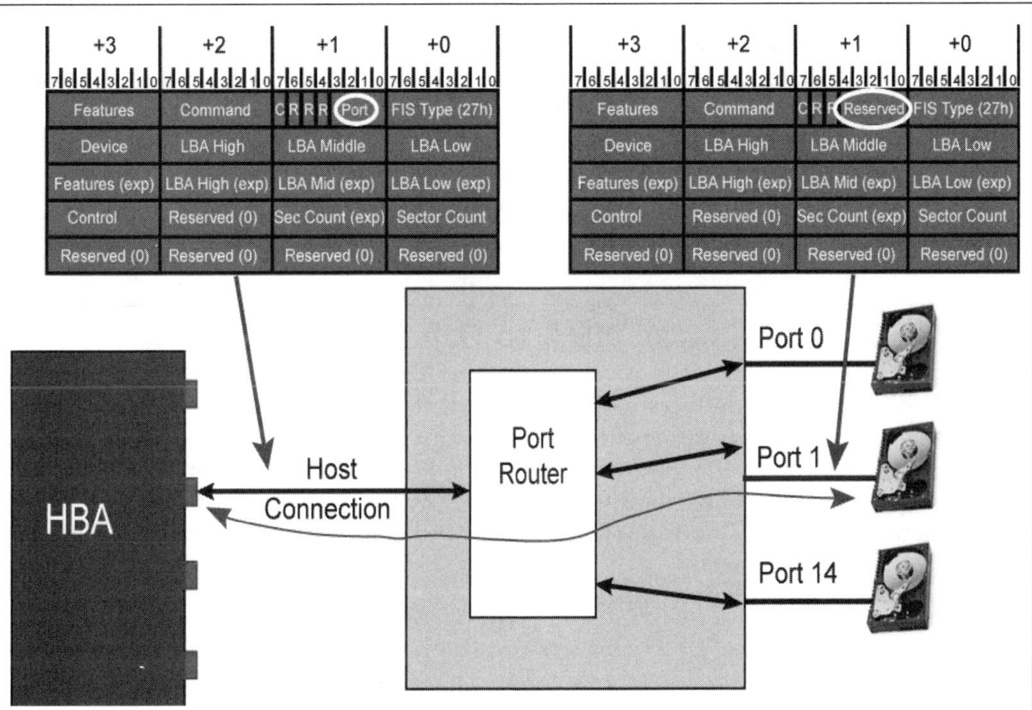

Device Port Numbers

A port multiplier may implement up to 15 ports to which SATA devices may be attached. These device ports must be numbered starting with device port zero and be assigned sequentially up to the maximum number of ports implemented. Because SATA is a point-to-point implementation, each device port interface performs many of the same functions associated with an HBA port interface. For example, each Port Multiplier port has the SATA-specific registers that are used to specify capabilities, control the link, and gather and report status and errors.

FIS Transmission

The complication associated with sending a FIS between the HBA and drive is that two separate SATA links are involved in the transfer. The HBA and drive are completely unaware of the Port Multiplier's existence, thus the Port Multiplier must appear transparent. The following sections discuss FIS transmission from Host to Drive and from Drive to Host. In addition, collisions can potentially occur when the HBA attempts to send a FIS to a drive that is also in the process of sending a FIS to the HBA. The Port Multiplier must manage such conflicts.

FIS Transmission HBA to Drive

When the HBA delivers a FIS to the PM it routes the FIS to the target drive based on the Port Number field within the FIS. The PM must ensure that the HBA receives verification of whether the FIS is received by the drive without errors. The following example describes how the PM handles the reception and delivery of the FIS and is able to report valid end status to the HBA.

Error Free FIS Transfer

To ensure that the HBA receives notification of successful delivery of the FIS across both links, the PM simply waits until the PM-to-drive transfer completes, before reports transmission results to the HBA. The protocol is handled as specified in the example below.

1. The HBA arbitrates for link ownership and starts transmission of the FIS.
2. As the PM receives the frame it returns primitives to the HBA. Note that all primitives are returned except the R_OK or R_ERR primitive, which must not be returned to the HBA until frame transmission completes to the drive.
3. When the PM detects the FIS type and port number, it determines the port to which the FIS must be transferred.
4. The PM arbitrates for link ownership and begins transmitting the FIS to the drive. The PM must send the FIS to the drive unaltered. (this including the Port number field). Furthermore, the PM is not required to check and recalculate CRC before sending the FIS to the drive. This reduces latency and buffering.
5. As the drive receives the FIS it returns primitives to the PM is normal fashion. At this point the PM is involved in two separate and independent link transmissions of the same FIS.

6. When the PM receives the FIS in its entirety it does not return R_OK.
7. Once FIS delivery completes to the drive, it returns R_OK to the PM, which in turn sends R_OK to the HBA thereby completing FIS delivery.

During transmission normal flow control is enforced at both interfaces. The flow control signaling latencies must also be met by the PM.

PM Error Detection and Handling - HBA FIS Delivery

Fundamentally, errors are handled at each interface as specified by the SATA protocol. Errors detected during FIS transmission generally result in a SYNC primitive being delivered by the PM in both directions. That is, whether the error occurs between the drive and PM or the PM and the HBA the SYNC primitive must be propagated to both the Drive and HBA. This ensures that both the drive and HBA understand that FIS transmission has failed.

The list below highlights several error scenarios and describes how they must be handled.

- When the PM checks the port number to determine routing, it is possible that the port number is invalid (e.g., destination port not implemented). In this case the PM must return a SYNC primitive to the HBA thereby, terminating the FIS transmission.
- If the X bit is set in the SError Register's Diagnostic field then there has been a change in device connection status. The PM is required to send a SYNC primitive in response, forcing FIS transmission to be terminated. The X bit indicates whether device connection status has changed. If the bit is set, a change has occurred but software may not have detected the change and has not cleared the bit.
- The Port Multiplier is permitted to check and recalculate the CRC, but these actions are not required and if implemented would increase latency in delivering the FIS to the drive.

FIS Transmission Drive to HBA

It is not the drive's responsibility to know the port number of the PM to which it is attached; thus, when a drive initiates a FIS transfer the Port number field is cleared (zero). Consequently, the PM must load the Port number field so software can determine which drive has delivered the FIS. The following description summarizes the general sequence of events associated with FIS delivery from the drive to the HBA and presumes that no errors are detected.

Error Free FIS Transmission

The following sequence describes error-free FIS delivery across a PM that originates at the drive.

1. The drive arbitrates for link ownership and starts transmission of the FIS.
2. As the PM receives the FIS it returns primitives to the drive in normal fashion, but it must not return R_OK until FIS transmission has completed to the HBA.
3. The PM begins to receive the FIS from the drive, but before sending the FIS on to the HBA, it loads the FIS's Port number field with the port number associated with the originating drive.
4. The PM arbitrates for link ownership and begins transmitting the modified FIS to the HBA. (Note: To reduce latency and buffer space requirements, the PM is allowed to arbitrate for ownership of the HBA link prior to returning R_RDY to the drive. Otherwise, the PM might need to buffer much of the incoming FIS while waiting to get ownership of the host port.)
5. As the HBA receives the FIS it returns primitives to the PM in normal fashion. At this point the PM is involved in two separate and independent link transmissions of the same FIS.
6. During delivery of the modified FIS to the HBA, the PM must calculate and deliver a new CRC value.
7. During FIS reception the HBA calculates and checks CRC. The PM also delays delivery of the R_OK primitive until it is received from the HBA.
8. When the HBA receives the FIS without error, it returns R_OK to the PM, which in turn sends R_OK to the drive thereby completing FIS delivery.

The PM must handle flow control conditions at both interfaces, including satisfying the latency requirements associated with flow control signaling.

PM Error Detection and Handling - Device FIS Delivery

Errors detected during FIS transmission generally result in a SYNC primitive being delivered by the PM in both directions. That is, whether the error occurs between the drive and PM or the PM and the HBA the SYNC primitive must be propagated to both the Drive and HBA. This ensures that both the drive and HBA understand that the FIS transmission has failed.

The following list highlights several error scenarios and describes how they must be handled.

- After receiving an X_RDY primitive from the device, the Port Multiplier determines if the X bit in the SError's Diag field is set. If set, the Port Multiplier must not return an R_RDY primitive to the drive until the X bit is cleared. The X bit indicates whether device connection status has changed. If the bit is set, a change has occurred but software may not have detected the change and has not cleared the bit.

- The PM must check the CRC of the FIS being received from the drive and if an error is detected, the PM must corrupt the CRC before forwarding it to the HBA to ensure that the HBA will also see an error.

Collisions

Collision can occur in a PM environment when the HBA is sending a FIS to a target drive that is also sending a FIS to the HBA. It is the Port Multiplier's job to handle the collision.

Background Information

Collisions can only occur when the HBA is sending a FIS to a target drive, while at the same time the target drive attempts to send a FIS to the HBA. Consequently, a collision should only occur when Native Command Queuing is in use, the drive has one or more commands outstanding, and the HBA is sending another command to the same drive.

In a single link implementation, collisions do not occur due to the specified arbitration priority. For review, if an X_RDY primitive is being signaled by the HBA, it awaits the return of an R_RDY primitive from the SATA drive. If at the same time the drive also signals X_RDY, the HBA is required to discontinue X_RDY transmission and send R_RDY, thereby giving priority to the drive.

The arbitration model described in the previous paragraph can fail in a PM environment. That is, the HBA may already have received R_RDY from the PM and started a FIS transmission to a target drive while at the same time the target drive sends X_RDY to the PM. The result is a collision!

Handling Collisions

The PM resolves a collision by completing FIS reception from the HBA, returning an R_ERR indication, and discarding the FIS. This allows the drive to deliver its FIS to the HBA, after which, the HBA performs a retry of the previously failed transmission.

Retries are permitted for all FIS types except a Data FIS. Fortunately, the Native Command Queuing protocol ensures that the drive will never send a FIS to the HBA while the HBA is delivering a Data FIS to the drive. This means that all collisions can be resolved with the HBA retrying the failed FIS.

Device Port Registers

Each Device Port of the PM implements a group of registers that are used to control the link and gather status and error information. This implementation depicted in Figure 15-6 also lists the registers that can be implemented. The registers are described is the following sections. Access to each device port's registers is provided via the Read PM register and Write PM register commands. See "PM Read and Write Commands" on page 276 for details.

Figure 15-6: Port-Specific SCRs (PSCRs)

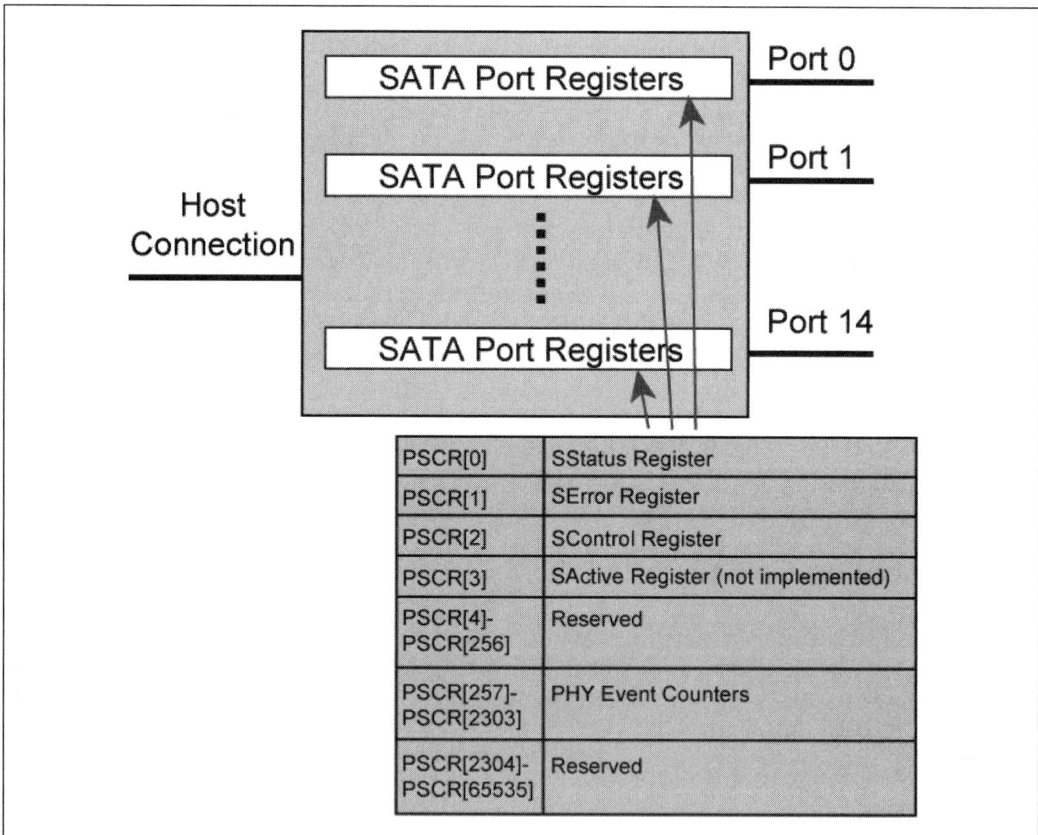

PSCR[0]	SStatus Register
PSCR[1]	SError Register
PSCR[2]	SControl Register
PSCR[3]	SActive Register (not implemented)
PSCR[4]-PSCR[256]	Reserved
PSCR[257]-PSCR[2303]	PHY Event Counters
PSCR[2304]-PSCR[65535]	Reserved

Port Status and Control Registers

Each device port interface implements SATA-specific registers, which are also implemented within the HBA. For reference purposes, the format and field definitions of each of these registers is included below.

SStatus Register - PSCR [0]

Figure 15-7 illustrates the format and content of the SStatus register. This register provides information regarding link interface power management, link speed, and device attachment and Phy communications.

Figure 15-7: SStatus Register Format and Field Definitions

31–12	11–8	7–4	3–0
Reserved	IPM	SPEED	DETECT

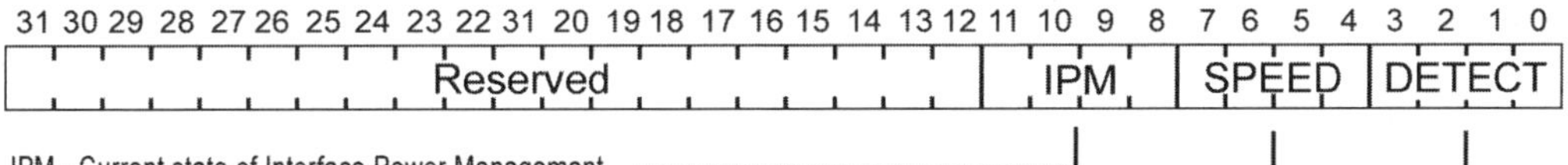

IPM - Current state of Interface Power Management
- 0000 = No device present or communication not established
- 0001 = Active PM state
- 0010 = Partial PM state
- 0110 = Slumber PM state
- Other values reserved

SPEED - Status of communication speed negotiated
- 0000 = No speed info; device not connected or no PHY communication
- 0001 = Base Communication rate established (Generation 1 speed)
- ***0010 = Generation 2 communication rate established***
- Other values reserved

DETECT - Reports Detect Status and the PHY State
- 0000 = Device not detected/no PHY communication
- 0001 = Device detected/no PHY communication
- 0011 = Device detected/PHY communicating
- 0100 = PHY offline (Interface disabled or running BIST Loopback)
- Other values reserved

SError Register - PSCR [1]

Figure 15-8 illustrates the SError register containing the Error and Diagnostic fields.

Figure 15-8: Error Field within the SError Register

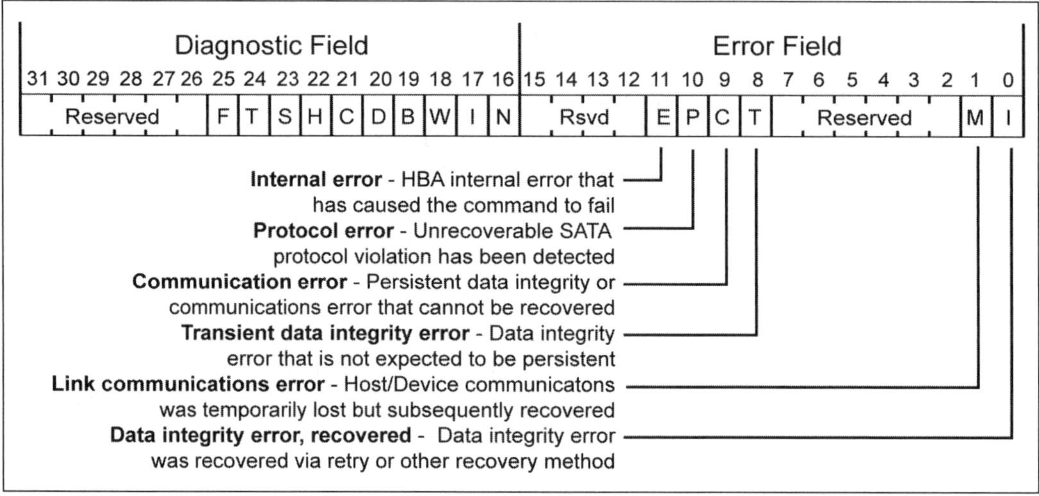

Figure 15-9: Diagnostic Field within the SError Register

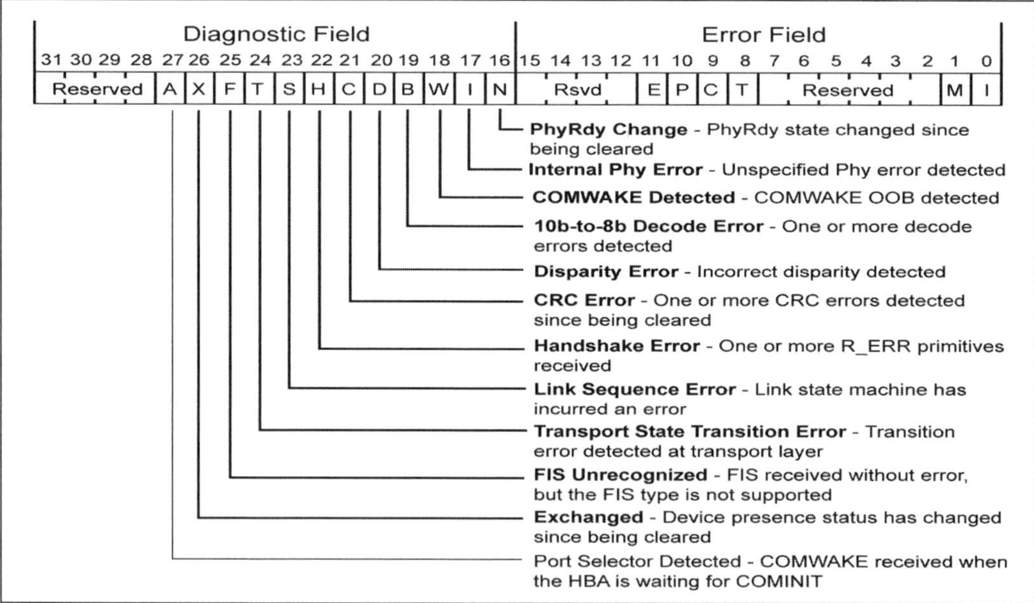

SControl Register - PSCR [2]

Figure 15-10 depicts the SControl register's format and field definitions. This register provides link control capability for enabling and disabling link power management, for limiting the link speed, and controlling the Phy and link interface as listed in Figure 15-10.

Figure 15-10: SControl Register Format and Field Definitions

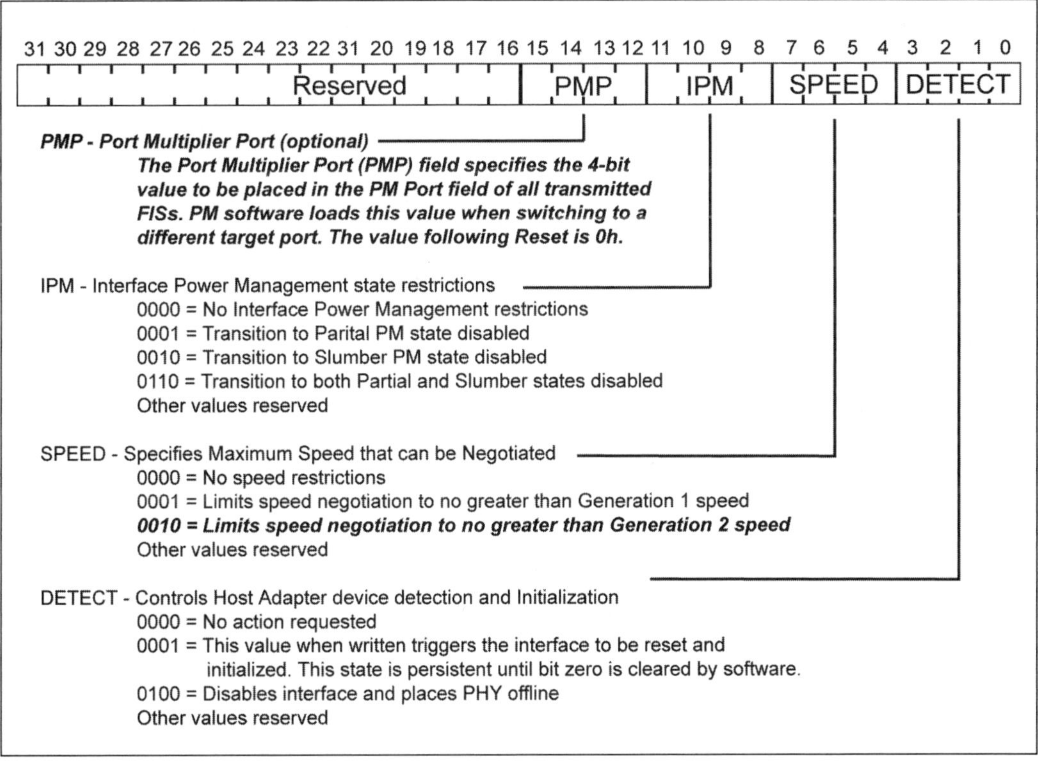

Port Event Counters - Port SCR [257-2303]

Port Event counters provide the ability to count and log various events associated with the transmission and reception of FISes between the PM port and the drive. Each Port Event Counter entry includes a 16-bit identifier that describes the specific event being monitored by the counter and reports the current value of the event counter. Figure 15-11 on page 270 illustrates the format of the identifier register.

Figure 15-11: Format of the 16-Bit Port Event Identifier Register

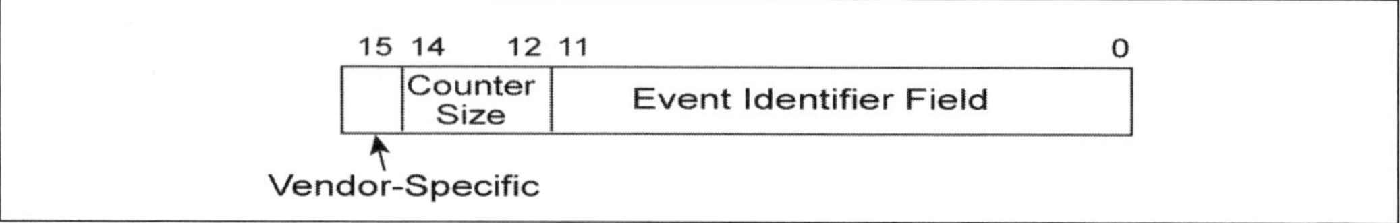

PHY Event Counter Identifiers. Table 15-1 lists the identifier values and defines the associated event. Any unused counter slots in the log page should have a counter identifier value of 0h. The log information can be returned in any order and is determined by the vendor. Software must simply associate the Event ID with the values returned. A value of zero means that there have been no occurrences of the corresponding event. Also note that any optional counters that are not implemented must not be listed or returned.

Table 15-1: PHY Counter IDs and Descriptions

Counter ID Bits (11:0)	Description
000h (Required)	Indicates end of counters in a given page
001h (Required)	Command failure and the ICRC error bit is set in the SError Register
002h	R_ERR response for Data FIS transmission
003h	R_ERR response from port for Device to Host Data FIS
004h	R_ERR response from port for Host to Device Data FIS
005h	R_ERR response from port for Non-Data FIS
006h	R_ERR response from port for Device to Host Non-Data FIS
007h	R_ERR response from port for Host to Device Non-Data FIS
008h	Device to Host Non-Data FIS retries
009h	Transition from Drive PHYRDY to Drive PHYRDYn
00Ah (Required)	Device to Host Register FIS sent due to COMRESET
00Bh	CRC Error detected in Host to Device FIS
00Dh	Non CRC Error detected in Host to Device FIS
00Fh	R_ERR response sent due to CRC error in Host to Device Data FIS
010h	R_ERR response sent due to Non-CRC error in Host to Device Data FIS
012h	R_ERR response sent due to CRC error in Host to Device Non-Data FIS
013h	R_ERR response sent due to Non-CRC error in Host to Device Non-Data FIS
C00h	PM only - R_ERR response due to Host to Device Non-Data FIS because of Collision
C01h	PM only - Device to Host Register FISes (Signature)
C02h	PM only - Corrupt CRC propagation, Device to Host FISes

PHY Event Counter Size. As illustrated in Figure 15-11 on page 270, bits 14:12 of the event counter identifier specifies the size of the counter. The values are specified in 16-bit intervals up to 64 bits as listed below.

- 1h 16-bit counter
- 2h 32-bit counter
- 3h 48-bit counter
- 4h 64-bit counter

Vendor-Specific PHY Event Counters Identifiers. Bit 15 of the identifier (when set to one) indicates that the counter is vendor specific. Consequently, the vendor-specific identifier range can be from 8000h to FFFFh.

Local PM Port

Port 15 is dedicated as a local port that permits access to the HBA Port interface Phy Event Counters, along with a collection of general registers that are internal to the Port Multiplier. Figure 15-12 depicts the register groups accessed via port 15.

Figure 15-12: Register Groups within the PM that are Accessed Via Port 15

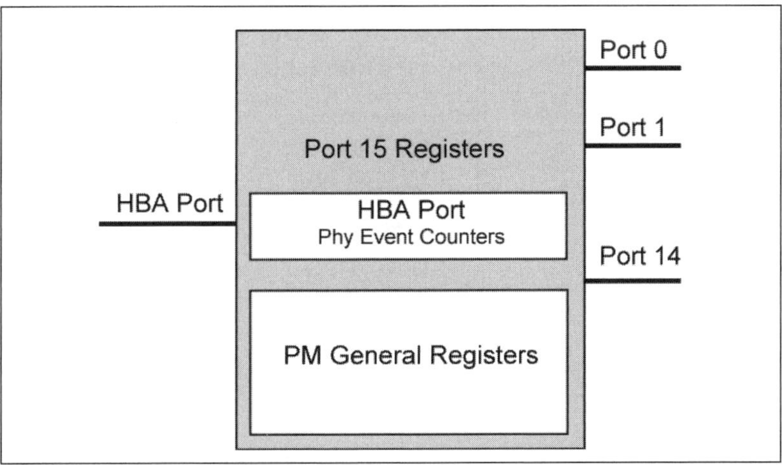

Local Port Registers

Local Port registers consist of 64k possible registers that are summarized in Table 15-2. Most of the registers are used to provide global capability, control and status information regarding the Device Ports. In addition the Local Port provides access to the Phy Event Counter Registers for the Host Port, which are mapped into GSCR[256-2303].

Table 15-2: Port Multiplier General SCRs

Register	O/M	F/V	Description
GSCR[0]	M	F	Product Identifier 31:16 Device ID specified by vendor 15:0 Vendor ID specified by the PCI-SIG
GSCR[1]	M	F	Revision Information 31:16 Reserved 15:8 Revision level of Port Multiplier 7:4 Reserved 3 1 = Supports PM spec 1.2 2 1 = Support PM spec 1.1 1 1 = Supports PM spec 1.0 0 Reserved
GSCR[2]	M	F	Port Information 31:4 Reserved 3:0 Number of exposed device ports
GSCR[3-31]	O	F	Reserved
GSCR[32]	M	 F V . . . V	Error Info: Bit map of SError register from all ports 31:15 Reserved 14 OR of selected bits of SError reg from Port 14 13 OR of selected bits of SError reg from Port 13 . . . 0 OR of selected bits of SError reg from Port 0
GSCR[33]	M	V	Error Information Bit Enable: Bit map corresponding to GSCR[32] 31:0 When set, corresponding bit in GSCR[32] is enabled and in use

Table 15-2: Port Multiplier General SCRs

Register	O/M	F/V	Description
GSCR[34]	O	V	Phy Event Counter Control: Bit map of ports used to individually reset (clear) all Phy Event counters of the selected PM port. Note that bit 0 enables the event counters of all PM ports. 31 Host port counter reset 30 Port 14 counter reset . . 16 Port 0 counter reset 15:1 Reserved 0 Phy event counters enabled when set
GSCR[35-63]	O	F	Reserved
GSCR[64]	M	F	PM Features Supported 31:5 Reserved 4 1 = Supports PHY event counters 3 1 = Supports asynchronous notification 2 1 = Supports dynamic SSC transmit 1 1 = Supports issuing PMREQ to the host 0 1 = Supports BIST
GSCR[65-95]	O	F	Reserved
GSCR[96]	M	 F V . . V	PM Features Enabled 31:4 Reserved 3 1 = Asynchronous notification enabled 2 1 = Dynamic SSC transmit is enabled 1 1 = Issuing PMREQ to the host is enabled 0 1 = BIST support is enabled
GSCR[97-127]	O	F	Reserved
GSCR[128-255]	O	X	Vendor Unique
GSCR[256-2303]	O	V	PHY Event Counter Regs for the host port
GSCR[2303-65535]	O	F	Reserved
M = Mandatory O = Optional F = Fixed (value doesn't change) V = Variable			

PM Initialization

Initialization begins in normal fashion with the HBA detecting Reset and beginning the link initialization process. PM-aware software must then verify presence of the PM and access the General PM registers to determine its capabilities and initialize each port.

PM Power-up State

During hardware initialization, the host will not detect the presence of a port multiplier. The HBA not knowing that a PM is attached will perform its normal initialization process. (See "Hardware Initialization" on page 305.) The PM will, upon detecting reset from the HBA, by default start the initialization of port zero. When initialization completes, the drive will return a Device-to-Host Register FIS that will be forwarded on to the HBA. This Register FIS contains the power-on signature of the drive. If no drive is connected to port zero, the HBA will detect a device attached, but no Register FIS will be returned.

Note that software that does not support Port Multipliers would only be able to access the drive attached to port zero. This mechanism also allows for booting from drive zero when using legacy software.

Detecting PM Presence

To discover whether a PM is attached to an HBA port, application software must initiate a soft reset and read the Register FIS that is returned from the device attached. The procedure for making the test is as follows:

- The host determines if communication is established on the host's Serial ATA port by checking the host's SStatus register.
- If a device is present, the host issues a software reset with the PM Port field set to the control port (15). This is accomplished by setting the SRST bit of the Shadow Control register, causing a Host-to-Device Register FIS to be delivered to the PM.
- The PM detects the reset and runs its internal diagnostics.
- Software clears the SRST bit of the Shadow Control Register triggering the HBA to send a second Host-to-Device Register FIS to the PM.
- At the conclusion of the reset, the PM will return a Register FIS. The FIS will have a signature associated with the device attached.

- If the signature matches the Port Multiplier Signature, the host knows that a Port Multiplier is attached.
- If the signature value does not match the PM signature, the host may proceeds with the normal initialization sequence for that device type.

Figure 15-13 illustrates the Register FIS signature that tells software that the device attached is a Port Multiplier.

Figure 15-13: Register FIS Signature of a Port Multiplier

Data	
Error	00h
Sector Count	01h
Sector Number	01h
Cylinder Low	69h
Cylinder High	96h
Device	00h
Status	

Configuring Device Ports

By default the Device ports associated with the PM are disabled (except port 0). This gives software the ability to enable each port individually, thereby staggering drive spinup.

Each device port on the PM must be configured. Host software performs the following procedure to a device attached to a PM Device Port:

1. Software uses a Write Port Multiplier command to enable the device by writing a value of 1h to the DET field of the port's PSCR[2] (SControl) register. This action causes a Phy Reset that triggers link initialization. Subsequently, software must clear the DET value to permit the initialization sequence to continue.

2. Software allows time for link initialization to complete and then uses a Read Port Multiplier command to check the DET value in the PSCR[0] (SStatus) register. If a device is present and communications has been established, the host checks the X bit (Device Present Change) in the PSCR[1] (SError) register and clears the bit, if set.
3. The Device Signature returned from the drive at the end of the initialization sequence is in some cases invalid. Consequently, software may choose to issue a software reset (via the Shadow Control register) to the device and check the signature returned at the completion of the software reset.

PM Read and Write Commands

The PM read and write commands provide access to both the port-specific and general registers within the PM. In addition to reading the contents of a selected register or writing a value to the register, other actions can also be performed. Details regarding each command and the actions that can be performed are described in the following sections.

PM Read Command

The Port Multiplier read command provides the ability to read from any register within the PM. This includes the Device Port registers, the Host Port register, and global registers that provide PM capability information, port control, and port status information. This section defines the command values, the values returned by the PM, and the values associated with PM Read command errors.

Command Setup

Figure 15-14 illustrates the Shadow register fields that must be setup prior to issuing a PM Register Read command. Only the Features and Feature (exp) registers and the Device register are used when setting up a PM Read command. The field definitions and use of these registers are specified in Table 15-3 on page 277.

Table 15-3: PM Read Command Input Fields and Definitions

Shadow Register Name	Field Name	Description
Feature Feature (exp)	PM Register [7:0] PM Register [15:8]	These fields selects the target PM register to be read.
Device	Port Number	Selects the PM port whose registers are to be read: 0 - Eh = Device Port Numbers Fh = Local Port
Device	RS2	Used only when accessing the Phy Event registers. 0 = Phy Event Counter Identifier returned 1 = Phy Event Counter value returned
Device	RS1	Used only when accessing the Phy Event registers. 0 = Normal register read 1 = Value returned and register cleared. Note that the register is not cleared until command completes successfully.

Figure 15-14: Input Values for PM Read Command

Register Name	7	6	5	4	3	2	1	0
Features	Port Multiplier Register Number [7:0]							
Features (exp)	Port Multiplier Register Number [15:8]							
Sector Count	Reserved							
Sector Count (exp)	Reserved							
LBA Low	Reserved							
LBA Low (exp)	Reserved							
LBA Middle	Reserved							
LBA Middle (exp)	Reserved							
LBA High	Reserved							
LBA High (exp)	Reserved							
Device	na	RS1	RS2	na	Port Number			
Command	E4h							

PM Register Read Command with Good Status

Figure 15-15 on page 278 illustrates the register contents and field names associated with a successful PM Read command. The selected register contents are returned in the PM Register Value fields. If the value returned is less than 64 bit wide then the upper bits not used must contain zeros. The values in the Status register will all be cleared except for the DRDY bit which must be set.

Figure 15-15: Read Values Returned to the Shadow Registers During PM Read Command

Register Name	7	6	5	4	3	2	1	0
Error	0							
Sector Count	PM Register Value [7:0]							
Sector Count (exp)	PM Register Value [39:32]							
LBA Low	PM Register Value [15:8]							
LBA Low (exp)	PM Register Value [47:40]							
LBA Middle	PM Register Value [23:16]							
LBA Middle (exp)	PM Register Value [55:48]							
LBA High	PM Register Value [31:24]							
LBA High (exp)	PM Register Value [63:56]							
Device	Reserved							
Status	BSY	DRDY=1	DF	na	DRQ	0	0	ERR=0

PM Register Read Command with Error Status

Figure 15-16 on page 279 illustrates the register definition when error are detected during execution of a PM Register Read command. The Status register must be set to indicate that an error has been detected, which also validates the contents of the Error register. The Error register bits are defined as:

- Port — Set to one if the Port specified is invalid
- Reg (Register) — Set to one if the Register specified is invalid
- ABRT (Abort) — indicates that an error has caused the command to abort.

Figure 15-16: Status Register Definition when Error is Detected

Register Name	7	6	5	4	3	2	1	0
Error						Abrt	Reg	Port
Sector Count	PM Register Value [7:0]							
Sector Count (exp)	PM Register Value [39:32]							
LBA Low	PM Register Value [15:8]							
LBA Low (exp)	PM Register Value [47:40]							
LBA Middle	PM Register Value [23:16]							
LBA Middle (exp)	PM Register Value [55:48]							
LBA High	PM Register Value [31:24]							
LBA High (exp)	PM Register Value [63:56]							
Device	Reserved							
Status	BSY	DRDY=1	DF	na	DRQ	0	0	ERR=1

PM Write Command

The Port Multiplier Write command provides the ability to write to any register within the PM that is not designated as read only. This includes the Device Port registers, the Host Port register, and General registers that provide PM port control and status information. This section defines the command values, the values returned by the PM, and the values associated with PM Read command errors.

Command Setup

Figure 15-17 illustrates the Shadow register fields that must be setup prior to issuing a PM Register Write command. All of the registers are used when setting up a PM Register Write command. The field definitions and use of these registers are specified in Table 15-4 on page 281.

Figure 15-17: PM Port Write Command Register Setup

Register Name	7	6	5	4	3	2	1	0
Features	Port Multiplier Register Number [7:0]							
Features (exp)	Port Multiplier Register Number [15:8]							
Sector Count	PM Register Value [7:0]							
Sector Count (exp)	PM Register Value [39:32]							
LBA Low	PM Register Value [15:8]							
LBA Low (exp)	PM Register Value [47:40]							
LBA Middle	PM Register Value [23:16]							
LBA Middle (exp)	PM Register Value [55:48]							
LBA High	PM Register Value [31:24]							
LBA High (exp)	PM Register Value [63:56]							
Device	na	RS1	na	na	Port Number			
Command	E8h							

Table 15-4: PM Read Command Input Fields and Definitions

Shadow Register Name	Field Name	Description
Feature Feature (exp)	PM Register [7:0] PM Register [15:8]	These fields select the target PM register to be written.
Sector Count Sector Count (exp) LBA Low LBA Low (exp) LBA Mid LBA Mid (exp) LBA High LBA High (exp)	Register Value [7:0] Register Value [39:32] Register Value [15:8] Register Value [47:40] Register Value [23:16] Register Value [55:48] Register Value [31:24] Register Value [63:56]	The value to be written into the selected register is loaded into the Register Value fields.
Device	Port Number	Selects the PM port whose registers are to be written: 0 - Eh = Device Port Numbers Fh = Local Port
Device	RS1	This bit must be set when writing to the Phy Event registers and is treated as "na" for all other register writes. If the RS1 bit is cleared during a Phy Event register write, error status will be returned.

PM Register Write Command with Good Status

Figure 15-18 illustrates the register definition when a PM Register Write command completes with error. The values in the Status register will all be cleared except for the DRDY bit which must be set.

Figure 15-18: Register Format and Value when Report Successful PM Register Write

Register Name	7	6	5	4	3	2	1	0
Error	0							
Sector Count	Reserved							
Sector Count (exp)	Reserved							
LBA Low	Reserved							
LBA Low (exp)	Reserved							
LBA Middle	Reserved							
LBA Middle (exp)	Reserved							
LBA High	Reserved							
LBA High (exp)	Reserved							
Device	Reserved							
Status	BSY	DRDY=1	DF	na	DRQ	0	0	ERR=0

PM Register Write Command with Error Status

Figure 15-19 on page 283 illustrates the register definition when error are detected during execution of a PM Register Read command. The Status register must be set to indicate that an error has been detected, which also validates the contents of the Error register. The Error register bits are defined as:

- Port — Set to one if the Port specified is invalid
- Reg (Register) — Set to one if the Register specified is invalid
- ABRT (Abort) — indicates that an error has caused the command to abort.

Figure 15-19: Error Status Fields Defined for PM Register Write Command

Register Name	7	6	5	4	3	2	1	0
Error	Reserved					Abrt	Reg	Port
Sector Count	Reserved							
Sector Count (exp)	Reserved							
LBA Low	Reserved							
LBA Low (exp)	Reserved							
LBA Middle	Reserved							
LBA Middle (exp)	Reserved							
LBA High	Reserved							
LBA High (exp)	Reserved							
Device	Reserved							
Status	BSY	DRDY=1	DF	na	DRQ	0	0	ERR=1

Hot Plug Support

Port Multipliers must also support Hot Plug capability. This solution requires that PMs support the requirements of the Hot Plug portion of the specification. Please refer to Chapter 21, on page 375, for details regarding Hot Plug operation.

Staggered Spinup/Drive Activity Indicator

Pin 11 of the SATA Power connector may be used to disable staggered drive spin-up or alternatively can be used as a drive activity signal to drive an LED to provide the user with comforting knowledge that the drive is active. These two features are mutually exclusive and the usage is determined at the host side. Pin 11 will either be connected to LED drive circuitry (pulled up) or will be grounded to indicate that staggered spin up is disabled.

Staggered Spinup

Designers of systems that include arrays of drives must consider the total power consumption during the power up sequence. If all drives spin up their media at the same time, the peak power consumption may exceed the supply limits. SATA drives are required to delay spin-up until they have completed their link initialization sequence and are ready to send and receive frames. This feature provides designers with a method to control when each drive spins up by staggering reset delivery to each drive. Please refer to Chapter 18, on page 303, for details regarding the reset and initialization sequence. Note that the specification does not define a specific mechanism for controlling when each drive receives reset. Instead, it is left as a vendor-specific solution.

Drives may optionally support the staggered spin-up disable feature. This feature allows drives to sample pin 11 of the SATA power connector to determine whether it should spin up its media immediately when power is applied. For example, pin 11 is normally grounded in a laptop or desktop system where immediate spin up is important, and is normally be pulled high in a server system where a staggered spin-up is important. When pin 11 is pulled up it can be used as a drive activity output signal following initialization.

Drive Activity

SATA drives may optionally support the READY LED signal (pin 11 in the power portion of the connector). This pin is designed to be an open-drain or open-collector transmitter used to pull down the cathode of an externally visible LED. This same pin may optionally be used by SATA drives as a staggered spin-up disable input.

16 Port Selectors

Previous Chapter

Port Multipliers provide a fan-out capability; whereby, up to 15 ports can be accessed via a single HBA port. This capability is useful in large rack mount implementations. The previous chapter detailed the hardware and software required to support the Port Multiplier solution.

This Chapter

A common goal of server implementations is non-stop operation. This typically includes some type of redundant capability that allows for failures to be managed without shutting down the entire system. Port Selectors provide access to SATA drives from two separate sources, thereby permitting a fail-over solution. This chapter discusses the Port Selector implementation and associated protocols.

The Next Chapter

Large arrays of drives are typically housed in cabinets called drive enclosures. Managing the environment within an enclosure such as temperature, fan speed, power, etc., is critical to the health of the drive array. SCSI systems have long incorporated hardware and software to help manage drive enclosures. Two SCSI standards are supported by SATA II. This chapter highlights the support that has been added by SATA to ease the implementation of enclosure services.

Overview

Port Selectors provide a method for connecting drives to one of two different host ports. The goal of this mechanism is to provide a way for system designers to create redundant implementations. The typical implementation would likely employ a RAID solution in combination with the Port Selector capability. Figure 16-1 on page 288 illustrates the Port Selector implementation; whereby, a standard SATA drive can be accessed by separate HBA ports or Systems.

Figure 16-1: Port Selector

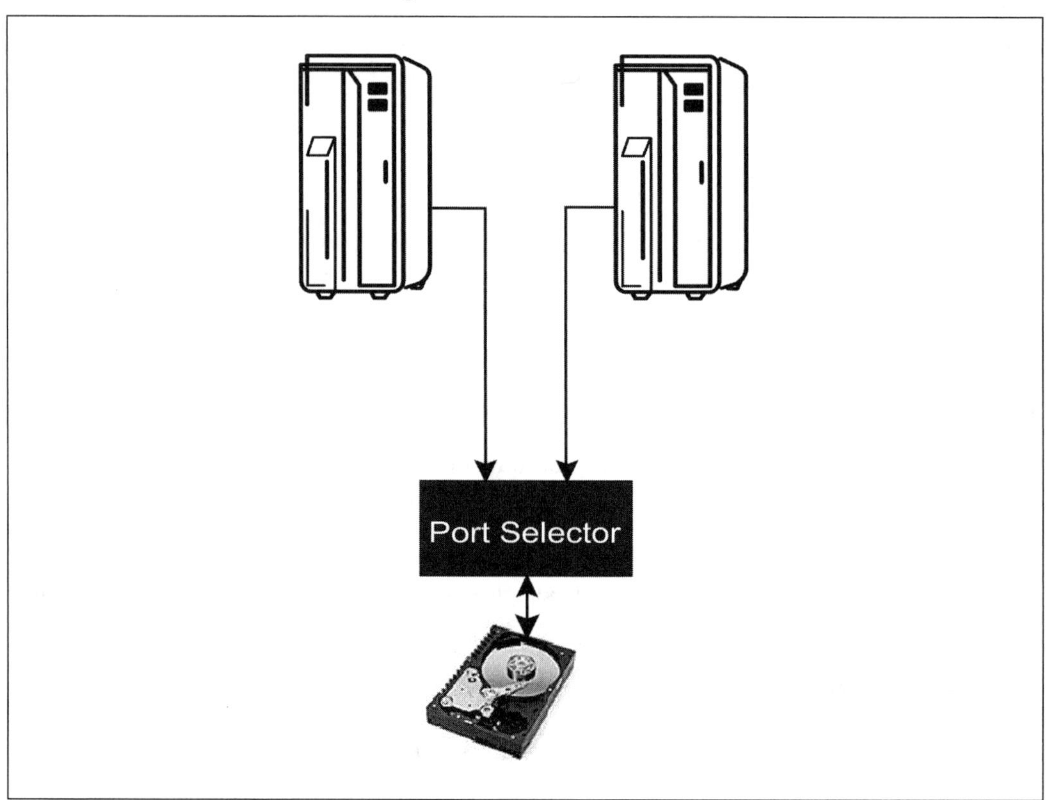

The overall design of the Port Selector was based on key design requirements including:

- No modifications to Serial ATA 1.0a compliant devices required
- No hardware modification required for Host Adapters (Some optional features do require modification)
- No new primitives needed
- No new FIS types needed
- Full-function link and transport layers not needed
- Support for only two host connections
- Only one port can be active at a time
- Port selectors cannot be cascaded
- New software required to manage fail-over

Port Selector Functions

Port selectors are switches that select which host port will be permitted access to the drive, and they also repeat frames between the HBA and drive. The block diagram in Figure 16-2 illustrates the primary element of a Port Selector. The following list describes the primary functions associated with a Port Selector:

- Port Selectors participate in the OOB (Out-Of-Band) sequence to establish link communications with both the active HBA and the attached drive.
- The HBA and Port Selector may optionally support a mechanism to detect the presence of a Port Selector based on OOB signaling.
- A Port Selector must support a mechanism that permits software to change the active port. The specification defines a protocol-based method of port selection and also permits side-band solutions (defined as implementation-specific).
- Port Selectors repeat frame and OOB traffic between the active host port and the drive, and in doing so must satisfy all of the protocol and timing requirements.

Figure 16-2: Simplified Block Diagram of a Port Selector

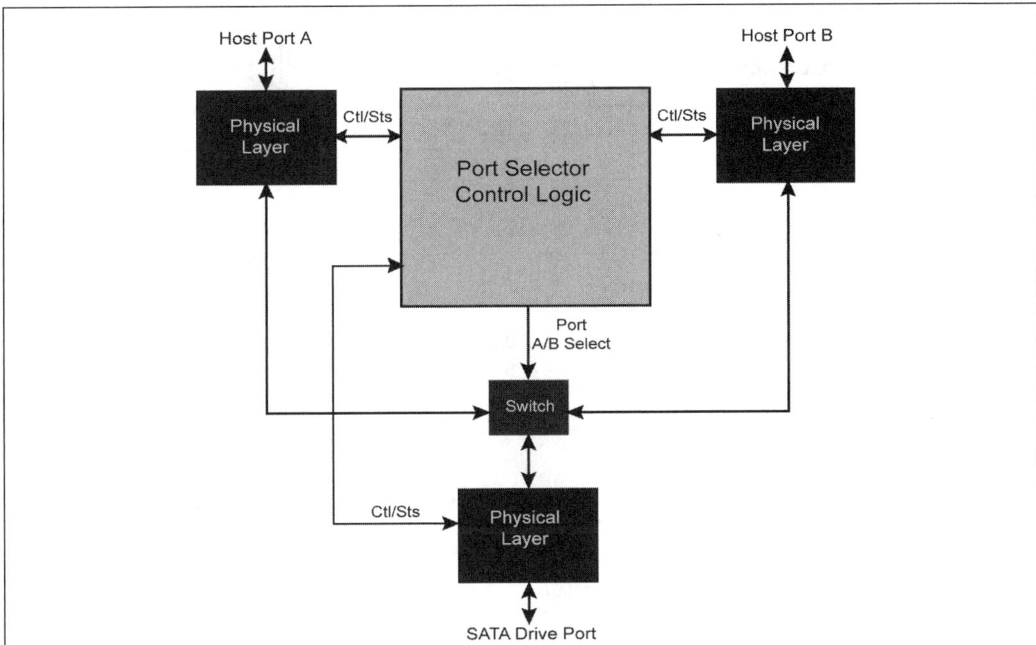

Detecting Port Selector Presence

Detecting whether a Port Selector is present is an optional capability and was defined for Port Selectors that support protocol-based port selection. Port Selectors may identify themselves via a variation of the standard OOB signaling sequence during link initialization. Normally the OOB sequence proceeds as illustrated in Figure 16-3; however, to identify itself as a Port Selector, a COMWAKE is inserted in front of the normal COMINIT after detecting COMRESET from the host (Figure 16-4). HBAs that are designed to detect the presence of Port Selectors will recognize this variation and update the SError register (Diag field) to indicate that a Port Selector is present. (See Figure 16-5 on page 291.)

Figure 16-3: Normal OOB Sequence

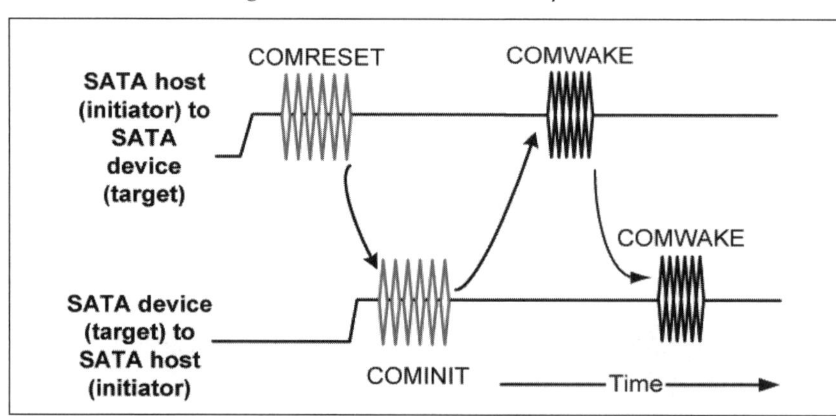

Figure 16-4: OOB Sequence Used for Port Selector Presence Detection

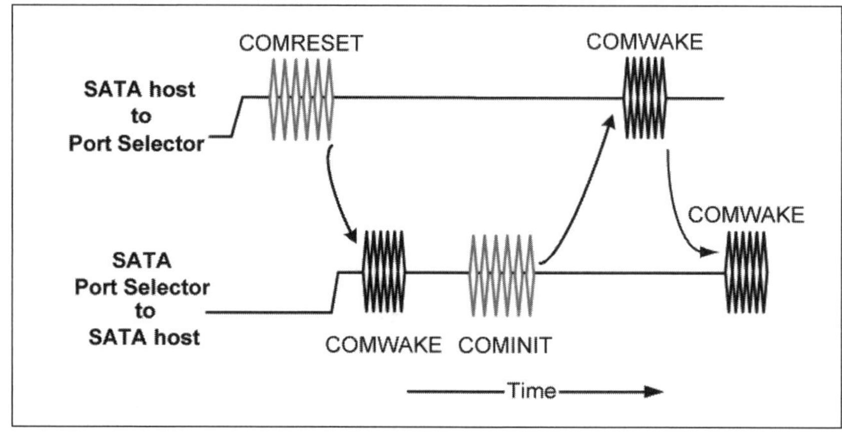

Figure 16-5: Port Selector Presence Bit

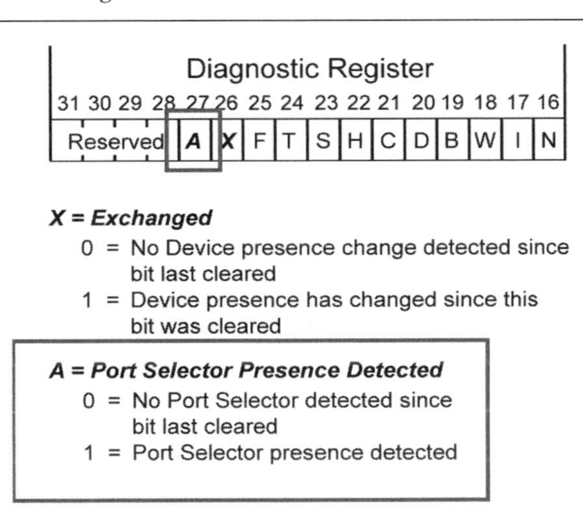

Port Selection

Two methods of port selection are defined for software to dynamically switch host ports. These methods include:

- Sideband signaling — this method requires that the Port Selector implement a pin that can be used to signal the Port Selector that the active port is to be switched. The specification considers this method to be implementation specific and provides a suggested implementation.
- Protocol-based switching — the specification defines a specific OOB (Out-OF-Band) signaling protocol that is sent to the inactive host port to notify the Port Multiplier to switch the active port.

One of these two methods must be employed but neither one is specifically required to be implemented.

The Active Port at Startup

Only one of the two host ports is permitted to be active at a one time. Thus, when the system is initially powered, one of the two host ports must in some way be designated as the active port. The active port may be pre-determined, selected by software, or may be selected dynamically.

The Pre-Selected Active Port

In some cases the active port is pre-selected (e.g., a strapping option or other hardware defined method). The specification does not define any particular solution. However, it is expected that this method of selecting the default active port would be typical of Port Selectors that use sideband port switching.

Dynamic Active Port Selection

Port Selectors that support the protocol-based method of port selection are not permitted to pre-select the active port at power up. In these implementations, the first COMRESET or COMWAKE received by one of the host ports selects that port as the default active port.

OOB Protocol Switching

Protocol-based port switching requires that software triggers the delivery of five COMRESET events with specified time intervals between them. The COMRESET bursts and the intervals are illustrated in Figure 16-6 on page 293. Note that the table specifies the duration (nominally 2.0ms) between the beginning of the first COMRESET and the beginning of the second COMRESET, called T1. Similarly, the second timing interval (nominally 8.0ms) is the time between the beginning of the second and third COMRESET bursts, called T2. The T1/T2 sequence is repeated twice follow by the fifth COMRESET burst, after which the port switch can occur.

This mechanism was specified such that no modification of the HBA is required to generate the OOB switching protocol. The sequence can be created using the SConrol register (refer to Figure 15-10 on page 269 for reference) as follows:

1. Place the HBA port into the offline state by setting the SControl Register's DET field to a value of 4h.
2. Put the HBA's Phy into the Reset state by setting the SControl Register's DET field to a value of 1h. (Note: because the Phy is offline no action can be

taken at this point).

3. Place the HBA port into the Online state (by setting the SControl Register's DET field to a value of 0), which triggers the delivery of COMREST and wait for 20 microseconds to allow for COMRESET to complete.
4. Once again place the HBA port into the offline state by setting the SControl Register's DET field to a value of 4h, and wait for the T1 time to elapse (1.975 milliseconds).
5. Repeat steps 2 and 3.
6. Place the HBA port into the offline state by setting the SControl Register's DET field to a value of 4h, and wait for the T2 time to elapse (7.975 milliseconds).
7. Repeat steps 2 through 6; thereby repeating the T1/T2 sequence.
8. Send one more COMRESET as specified in steps 2.
9. Place the HBA port into the offline state by setting the SControl Register's DET field to a value of 4h, thus ending the sequence.

Figure 16-6: OOB Sequence for Switching the Active Host Port

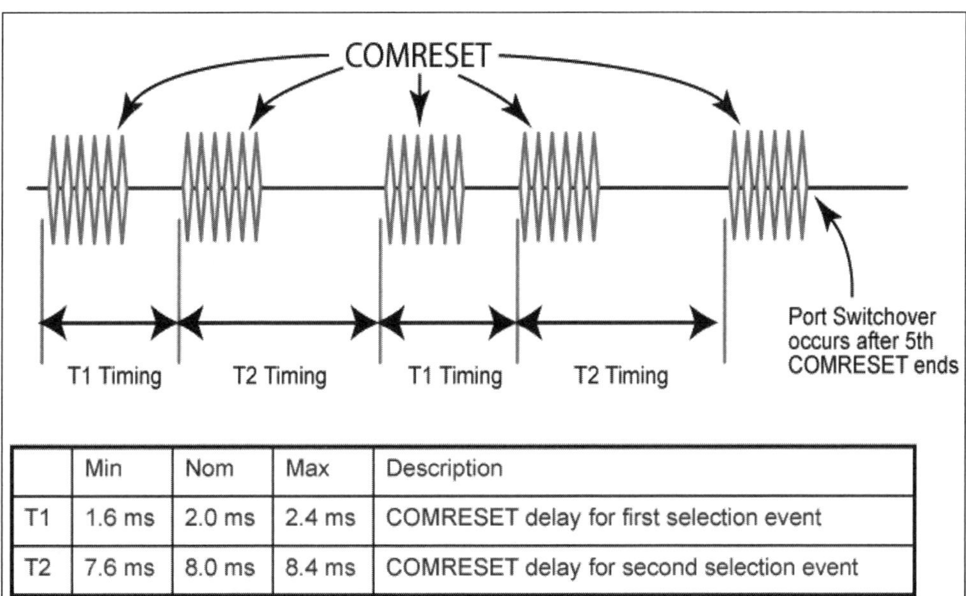

	Min	Nom	Max	Description
T1	1.6 ms	2.0 ms	2.4 ms	COMRESET delay for first selection event
T2	7.6 ms	8.0 ms	8.4 ms	COMRESET delay for second selection event

Side-Band Signal Switching

The definition of a side-band method of switching the active port is simply that the mechanism is "outside of the Serial ATA protocol." This of course leaves considerable latitude for implementing a solution. As mentioned in the introduction to this section, the solution might simply consist of a single signal used to select the active port.

17 Enclosure Services

Previous Chapter

A common goal of server implementations is non-stop operation. This typically includes some type of redundant capability that allows for failures to be managed without shutting down the entire system. Port Selectors provide access to SATA drives from two separate sources, thereby permitting a fail-over solution. The previous chapter discussed the Port Selector implementation and associated protocols.

This Chapter

Large arrays of drives are typically housed in cabinets called drive enclosures. Managing the environment within an enclosure such as temperature, fan speed, power, etc., is critical to the health of the drive array. SCSI systems have long incorporated hardware and software to help manage drive enclosures. The SCSI standards are supported by SATA II. This chapter highlights the support that has been added to ease the implementation of enclosure services.

The Next Chapter

The next chapter describes the hardware link initialization process. To begin communicating, link neighbors must go through a sequence of steps after reset to recognize that a proper device type is attached and is working at a supported speed. The process is relatively simple compared to other serial protocols because the devices have defined roles: one acts as the host/initiator while the other behaves as the target device. New device types added with the SATA II definition have necessitated some new initialization protocols as well.

Overview

This chapter provides an overview of the primary features associated with the enclosure management features included in the SATA II specification. This chapter does not detail the protocols and additional information defined by the two industry standards that the SATA II specification supports. These two standards (listed below) provide support for managing drive enclosures:

- SAF-TE (SCSI Accessed Fault-Tolerant Enclosures)
- SES (SCSI Enclosure Services)

These SCSI specifications define the services for managing storage subsystems, and can also be applied to SATA Storage subsystem. The elements involved in Storage enclosure management are illustrated in Figure 17-1. The specific implementation illustrated shows a portion of the Storage Enclosure function embedded within a Port Multiplier and accessible by the HBA via port 2. The Storage Enclosure elements include:

SEP (Storage Enclosure Processor) — This device interfaces with various sensors and indicators within a storage enclosure subsystem and responds to enclosure service commands. The SEP may support both the SAF_TE and SES protocols. The required interface to the SEP is the I2C bus, over which the commands and data are passed.

SEMB (Storage Enclosure Management Bridge) — This device is the interface (bridge) between the SATA host and the Storage Enclosure Processor (SEP). SEP commands are delivered via the standard SATA programming interface and sent to the SEMB. The SEMB converts the SATA commands into I^2C packets that are then delivered to the SEP.

Figure 17-1: Enclosure Management Elements

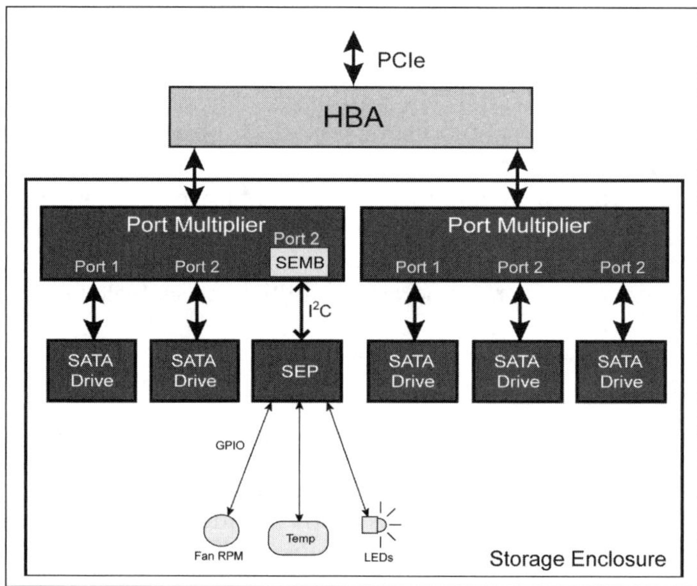

Enclosure Services

This section briefly describes the two industry standards that provide service for managing storage enclosures, and discusses the relationship between them.

SAF-TE (SCSI Attached Fault-Tolerant Enclosure)

The SAF-TE (SCSI Attached Fault-Tolerant Enclosure) was implemented as an inexpensive SCSI target that provided enclosure control and monitoring. The target is called an SEP (SCSI Enclosure Processor) and only acts in a target role. It does not include asynchronous notification of events and requires periodic polling to detect changes. It allows for access to enclosure information such as number and status of fans, power supplies, sensors, etc.

The problem with the SAF-TE specification was that it was not owned by any existing standards body and consequently was not extensible. In the mid 1990s the SAF-TE working group agreed to merge the architecture with the SCSI ESI (Enclosure Services Interface) definition to create a single standard called SES.

SES (SCSI Enclosure Services)

The SES (SCSI Enclosure Services) command set is used to communicate with a separate enclosure service processor intended to be implemented in high-end enclosures for sensing and managing resources that are relevant to an enclosure, such as fans, temperature sensors, and LEDs. The SES command set defines a series of Diagnostic Pages to allow devices to communicate with the enclosure processor over SCSI. The SCSI commands for this purpose are SEND DIAGNOSTIC and RECEIVE DIAGNOSTIC RESULTS.

SATA Storage Enclosure Services Commands

SATA defines a standard interface for software to pass enclosure commands to SEMB devices via the Shadow Registers. The SEMB passes these commands to the SEP via the I^2C interface. Software may use either the SAF-TE or SES command protocol to communicate with the SEP. Because these protocols are in widespread use, implementers can leverage existing software and hardware.

SATA II defines the new Read SEP/Write SEP commands to originate the enclosure management commands. Figure 17-2 on page 298 illustrates the Shadow register field definitions when performing both the Read and Write SEP commands.

Figure 17-2: Format and Field Definitions for SEP Commands

Register Name	7	6	5	4	3	2	1	0
Features	SEP_CMD							
Features (exp)	Reserved							
Sector Count	LEN							
Sector Count (exp)	Reserved							
LBA Low	CMD_TYPE (80h or 82h)							
LBA Low (exp)	Reserved							
LBA Middle	Reserved							
LBA Middle (exp)	Reserved							
LBA High	Reserved							
LBA High (exp)	Reserved							
Device	Reserved			0	Reserved			
Command	SEP_ATTN (67h)							

Read SEP Command

Register Name	7	6	5	4	3	2	1	0
Features	SEP_CMD							
Features (exp)	Reserved							
Sector Count	LEN							
Sector Count (exp)	Reserved							
LBA Low	CMD_TYPE (00h or 02h)							
LBA Low (exp)	Reserved							
LBA Middle	Reserved							
LBA Middle (exp)	Reserved							
LBA High	Reserved							
LBA High (exp)	Reserved							
Device	Reserved			0	Reserved			
Command	SEP_ATTN (67h)							

Write SEP Command

Table 17-1 lists and defines the fields associated with the SEP commands.

Table 17-1: Register Content and Descriptions for SEP Commands (Reserved Regs not shown)

Shadow Reg	Field Name	Description
Features	SEP_CMD	SEP Command — Defines parameters related to the SES and SAF_TE command protocol.
Sector Count	LEN	Length — defines the length of the data payload
LBA Low	CMD_TYPE	Command Type — encoding as follows: Upper nibble bits (7:4): 0 = SEP to Host Data Transfer 8 = Host to SEP Data Transfer Lower nibble bits (3:0): 0 = SAF-TE protocol used 2 = SES protocol used
Device	NA	Value specified is listed in Figure 17-2, above.
Command	SEP_ATTN	SEP Attention Command (67h) — indicates that the SEMB that a SEP command is being issued

Topologies

The only topology presented in this chapter is illustrated in Figure 17-1 on page 296, where the SEMB resides within a Port Multiplier and the SEP is attached to an I^2C port provided by the Port Multiplier. The specification provides examples of several other topologies that simply illustrate that the location of the SEMB and SEP can vary widely depending on the storage application.

Part Five

Physical Layer Details

18 SATA Initialization

The Previous Chapter

The last chapter highlighted the support that has been added to ease the implementation of enclosure services. Large arrays of drives are typically housed in cabinets called drive enclosures. Managing the environment within an enclosure such as temperature, fan speed, power, etc., is critical to the health of the drive array. SCSI systems have long incorporated hardware and software to help manage drive enclosures. The SCSI standards are supported by SATA II.

This Chapter

This chapter describes the hardware link initialization process. To begin communicating, link neighbors must go through a sequence of steps after reset to recognize that a proper device type is attached and is working at a supported speed. The process is relatively simple compared to other serial protocols because the devices have defined roles: one acts as the host/initiator while the other behaves as the target device. New device types added with the SATA II definition have necessitated some new initialization protocols as well.

The Next Chapter

The next chapter describes the physical layer logic and the electrical characteristics of the SATA interface. The chapter specifically discusses the electrical characteristics of the differential transmitter and receiver used to transmit the bits across the wire. It also covers the changes in the electrical signaling as different interface environments are used.

Introduction

After reset, the hardware in devices on both ends of a link automatically begins the process of detecting whether another device is present and at what speed the interface can run. This initialization takes place using OOB (out of band) signaling even before the devices are able to recognize dwords as information from the transmitter. OOB uses the same signal path as every other bit from the transmitter, meaning they are not side-band signals, but occurs before the link is trained. Once the link is trained, application software reads the signature returned by the target device in the first Device-to-Host Register FIS and determines the device type. Software can then write configuration information into the device registers and set up the desired parameters.

The overall process associated with link initialization is illustrated in the diagram in Figure 18-1. OOB signaling involves bursts of signal activity followed by periods of idle time. The timing of these sequences vary and have given names that in some cases designate whether the HBA or the SATA Device is sending a particular sequence. During the sequence the HBA and SATA Device engage in the handshake sequence shown below. Details regarding the process are discussed later in this chapter.

Figure 18-1: Overview of Link Initialization Sequence

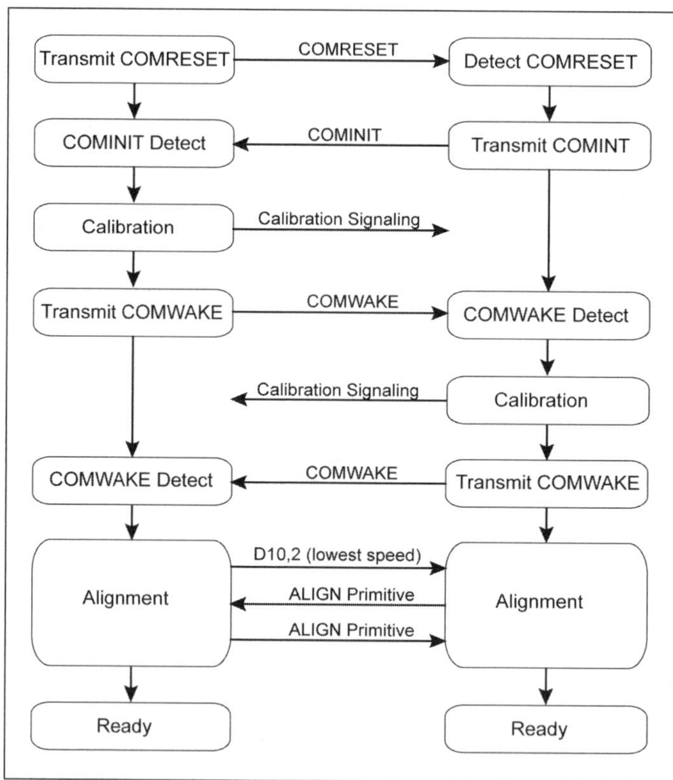

The definitions and protocols associated with initialization are defined by the Phy Initialization state machine. This state machine supports Port Multipliers, Hot Plug, and speed negotiation. Authors of the standard did not use the conventional bubble diagrams to describe the state machine because they are difficult to modify and update regularly. Instead, they chose a table format, which is precise and easy to update but unfortunately not very good at giving an overall understanding of the behavior. They also chose later not to convert the tables into bubble diagrams so as to avoid the risk of introducing errors. Rather than attempting to redraw the state diagrams here and take the same risk of introducing errors in the details, the author believes the reader will be better served by a discussion of the overall behavior of both host and target devices as they go through the initialization process.

Hardware Initialization

General

SATA host and target devices have a fixed role in hardware initialization because they only expect to be attached to each other. This makes the process simpler than it would be if there were other configurations possible. There are two basic steps of hardware initialization:

1. Detect the presence of an attached device.
2. Negotiate the highest transmission rate supported by both devices.

The first step is accomplished using OOB signaling, in which both nodes send a pattern and then wait for a response. If the proper response is seen, the second step is to negotiate the transfer speed on the link by sending a steady stream of patterns from both nodes. Modifying and observing this pattern allows devices to negotiate a common speed, recover the transmitter's clock, and achieve dword synchronization. At that point devices can begin to detect valid symbols and meaningful dwords in the data stream.

The Physical Plant

The SATA standard provides a suggested Phy implementation, referred to as the physical plant, and this is recreated in Figure 18-2 on page 307. This diagram is described more fully in the SATA 1.0a standard, but it's useful to discuss several of the definitions here in the context of initialization.

Physical Plant Signal Definitions

Align Source — refers to the ALIGN patterns sent for initialization during OOB, and for clock compensation after initialization. The receiver has squelch logic in the analog front end to detect the two OOB patterns. For more on these patterns, see "OOB (Out of Band) Signaling" on page 307.

PhyReset — causes the phy to initialize itself, after which a host will send COMRESET and a target device will send COMINIT.

PHYRDY — indicates that the phy has succeeded in establishing communications. This means that OOB and speed negotiation worked properly, and Dword synchronization has been achieved.

SPDSEL — a vendor-specific signal instructing the phy to negotiate the speed or to set a particular speed.

SPDMODE — a vendor-specific signal indicating the current speed setting.

COMMA — indicates that a K28.5 value was detected in the incoming data stream, identifying the beginning of both a 10-bit symbol and a 40-bit primitive.

COMINIT/COMRESET and COMWAKE — outputs of the squelch logic in the analog front end that report the detection of these OOB patterns to the state machines and higher level logic.

Slumber/Partial — Link power management states that reflect the degree of power savings.

ANELB — Test feature that places the near end (local) transceiver into to a silicon loopback where the transmitter is looped back to the receiver.

AFELB — Test feature that places a far end (remote) transceiver into a silicon loop back mode where the receiver is looped back to the transmitter. Two version of this loopback exist: one that is retimed and one that is not.

Figure 18-2: Physical Layer Detailed Block Diagram

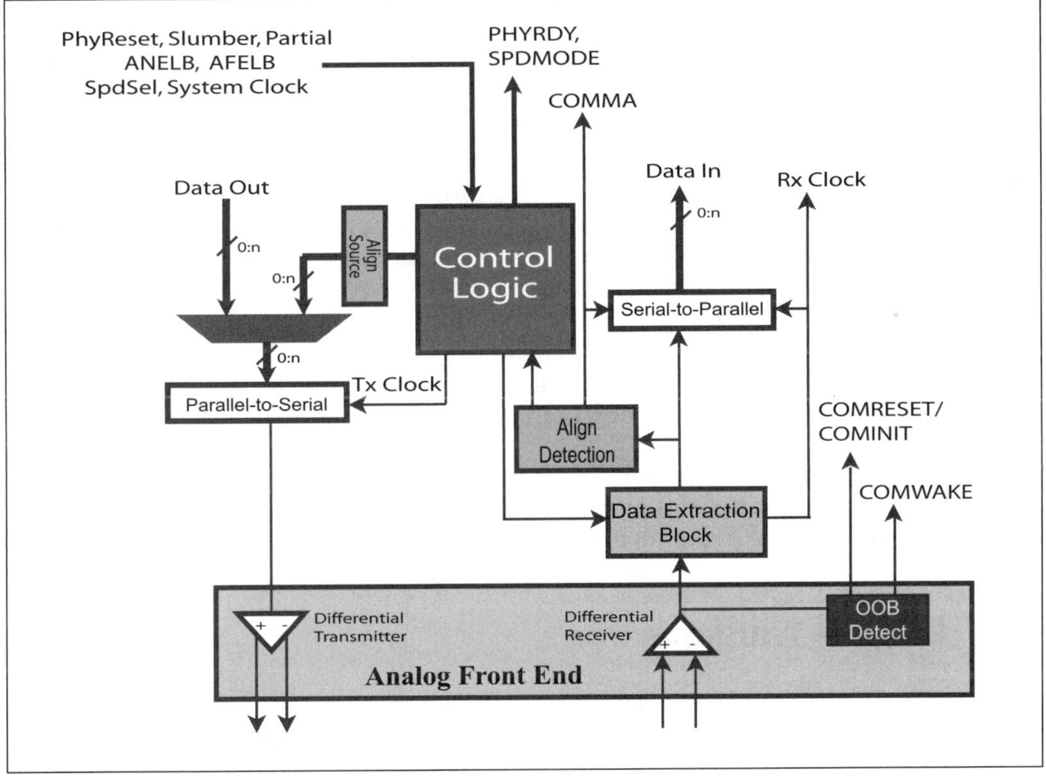

OOB (Out of Band) Signaling

Before the link has been trained devices cannot recognize bit patterns in the signal and are unable to communicate. Early in the SATA definition the designers considered a simple OOB that used steady-state signals: TX+ high meant one thing and low meant another, for example. However, when the AC-coupled solution was added later, that method no longer worked because the coupling capacitor blocked that DC signal, so a "chirp" method was developed instead. To accomplish this the transmitter alternates sending repeated ALIGN primitives (the chirp) followed by periods of no activity. Even though bit patterns can't be understood, a receiver can still detect that there is activity on the link by using a squelch-detect circuit. The timing of the pattern of activity and idle conveys the needed information.

Special Note Regarding OOB Timing and Terms

OOB timing is specified in terms of Unit intervals (UI). An OOB UI is perhaps easier to understand by noting that 10 bits represent one byte, so 160 bits or Unit Intervals equate to 16 bytes or 4 dwords. For the quiet time (idle time), 480 UI translates to 12 transmitted dwords. Since OOB is intended to establish communications, the detection process is fairly relaxed. For example, as discussed later, the receiver does not have to verify the proper burst time and only measures the idle times. The receiver also only needs to see 4 of the 6 required bursts to detect the pattern. The receiver cannot yet understand the content of what is being sent so, in a sense, it doesn't matter what the transmitter does as long as it shows the proper burst/idle sequence. However, to eliminate one variable, the standard writers decided that the pattern to be sent would be the ALIGN primitive. Since a primitive is defined as one dword, that means the ALIGN will be sent four times in an OOB burst of 160 UI.

Also note that the Gen 1 UI and OOB UI are the same duration.With Gen 2 and higher speeds, the OOB UI remains the same as Gen 1, but of course the UI changes with the higher transmission rate of the selected interface speed.

OOB — Transmission

SATA OOB only uses two patterns: COMWAKE and COMINT/COMRESET. COMINIT and COMRESET are actually the same pattern; the different terms used for the pattern depends on the direction of transfer, as described in "OOB Protocol Sequence" on page 311. In short, the HBA sends COMRESET and a drive sends COMINIT. The timing for these patterns is listed in Table 18-1 and illustrated in Figure 18-3. From the table it can be readily seen that the burst time is the same for both patterns and only the idle and negation times differ. To send one of the patterns, the transmitter repeats the pattern of burst and idle six times and follows that with the negation quiet time on the link.

Note that the values listed in Table 18-1 were calculated based on the tolerance allowed for the OOB UI which ranges from 646.67ps - 686.67ps specified in the 1.0a version of the specification.

Table 18-1: SATA OOB Transmission Timing

OOB Signal	Burst Time	Idle Time	Negation Time
COMWAKE	160 OOB UI (103.47 - 109.87ns)	160 OOBI (103.47 - 109.87ns)	280 OOBI (181.07- 192.60 ns)
COMINIT/ COMRESET	160 OOBI (103.47 - 109.87ns)	480 OOBI (310.40 - 329.60 ns)	800 OOBI (517.33 - 549.34 ns)

Figure 18-3: OOB Transmission Timing

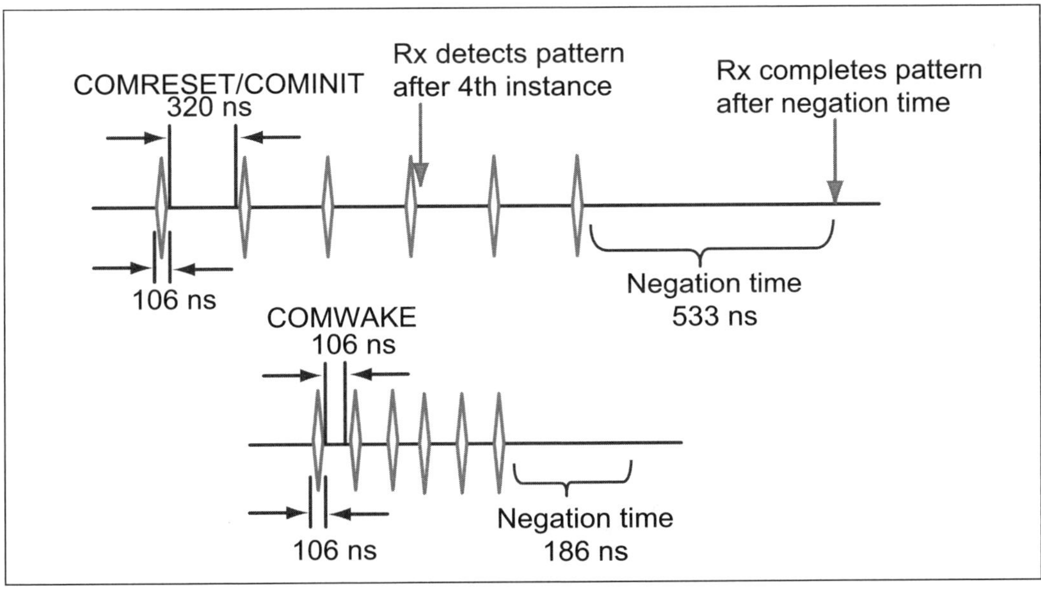

OOB — Reception

Since the OOB patterns are the first thing a device sees after a reset, there is no expectation that it can recognize any data. In fact, the requirements for what it must be able to understand are fairly relaxed, so as to increase the likelihood of successful detection. As shown in Figure 18-3, the receiver logic detects an OOB pattern when it sees just four idle-burst pairs with the proper timing, and then it completes the pattern when the proper negation time is seen sometime after that. The receiver's limits for the idle times are shown in Table 18-2 and the negation detect times are given in Table 18-3.

Table 18-2: SATA Receiver OOB Idle Detection Timing

OOB Signal	May Detect	Shall Detect	Shall Not Detect
COMWAKE	55 to 175 ns	101.3 to 112 ns	outside the range 55 to 175 ns
COMINIT/ COMRESET	175 to 525 ns	304 to 336 ns	outside the range 175 to 525 ns

Table 18-3: SATA Receiver OOB Negation Detection Timing

OOB Signal	Shall Detect
COMWAKE	> 175 ns
COMINIT/ COMRESET	> 525 ns

The detection of either OOB pattern is indicated by an output from the squelch logic of the receiver. For example, the COMWAKE detector output would be asserted when 4 bursts with the proper timing have been received. It would be deasserted if a burst with invalid timing occurs or when the pattern is properly negated.

OOB Protocol Sequence

The OOB initialization sequence is shown in Figure 18-4, where it can be seen that the host and target device exchange the COMRESET/COMINIT pattern to start. As was mentioned earlier, COMRESET and COMINIT both use the same pattern; the difference in meaning depends on which device is receiving them. When received by the target device the pattern is called COMRESET and resets the target; when received by the host it's called COMINIT and indicates the target's readiness for the next step.

Avoiding Confusion

It might seem that there could be confusion about the time when both devices are ready after power-up, but such is not the case. While it's being reset, the host repeatedly sends COMRESET. Once released from reset, it stops sending COMRESET and begins to listen for COMINIT coming from the target. If the target sent COMINIT while the host was still in reset and unprepared to respond, the host will still be sending COMRESET, which will reset the target and cause it to send COMINIT again, so the order of events will end up being the same. On the other hand, if the host becomes active first and finishes sending COMRESET before the target is ready then the target won't have seen it. But when the target comes out of reset and sends COMINIT, the host will recognize that the target is ready and move on to the next step. As an aside here, it's interesting to point out that a COMRESET can be used to reset a device that is not communicating.

Figure 18-4: Initial SATA OOB Sequence

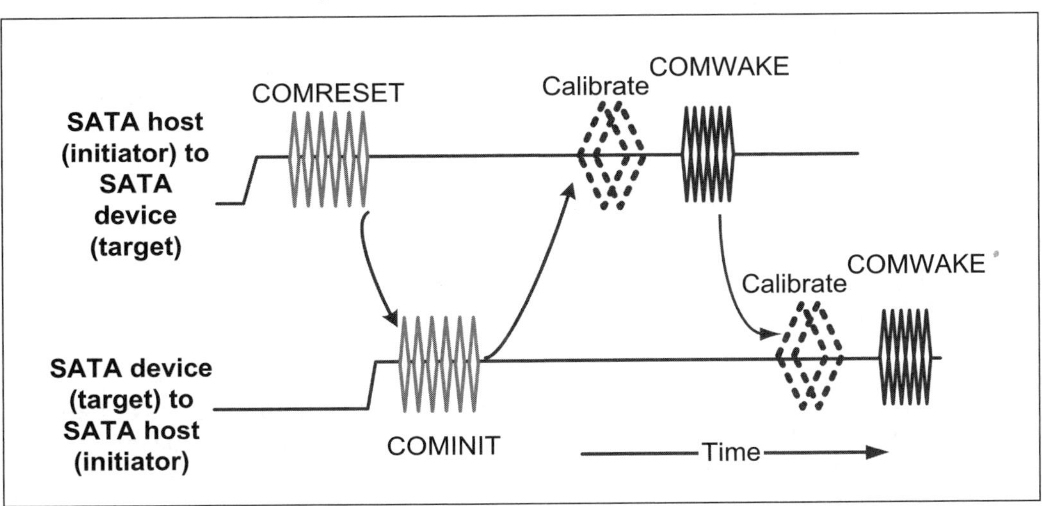

The target only sends COMINIT once, after which it waits for COMWAKE to be returned from the host. When the host sees COMINIT it goes to the calibration state, where After that, the host sends COMWAKE and waits for it to be returned from the target.

Device Detection

When COMRESET is delivered by the HBA, the control logic must clear its internal "Device Detect" bit. When the HBA detects a COMINIT from the attached device, the "Device Detect" bit must be set to indicate a device is attached. This indication is reflected in the SStatus register.

Optional Calibration

Once the host succeeds in receiving COMINIT, its next step is to optionally calibrate for the signaling environment and allow its transceivers to make adjustments. The standard suggests that this might be done with a TDR (time-domain reflectometer) test, in which a step is transmitted on the wire and the reflections on the signal are observed. One advantage of this approach is that, since the host must do its calibration process first, it can't depend on the receiver being calibrated and thus can't use it as a reference. Using the TDR approach essentially uses the connecting cable as the reference and avoids that problem. The purpose is to let the host make adjustments to achieve the best signal quality.

This adjustment might be as simple as selecting from among different internal termination resistor values to get a good impedance match. The differential impedance is specified as 100 ohms +/- 15%, so a range of values is possible on the line. The transmitter and receiver terminations must closely match that value to avoid discontinuities and achieve the best signal integrity. The termination could consist of external resistors, but it's cheaper to put the resistors on the transceiver chip itself. However, it's difficult to reliably create integrated resistors of a specific value, so vendors will sometimes build in a few different resistor pairs and allow one of them to be chosen that best matches the environment. Calibration might also mean setting signal compensation parameters like the amount of signal de-emphasis to apply to the signal. Any activity the host chooses to do on the link is legal, so long as it doesn't appear to the target like OOB signals. It should be noted here that, although calibration is allowed, it isn't required and consequently wasn't commonly used by devices at the time of this writing.

When the host is satisfied with the results of the calibration process (if any), it sends COMWAKE and waits for COMWAKE to be returned by the target. Now the target has an opportunity to run its own optional calibration routine. When it's finished, it sends COMWAKE back to the host and both devices recognize that this stage is complete and they can move on to the speed negotiation step.

OOB Problems

Of course, if the OOB patterns are not correctly seen by a device, communication over the link will not be possible. This kind of problem could be caused by a link neighbor that is not a SATA device or by one that is broken and not responding properly. Interestingly, there are no time-out conditions for the OOB sequence in the Phy. If a device is present the Phy should detect it within 10ms, since the standard states that a COMINIT must be returned by the target within 10ms of a COMRESET, but there are no other timing constraints given. If no device is present there is no time-out mechanism and the Phy can stay in the reset state indefinitely unless software changes it. This condition would be detected in software by reading the SStatus register and observing that no device is detected.

Speed Negotiation

After the initial OOB patterns are sent and the device recognizes that the proper host or target is attached, the next step is to negotiate the speed of the link. This is accomplished by sending a pattern at the desired rate to the neighbor and listening for the response.

Roles During Speed Negotiation

The target device is in control of this process and the host acts as the responder. Once the target has sent COMWAKE, it begins speed negotiation by sending ALIGN primitives at the fastest rate it can support. If the host can support that speed, it will respond with ALIGNs coming back. If no ALIGNs are received from the host during the rate window, the target will shift down to the next lower speed and try the process again. This is repeated until a mutually-agreeable speed is found or the process times out.

After the host has both sent and received COMWAKE, its part in the negotiation is to send the D10.2 value repeatedly while it waits to recognize incoming ALIGN primitives at its receiver. Once incoming ALIGNs are detected, ALIGNs are sent back to the target as a confirmation that the current link speed is working, and that completes the negotiation.

D10.2 Used as a "Dial Tone"

As a side note for historical background, the D10.2 symbol was evidently chosen for the host to send during this initialization time because it provides an alternating 1s and 0s pattern on the wire and therefore appears like an input clock to the target device. Evidently, one reason for doing this is that when SATA was first introduced it had to compete on cost with parallel ATA. Unlike parallel designs, serial transports need an accurate clock (+/- 350 ppm for SATA), and that requires the use of a relatively expensive crystal oscillator. Parallel ATA drives did not have this requirement and were able to use a less accurate and less expensive ceramic clock. The cost difference was considered sufficient to conclude that SATA targets should also use the ceramic oscillators as a base clock and then use a "clock" from the host to establish a more accurate clock version during the link reset sequence. Even though this incoming clock only runs at the slowest rate supported by the host, the host was not cost-constrained and therefore would have a crystal oscillator. That means it could provide a more accurate reference until the data stream was established. For a modern design today it seems unlikely this would be necessary, as clock sources have become less expensive since the first SATA standard was written, but it's interesting to understand this background.

Speed Negotiation Example

In the example shown in Figure 18-5 on page 315, the SATA target first tries the highest rate it can support. In this example, the host does not support that rate and continues to send D10.2 as an indication that it is still working but has not yet seen a recognizable pattern from the target. Each rate window takes 54.6µs, and the target sends the number of ALIGNs that can be sent during that time, meaning there will be more ALIGNs at higher rates and fewer at slower rates. For example, 1.5 Gbps for 54.6 µs equals 81,900 bits or 8,190 encoded characters, and dividing that by 4 gives 2048 dwords. At a higher rate like 3.0 Gbps, the number of ALIGNs that could be sent would therefore be twice that many, or 4096.

Figure 18-5: SATA Speed Negotiation Example

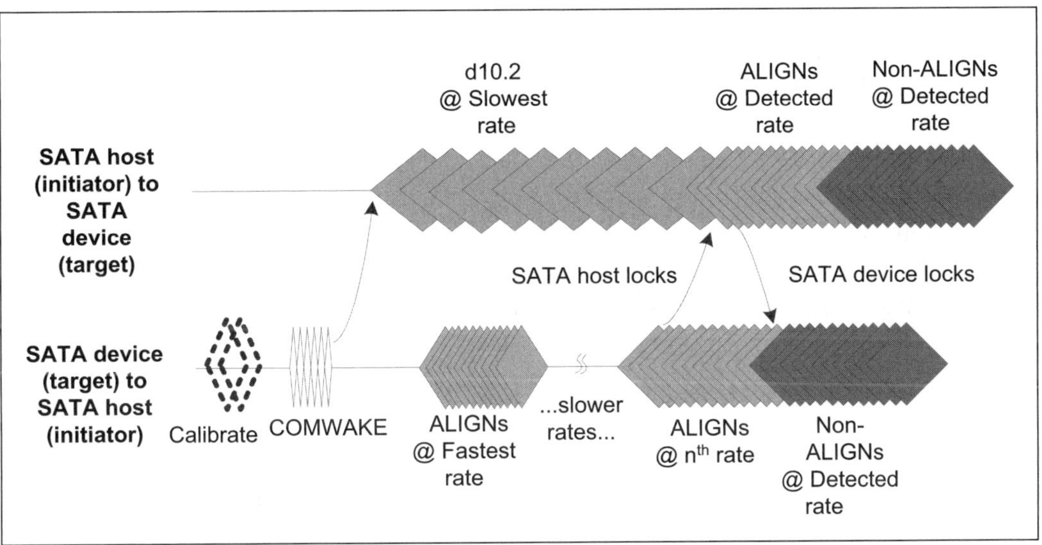

If the target doesn't see the correct response from the host within the time-out period, the target switches to the next lower speed it supports and repeats the process. Eventually a compatible speed is attempted and the host does recognize the ALIGN primitives, and it indicates this by sending ALIGNs back to the target. The target then begins to send SYNC primitive, indicating the idle condition to the host, who also sends SYNC and that completes the negotiation. One advantage of always starting at the highest rate and working down is that future devices will not have to maintain support for the slower speeds, since the slower speeds will not be required to operate in order to complete the negotiation.

Asynchronous Signal Recovery

When communication is lost between the Host and SATA device (i.e., no signals are received), a phy that supports asynchronous signal recovery will attempt to re-establish communication. Phys that support asynchronous signal recovery implement use a variable named the RetryInterval. This parameter determines the rate at which signal recovery polling is attempted, and cannot be shorter than 10 ms. This condition can occur when the signal connector is unplugged during normal operation and then replaced while power is still present.

The 1.0a specification did not define any state transitions associated with losing link synchronization. The only action specified is that the PhyRdy signal will be deasserted.

Host Phy Asynchronous Signal Recovery

Host Phy Sends COMRESET. When the host phy is in the Ready state and the receiver no longer detects a signal, the host will attempt to recover communications by sending COMRESET. The phy then awaits receipt of COMINIT from the device. If COMINIT is not received when the RetryInterval elapses, the phy transitions back to the Reset state causing COMRESET to be sent again. This process continues until communications is re-established, if at all.

Unsolicited COMINIT. In some cases, the host phy may receive an unsolicited COMINIT; that is, COMINIT is send by the device even though the host has done nothing to trigger the device to send it. Upon detecting an unsolicited COMIINIT in any state, except for the AwaitCOMINIT state, the host phy transitions to the Reset state. This of course, causes the host phy to deliver a COMRESET.

Upon detecting an unsolicited COMINIT the shadow Status register value must be set to 7Fh, while the other shadow command block registers are set to FFh. A solicited COMINIT (i.e., one in response to the COMRESET) causes the host to set the shadow Status register value to FFh or 80h. This indicates that a device is attached.

Note: A host that does not support asynchronous signal recovery, and that detects an unsolicited COMINIT simply awaits the end of COMINIT and sends a COMWAKE and attempts to continue the initialization sequence.

Device Phy Asynchronous Signal Recovery

SATA devices also attempt signal recovery by transitioning to the Error state when the received signal disappears. Once in the Error state the device phy will transition to the Reset state after the RetryInterval elapses. When in the Reset state the Drive sends a COMINIT and awaits a response from the Host.

Software Initialization

After hardware initialization has completed, the next step is software initialization. The preparation for this process occurs after the Phy reset sequence, when the target device runs diagnostic tests and reports the results to the host with its first Device-to-Host Register FIS. Software can read the contents of the shadow registers in the host at that point and see what is referred to as the device's power-on signature (Figure 18-6 on page 317 shows an example). One thing the signature indicates is the type of the device and whether it supports the basic ATA protocol or the ATAPI protocol (ATA Packetized Interface — used to encode SCSI commands into the data portion of a SATA FIS). Another example of information found in the signature is whether the device is a System Enclosure Management Bridge (SEMB).

Figure 18-6: Example Power-On Signature - Good Status

Command Register
(Non-ATAPI device)

Register	Value
Sector Count	01h
Sector Number	01h
Cylinder Low	00h
Cylinder High	00h
Device/Head	00h
Error	01h
Status	00h-70h*

* Bits 4 to 6 are device specific

To finish initializing the device, system software uses the Identify Device and Set Features commands to configure the device. For clarification the Device Configuration Command Overlay feature is intended to be a one time, factory only, configuration that allows a system manufacturer to reduce the supported feature set and/or capacity on low-end drive models, while using the same base HDD. The overlay changes persist across power cycles.

Changes for SATA II

The second generation of SATA introduced two new device types to facilitate the use of SATA in the server market, where scalability and reliability are important. Two devices (Port Multipliers and Port Selectors) were devised that act as intermediaries between the host and target device to help achieve those goals. Both introduce a few variations in the initialization process as discussed in this section.

Port Multiplier

A Port Multiplier (illustrated in Figure 18-7) allows one host port to access up to 15 target devices (ports 0 through 14). This requires the use of a previously reserved 4-bit field in the FIS header to indicate which port is being selected for service by the host.

Figure 18-7: Port Multiplier

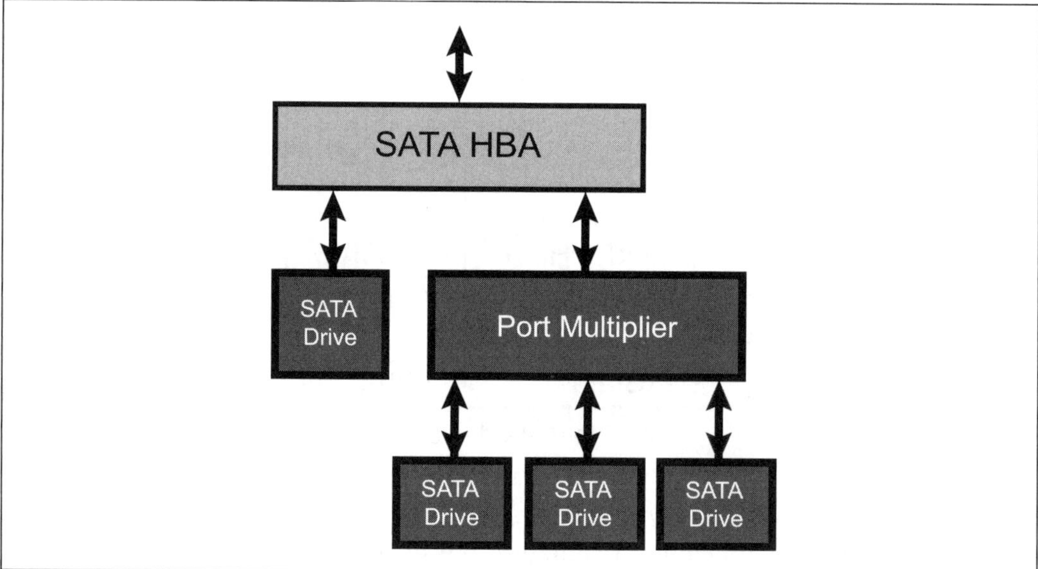

PM Default Active Port

During normal hardware initialization the host cannot detect the presence of a port multiplier (PM). Instead, the host will be communicating by default with whichever device is attached to port zero of the PM. Consequently, the Device-to-Host register FIS that occurs once the link is working returns the power-on signature from the device attached to port 0 (since PMs cannot be cascaded, that device will never itself be a PM).

PM Discovery

To discover whether a PM exists on a Phy, application software must initiate a soft reset by sending a Host-to-Device Register FIS with the SRST bit set and the port value set to 15, which is the internal target of the PM (see Figure 18-8). This would then be followed by another Host-to-Device Register FIS with the SRST bit cleared. The resulting reset will cause the internal target of the PM to run its diagnostics and return a Device-to-Host Register FIS with the power-on signature of the Port Multiplier, which is shown in Figure 18-9 on page 320. Software can look for this signature and then read the General Status and Control Register GSCR[2] to learn the number of ports.

Enabling PM Ports

Software enables each port by setting the DET field in the device Port Status and Control register PSCR[2] using a Write Port Multiplier command. After allowing for communication to be established, the host would read the SStatus register PSCR[0] using the Read Port Multiplier command. If a device is present on that port, the host can read the SError register PSCR[1] of the port and clear the X bit showing that device presence has changed. Finally, sending a soft reset to the port will cause the device to return its signature. If the signature is valid, the software can proceed with the normal initialization for that device.

Figure 18-8: Port Multiplier Registers

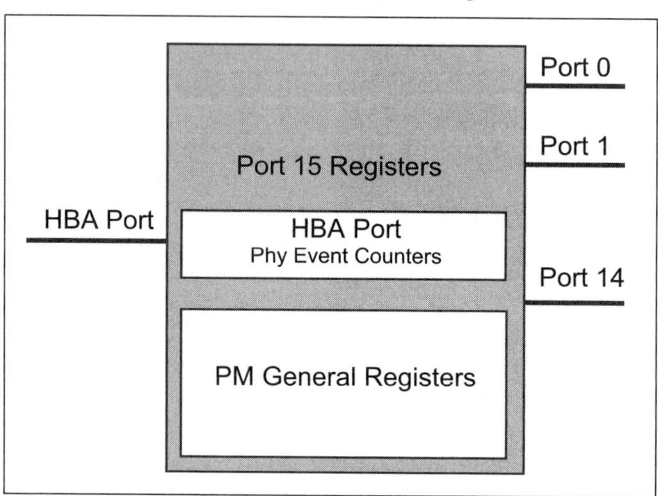

Figure 18-9: Port Multiplier Power-On Signature

Data	
Error	00h
Sector Count	01h
Sector Number	01h
Cylinder Low	69h
Cylinder High	96h
Device	00h
Status	

Port Selector

A Port Selector allows two hosts to access one device and thus provide a fail-over mechanism to prevent a single point of failure (see the example in Figure 18-11 on page 322). Since two hosts may attempt to access the Port Selector after reset, the Port Selector only completes the initialization with the first host to start the process and ignores the latecomer. Later, if software chooses to change from one host to the other, there are two possible ways to do it. First, a side-band signal can be used, which could be as simple as a single line that is either high or low to select one port or the other. The second option is to use an in-band method, which is also called protocol-based port selection. To use this method, the new master executes a sequence of five COMRESET patterns with a particular timing, as shown in Figure 18-10. The device will detect a reset after the fourth COMRESET, and the fifth one, with the proper timing (see Table 18-4), indicates that the host generating this pattern is now going to be the active host.

Figure 18-10: Port Selection In-Band Timing

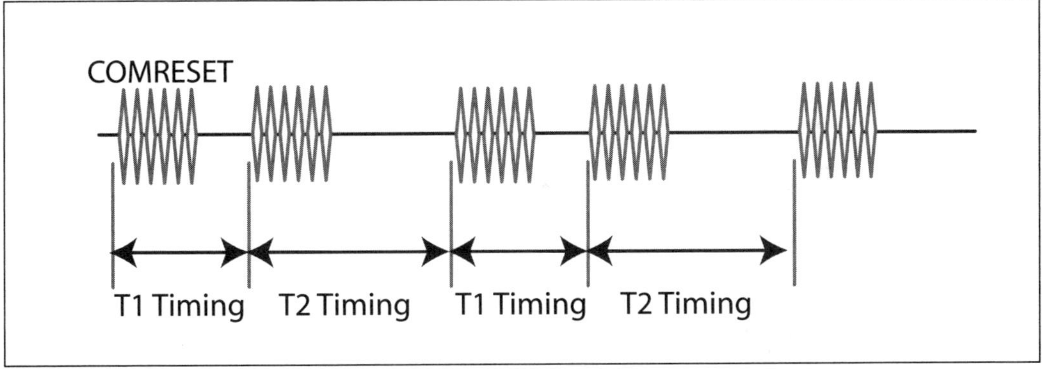

Table 18-4: Timing of Port Selector Switch Using In-Band Signaling

	Min	Nom	Max	Units	Comment
T1	1.6	2.0	2.4	ms	Timing of first event of the selection sequence
T2	7.6	8.0	8.4	ms	Timing of second event in selection sequence

Figure 18-11 illustrates an example Port Selector implementation. Port Selector may be implemented in a variety of ways. The key aspects of Port Selectors are summarized below:

1. A Port Selector is normally transparent to the host and device, so a host can't be certain whether a Port Selector is installed or not.
2. A Port Selector using the protocol-based selection can be designed to identify itself during the OOB reset sequence. This is optional.
3. A system using Port Selector sideband switching is presumed to have a separate way to detect the Port Selector, but the solution is implementation specific.

Figure 18-11: Port Selector Example

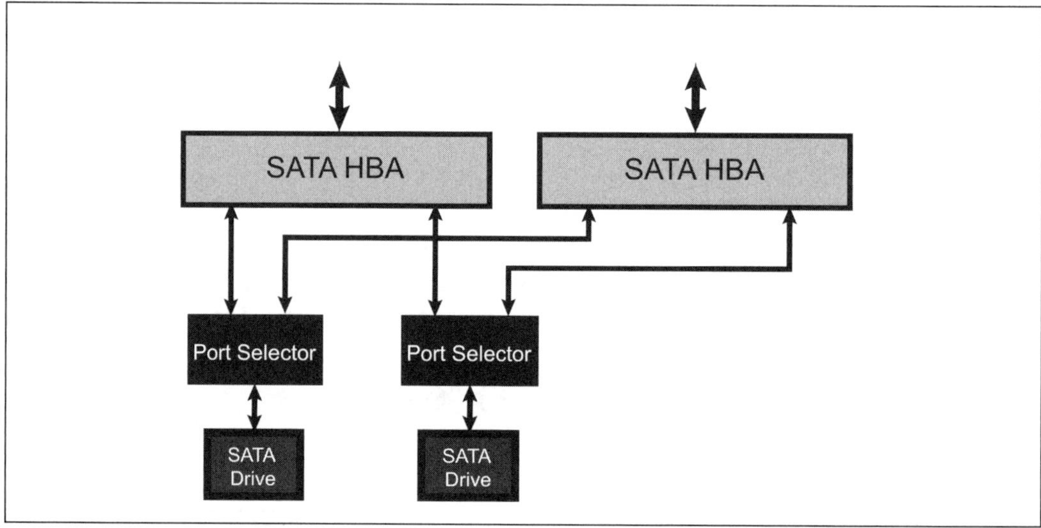

If a Port Selector the optional host detection feature, can be detected by the host during the OOB reset sequence. These Port Selectors return COMWAKE to the HBA in response to detecting COMRESET, rather than the normal COMINIT, as shown in Figure 18-12 on page 323. The hardware only needs to know that this is not an error condition and that it should set the Port Selector Presence Detected bit in the Diagnostics register (the upper 16 bits of the SError register - see Figure 18-13).

Figure 18-12: Port Selector Detection OOB Sequence

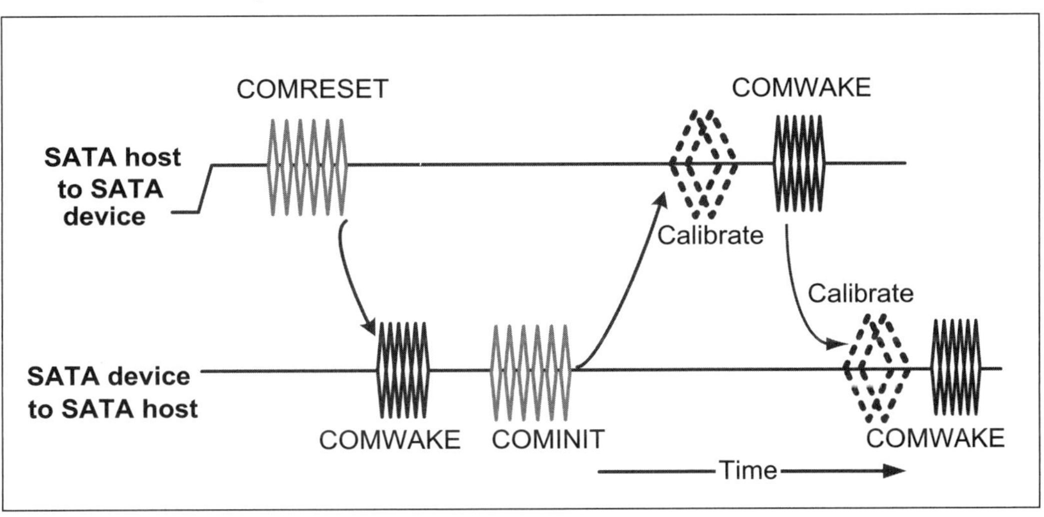

Figure 18-13: SATA Diagnostic Registers

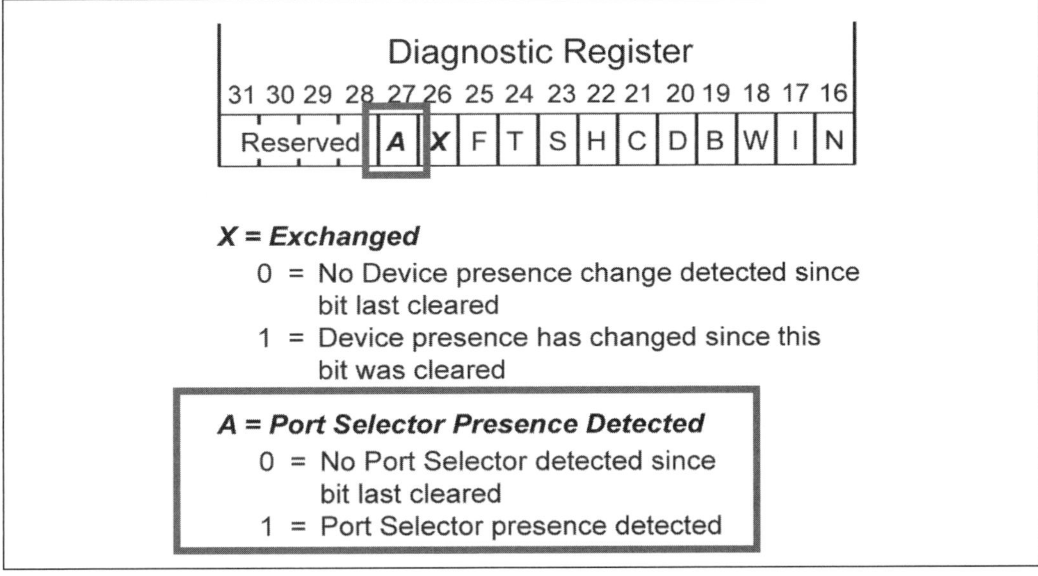

19 Physical Layer

The Previous Chapter

The previous chapter described the hardware link initialization process. To begin communicating, link neighbors must go through a sequence of steps after reset to recognize that a proper device type is attached and is working at a supported speed. The process is relatively simple compared to other serial protocols because the devices have defined roles: one acts as the host/initiator while the other behaves as the target device. New device types added with the SATA II definition have necessitated some new initialization protocols as well.

This Chapter

This chapter describes the physical layer logic and the electrical characteristics of the SATA interface. The chapter specifically discusses the electrical characteristics of the differential transmitter and receiver used to transmit the bits across the wire. It also covers the changes in the electrical signaling as different interface environments are used. This includes internal cabling, external cabling, backplane environments.

The Next Chapter

The next chapter covers the various form factors, cables and connectors that are described in the SATA specifications. The SATA II specification added several new cable and connector types in support of SATA-based server implementations.

Introduction

After all the work has been done to create a FIS for transmission, the Physical Layer, sometimes called just the Phy, is the final piece of logic that this packet will pass through. This layer resides hierarchically at the bottom of the SATA layered architecture (see Figure 19-1 on page 326) and can be described in two parts. The first part represents the logic needed to prepare the 10-bit encoded data for transmission or to recover it properly at the receiver. The second part consists of the high-speed electrical interface and is made up of the differential transmitter, receiver, and transmission line.

Figure 19-1: Physical Layer

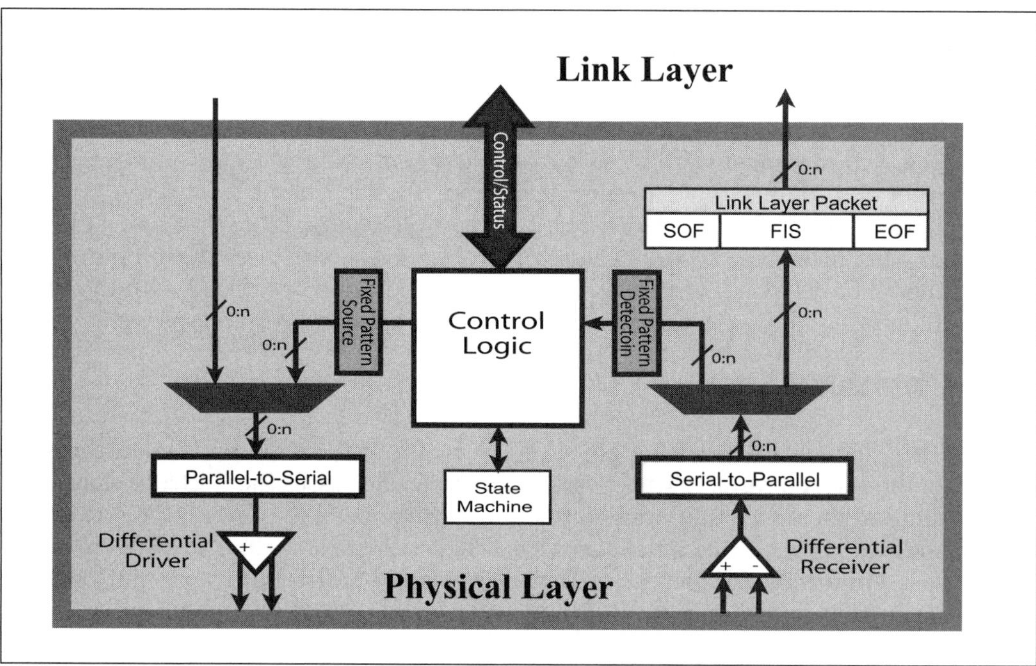

Logical Interface

It should be noted that the SATA standard does not require a particular implementation, specifying instead the behavior that must be carried out by each layer. The responsibilities of the logical part of the physical layer on the transmit side include:

- Serialize the data for transmission
- Insert primitives for clock management
- Initialize the link using OOB (described in the Initialization chapter)

The responsibilities on the receive side are:

- Data and Clock recovery
- Manage the elasticity buffer for clock skew compensation
- Detect OOB signals and speed negotiation primitives (described in the Initialization chapter)
- Deserialize the bitstream
- Detect the K28.5 Comma value and align the parallel output with it
- Optionally support power management modes

Transmit Side

Each SATA interface consists of a transmit side and a receive side, as shown in Figure 19-2. For normal transmission, the Physical Layer takes the output from the Link layer and it's expected that many vendors will implement the transmit path as four bytes wide, as shown here, to simplify the design. This would also mean that the internal clock would only need to be 1/40th of the transmit clock, so if the serial data rate is 3.0 Gb/s, then the internal dword rate would be 75 MHz.

Figure 19-2: Physical Layer Transmit Block Diagram

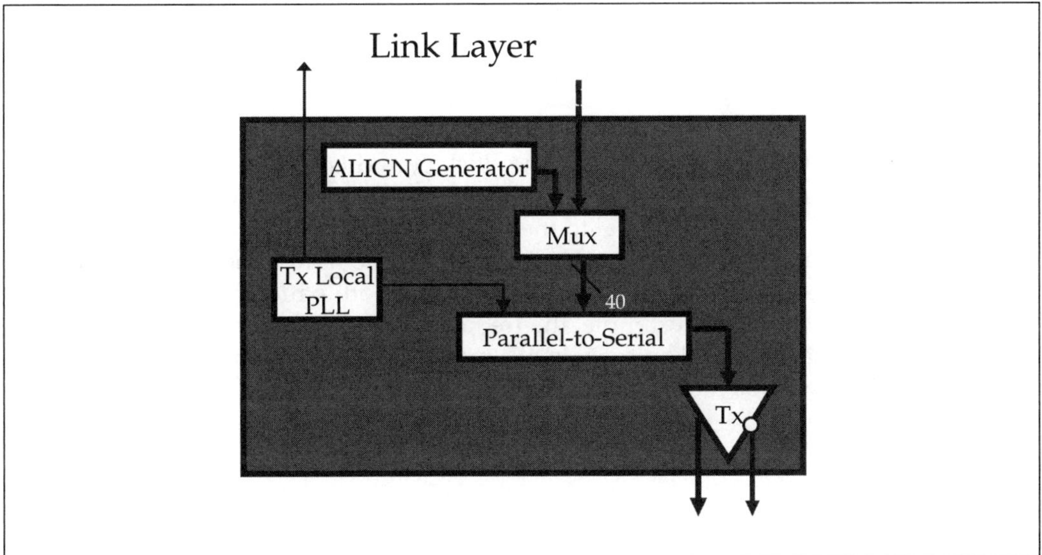

Selecting Frames or OOB Primitives

A mux is shown on the transmit side because ALIGN primitives will be needed for initialization before the normal data path will be useful. The Physical Layer generates and injects these primitives for the OOB sequence and link initialization automatically after the device is reset. The output from the mux passes to the serializing buffer, which takes in a dword and shifts the bits out serially to the differential transmitter based on the transmit clock frequency that was selected during speed negotiation on the link.

Reducing EMI by Using SSC

The data is clocked out of the serializer using the internal transmit clock running at either 1.5 GHz or 3.0 GHz. The clocks must be accurate to within +/- 350 ppm, for a total maximum separation of 700 ppm. The use of SSC (Spread Spectrum Clocking) adds another 5000 ppm, resulting in a total difference between the clocks that could be as high as 5,700ppm. SSC varies the clock over a range of frequencies rather than keeping it fixed as a pure reference clock, for the purpose of reducing EMI (electro-magnetic interference). For that reason, it is commonly used in devices that operate in consumer environments where stricter EMI requirements must be met. While varying the operating frequency does not actually reduce the overall radiated energy of the device, it spreads the energy across a wider range of frequencies and therefore reduces the peak output that may be seen at any one given frequency. Since governmental emissions tests like those used in the U.S. test for energy thresholds at certain frequencies, the goal is to ensure that none of the frequencies has so much radiated energy that it would fail the threshold test. SATA is intended for use in consumer environments and so SSC is optional for SATA transmitters, while SATA receivers must tolerate it.

The SATA standard specifies that the clock period is never allowed to go below the minimum value specified, meaning the frequency shift can only be frequencies that are less than or equal to the nominal rate (referred to as "down-spreading"). The method of frequency modulation to be used is not specified, but an example is shown in the standard using a sawtooth pattern as reproduced here in Figure 19-3. In that example, the frequency ranges from its nominal value to 0.5% less than that and back again at a rate between 30 and 33 KHz (modulation period between 30 and 33ns).

Figure 19-3: Sawtooth Wave SSC Frequency Modulation

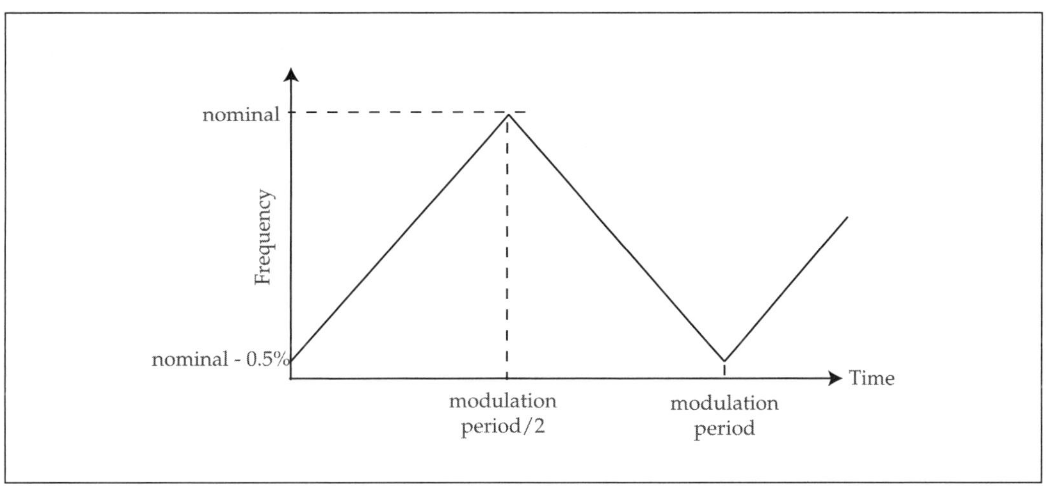

Figure 19-4: Results of SSC in Frequency Analysis

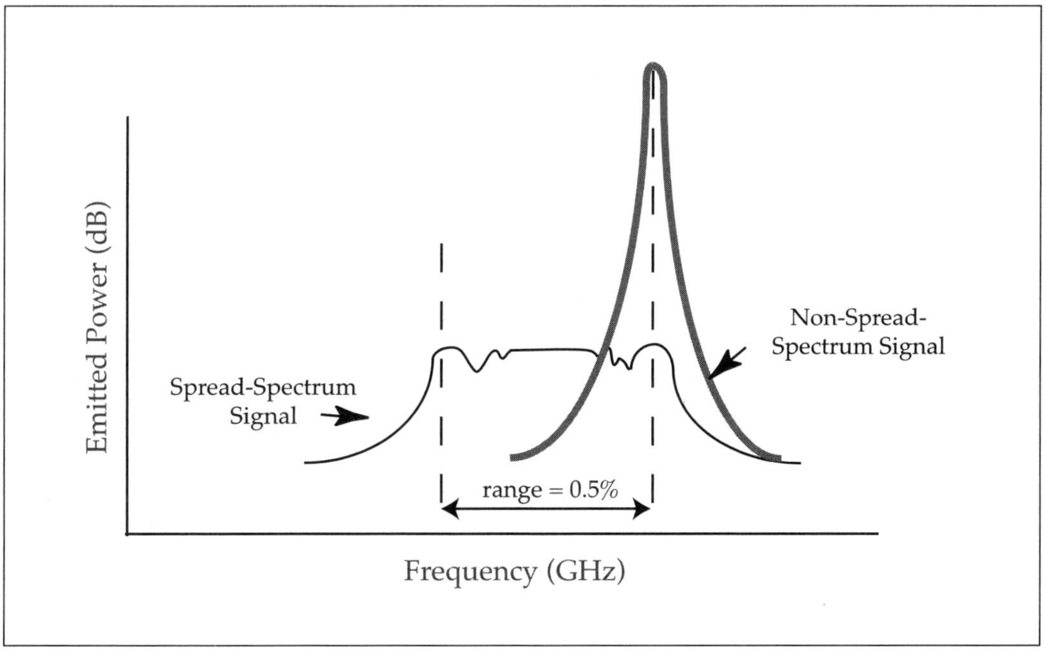

Bit Frequency

An interesting observation to make here is that the frequency of the signals seen on the wire using NRZ encoding must necessarily be less than or equal to half of the transmit frequency. This is shown in Figure 19-5, where two rising edges of the internally-generated transmit clock are required to generate one rising edge on the output signal. The reason for mentioning this is that the frequencies radiated by the system are most often those that appear on the transmission medium, meaning the frequency of concern for EMI in a 3.0 Gbps SATA system would actually be 1.5 GHz.

Figure 19-5: Output Frequency

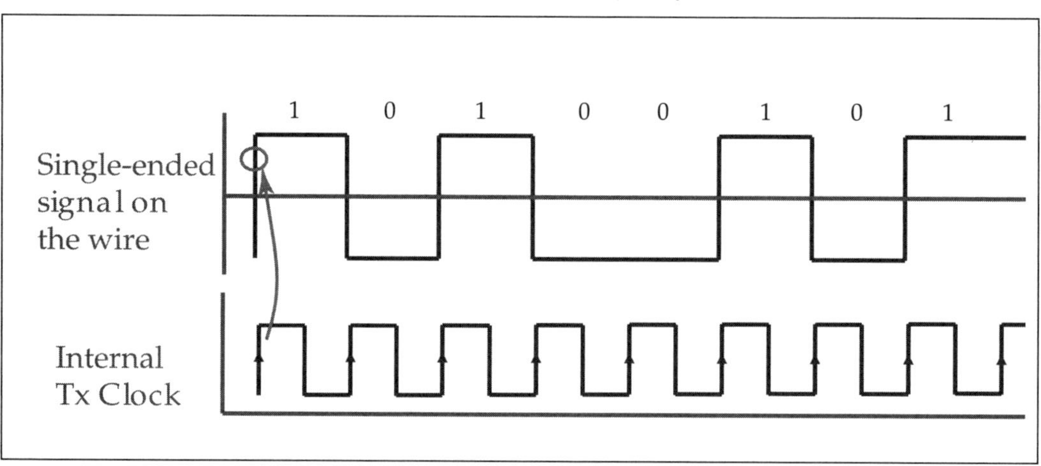

Receive Block

On the receive side (see Figure 19-6), the data stream passes through the differential receiver and is converted back into the stream of dwords that was sent by the transmitter. After a reset or power-up event, the receiver logic is unable to recognize primitives or other structures. That's not a problem, though because the logic only needs to behave as a squelch-detect circuit, observing whether the incoming stream is active or quiet (above or below a voltage threshold). Once transitions above the threshold are seen, the circuit then measures the idle time between bursts of activity to determine the OOB pattern from the transmitter.

After the OOB sequence is complete, the next step will be speed negotiation, and one of the things that the receiver needs to accomplish during that process is to recover the clock that was embedded in the bit stream.

Figure 19-6: Receive Block Diagram

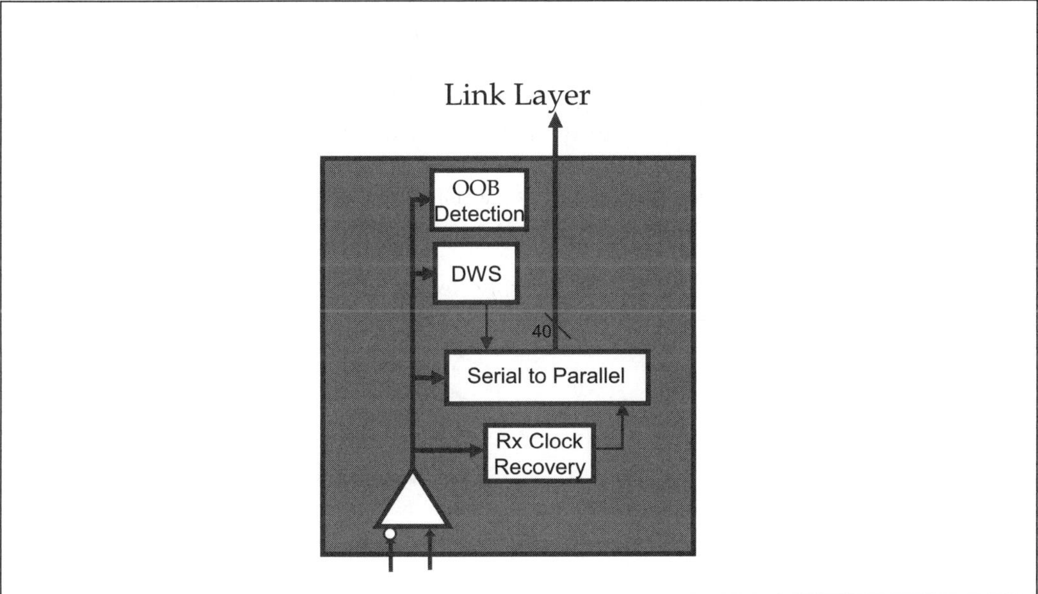

Recovering the Clock

A significant advantage of a high-speed serial design is the elimination of the constraints that limit parallel data transfer speeds, such as signal skew, flight time, and clock skew. Skew between signals is eliminated because there is now only one signal to transfer. Flight time and clock skew are also eliminated because serial designs don't use a separate signal dedicated as a strobe or clock. Instead, the clock is embedded into the bit stream by the transmitter and then recovered at the receiver. Consequently, flight time is irrelevant because the data always arrives at the same time as the clock, regardless of how long it took it to get there. And since the recovered clock matches the transmitter clock, there is no skew between the clock used to transmit the bits and the clock used to receive them. Once the clock has been recovered, it's used by the receiver to latch the incoming bit stream.

To recover the clock, the receiver uses a local PLL or oversampling circuit to lock onto the frequency in the incoming bit stream. Locking onto the clock is a straight-forward process that involves adjusting the phase of the recovered clock relative to the bit stream. That allows the logic to move the clock edges away from transitions in the data, as shown in Figure 19-7 on page 332, enabling it to reliably latch the incoming data. This illustration is also purposely drawn with the longest legal run length of 5 bits of the same polarity to show the trouble that the receiver needs to avoid. The longer the run length (number of bits without a transition), the longer the recovered clock must run without a reference and the more opportunity it has to drift from the actual frequency or phase. That makes subsequent bit positions more and more a matter of guesswork. The way trouble is avoided is by using 8b/10b encoding at the transmitter, which always ensures a maximum run length of only 5 bits.

Figure 19-7: Recovering Receiver Clock

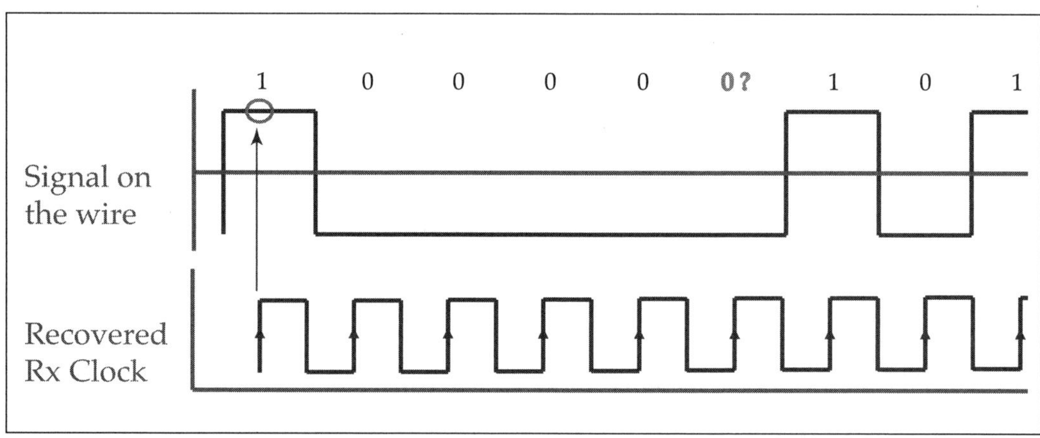

Clock recovery is simplified by the fact that the receiver knows the operational frequency once OOB and speed negotiation are complete, and simply needs to adjust the phase of its clock to align it with the incoming embedded clock. The SATA standard doesn't specify a particular method for recovering the clock, but describes two basic forms: tracking (using a PLL) and non-tracking or oversampling (typically using a DLL).

Tracking Architecture

A tracking receiver typically uses a PLL (phase-locked loop) or DLL (delay-lock loop) to generate the recovered clock based on the bit stream coming into its receiver. A PLL can be a fairly sophisticated design, but for now we just want to cover the basics. Figure 19-8 shows a simple block diagram of a PLL, which consists of a voltage-controlled oscillator (VCO) designed to generate a clock of a certain frequency based on an input voltage. The output of the VCO goes to a logic block that compares its phase with a reference clock, in this case the bit stream. The resulting phase error information is fed back to the VCO as a change in voltage, causing it to adjust the frequency. When the phase error is zero, the output clock is steady and the PLL is "locked".

Figure 19-8: Simplified PLL Diagram

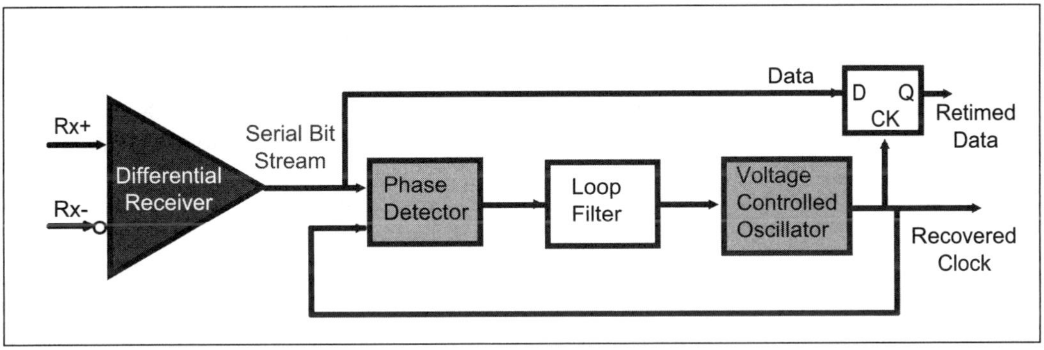

A DLL (delay-locked loop) works in much the same way except that the VCO is replaced with a variable delay line, as shown in Figure 19-9. This allows the DLL to add or remove delay to the reference clock to align the phase with the input signal. The advantage of a PLL is that it allows frequency synthesis, or multiplying the input clock. Its disadvantage is that the VCO introduces some instability and phase error that degrade its performance. A DLL design, on the other hand, is stable and doesn't accumulate phase error, but it can't be used to synthesize new frequencies from the reference input.

Figure 19-9: Simplified DLL Diagram

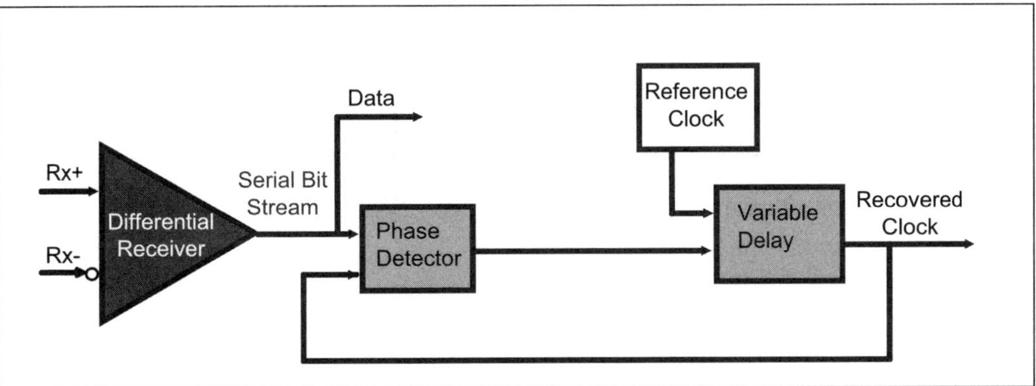

Non-Tracking (Oversampling) Architecture

An oversampling receiver uses a different approach to recover the clock from the incoming bit stream and latch in the bits. Oversampling simply means sampling the input at a rate that is higher than the bit rate as a way of determining the timing of the bits. Figure 19-10 illustrates how this might work when the incoming data is sampled at 8 times the bit rate. The sampled data will show a high value or a low value and when a transition is detected that can be used to infer that the transmitter's clock edge must have been near the time of the change. In this example, the clock rising edge must have been between samples 4 and 5 because that's where a change in the input value occurred. The output clock rising edge can therefore be assigned to sample time 5, for example, and that fixes the phase relationship of the recovered clock. To avoid any risk of latching an incoming bit at a transition time and getting the wrong value, the receiver now simply needs to select a sample point safely away from the inferred clock edge as the time to latch the data bit, such as sample point 1 in this example. This approach is sometimes referred to as "phase picking" for obvious reasons.

Figure 19-10: Oversampling Example

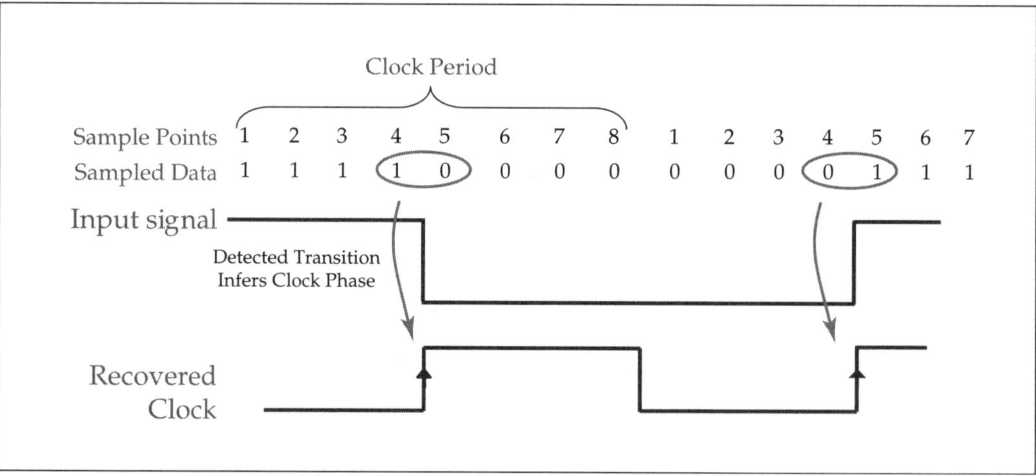

Clock Compensation

The recovered clock matches the transmitter's clock very closely, but doesn't exactly match the receiver's local clock. In fact, the receiver's local clock is technically in a different clock domain, with the result that the input is considered asynchronous to it. As a result, a mechanism to compensate for the difference is needed and that's where the elasticity buffer comes into play. The elasticity buffer enables the receiver to accept a slightly different incoming frequency and still avoid buffer overruns or under-runs. This buffer is essentially a FIFO whose inputs and output are clocked with separate clocks.

Because these clocks are imperfectly matched, one may be slightly faster than the other by as much as the maximum skew allowed in the standard, listed as +/- 350ppm (parts per million). Dividing 350 by one million and then multiplying by 100 converts it to a percentage: +/- 0.035%. It's also possible that one device implements SSC while the other does not, and this must be taken into account. For SATA, SSC means "down-spreading" the clock by as much as 5000ppm, meaning the frequency will never be higher than the nominal value, but could range lower by as much as 0.5%. In the worst case this gives an overall range from +350 to -5350ppm, resulting in a maximum separation of 5700ppm or 0.57%. Taking the inverse of this value indicates that the clock can gain or lose at most one cycle after every 175 clocks, regardless of the link speed. For simplicity, we can also think of this as gaining or losing up to one dword after every 175 dwords.

To compensate for this difference, the elasticity buffer needs to be able to add or remove some bits from the incoming bit stream. If the local clock is running faster, the contents of the buffer will drain out too quickly, leading to a buffer dry condition. This is remedied easily enough by having a control circuit that watches for this condition and adds an ALIGN primitive when it occurs. The ALIGN will be discarded when it reaches the Link layer, so this is harmless and solves the problem. On the other hand, if the recovered clock is running faster then the buffer will eventually reach an overflow condition. Again, the control logic can watch for this, but now something has to be removed from the buffer. That something is again the ALIGN primitive, which is added into the bitstream by the transmitter for this purpose. This scheme requires that the transmitter periodically inject ALIGN primitives for use as throw-away values in the elasticity buffer, at a specified rate of two ALIGNs (always sent in pairs) within at least every 256 dwords. That works out to an average of one ALIGN for every 128 dwords, and exceeds the requirement for the worst-case clock difference of one dword for every 175.

Figure 19-11: Elasticity Buffer - Dry Condition

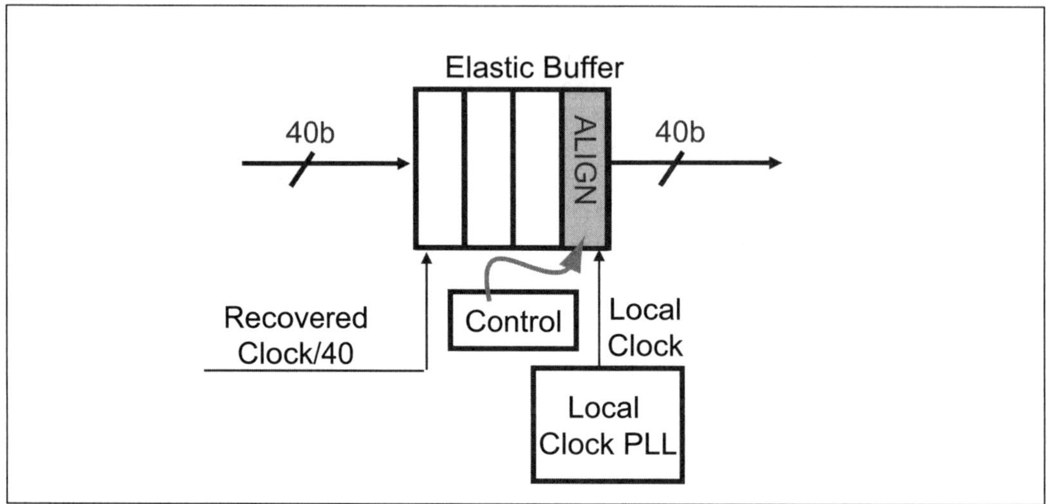

Figure 19-11 on page 336 illustrates the case in which the elasticity buffer runs dry. The buffer is shown as 40 bits wide even though the standard doesn't specify a width because it makes the illustration easier. In this case, the local clock is ready to take the next dword, but the buffer is empty. To forestall a problem, the control logic detects this condition and injects an ALIGN primitive so the receiver logic latches a valid dword even though the next one has not yet arrived. Figure 19-12 on page 337 illustrates the opposite case of an overflow condition. Here, the recovered clock is about to latch in another dword but the local clock has not yet taken out the next one and the buffer is full. To make room in the buffer, an ALIGN will be deleted, and the transmitter guarantees that one will be available by injecting them at the required rate.

Figure 19-12: Elasticity Buffer - Overflow Condition

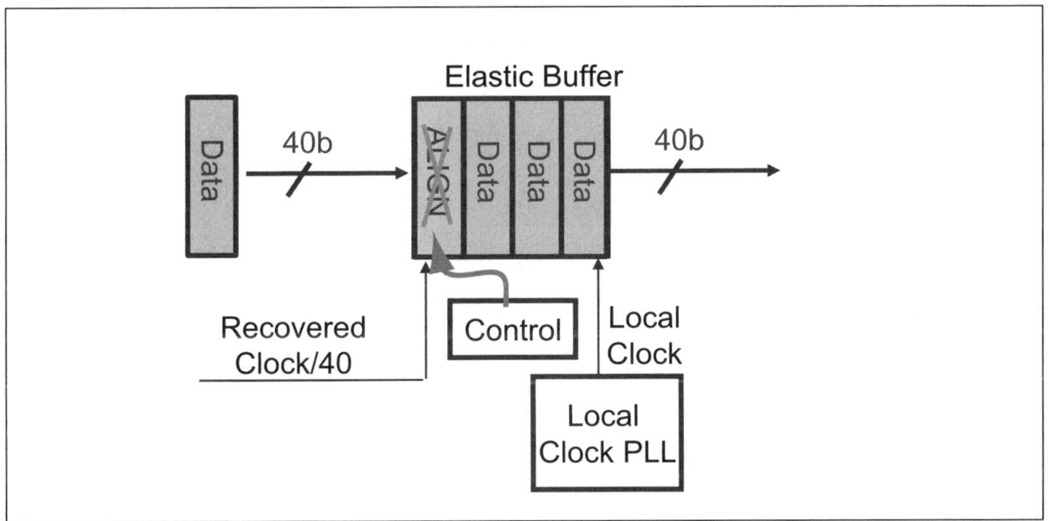

Achieving Dword Synchronization

Once the recovered clock is stable, it's used to latch the incoming bits into a buffer at the negotiated data rate. This buffer groups the bits together to create a parallel output for the next stage in the link layer. Although the standard doesn't specify the size of this parallel output, the flow of information is measured in dwords and that's the boundary that must be located regardless of the width of the data going to the Link layer. Since each byte has been encoded into 10 bits for transmission, a four-byte dword will consist of 40 bits. In order to correctly find the dword boundaries, the logic watches the incoming bit stream and searches for a recognizable pattern. As it turns out, the K28.5 control value used in ALIGN primitives works well for this, because it's the only legal 10-bit pattern that begins with 2 bits of one polarity followed by 5 bits of the other polarity. The detection of this pattern establishes both the bit position for the incoming bytes (groups of 10 bits), and the byte position for grouping them into dwords (groups of 40 bits), since K28.5 is required to be in the first byte position of an ALIGN primitive dword. Placing that byte into the first byte position and filling in the next three from there recovers the dword. Once achieved, the logic need not go through this dword synchronizing search again unless synchronization has been lost for some reason.

Figure 19-13 on page 338 illustrates this process. When the "comma" pattern is received the next 3 bits should complete the 10-bit value, identifying the value boundary. Since the K28.5 value is required to be the first in the group of 4 values that make up an ALIGN dword, this also identifies the dword boundaries. Placing it in the first position and then checking the next 3 values verifies the arrival of a valid ALIGN primitive dword.

Figure 19-13: Dword Synchronization

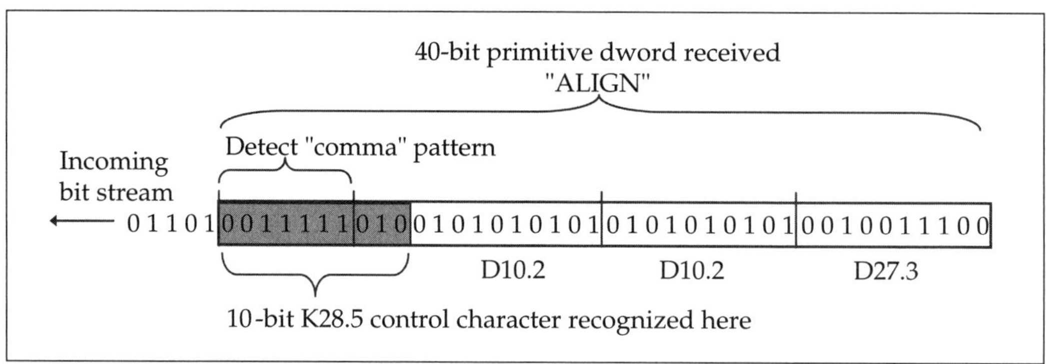

Implementation Example

An example of a clock recovery block at the receiver is shown in Figure 19-14. The clock recovery logic locks onto the frequency of the incoming bit stream to create a recovered clock and uses that to latch the bits into a deserializing buffer that groups the bits into 40-bit dwords. To find the 40-bit boundaries, a K28.5 detector indicates when the "comma" pattern has arrived. When that happens, the K28.5 value is moved to the front end of the buffer and the next 30 bits are used to fill in behind it. Once the dword boundary is established, the 40 bits can now be clocked into an elasticity buffer with a version of the recovered clock that is divided by 40. Data is clocked out of the elasticity buffer with the receiver's local clock, which will be a slightly different frequency. This frequency difference may result in the elasticity buffer approaching an overflow condition (if the local clock is slower than the recovered clock) or an underflow condition (if the local clock is faster). To compensate for this, the transmitter injects extra ALIGN primitives and the elasticity buffer's control logic watches for them. When the ALIGNs arrive, the logic will check the status of the buffer. If the buffer is approaching an overflow, the logic will remove the ALIGNs; if it's approaching an underflow, the logic will add more ALIGNs. The Link layer receiving the data from this buffer will simply discard any ALIGNs that it sees anyway, so it doesn't matter how many of them make it through.

This process allows the receiver to compensate for the worst-case difference between the two clocks that would occur if one supported SSC and the other did not. Essentially, it slows the transmitted data rate down to the slowest allowed rate by forcing the insertion of some extra ALIGNs.

Figure 19-14: Receiver Block Diagram

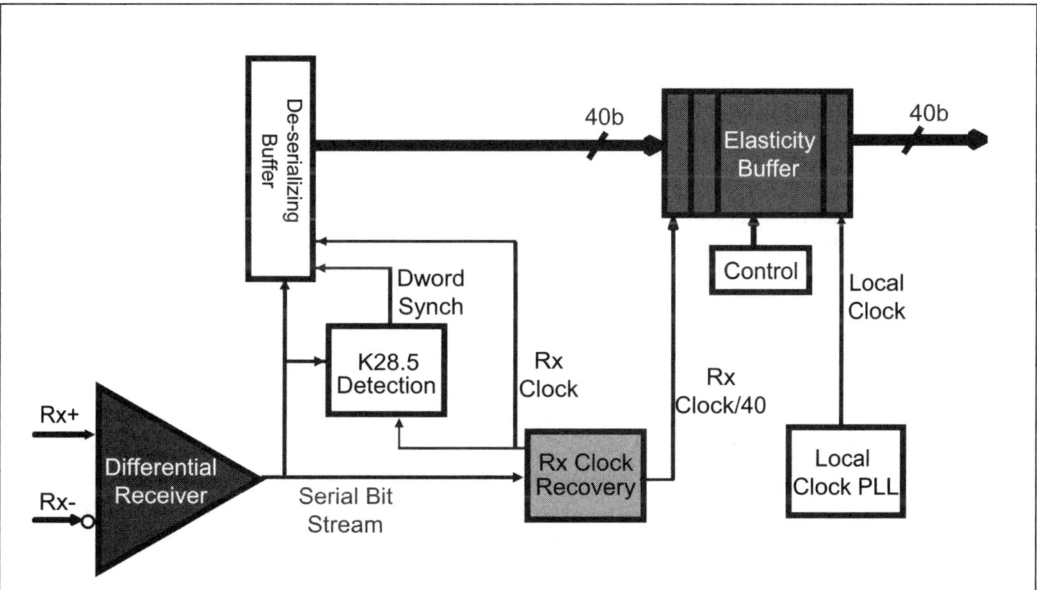

Power Management

The physical layer has some responsibilities regarding power management. When informed of a transition to the Partial state, the Phy logic remains powered, but at a reduced level. The transmitter outputs are held at the common-mode voltage and the recovery time is specified as no more than 10 us. When the Slumber state is indicated, the Phy response is similar to the Partial state, but now the recovery latency can be up to 10ms, suggesting that more logic, such as the clock recovery circuit, could be powered off to achieve a deeper power savings. No power values are specified for any of the states.

Electrical Interface

The SATA transmitter changes the serialized bits received from the Phy layer into a differential, NRZ (non-return to zero) encoded signal with a peak-to-peak voltage between 400 and 600mV. There are many other signal encoding schemes that might have been chosen. For example, PAM-4 (Pulse Amplitude Modulated) encoding uses a multi-level voltage scheme to increase bandwidth by increasing the number of bits visible in each time interval. The problem with such schemes is that they make both transmitter and receiver more complex, and recovering multi-level signals is more difficult and more susceptible to noise. The SATA standard writers chose NRZ because of its simplicity and robust operation and because it has been used successfully in many earlier serial architectures. Another signal encoding scheme may yet be needed for future generations of SATA, but the consensus seems to be that it will be acceptable for the planned next generation speed of 6.0 Gbps.

Differential Signaling

The SATA interface uses a low-voltage differential signaling scheme to transmit the bit stream. Differential transmitters use mirror-image positive and negative versions of the same signal to transmit the bits across a link, while the receiver recovers the transmitted bits by evaluating the difference between the two signals. Although this requires twice as many pins to implement as a single-ended signaling environment, differential offers several advantages.

Common-Mode Noise Rejection

Perhaps the most important of these advantages is common-mode noise rejection, and a little background may be helpful here. First, differential signals use much smaller voltage swings on each signal, because the receiver subtracts the negative signal from the positive signal to find the differential voltage value. As shown in Figure 19-15 on page 341, that means the receiver always perceives twice the voltage level (referred to as the peak voltage) compared with looking at only one of them.

The trouble with low-voltage signaling is that the smaller the signal swing, the more susceptible it is to noise. Fortunately, differential signaling reduces that susceptibility because noise that affects the one signal is very likely to affect the other signal by the same amount. The signals have to be routed as a pair, side by side, to achieve the proper transmission line impedance, so there is very little difference between what one signal experiences compared to the other one. In other words, changes to one signal tend to be balanced by changes in the other, with the result that the difference between them stays effectively the same.

Figure 19-15: Differential Voltages

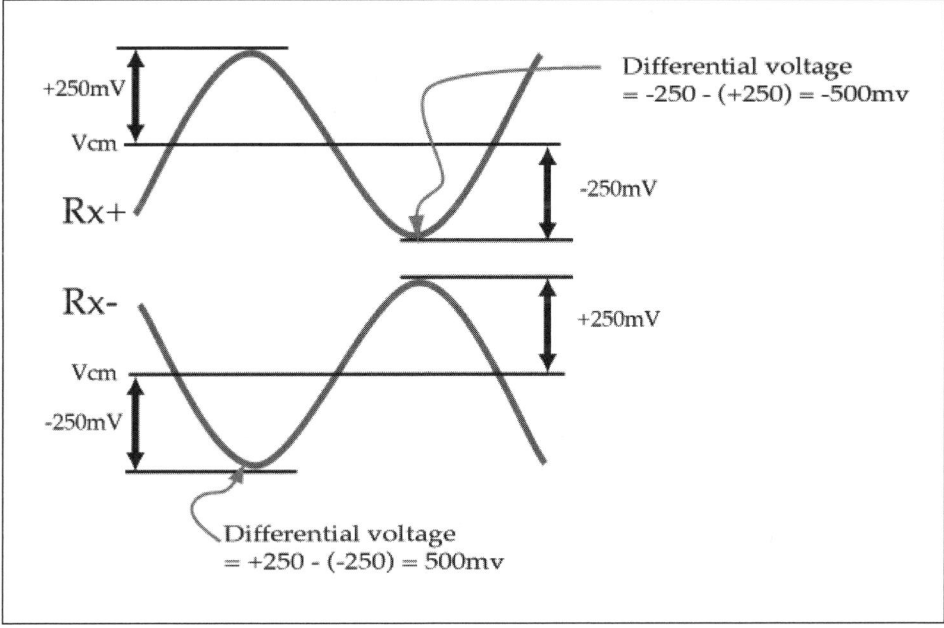

Consider the example shown in Figure 19-16 on page 342, which shows a differential transmission line affected by two types of voltage noise. In one case, ground bounce or some other noise has momentarily changed the reference voltage used for single-ended signals. The differential receiver is unaffected by this because, in the end, it's comparing the signals to each other and their relationship hasn't changed. In the second case, transient environmental noise causes a voltage spike. Since both signals are affected by such events to approximately the same degree, the receiver is again able to see the intended signal and remains largely unaffected by the noise. Single-ended signals could easily suffer loss of signal integrity in either of these cases, but a differential receiver sees very little change.

Figure 19-16: Differential Signaling Rejects Common-Mode Noise

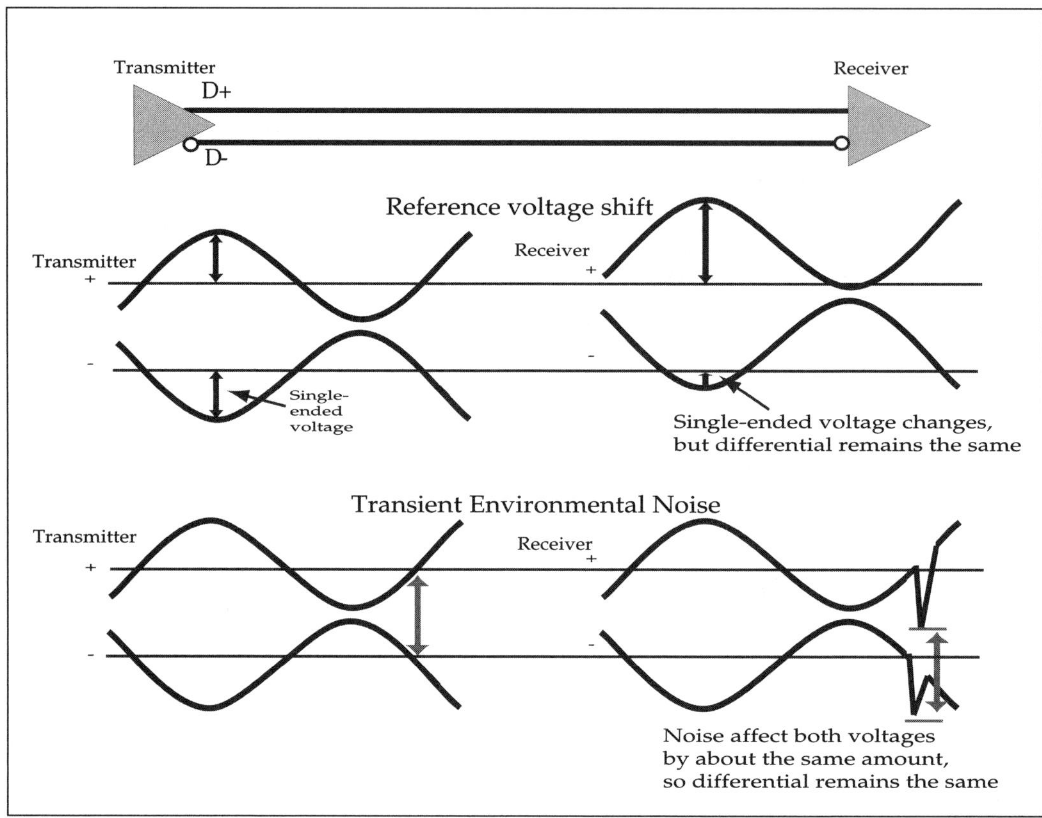

Clearly, system designers should make the effort to build margin into their systems wherever possible so as to leave more timing or voltage budget available for devices with tight constraints. One way to do that is to put stricter requirements on the transmission medium and termination used. For example, the differential impedance is listed as 100 ohms nominal but, for a variety of reasons, many board designs vary from that quite a bit. Getting this value as close as possible to exactly 100 ohms will improve the transmission characteristics and thus improve the budget for other parts of the system. Similarly, the receiver single-ended impedance is listed as 40 ohms minimum, but designers should make an effort to get the values balanced between the differential pair as much as possible. Balancing the impedance of the two signals helps ensure that environmental noise affects both signals in the pair by the same amount. If these are not evenly matched, it will increase the perceived noise at the receiver.

Other Advantages of Differential signaling

A second advantage of differential is that, since the two signals switch in opposite directions and the traces must be in close proximity to each other, the signals tend to cancel out each other's EMI and crosstalk effects. This benefit becomes more important as the transmission frequencies increase, adding to the desirability of using differential in serial interface designs that have high switching speeds. This also reduces the need to shield the signals and, as a result, can allow tighter routing densities.

A third important advantage is that the lower voltages used in differential switching allow both faster switching times and reduced power consumption, because the voltage change that must be driven by the transmitter is smaller.

Transmission Characteristics

The SATA standard specifies the transmitter and receiver characteristics, a few of which are listed in Table 19-1. In Figure 19-17 on page 344, an in-line capacitor is shown at each end of the transmission line to create an AC-coupled solution. AC coupling is required for the Gen1x and all of the Gen2 signaling environments. (See "Extreme Signalling Environments" on page 354.) The SATA specification allows the link to be DC-coupled for the friendlier Gen1i and Gen1m signaling environments, meaning there would be no in-line capacitors at all, as shown in Figure 19-18 on page 344. The purpose of AC coupling is to allow the high-frequency components of a signal (the AC part) to pass through, but block the low-frequency components (the DC part). This allows the common-mode voltages at the transmitter and receiver to be different, and this is desirable in cases where maintaining common voltages would be more difficult, such as when the devices are not in the same physical enclosure. However, for the common SATA implementation using a short (1m) internal cable, a DC-coupled solution works just fine.

Table 19-1: Link Characteristics

Characteristic	1.5 Gb/s (Gen-1)	3.0 Gb/s (Gen-2)
Physical Link Rate	150 GB/s	300 GB/s
Unit Interval (UI) (Nominal)	666.66 ps	333.33 ps
Differential Impedance (Nominal)	100 ohms	

Table 19-1: Link Characteristics

Characteristic	1.5 Gb/s (Gen-1)	3.0 Gb/s (Gen-2)
A.C. Coupling capacitor (max)	12 nF	

In a DC-coupled environment, the transmitter and receiver are required to maintain a nominal common-mode voltage of 250mV. In an AC-coupled environment there is no fixed common-mode voltage; instead, the Vcm at transmitter and receiver in that case can vary over a much larger range from 0 to 2 Volts.

Figure 19-17: Optional AC-Coupled Solution

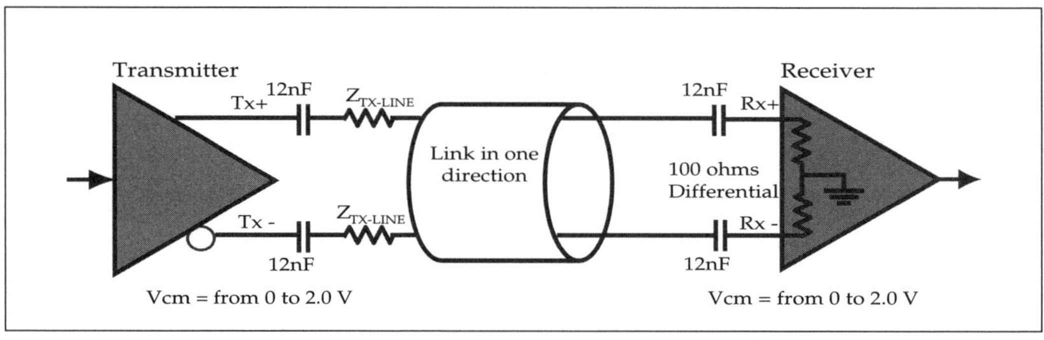

Figure 19-18: DC-Coupled Solution

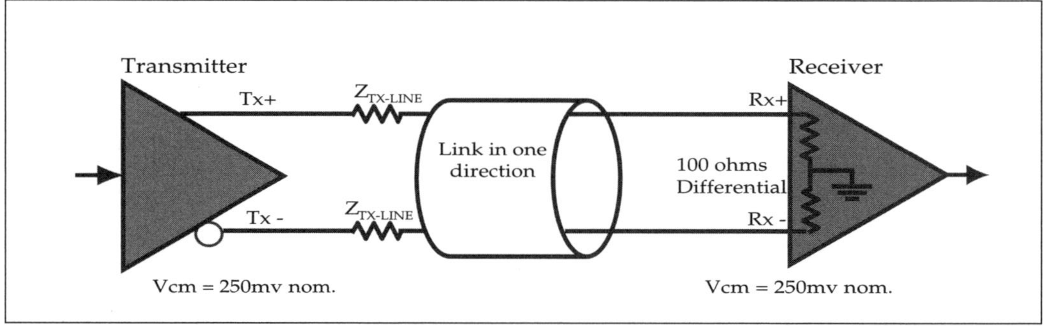

A 100 ohm differential termination is required at the receiver and could be created with external components, but it's expected to be implemented internally for reasons of cost, reduced part count, and improved signal integrity. There is evidently a wide range of opinions on the best way to do this. Some engineers with whom the author has spoken on this topic recommended external resistors tied to ground. One vendor recommended that both Rx+ and Rx- should each be independently connected to V_{DD} through a 1K ohm at 100 MHz ferrite bead, then a 0.01 μF capacitor. Another vendor states that, "Ferrite beads are not advisable in digital switching circuits because inductive spiking (di/dt noise) is introduced into the power rail." Still another vendor says, "No external resistor terminations are necessary on the high-speed I/O." Clearly, it will be incumbent on a designer to become familiar with the high-speed signaling issues affecting a given implementation. For more on this topic, refer to materials such as the book *High-Speed Signal Propagation: Advanced Black Magic* (Howard Johnson and Martin Graham, 2003 Prentice Hall Professional Technical Reference (PTR)).

More of the electrical characteristics of the link are listed in Table 19-2. The term "mV_{p-p}" appears several times there and means peak-to-peak millivolts. Peak-to-peak is defined as the difference between the voltage for representing a logical 1 versus that for representing a logical 0. The voltage for single-ended signals is measured as a peak value, meaning the overall range of voltage it can cover, while differential voltages are measured as the combination of two single-ended signals and are thus twice the value.

Table 19-2: Selected Electrical Characteristics

Characteristic	Min	Nominal	Max	Units
Link rate tolerance	-5350		+350	ppm
Receiver A.C. common-mode voltage tolerance			100	mV
Squelch Detector Threshold	50	100	200	mV_{p-p}
Differential impedance - Tx and Rx	85	100	115	ohms
Common-mode impedance	40			ohms
Vcm - DC coupled	200	250	450	mV
Vcm - AC coupled	0		2000	mV
Rx Vdiff	325	400	600	mV_{p-p}
Tx Vdiff	400	500	600	mV_{p-p}

This idea is illustrated in Figure 19-19. Two single-ended signals are shown, and for each one we can see the peak value: the sum of the positive and negative excursions from the common-mode voltage. The differential excursion, which is the result of subtracting the negative signal from the positive signal, will be double what it is for just one of them. To clarify which case is being described, the differential voltage isn't described as a peak voltage, but rather as peak to peak, to distinguish it as differential and highlight that it represents the sum of the peak values for both single-ended signals.

Figure 19-19: Single-Ended and Differential Voltages

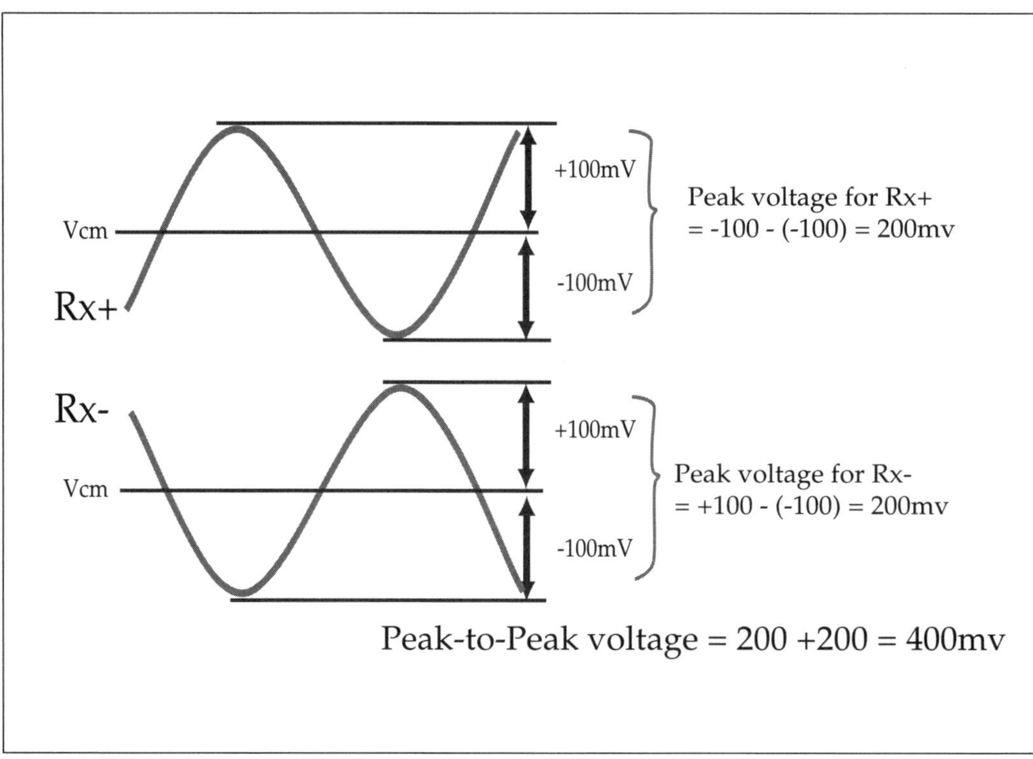

For another view of this, consider Figure 19-20 on page 347. Here the peak-to-peak voltage is illustrated by an overlay picture of the two single-ended signals that make up the differential pair. The measurement and result is still the same, adding the full voltage swing of one signal (250mV in this illustration) to the full voltage swing of the other signal which is also 250mV.

This view is commonly used when creating eye diagrams by sampling the signals over a long period of time. Judging by the number of questions this generates in classes, though, this view can also be confusing because it's easy to misinterpret the peak-to-peak voltage as being just Vp1 alone, for example. To clarify this, it helps to think of the peak-to-peak voltage as the sum of the total voltage swing for the positive signal (labeled as Vp1) and the total voltage swing for the negative signal (labeled as Vp2).

Figure 19-20: Differential Voltages Overlay View

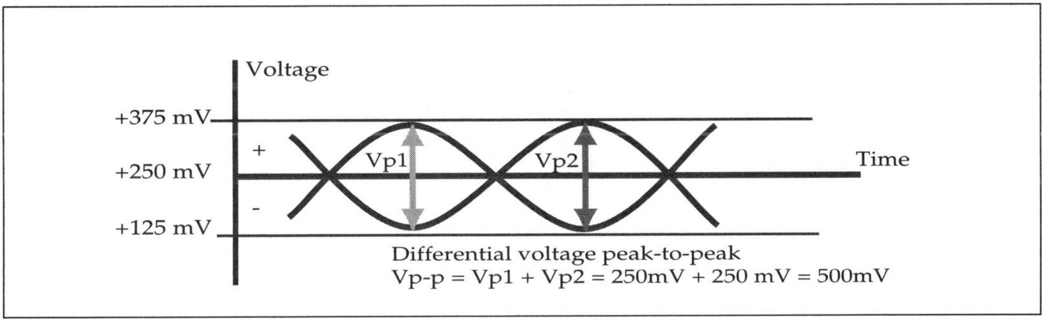

Eye Diagram

An eye diagram test involves setting up a sampling scope to capture a history of waveforms on the link and verifying that the voltage range and jitter are within specified tolerances. The standard points out that it's not realistic to try to capture enough edges to be able to guarantee the design goal of a 10^{-12} BER (bit error rate). Still, the eye diagram is helpful because "a quick health check may be performed with minimal setup". The eye diagram in Figure 19-21 on page 348 shows the voltage ranges as well as the jitter allowed. The signal, and thus the size of the eye opening, is affected in terms of voltage (vertically) by transmission line attenuation and noise. The eye is affected in terms of timing (horizontally) primarily by jitter.

An example of what this looks like in a real system is illustrated in Figure 19-22 on page 349 where a trace capture from the transmitter is shown at the top and from the receiver at the bottom. The illegal area is drawn to scale in the pictures, so this transmission line would appear to have acceptable performance. The pattern generated for this test is not a normal data pattern but is a Pseudo-Random Bit Sequence (PRBS-7) standard polynomial generated by test equipment.

Because it generates patterns that would be illegal during normal operation (e.g., 10 zeros in a row), it's actually worse than any legal pattern.

Figure 19-21: Transmitter and Receiver Eye Diagram

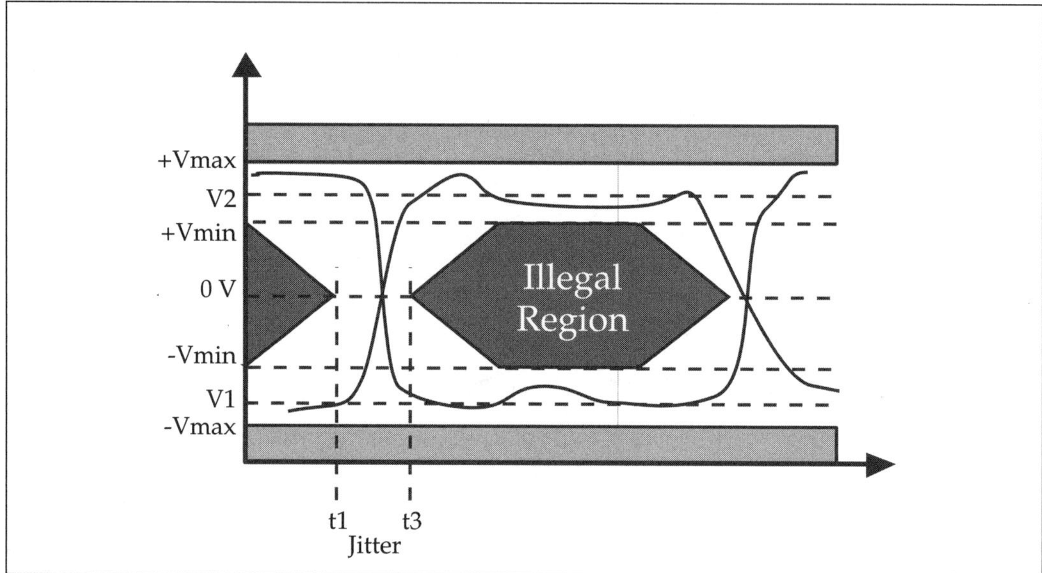

Consequently, a system that passes when using this pattern should work with any legal patterns. As expected, the signals suffer some loss in propagation through the cable, resulting in a reduced eye opening at the receiver. Since this is a relatively short transmission path, the loss is not so great as to encroach on the limits for the eye mask, but it can be seen that the signal experiences reduced voltage and increased jitter. Longer paths make this problem worse because both attenuation and phase shift are proportional to distance. Consequently, chip designers typically must take steps to compensate for this loss and the amount of compensation depends on the expected system environment (See "Signal Compensation" on page 350.)

The reader interested in learning more about this topic may wish to refer to the ANSI/INCITS spec TR-35-2004 titled *Methodologies for Jitter and Signal Quality* (MJSQ) for more details on verifying compliance.

Figure 19-22: Eye Diagram Measured On a Short Cable

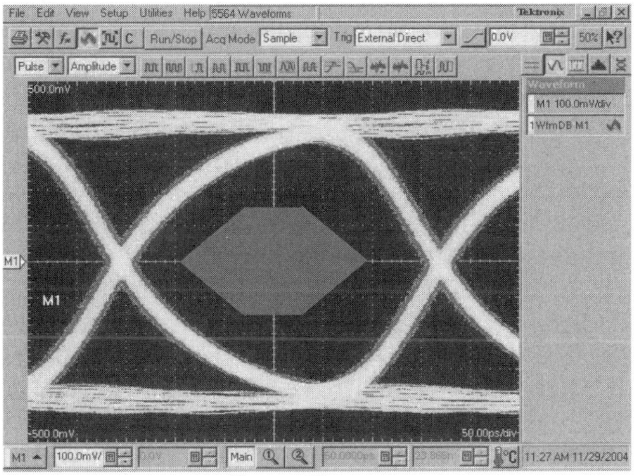

Transmitter

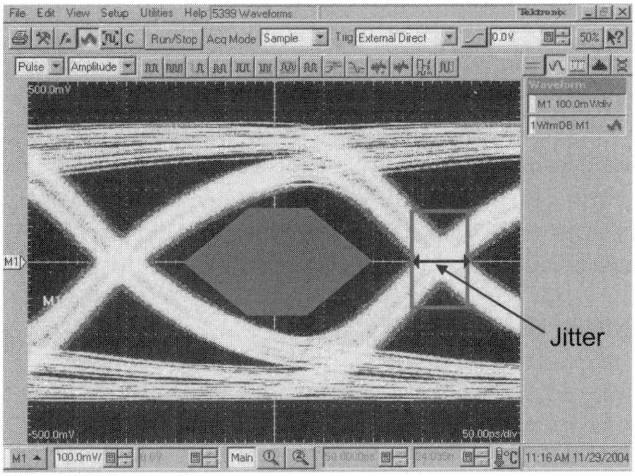

Jitter

Receiver

Signal Compensation

Signal loss for an internal SATA environment is not ordinarily a problem because the cables are limited to just one meter and don't cause much attenuation. Still, a brief discussion of the problem and common solutions is included here for those dealing with more demanding environments than the consumer machines that represent SATA's biggest market. External cables or backplane implementations would be examples of those environments.

The simplest form of compensation would be to have the transmitter just drive the voltage a little higher and make the receiver a little more sensitive than required by the standard. If that isn't enough, compensating for signal loss typically takes two forms: de-emphasis at the transmitter, or equalization at the receiver. Neither of these techniques is required by the SATA standard or even mentioned in it. However, they are common in other serial transports that target the server market or noisier environments and longer transmission lines.

De-emphasis

De-emphasis (or its cousin, pre-emphasis) is a method by which the transmitter attempts to compensate for the anticipated distortion a signal will experience during transmission by distorting it in the opposite way as it's sent. The loss of power a signal experiences in transmission is not uniform but is predictable: the high frequency components are reduced more than the others. Compensation for that loss can be achieved by either boosting the power of the high frequencies (pre-emphasis), or reducing the power of the lower frequencies (de-emphasis). Either approach helps alleviate this problem, which is largely created by electrical issues such as skin effects and dielectric loss.

Overcoming ISI

Loss and jitter in a signal can prevent the bits from reaching their full strength in time, causing them to spill over somewhat into the next bit time. The magnitude of this problem depends on the bit patterns on the wire. This pattern-dependent jitter is called inter-symbol interference (ISI) because it results when the pattern of the previous bits interferes with proper reception of the current bit. As an example of ISI, consider the diagram in Figure 19-23 on page 351. In this picture, the waveform on the left shows the transmitter's output of one of the two differential signals (single-ended), while the picture on the right shows the same signal at the receiver. At the receiver, the transitions have experienced attenuation and one effect that can be readily observed is that repeated bits of the same polarity tend to charge up the line, causing it to reach a higher voltage than it otherwise would and making it more difficult to switch to the proper level for a bit transition within the given time.

Figure 19-23: Inter-Symbol Interference (ISI)

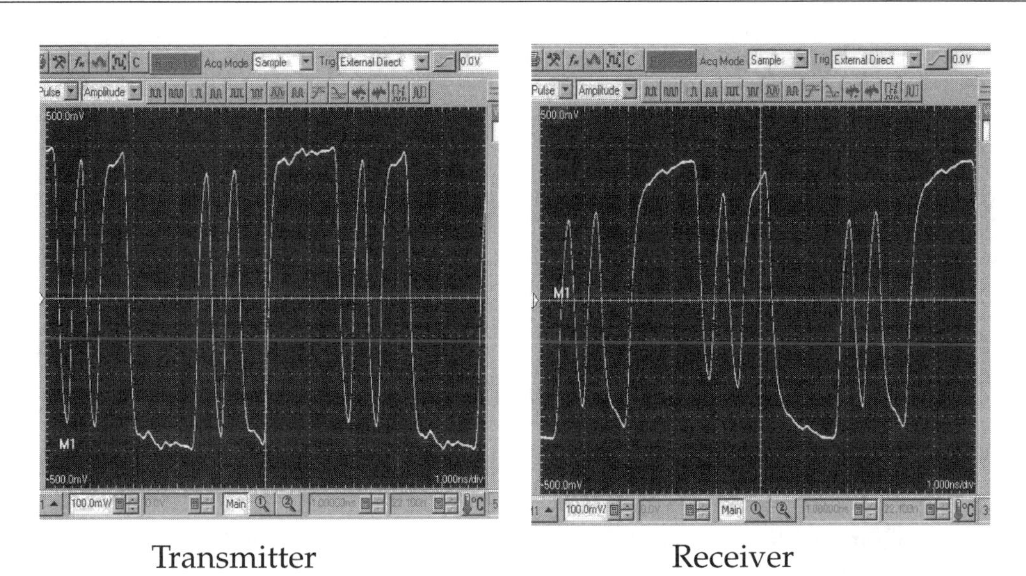

In Figure 19-24 on page 352, this effect is reduced by de-emphasizing the transmitter waveform to compensate for the expected distortion of the signal during transmission. Note that the transmitter's waveform shows pre-emphasized transitions (the high-frequency components of the signal), or de-emphasized bits when they do not change state to prevent the "charge up" effect on the line. The amount of pre-emphasis or de-emphasis applied to the signal is typically programmable within the transmitter, allowing the system to increase it for longer transmission environments or reduce it for shorter transmission lengths.

Figure 19-24: ISI Reduced by Use of De-emphasis

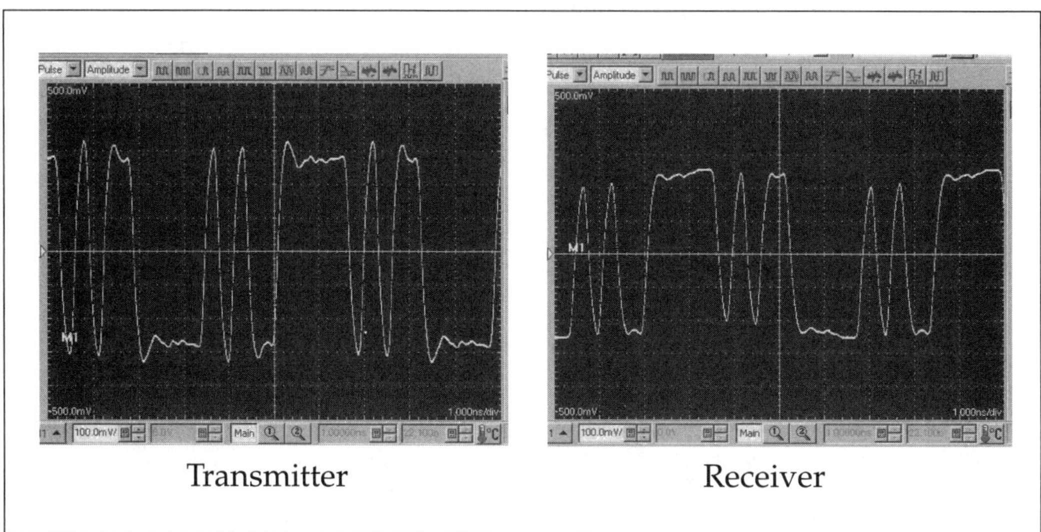

Programmable compensation will be important if the signaling environment is not known ahead of time, since applying de-emphasis on a short path would actually make it worse. Figure 19-25 shows a trace capture for the short cable with de-emphasis applied. At the top, it can be seen that the output at the transmitter has been markedly distorted. If the transmission path was short and didn't actually affect the signal much, that distortion would also appear almost unchanged at the receiver. In the lower picture, though, the signal has experienced attenuation, so the compensation improves both the signal and the eye opening at the receiver (compared to the way it looked in Figure 19-22).

Figure 19-25: Eye Diagram Showing De-Emphasis

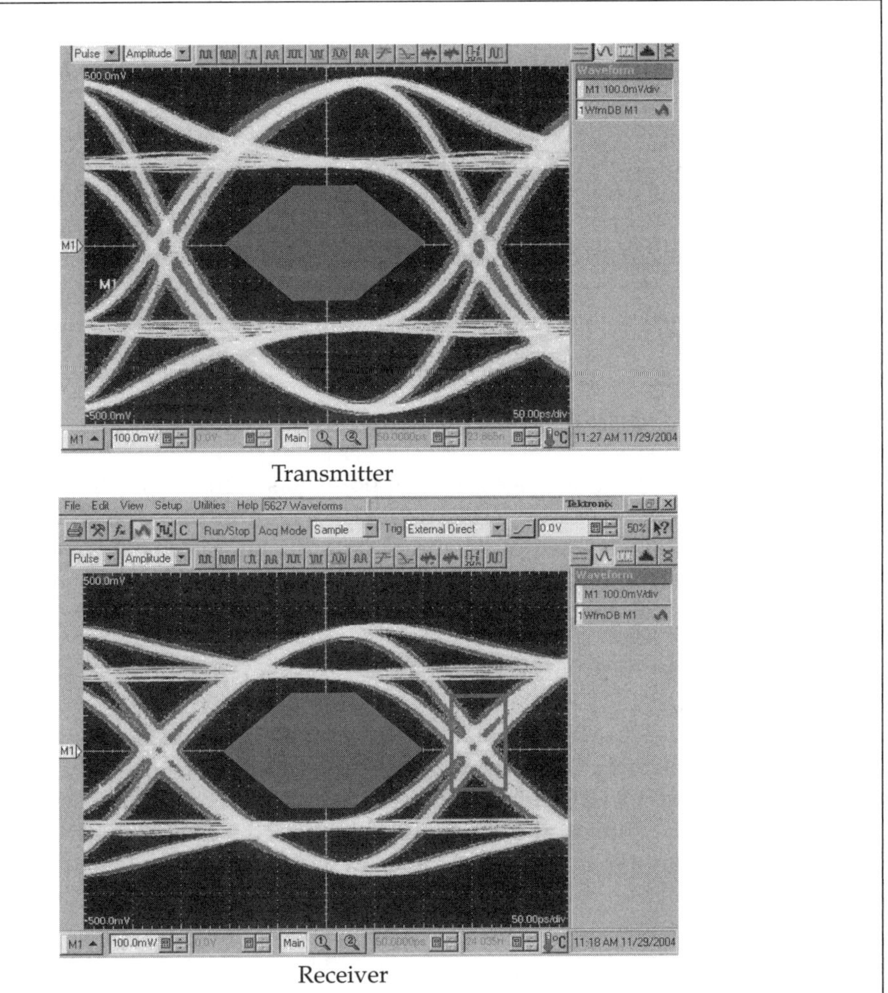

Equalization

Equalization involves applying a high-pass filter at the receiver and then amplifying the result to recover the original signal. Since this method is applied inside a device, no waveforms are available to show the results, but simulations indicate a similar improvement in the eye opening. The advantage of this approach is that the receiver can detect how well the applied compensation is working and adjust the equalization parameters to improve the results as needed. A disadvantage is that when the signal is amplified, all the noise associated with it is also amplified, and the logic can also be more complex to implement.

Comparing the Methods

Comparing the two types of compensation, it can be seen that each has advantages and disadvantages. De-emphasis has no feedback mechanism to detect how well it's working, can cause increased cross-talk by amplifying high frequencies, and uses more power. Equalization allows for performance feedback but, because it also amplifies the noise, if the signal to noise ratio is low enough it might make matters worse. Reliable system operation might involve using both of these techniques together to minimize transmission line loss effects.

Extreme Signalling Environments

The information discussed to this point has focussed on the electrical parameters defined for the Generation 1 and Generation 2 internal signaling environment. SATA also supports more difficult electrical environments associated with server-type applications. The three environments defined by the specification are:

- Internal (i) Environment (Gen1i and Gen2i) — internal electrical specification for 1.5 Gb/s and 3.0 Gb/s phys with a maximum cable length of 1 meter. (This environment was discussed previously in this chapter.)
- Intermediate (M) Environment (Gen1m and Gen2m) — electrical specification for 1.5 Gb/s and 3.0 Gb/s phys used in the Short Backplane and External Desktop applications with cable lengths up to 2 meters.
- Extreme (X) Environment (Gen1x and Gen2x) — electrical specification for 1.5 Gb/s and 3.0 Gb/s phys used in long backplane and longer cabled environments.

Direct Versus AC Coupling

The specification makes the following statement regarding coupling:

- Gen1i implementations may be either DC or AC coupled.
- Gen1m implementations are allowed to be DC coupled, but AC coupling is recommended.
- Gen1x, Gen2i, Gen2m, and Gen2x implementations must be AC coupled.

Drive Electrical Interface

The electrical interface at all SATA drives must be compliant with the Gen1i or Gen2i electrical specifications. No requirement is made of drives for them to be placed into the M and X environments.

HBAs Manage Extreme Environments

The more challenging electrical environments (designated M and X) must be managed at the host side. That is signals transmitted by the host must compensate for the increased attenuation of the environment and drive signals with greater amplitude. Similarly, the host side receiver must have greater sensitivity to compensate for the attenuation of the signals transmitted by the drives (at the standard 400-600 mvpp level).

Electrical Parameters

Table 19-3 lists key transmitter parameters required for the three environments and Table 19-4 lists the key receiver parameters.

Table 19-3: Key Transmit Parameters for Internal, Intermediate and Extreme Environments

<table>
<tr><th>Parameter</th><th>Limit</th><th>Gen1i</th><th>Gen1m</th><th>Gen1x</th><th>Gen2i</th><th>Gen2m</th><th>Gen2x</th><th>Units</th></tr>
<tr><td rowspan="3">Tx Diff. Output Voltage</td><td>Min</td><td>400</td><td>500</td><td>800</td><td>400</td><td>500</td><td>800</td><td rowspan="3">mVppd</td></tr>
<tr><td>Nom</td><td colspan="2">500</td><td>--</td><td colspan="3">--</td></tr>
<tr><td>Max</td><td colspan="2">600</td><td>1600</td><td colspan="2">700</td><td>1600</td></tr>
<tr><td>Tx Min Voltage Meas. Interval</td><td></td><td colspan="2">--</td><td>0.5</td><td colspan="2">0.45 – 0.55</td><td>0.5</td><td>UI</td></tr>
<tr><td rowspan="2">Rise/Fall Time 20-80%</td><td>Min</td><td colspan="2">100 (.15)</td><td>67 (.10)</td><td colspan="3">67 (.20)</td><td rowspan="2">ps
(UI)</td></tr>
<tr><td>Max</td><td colspan="2">273 (.41)</td><td>273 (.41)</td><td colspan="3">136 (.41)</td></tr>
<tr><td>Diff. Skew</td><td>Max</td><td colspan="3">20</td><td colspan="2">20</td><td>15</td><td>ps</td></tr>
<tr><td>AC Common Mode Voltage</td><td>Max</td><td colspan="3">--</td><td colspan="2">50</td><td>--</td><td>mVp-p</td></tr>
<tr><td>OOB Differential Delta</td><td>Max</td><td colspan="2">--</td><td>25</td><td colspan="3">25</td><td>mV</td></tr>
<tr><td>OOB Common Mode Delta</td><td>Max</td><td colspan="2">--</td><td>50</td><td colspan="3">50</td><td>mV</td></tr>
<tr><td>Rise/Fall Imbalance</td><td>Max</td><td colspan="3">--</td><td colspan="2">20</td><td>--</td><td>%</td></tr>
<tr><td>Amplitude Imbalance</td><td>Max</td><td colspan="2">--</td><td>10</td><td colspan="3">10</td><td>%</td></tr>
</table>

Table 19-4: Key Receive Parameters for Internal, Intermediate and Extreme Environments

Parameter	Limit	Gen1i	Gen1m	Gen1x	Gen2i	Gen2m	Gen2x	Units
Diff. Impedance	Min	85			--		85	Ohms
	Max	115			--		115	
Single-Ended Impedance	Min	600		1600	700		1600	
Differential Input Voltage	Min	325	240	275	275	240	275	mVppd
	Nom	400		--				
	Max	600		1600	750	750	1600	
Rise/Fall Time 20-80%	Min	100 (.15)		67 (.10)	67 (.20)			UI
	Max	273 (.41)			136 (.41)			
Voltage Meas Interval	Min	--		0.5	0.5			UI
Diff. Skew	Max	--		80	50	75		ps
AC Common Mode Voltage	Max	100		150	100		150	mVp-p
AC Common Mode Frequency	Min	2			2			MHz
	Max	200			200			

SAPIS

As is true with many serial designs, the high-speed electrical interface in the physical layer is a good candidate for a separate design module. Digital logic ASIC designers may not have the necessary expertise to develop a robust high-speed circuit of this type, and may prefer instead to purchase it as a module from another vendor. Defining a separate interface facilitates this division of labor and thus the adoption of the SATA interface, so a separate Intel specification has been created called SAPIS (SATA Physical Interface Specification).

SAPIS provides a standard interface to which a chip designer can design that will be functionally compatible with what is called the AFE (analog front end) in the SATA standard and is called the Phy Component in SAPIS. That very short 12-page spec provides a block diagram and a description of the interface signals between the Phy Component and the Link layer of the design. The diagram is repeated here for convenience in Figure 19-26 on page 359 and is followed by a brief description of each of the interface signals.

The SAPIS signals are explained in the spec and many are fairly intuitive. For example, the 10 transmit data bits are the output of the 8b/10b encoder of the link layer. For convenience, these signals are briefly described here as well:

- **Tx_Data (0:9)** - the 10-bit "byte" that is clocked out of the ASIC on both rising and falling edges of the TBC.
- **TBC (0:1)** - Transmitter Byte Clocks, used to clock 10-bit "bytes" into the transmit block. For the Generation-1 speed of 1.5 Gbps, this frequency would be expected to be 150 MHz but, in fact, both edges of this clock are used to send data, so it only runs at half that speed or 75 MHz for Gen-1 and 150 MHz for Gen-2.
- **Data Rate** - a low level selects Gen-1 and a high level selects Gen-2. Support for Gen-2 is optional, and a Phy that doesn't support it won't have this input.
- **Tx_Enable** - when high the output buffer generates normal drive levels; when low, the outputs are idle and just maintain the common-mode voltage as specified.
- **V_REF_TX** - voltage reference for signals driven by the ASIC to the Phy.
- **Rx_Data (0:9)** - the 10-bit "byte" that is clocked out of the Phy on both rising and falling edges of the RBC.
- **Rx Data Valid** - used for flow control, this indicates that the incoming data is valid. If this is not active, the data should be ignored. Recall that the Phy can insert or remove ALIGN primitives as needed to prevent elastic buffer underflow or overflow because the link layer ignores them anyway, and this signal tells the link layer not to latch the current data.
- **RBC (0:1)** - Receiver Byte Clocks, used to latch the 10-bit data values into the link layer buffer. This clock is phase locked to the incoming data stream for a tracking receiver, or frequency locked to the differential REF_CK for an oversampling receiver. Note that the RBC clocks are not expected to be synchronous to the ASIC_CK, which means the link layer will need to implement the necessary elasticity buffer.
- **K28.5_Detect** - indicates this control value is present on the Rx Data pins. This is used to define the byte alignment (dword boundaries) in the incoming bit stream. If the Phy removes an ALIGN primitive for clock compensation, the K28.5 at the beginning of the primitive would also be removed. In that case, the K28.5_Detect signal still goes active, but on the next byte.
- **V_REF_RX** - reference voltage for the signals driven by the Phy.
- **RX_LOCKED** - indicates that three conditions are all true:
  - The differential input signal exceeds the squelch detector threshold.
  - The receiver is locked to the incoming signal.
  - The receiver byte alignment is correctly established.

  (For more on these topics, see chapter *.* on Initialization.)
- **RX_ERROR** - indicates that a data reception error such as an elastic buffer overrun or underrun has occurred.
- **ASIC_CK** - this is a clock to the ASIC that runs at 150 MHz for Gen-1 or 300 MHz for Gen-2.

- **ASIC_CK_RATE_SELECT** - low value selects Gen-1 and high selects Gen-2 clock rate. If the Phy doesn't support the Gen-2 clock, it won't have this input.
- **SIGNAL_LEVEL_VALID** - indicates that the differential input exceeds the squelch detector threshold. This can be used to awaken the link layer ASIC from a suspended state.
- **COMWAKE_DETECT** - indicates that the criteria for detecting a COMWAKE were met (see the chapter on Initialization for details).
- **COMINIT_DETECT or COMRESET_DETECT** - indicates that the criteria for detecting a COMINIT or COMRESET were met (see the chapter on Initialization for details).
- **REF_CK (0:1)** - differential reference clock (REF_CK1 is positive and REF_CK0 is negative). A "rising edge" is seen when REF_CK1 rises and REF_CK0 falls. This clock is used by the PLL of tracking receivers or by the DLL of oversampling receivers. The frequency can be either 100MHz, which must be supported, or 25MHz, which is optional. It's strongly recommended that the Phy use this clock as the reference for its PLL to generate its transmit clock.
- **REF_CK_Rate** - indicates which of the two possible frequencies is being used (low means 25MHz, high means 100MHz). If the Phy doesn't support the lower speed, it won't have this input.
- **Partial** - places the Phy into its partial power state, during which the Phy leaves the ASIC_CK output active.
- **Slumber** - places the Phy into its slumber power state, during which the Phy turns off the ASIC_CK signal to save power.
- **Reset** - re initializes all internal state information, with the exception of conditions that were set using the Vendor-Specific Port. Those conditions are cleared by a power cycle.

Figure 19-26: SAPIS Block Diagram

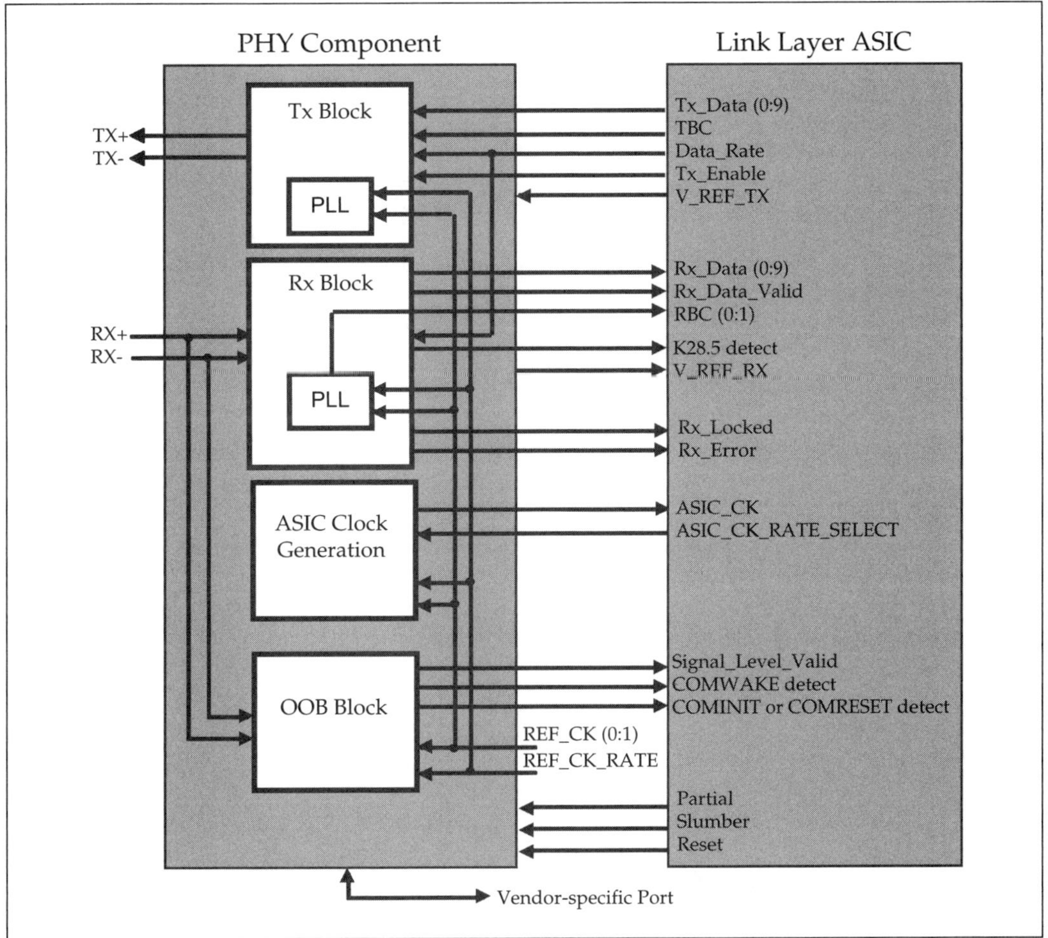

20 *Cables & Connectors*

The Previous Chapter

The previous chapter described the physical layer logic and the electrical characteristics of the SATA interface. The chapter specifically discusses the electrical characteristics of the differential transmitter and receiver used to transmit the bits across the wire. It also covers the changes in the electrical signaling as different interface environments are used. This includes internal cabling, external cabling, backplane environments.

This Chapter

This chapter covers the various form factors, cables and connectors that are described in the specification. The SATA II specification added several new cable and connector types in support of SATA-based server implementations. Also, the particular requirements associated with a given cable/connector type are discussed.

The Next Chapter

The SATA specifications add several key features intended to enable hot pluggable drive platforms. These features include a Hot Plug connector definition, detection of drive insertion and removal, asynchronous signal recovery, and more. The next chapter discusses the requirements necessary for SATA Hot Plug compliance.

Introduction

SATA's mechanical specifications define each connector (plug and receptacle) in detail, but the cable construction is purposely not specified. This allows manufacturers to make trade-offs between performance and cost; thereby giving the flexibility to design for different market segments.

Many of the original SATA cable and connector characteristics were based on the shortcoming and difficulties associated with the ATA implementation. The

SATA connections are superior to ATA in a variety of ways, including:

- smaller and thinner
- easier to manage
- smaller cables promotes better airflow through the system, potentially reducing overall system cost (e.g., fewer/smaller fans).
- blind connector mating capability
- use of edge contacts rather than pins that were prone to bending and breaking
- longer cables (up to one meter in length)
- hot pluggable connector at the drive

The specification states the following design goals for SATA connections:

- Support data rates of 1.5 Gbps and 3.0 Gbps. Clearly, supporting higher speeds would also be desirable since higher bit rates are likely in the future.
- Cost competitive with Ultra ATA. Cost is always an issue for the consumer market that was the first target for SATA, and the cost must be comparable with the cost of ATA.
- Facilitate smooth migration from ATA to SATA, meaning at least equal, and preferably better, cost and performance.
- Provide a common interface for both 2.5-inch and 3.5-inch devices

Usage Models and Form Factors

Cabled connections and direct connect solutions are based on a variety of usage models and related form factors. This section is a brief review of several of these models:

- Internal 1 meter Cabled Host to Device — This is the typical PC desktop application in which a drive is connected by cable to an HBA port. This application is not intended for hot plugging and uses the Gen1i or Gen2i electrical definitions.
- Internal 4-lane Cabled Disk Arrays — Rather than routing four separate cables, as defined in the previous example, a 4-lane cable can be implemented. The HBA connection is a single connector that support the four lanes and the drive end of the cable separates into four single drive connectors. The drive side of the cable may also be a single connection that attaches to an internal proprietary backplane that may have an IC that ensures that the proper Gen1i/Gen2i signal levels are met. Otherwise the characteristics are the same as the single cable solution.
- System to Device External Interconnect (long) – These types of intercon-

nects are anticipated for external drive enclosures that are relatively close to the PC (no longer than 2 meters). The single lane cable must operate at both Gen1 and Gen2 speeds and the HBA must support The Gen1x/Gen2x electrical requirements. Note that a single device may be attached to the cable or a Port Multiplier and multiple-drive enclosure.

- Short Backplane to Device — This application is intended for small drive arrays, in which drives are placed into drive canisters that plug directly into a backplane. Hot plug may or may not be supported and the Gen1m or Gen2m electrical specifications are used.
- Long Backplane to Device — similar to the short backplane implementation, but supporting larger disk arrays and requiring Hot Plug support. Because of the much greater signal attenuation the HBA must use the Gen1x or Gen2x electrical definitions. In addition, the signal levels may be too low to be used; consequently, an intermediate IC may need to be implemented (such as a Port Selector).
- System to System Interconnects (very long) – These connections may be used in applications such data centers where large drive arrays are required. These cabled connections are much longer than a normal external PC application and require higher quality and typically support multiple lanes (four and eight lane cables are defined). The HBA electrical interface requires Gen1x/Gen2x signaling.

It is apparent that many other applications and solutions can be implemented beyond those listed above.

Cables and Connectors — A Review

Detailed mechanical and electrical requirements are defined in the SATA 2.5 specification. This section describes the basic connection types and does not attempt to provide the detailed information that is the province of the specification.

The SATA Device Connector

Hard drives today use either a 3.5-inch or 2.5-inch format. While the SATA signaling connector is the same in either case, the power interface can vary depending on its size. For 3.5 inch drives there is still room for a legacy power connector, which many of the early SATA drives used. On the 2.5 inch drives that's no longer true and the newer power connector must be used.

The drive connector is actually implemented as a plug as illustrated in Figure 20-1 on page 364. Drives can be either plugged directly into a receptacle mounted in a backplane or drive bay or may be connected to the HBA via a cable receptacle. Several features can be seen in this figure, including the separate power and signal portions of the connector. The signal portion contains only 7 pins made up of 3 ground pins and 2 differential signal pairs, one pair for transmitting and the other pair for receiving, while the power portion contains 15 pins. Table 20-1 on page 365 lists each pin by number and name and describes its function where necessary. Note also that the drive contact includes two lengths to support Hot Plug solutions. Refer to Chapter 21, entitled "Hot Plug," on page 375 for more information.

Figure 20-1: Internal Backplane Connectors

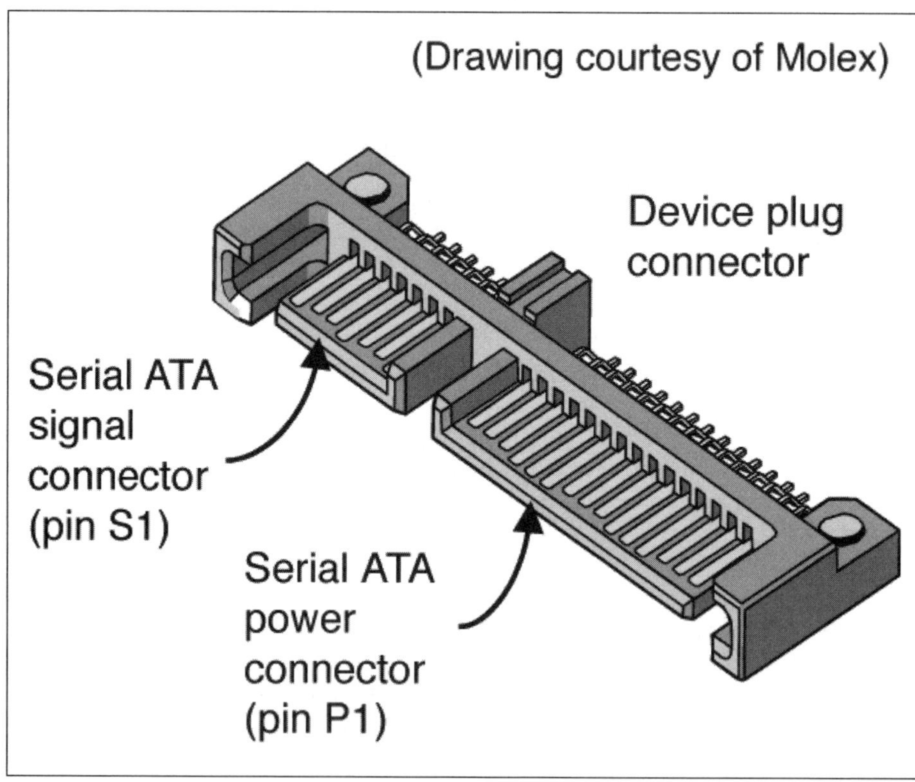

Table 20-1: SATA Drive Plug Contact Designation and Pinout

Contact	Name	Description
S1	GND	
S2	A+	Differential Signal Pair (A)
S3	A-	
S4	GND	Differential Signal Pair (B)
S5	B+	
S6	B-	
S7	GND	
Key (Slot between Signal and Power portion of the plug)		
P1	V_{33}	3.3V Power
P2	V_{33}	3.3V Power
P3	V_{33}	3.3V Power (Pre-charge)
P4	GND	
P5	GND	
P6	GND	
P7	V_5	5.0V Power (Pre-charge)
P8	V_5	5.0V Power
P9	V_5	5.0V Power
P10	GND	
P11	DAS/DSS	Device Activity Signal/Disable Staggered Spinup
P12	GND	
P13	V_{12}	12V Power (Pre-charge)
P14	V_{12}	12V Power
P15	V_{12}	12V Power

Internal cables and connectors

Platforms such as PCs may have entirely internal SATA drive connections. For this application the specification includes two primary connection types:

Direct-connects — a drive plugs directly into a receptacle within a drive bay or internal backplane.
Cable connections — a SATA cable has receptacles at both ends, thus providing the connection between drive plug and HBA plug.

Figure 20-2 on page 366 illustrates both types of connection. The following sections describe the various cable types defined by the specification.

Figure 20-2: Internal Cables and Connectors

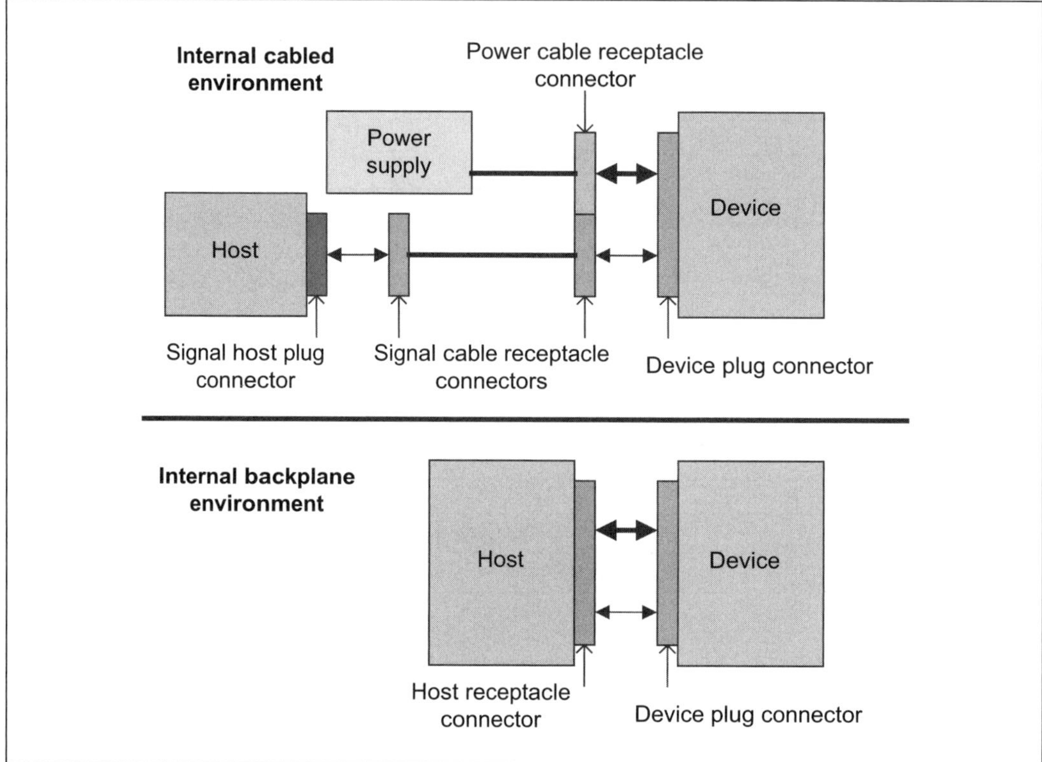

Single Lane Cables

The internal cable connectors defined for SATA are shown in Figure 20-3 on page 367. The pins for the signal and power connectors are the same as they were for the direct-connected case, and they can be attached separately or both together as one unit. The signal cable is not tightly specified in the standard so as to allow vendors to differentiate their products. The cable length is limited to a maximum length of one meter.

One thing to note about the internal cable design is that, unlike the backplane connectors, it's not rated for hot plugging. The reason is the expectation that access to these cables will require opening an enclosure. An operator could certainly do that, but wouldn't do so for a hot-plug operation. Consequently, the connectors are not robustly blind mated or self aligned, and the connectors are not designed to tolerate multiple make and break cycles. The expectation for these cables is that the manufacturer would install these at the factory and the user would change them only rarely.

Figure 20-3: Internal Signal/Power Cable - Receptacle to Receptacle

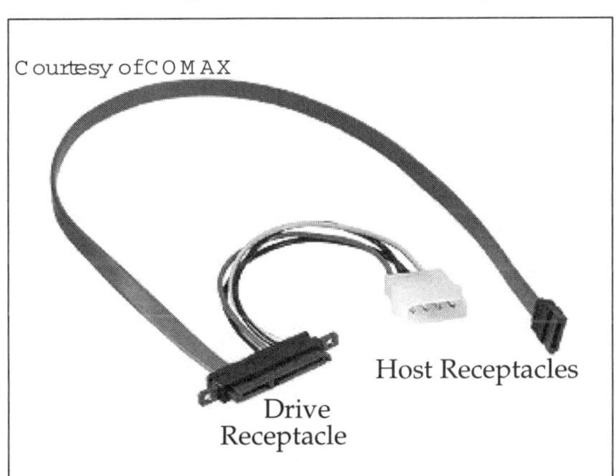

Note that some implementations may use a receptacle at the host side rather than a plug. In these implementations, the cable will have a plug on the host side as shown in Figure 20-4.

Figure 20-4: Internal Signal/Power Cable - Receptacle to Plug

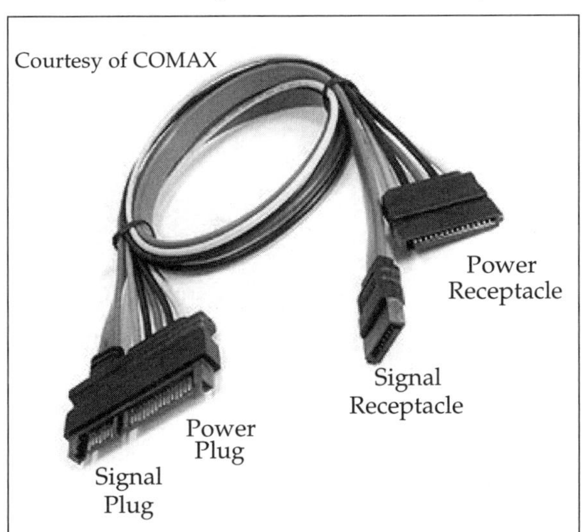

Multiple-lane Cables

In perhaps the most simple implementation, a multiple-lane cable can be used for connecting multiple SATA links from an HBA to individual drives. Other applications include connecting a RAID controller (Perhaps built into a Port Multiplier) to a backplane within the same enclosure. The specification defines 2-lane and 4-lane cable widths, and specifies the pinouts and dimensions associated with these connectors.

Backplane connectors

The connectors defined for a directly-connected host and device are shown in Figure 20-1 on page 364.

Figure 20-5: Direct Connect Drive Plug and Receptacle Connectors

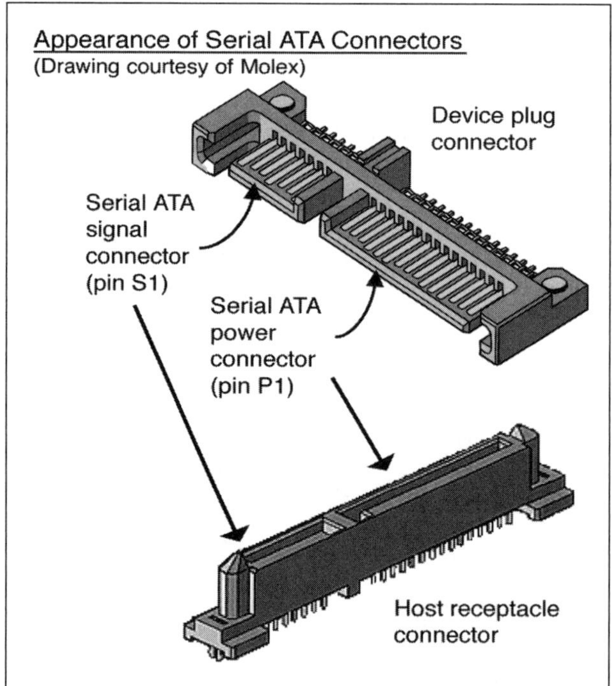

External cables and connectors

SATA was originally developed as a replacement for the legacy ATA environment. The specification for internal connections satisfies these PC applications in which connectors are expected to be unplugged/plugged on a very occasional basis, and leading to designs that are required to withstand 50 plug/unplug cycles. Furthermore, the maximum cable length of one meter will typically exceed the requirements originally anticipated by standard applications.

With the growing desire to move SATA drives into very large storage applications, the original SATA cable definition was insufficient in nearly all respects. The new cables and connectors designed for external applications needed to support a variety of features including:

- Connectors designed to handle many unplug/plug cycles
- Improved connector retention
- Support for faster transmission rates
- Improve transmission characteristics
- Longer cables (2 meters and beyond)
- Support for hot plugging
- Improved ability to control Electromagnetic Interference (EMI)
- Requirements for handling electrostatic discharge (ESD)

In summary, the external connections required a more robust mechanical design to help prevent the cable from being accidentally disconnected. With this in mind, the external SATA (eSATA) connectors were designed with a variety of features including spring clips in the receptacle and indentions in the cable connectors where it springs fit. Also, measures were taken to meet the requirements for electrostatic discharge (ESD) and electromagnetic interference (EMI) emission. For example, an additional layer of shielding is added around the differential signal pairs, and the cable connectors and drive enclosure/PC connectors are all shielded with a metal all four sides of the signal conductor.

Two cable and connector types are defined by the specification:

- Single-lane cable — The cable ends have identical plugs that fit into receptacles at a SATA drive enclosure and into a receptacle at the host side. The maximum cable length is specified at 2.0 meters.
- Multi-lane cables — This cable type is based on the Infiniband SFF-8470 specification. The SATA and Serial-Attached SCSI (SAS) both use this cable, but SATA defines optional blocking keys that present the modified eSATA cable from being plugged into a SAS receptacle.

eSATA Single Lane Cable and Connectors

Figure 20-6 pictures an eSATA single-lane cable. The cable ends are plugs that fit into the receptacles at the host and drive enclosure. The external cables consist only of the do not include power. The cables and connectors have a total of seven contacts:

- Two signal pairs (4 contacts)
- Three ground contacts

Figure 20-6: eSATA Single-Lane Cable

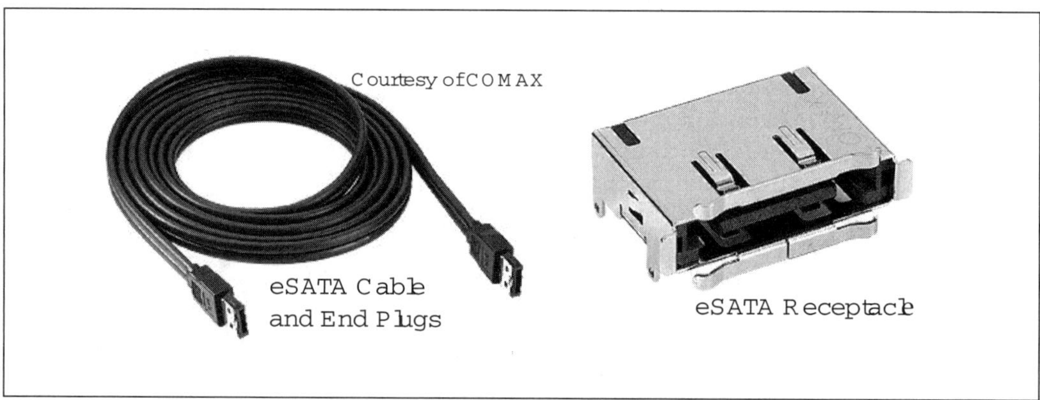

eSATA Multiple-Lane Cable and Connectors

Figure 20-7 on page 371 illustrates the SFF-8470 infiniband cable and connectors that are used by SATA and SAS. If fact, the example illustration chosen is of a SAS cable. The one variable defined by SATA is the possibility of adding blocking keys to the cable-end plugs that would prevent a keyed SATA cable from being plugged into a SAS receptacle. The placement of the keys are illustrated in Figure 20-8 on page 371.

Figure 20-7: eSATA Connectors for Multiple-Lane Cables

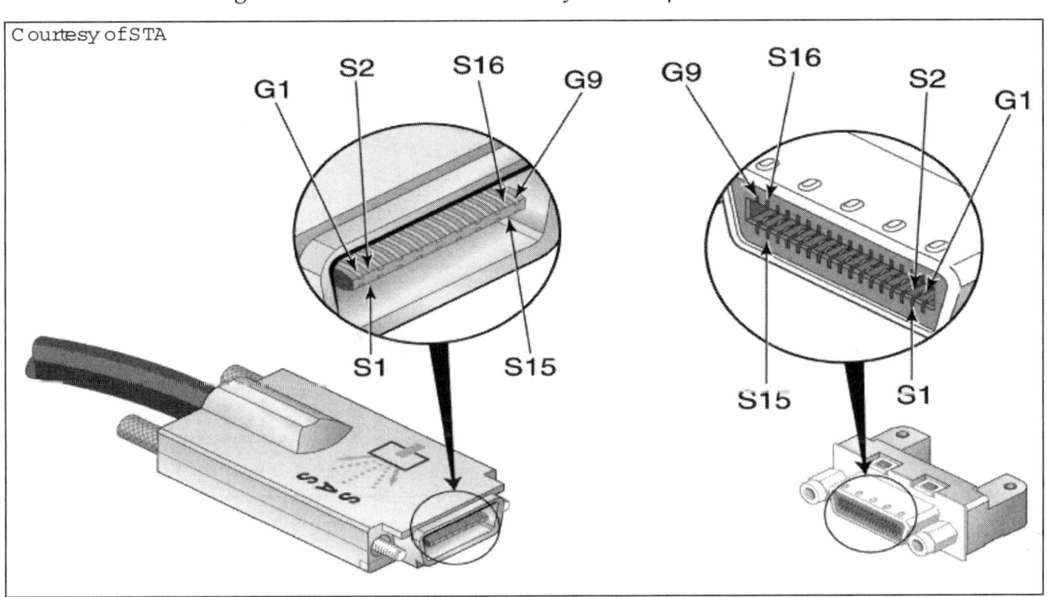

Figure 20-8: Keying Locations Inside the eSATA Multiple-Lane Cable Plug

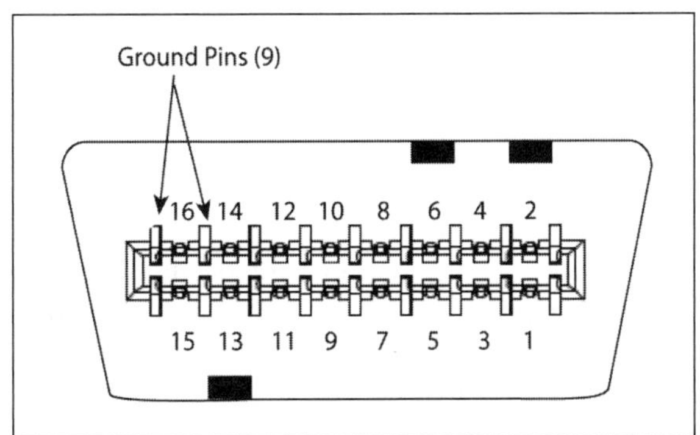

Hot Plug Support

Hot Plugging is required the form factors and applications that require the Gen1m/Gen2m and Gen1x/Gen2x electrical characteristics. In these cases the receptacles to which a SATA drive is connected, must also included contacts that are longer than others. This allows the contacts to mate and break at three different times (long to long, long to short, and short to short). The Hot Plug connections are illustrated in Figure 20-9.

Figure 20-9: Hot Plug Three-Step Mating

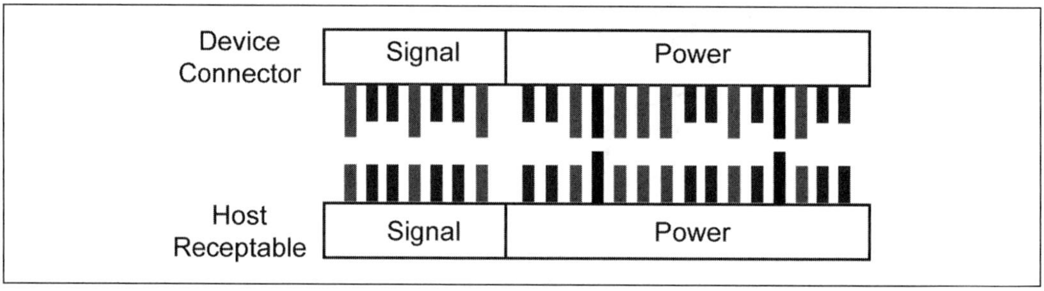

The case of a long pin mating to another long pin results in the first contact when a device is plugged in. These long pins are connected to ground so that any static charge that may be present at either connector can be discharged before any other pins make contact. The next set of pins to make contact will be one long and one short pin. These pins are defined as current limiting power pins (i.e., they include a current-limiting resistor installed serially in the path). This allows the power to begin charging any lines or capacitors that might be present on the other device while still limiting the risk of a large in-rush of current. Finally, the short-to-short pins make contact, and these will connect the remaining power pins (that do not include a current-limiting resistor) as well as the signal pins.

Still another aspect of Hot Plug connectors are the guides on either end that are designed to support blind-mating and self-aligning connections. This would be useful under any conditions, but is more so in a hot-plug environment where the pins must make contact in a certain order. If it were possible for the connector to be plugged in at an angle, the pins might make contact in a different order and defeat the hot-plug goal.

Facilitating hot-plug operations in these ways is important for a backplane environment, where the expectation is that drives could be externally installed without the need to open any enclosures.

Host Bus Adapters

There are HBA products on the market today that are designed for external cabling, others use internal connections, and some implement both types. Most of these were created to connect with PCI, PCI-X, and PCIe buses and use the standard PCI-type form factor, but some were designed for the mobile market and use the older CardBus or newer Express Card interface associated with PC Card slots.

Port Multipliers

Port multipliers are available as stand-alone devices or may be incorporated into a storage unit. Combining features like port multipliers, RAID controllers, and other functions into a single package is a popular option. See Chapter 15 for details on Port Multiplier operation.

21 Hot Plug

Previous Chapter

The previous chapter covers the various form factors, cables and connectors that are either described in the standard. The SATA II specification added several new cable and connector types in support of SATA-based server implementations.

This Chapter

The SATA specifications add several key features intended to enable hot pluggable drives. These features include a Hot Plug connector definition, detection of drive insertion and removal, and asynchronous signal recovery. This chapter discusses these and other features that support a Hot Plug solution.

The Next Chapter

SATA defines two levels of power conservation for the link, called Slumber and Partial. The next chapter describes the protocol associated with forcing the link into a low power state and recovering back to normal power and operation.

Overview

Whether Hot Plug is required or not, depends upon the particular platform. A wide variety of SATA Hot Plug solutions may be implemented. The specification defines three sets of electrical parameters based on the environment into which a SATA subsystem is implemented. The definition of these environments also determine whether the Host Controller must support the Hot Plug electrical requirements:

- Gen1i/Gen2i Implementations do not require Hot Plug support; however, if implemented in a short backplane implementation, Hot Plug capability is required.
- Gen1m/Gen2m Implementations require support for Hot Plug.
- Gen1x/Gen2x Implementations are required to support Hot Plug.

Platforms designed for Hot Plug-aware software may implement hardware that under software control can remove power from the connector prior to inserting or removing a drive. This chapter focuses on the features provided by SATA to assist in implementing Hot Plug platforms. The SATA specifications define the following key features that may be implemented in Hot Plug solutions:

- Asynchronous Signal Recovery (SATA II)
- Two Connector Contact Lengths to support Hot Plug Connectors
- In-rush Current Limiting Definition (SATA II)
- Drive Presence Detect (SATA II)
- Asynchronous Event Notification (SATA II)

Hot Plug Connector

Perhaps one of the most fundamental elements of a Hot Plug solution is a connector that reduces the likelihood that hardware damage will result from plugging or unplugging a device while the interface is powered and active.

Two types of Hot Plug connectors are defined:

- Cable-based connectors have two contact points
- Backplane-based connectors have three contact points

When a Hot Plug operation is performed two possibilities exist:

1. Power is present at the connector — insertion and removal is considered a surprise event because software has no prior notice of the Hot Plug event. When the surprise insertion or removal occurs, software either polls registers to detect the event or hardware may notify software directly.
2. Software has previously been notified by the user that a Hot Plug operation is requested. Under software control power is removed prior to the drive being removed and replaced.

The specification supports either of these types of Hot Plug operation.

Cable Hot Plug Connection

A SATA device connector has short and long contacts and the cable connector has all short contacts as illustrated in Figure 21-1 on page 377. This results in only two mating points. Table 21-1 on page 377 lists the mating order of the contacts. The specification does not consider the cable connection to be Hot Plug compliant, in that it is not qualified to support insertion and removal while power is applied.

Figure 21-1: Pin Lengths and Mating for Cable Hot Plug Connection

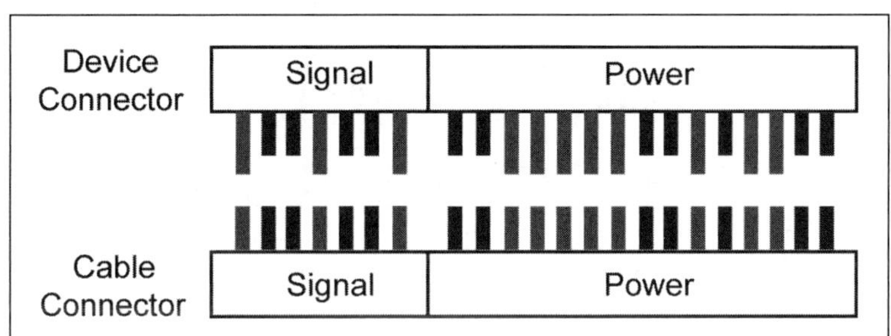

Table 21-1: Contact Mating When Drive is Plugged into Receptacle

Contact Combinations	Mating Points	Contact Assignments
Long to Short	First	3.3vdc Precharge Contact 5vdc Precharge Contact 12vdc Precharge Contact All ground Contacts
Short to Short	Second	Other 3.3vdc Contacts (2) Other 5vdc Contacts (2) Other 12vdc Contacts (2) Device Activity/Staggered Spinup disable Differential Signal Pairs (4 contacts)

Backplane Hot Plug Connector

Figure 21-2 illustrates the contact points of a backplane-based Hot Plug connector. Notice that the illustration shows the standard short and long contacts at the device connector and two long contacts at the host receptacle. The layout of contacts provide three mating points as a drive is plugged or unplugged from the backplane receptacle. Please also see Table 21-2.

Figure 21-2: Pin Lengths and Mating for Backplane Hot Plug Connections

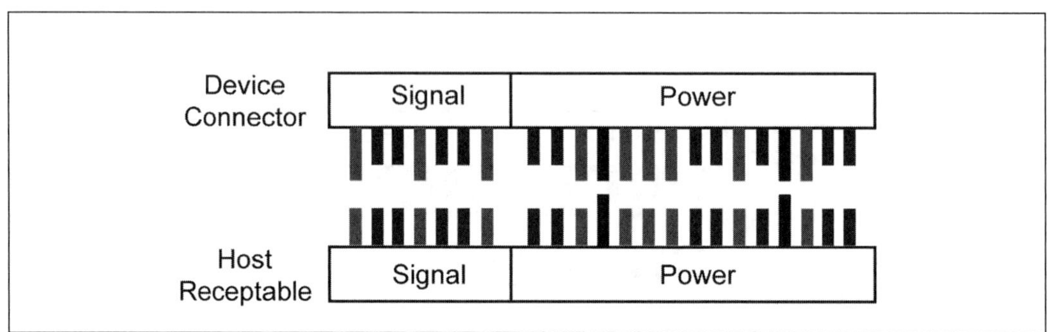

Table 21-2: Contact Mating When Drive is Plugged into Receptacle

Contact Combinations	Mating Points	Contact Assignments
Long to Long	First	Two Ground Contacts
Long to Short	Second	3.3vdc Precharge Contact 5vdc Precharge Contact 12vdc Precharge Contact All Other Ground Contacts (6)
Short to Short	Third	Other 3.3vdc Contacts (2) Other 5vdc Contacts (2) Other 12vdc Contacts (2) Device Activity/Staggered Spinup disable Differential Signal Pairs (4 contacts)

Drive Plug/Unplug Detection

The ability to detect the insertion or removal of a drive can be implemented by a Hot Plug compatible host or PM device port interface. Figure 21-3 illustrates an example circuit for detecting drive attachment and removal, which is provided by the specification.

To support hot insertion and removal, the specification requires that SATA devices bus the power contacts together for each supply voltage as is illustrated in Figure 21-3. The contact assignments are:

- P1, P2, and P3 -- 3.3V power contacts
- P7, P8, and P9 -- 5V power contacts
- P13, P14, and P15 -- 12V power contacts

When device attachment or removal is detected, the host interface sets the "X" bit in the SError register's DIAG field (Figure 21-4).

Figure 21-3: Example Drive Attachment/Detachment Detection Mechanism

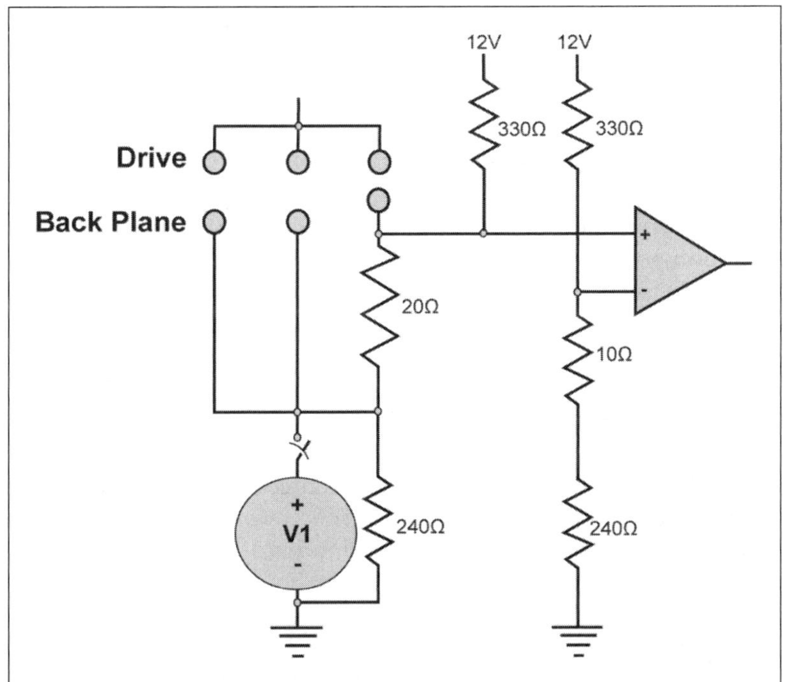

Figure 21-4: Exchanged Bit of DIAG Field of SError Register

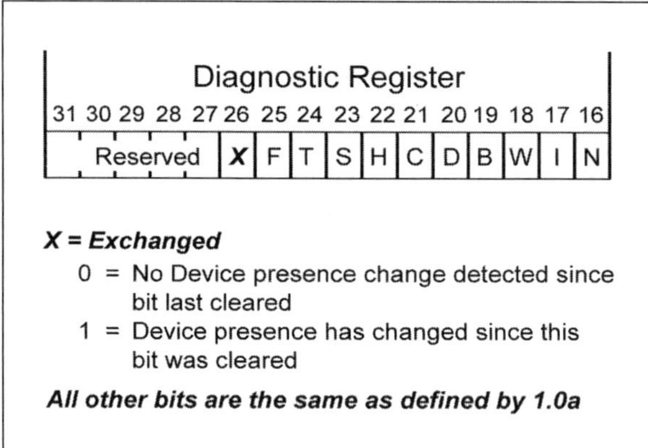

In-Rush Current Limiting

Figure 21-3 on page 379 also illustrates the In-Rush current limiting when a drive in plunged into the host receptacle. The power line with the current limiting resistor makes contact with the drive's power rail prior to the other two power contacts; thereby reducing the in-rush current.

Asynchronous Event Notification

Asynchronous Notification is a feature that could be used in a hot plus implementation. For example, a Port Multiplier implementation could notify software of drive insertion or removal. Figure 21-5 on page 381 illustrates this solution.

When an event occurs at a PM port, the PM notifies the host by sending a Set Device Bits FIS with the notification (N) bit set. It also sets the bit in the second DWord corresponding the PM port number sending the notification. In this example bit 1 is set. When the HBA receives the Set Device Bits FIS is recognizes the notification and updates the corresponding bit in it's SNotification register. An interrupt may be generated to notify software of the event or software may simply periodically poll the register.

Figure 21-5: Drive Removal Triggers Asynchronous Event Notification

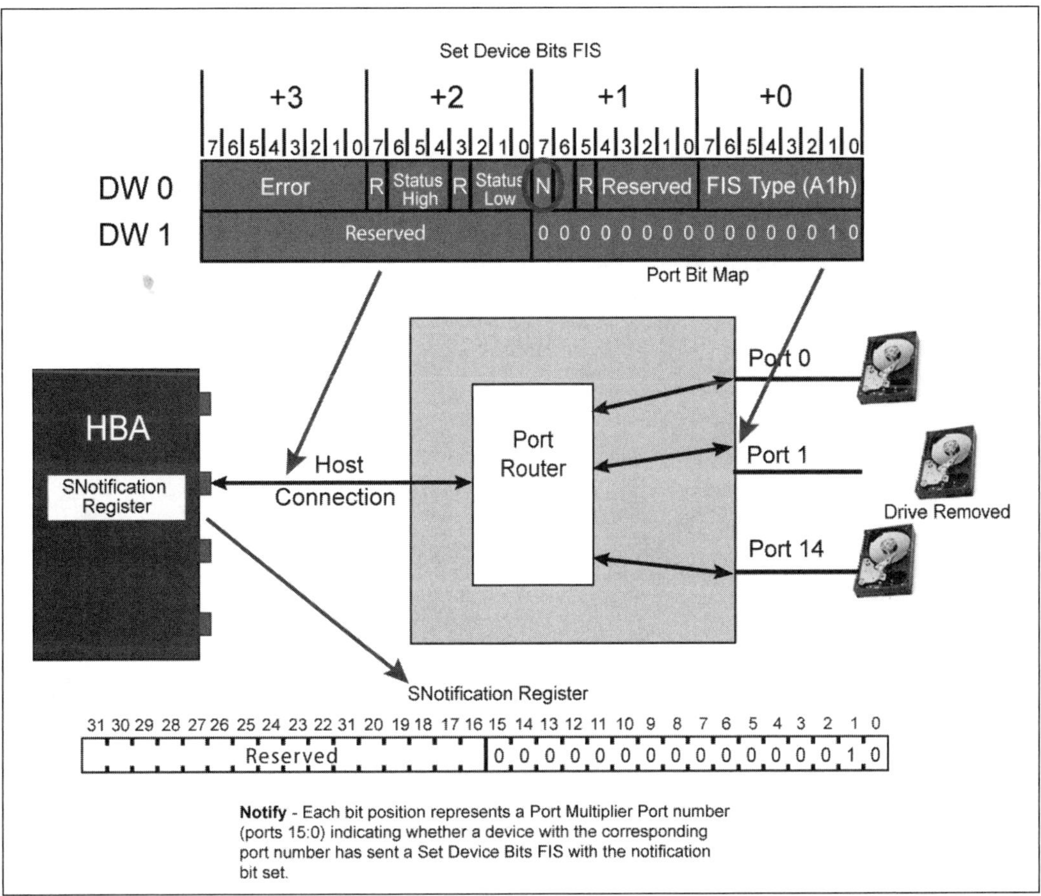

22 Link Power Management

Previous Chapter

The SATA specifications add several key features intended to enable hot pluggable drives. These features include a Hot Plug connector definition, detection of drive insertion and removal, and asynchronous signal recovery. The previous chapter discussed these and other features that support a Hot Plug solution.

This Chapter

SATA defines two levels of power conservation for the link, called Slumber and Partial. This chapter describes the protocol associated with transitioning the link into a low power state and recovering back to normal power and operation.

The Next Chapter

A variety of features built into the SATA subsystem assist in diagnosing problems, ensuring compliance, and validating proper operation of the SATA interface. The next chapter discusses these Built In Self Tests (BIST) some of which are required, while others are optional.

Overview

Like other serial interfaces based on 8b/10b encoding, SATA Phys are normally in the Phy Rdy state and are continuously sending and receiving information to keep the interface in the communicating state. Even during long periods of disk inactivity the SATA interface continues to send SYNC primitives (logical idle) to keep the interface ready to handle commands with very little latency when they are issued. Of course, the downside to this approach is that power continues to be consumed even when no work is being performed. The SATA specification defines an optional mechanism for placing the interface into the electrical idle state to conserve power and back into the normal operating state.

SATA defines two levels of link power conservation where the Phy is powered, but is dissipating less power than when in the PhyRdy state.

- Partial — Link power consumption is reduced by some vendor-specific level and the exit latency back to the PhyRdy state must be 10µs or less.
- Slumber — Link power consumption is reduced by some vendor-specific level less than that of the Partial state, and the exit latency from this state must be no longer than 10ms. As in the Partial state a zero differential voltage must be maintained unless a transmitter is AC coupled.

Even though the specification does not define a specific amount of power savings, the vendor may (the spec. says "should") publish the "not to exceed" power when in the Partial and Slumber states.

Configuring Link Power Management

Because link power management is an optional feature, the host implementation may or may support power management and the same is true of the drive. Whether a SATA host system supports link power management will likely depend on the operation environment; the two extremes being, battery-powered notebook computers where power saving is crucial and server-based platforms where the emphasis in on non-stop operation and low-latency disc access.

Detecting/Enabling Drive Link Power Management

Whether a drive supports the Partial or Slumber states is reported in the Identify Drive data. A drive may support:

- receipt of Host-initiated commands to enter Link Power Management
- initiation of commands that place the link into the partial or slumber states

Table 22-1 on page 385 lists the Identify Data information related to link power management, including its Link Power Management capabilities and whether these features are enabled.

Drives that report they can receive requests to enter the Partial or Slumber states are enabled to do so by default. However, drives that report the ability to initiate entry into a low-power link state are disabled to do so by default. Software must enable this feature via the SetConfiguration command.

Table 22-1: Identify Data Defines Drive's Support for Link Power Management

Word Offset	R/O	Description
76		**Serial ATA Capabilities** 15-11 Reserved 10 Phy event counters supported *9 Receiving Link Power Management requests supported* 8 Native Command Queuing supported 7-4 Reserved 3 Reserved for SATA 2 Supports Serial ATA Gen-2 signaling 1 Supports Serial ATA Gen-1 signaling 0 Reserved (0)
77		**Reserved for SATA**
78	Optional	**Serial ATA Features** 15-7 Reserved 6 Software settings preservation supported 5 Reserved 4 In-order data delivery supported *3 Drive initiation of Link Power Management requests supported* 2 DMA Setup FIS Auto-Activate optimization supported 1 DMA Setup FIS non-zero buffer offsets supported 0 Reserved (0)
79	Optional	**Serial ATA Features Enabled** 15-7 Reserved 6 Software settings preservation enabled 5 Reserved 4 In-order data delivery enabled *3 Drive initiates Link Power Management requests* 2 DMA Setup FIS Auto-Activate optimization enabled 1 DMA Setup FIS non-zero buffer offsets enabled 0 Reserved (0)
80-255		**Defined in ATA/ATAPI-7**

Link Power Management Protocol

The protocol associated with Link Power Management uses the primitives listed in Table 22-2. As discussed in the previous section, both the HBA and Drive may be able to initiate the protocol that will place the link into the Partial or Slumber states. The protocol is the same regardless of who initiates the sequence. The final aspect of this protocol is returning the link to its fully powered and communicating state, which is initiated by COMWAKE OOB signaling.

Table 22-2: Primitives Used in Link Power Management Protocol

Primitive	Name	Description
PMREQ_S	Power Management Request to enter Slumber state	This primitive is sent continuously until PMACK or PMNAK is received. When PMACK is received, current node (host or device) will stop sending PMREQ_S and enter the Slumber power management state.
PMREQ_P	Power Management Request to enter Partial state	This primitive is sent continuously until PMACK or PMNAK is received. When PMACK is received, current node (host or device) will stop PMREQ_P and enter the Partial power management state.
PMACK	Power Management Acknowledge	Sent in response to a PMREQ_S or PMREQ_P when the receiving node is prepared to enter either partial or slumber state.
PMNAK	Power Management No Acknowledge	Sent in response to a PMREQ_S or PMREQ_P when the receiving node is not prepared to enter a low-power state or when power management is not supported.

Host Initiated Entry into Partial/Slumber

The protocol associated with entry into either the Partial or Slumber state is described in this section. Figure 22-1 on page 388 illustrates the handshake performed between the HBA and Drive that causes the link to enter a low-power state. The sequence of events are described below and assumes that the link is currently in the logical idle state (i.e., transmitting and receiving SYNC primitives) and that the power modes are supported.

1. The Application layer initiates requests for entering either the Partial or Slumber state. The specification does not define a mechanism that triggers the Application layer to issue a request and is left as implementation specific. For example the AHCI provides registers that give software the means to both direct the HBA to initiate request to enter a low-power link state, and to enable the HBA hardware to initiate entry into a link low-power state autonomously.
2. The Transport layer receives and forwards the Power Management Request to enter Partial or Slumber to the link layer.
3. The power management request causes the Link layer to enter its Partial or Slumber state (L_TPMPartial or L_TPMSlumber). In this state PMREQ primitives are sent to the Phy layer. PMREQ primitives are delivered continuously until the Power Management Acknowledgement (PMACK) or Power Management No Acknowledgement (PMNAK) primitives are received from the drive.
4. The HBA physical layer transmits the primitives across the physical link.
5. The drive's Phy layer forwards all link traffic to the Link layer where it is decoded.
6. Upon detecting the PMREQ primitives, the Link layer enters its PMOff state.
7. While in the PMOff state the Link layer sends PMACK primitives for transmission by the Phy layer. Note that a minimum of four and a maximum of 16 PMACK primitives must be sent, after which the Link layer enters the ChkPhyRdy state. When in the ChkPhyRdy state the Link layer signals the Phy to enter the Partial or Slumber state.
8. The Phy layer transmits the PMACK primitives to the HBA.
9. The Phy layer detects either the Partial or Slumber signal from the Link layer and transitions to the electrical idle state.
10. The HBA receiver continues forwarding primitives to the Link layer where they are decoded.
11. When the HBA Link layer detects PMACK primitives it transitions to the ChkPhyRdy state and the transmit side discontinues PMREQ transmission.

12. During the ChkPhyRdy state the Link layer signals Partial or Slumber to the Phy layer. This cause the HBA's Phy to transition to its electrical idle state.

Figure 22-1: Host-Initiated Handshake Sequence for Entering Partial/Slumber State

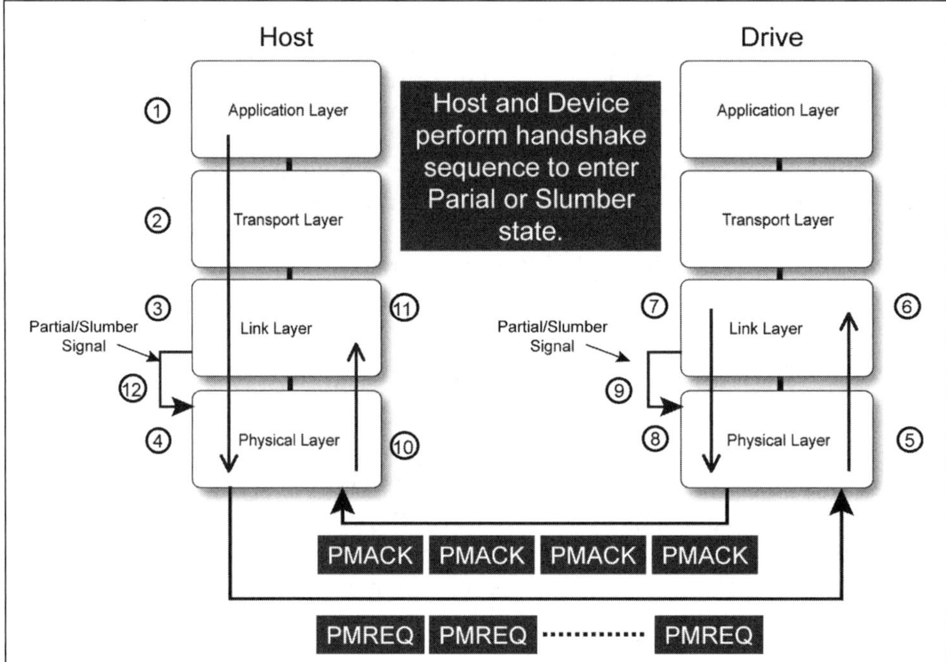

Drive Initiated Entry into Partial/Slumber

A drive must be enabled by software to initiate requests to enter either of the low-power link states. This is accomplished with the Set Feature command with a Sector Count value of 03h. Once enabled the Application layer initiates the Power Management request. The actual protocol is identical to that used when the HBA initiates the Power Management request, except the roles of the initiator and target are reversed.

COMWAKE Protocol

When in the Partial or Slumber states the transmitters at each end of the link are in the electrical idle state. COMWAKE OOB signaling initiates the link wakeup sequence. The wakeup protocol is different depending on whether the HBA or drive initiate wakeup. The Phy layer state machine defines the actions to be taken. The transmission of the COMWAKE OOB signaling causes entry to the state machine at the COMWAKE transmission state. The state machine actions are followed normally except that calibration and speed detection are skipped. The wakeup signaling is performed at the previously negotiated speeds.

Host Initiated Wakeup

Figure 22-2 illustrates the sequence of events that are taken when a wakeup is initiated by the HBA. The HBA triggers the wakeup by sending the COMWAKE OOB sequence. Upon detecting COMWAKE, the SATA device responds with COMWAKE. The HBA detects the end of COMWAKE from the Device and transmits D10.2 values until it detects ALIGN primitives. In response, the HBA transmits ALIGN primitive. When the HBA and Device are both transmitting and receiving ALIGN primitives PhyRdy is asserted and the link is in its communicating state.

Figure 22-2: Wakeup Initiated by HBA

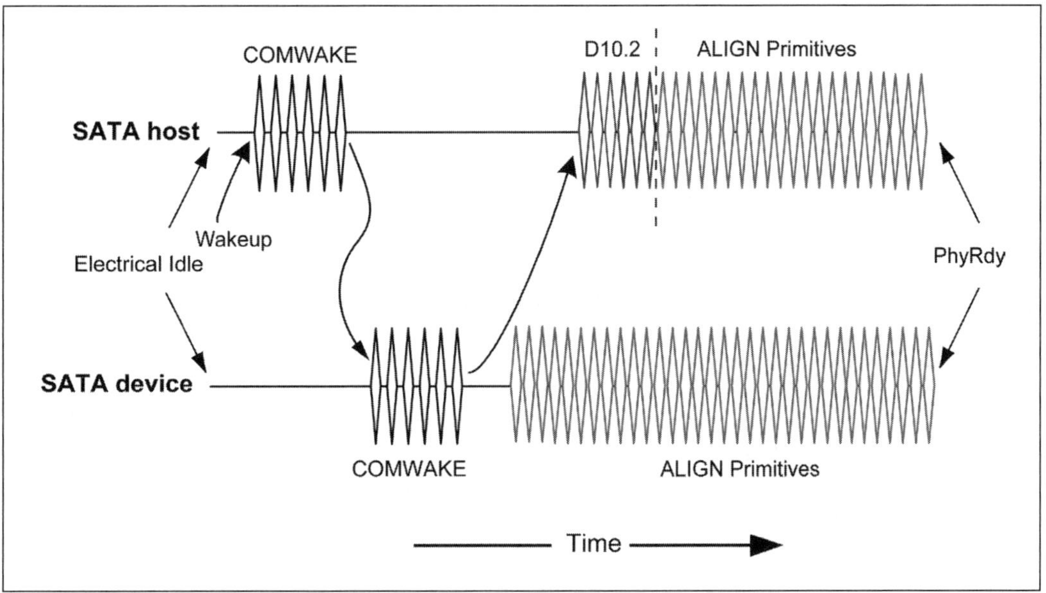

Device Initiated Wakeup

A SATA Device also initiates wakeup by transmitting a COMWAKE sequence followed by ALIGN primitives. Upon detecting COMWAKE from the Device, the HBA transmits the D10.2 values and then ALIGN primitives after detecting ALIGN primitives from the Device. When the HBA and Device are both transmitting and receiving ALIGN primitives, the Phy layer is ready to continue normal communications.

Figure 22-3: Wakeup Initiated by SATA Device

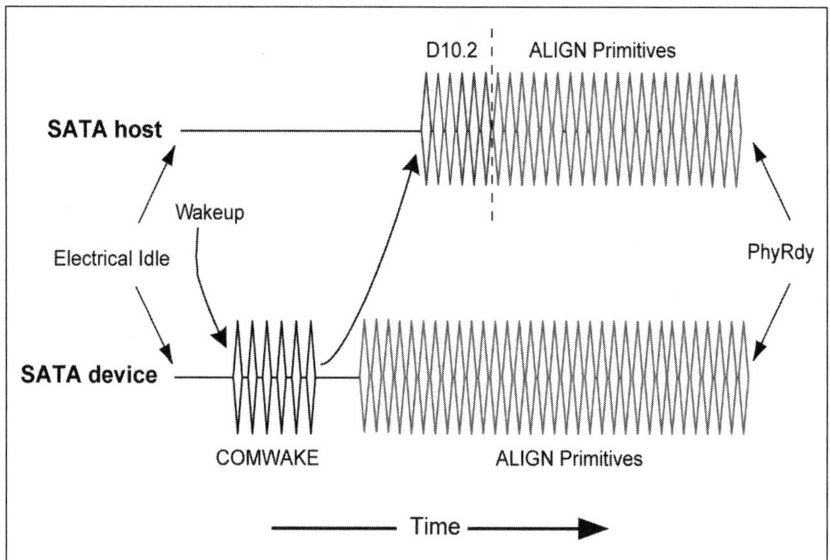

Electrical Idle Conditions

Idle requirements vary depending on whether the link is DC coupled or AC coupled and whether the Partial or Slumber state has been selected.

Idle Requirements

When in the Partial and Slumber states, the Phy must maintain the normal common-mode voltage levels on the signal lines with a zero differential voltage. The specification specifically requires that all four conductors of the signal pairs be held at 250mV. This requirement also applies to AC coupled transmitters when they are in the Partial state.

Special Condition for AC Coupled transmitters

When AC-coupled transmitters are in the Slumber state they are allowed to float the differential pairs, but a zero differential voltage must be maintained.

23 *BIST Features*

Previous Chapter

SATA defines two levels of power conservation for the link, called Slumber and Partial. The previous chapter described the protocol associated with transitioning the link into a low power state and recovering back to normal power and operation.

This Chapter

A variety of features built into the SATA subsystem assist in diagnosing problems, ensuring compliance, and validating proper operation of the SATA interface. This chapter details these Built In Self Tests (BIST) some of which are required, while others are optional.

Overview

The SATA specification defines several Built-In Self Tests that can be entered under either HBA or Drive control. These tests include:

- Far End Retimed Loopback
- Far End Analog Loopback (optional)
- Far End Transmit Only (optional)
- Near End Analog Loopback (optional)

These tests are intended to assist in a variety of testing environments including:

- Laboratory testing using conventional equipment
- Inspection testing
- Observation testing

These tests were not designed with in-system automated testing in mind.

BIST FIS

Entry into the test modes listed in the overview (except Near End Analog Loopback) requires a BIST (Built-In Self Test) Activate FIS be delivered from the Application layer of the node initiating the test. The device on the opposite end if the link (the far-end device) receives the BIST and enters the appropriate test mode. The specification does define the associated protocols and requirements for BIST. However, no method is specified for triggering the BIST Activate delivery. That is, there is no BIST command defined.

BIST Format and Contents

The BIST Activate FIS is defined as bidirectional; thereby allowing either the HBA or Drive to initiate entry into a particular BIST mode of operation. Figure 23-1 illustrates the content of the BIST Activate FIS and Table 23-1 describes each of the fields.

Figure 23-1: Format of the BIST Activate FIS

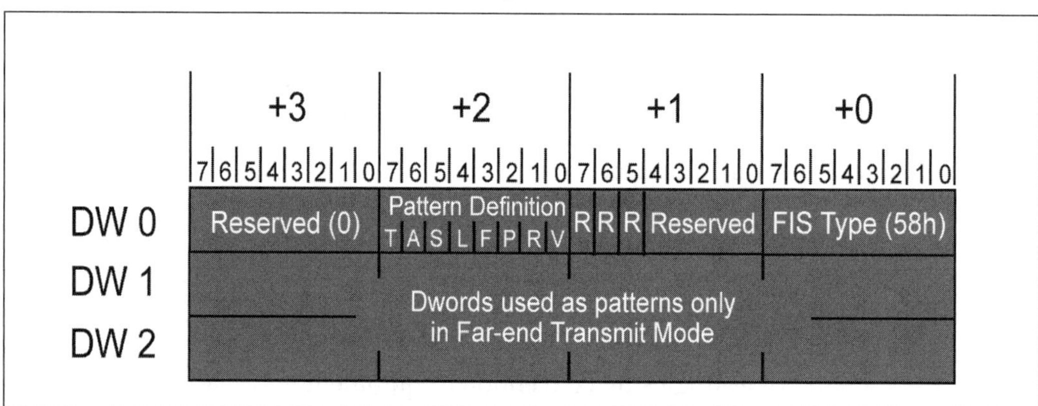

Table 23-1: BIST Activate FIS Field Descriptions

Field	Name	Description
FIS Type	FIS Type	A value of 58h identifies this FIS as a BIST Activate.
PM Port	Port Multiplier Port	This field allows a BIST Activate FIS to be directed to a drive attached to a Port Multiplier port and is only used by the HBA.
V	Vendor-Specific Test Mode	When this bit is set all other Pattern Definition bits must be ignored.
R	Reserved	Bit fields are always zero.
P	Primitive bit	Optional bit that is only valid when the T bit is set. When the P bit is set the DATA1 and DATA2 values are set up as primitives. The lower byte (D7:D0) of each DATA field contains a control (K) value followed by data values that define a valid primitive.
F	Far End Analog Loopback	This optional bit causes the node on the opposite end of the link to enter its analog loopback state (if supported). In this mode the raw data is received and retransmitted without clocking the data using the local receive clock and is intended to simply verify connectivity between the transmitting and receiving nodes.
L	Far End Retimed Loopback	This bit when set causes the node at the opposite end of the link to enter its Retimed loopback state. When data is received it re-clocks and re-transmits the data.
S	Scrambling Bypass	This bit may only be set when the "T" bit is set and must be ignored if the "P" bit is also set. The S bit is set when the node originating the Far End Transmit test wishes the data being returned to be left unscrambled.
A	ALIGN Bypass	This bit is only valid when the "T" bit is set. Setting the bit suppresses the delivery of ALIGN primitives. Otherwise ALIGN primitives are delivered periodically as required by the SATA protocol.
T	Far End Transmit Only	Setting this bit causes the Far End node to transmit repeatedly the contents of the DATA1 and DATA2 fields.

Table 23-1: BIST Activate FIS Field Descriptions

Field	Name	Description
DATA1	Dword One	This 4-byte field is only valid when the "T" bit is set and can be loaded with any value by the node that initiates the Far End Transmit Only mode.
DATA2	Dword Two	This 4-byte field is only valid when the "T" bit is set and can be loaded with any value by the node that initiates the Far End Transmit Only mode.

Table 23-1 makes apparent the requirement that only one test mode can be enabled at a time and that some bits have meaning only for a given BIST mode. The specification provides a clear explanation of the bit combinations that are legal. These combinations are presented in Table 23-2 on page 396 and the specified actions taken are summarized.

Table 23-2: Legal Pattern Definition Bit Combinations

BIST Mode	F	L	T	P	A	S	V
Far End Retimed Loopback	1	0	0	0	0	0	0
Far End Analog Loopback	0	1	0	0	0	0	0
Far End Transmit Only with ALIGN primitives and scrambled data	0	0	1	0	0	0	0
Far End Transmit Only with ALIGN primitives but without scrambled data	0	0	1	0	0	1	0
Far End Transmit Only without ALIGN primitives but with scrambled data	0	0	1	0	1	0	0
Far End Transmit Only without ALIGN primitives and without scrambled data	0	0	1	0	1	1	0
Far End Transmit primitives with ALIGNs	0	0	1	1	0	na	0
Far End Transmit primitives without ALIGNs	0	0	1	1	1	na	0
Vendor Specific BIST mode	na	na	na	na	na	na	1

BIST Transmission/Reception

BIST delivery is initiated by the Application layer in an application-specific manner. Transmission of the BIST FIS is intended to setup the test modes within both the near and far end nodes.

Far End Node Setup

When the far-end node receives the BIST FIS, it first verifies that the FIS has been received successfully and then returns the R_OK primitive to notify the transmitter that the BIS has been received. In addition the Application layer is notified of BIST FIS reception, evaluates the Pattern Definition and sets up the device to fulfill the BIST request. This setup is directed by the local application, which must place the transport, link, and physical layers into the states required for transmitting the requested data stream.

Near End Node Setup

Once successful transmission of the BIST FIS is received (R_OK), the near-end node should transmit SYNC primitives until it is ready to perform the specified operation. In addition, the near-end node notifies its Application layer that R_OK has been received from the far-end node. The local application then places its own Application, Transport, Link and Physical layers into the states necessary to deliver/receive the appropriate data stream.

Far End Retimed Loopback

This test is the only one whose implementation is required by both HBAs and devices. Entry into this test is course achieved by via the BIS FIS with the Pattern Definition field set as listed in Table 23-3 on page 398. Figure 23-2 on page 398 illustrates entry into the Far End Retimed loopback mode and the far-end node's actions. When in this state, data received by the far-end node is extracted by the receiver and associated logic as it does normally. The far-end node forwards the resulting parallel data to the transmit side where it is serialized and re-transmitted using its local clock. The Far-End Interface remains in the Far-End Retimed Loopback state until the originating node initiates a COMRESET sequence.

The data patterns delivered from the origination node must include delivery of the ALIGN primitives to allow for clock compensation at the receiving node.

Table 23-3: Pattern Definition for Far End Retimed Loopback

BIST Mode	F	L	T	P	A	S	V
Far End Retimed Loopback	1	0	0	0	0	0	0

Figure 23-2: Far-End Re-timed Loopback Test

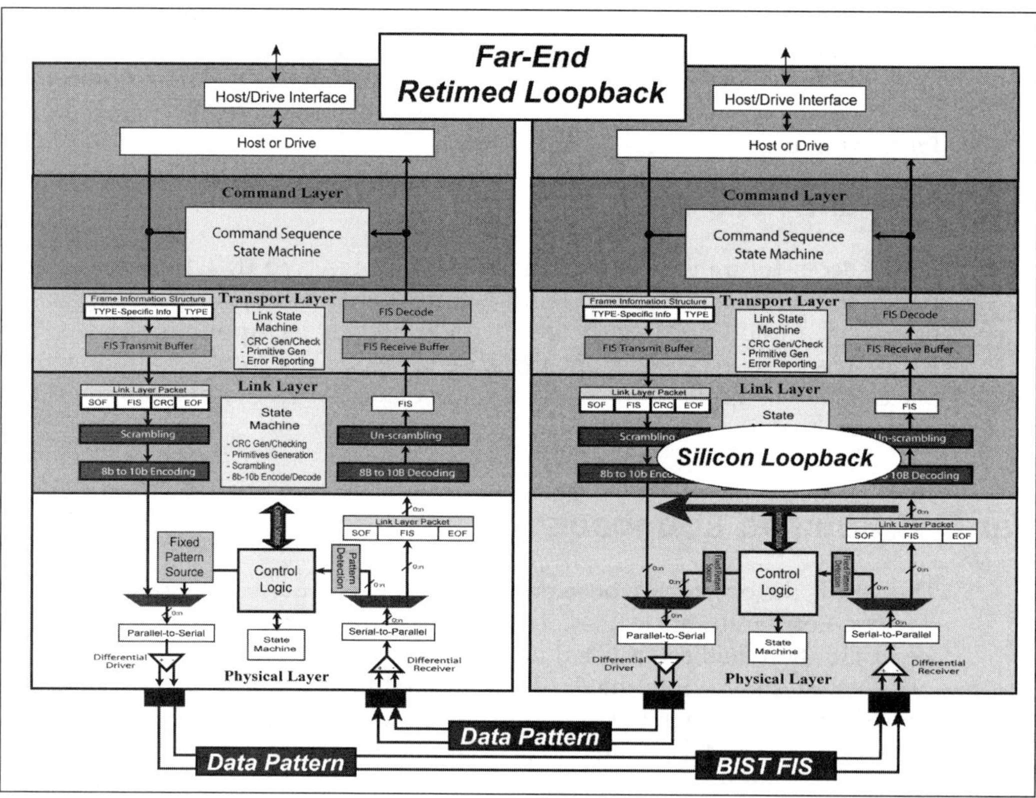

The receiving node may elect to include the link layer decode/encode and unscrambler/scrambler stages in the loopback sequence. This requires that the same unscrambling and scrambling pattern be used during the loopback. Note that the currently running disparity of the 8/10 bit decode and encode of the loopback node may have started with different initial disparity value. If so, the encoded data received from the originating node will not be the same as the data being returned to the originating node. However, the data values at the originating node prior to encoding will match the data received from the loopback node after it has been decoded.

Figure 23-3: Far-End Retimed Loopback with Extended Coverage

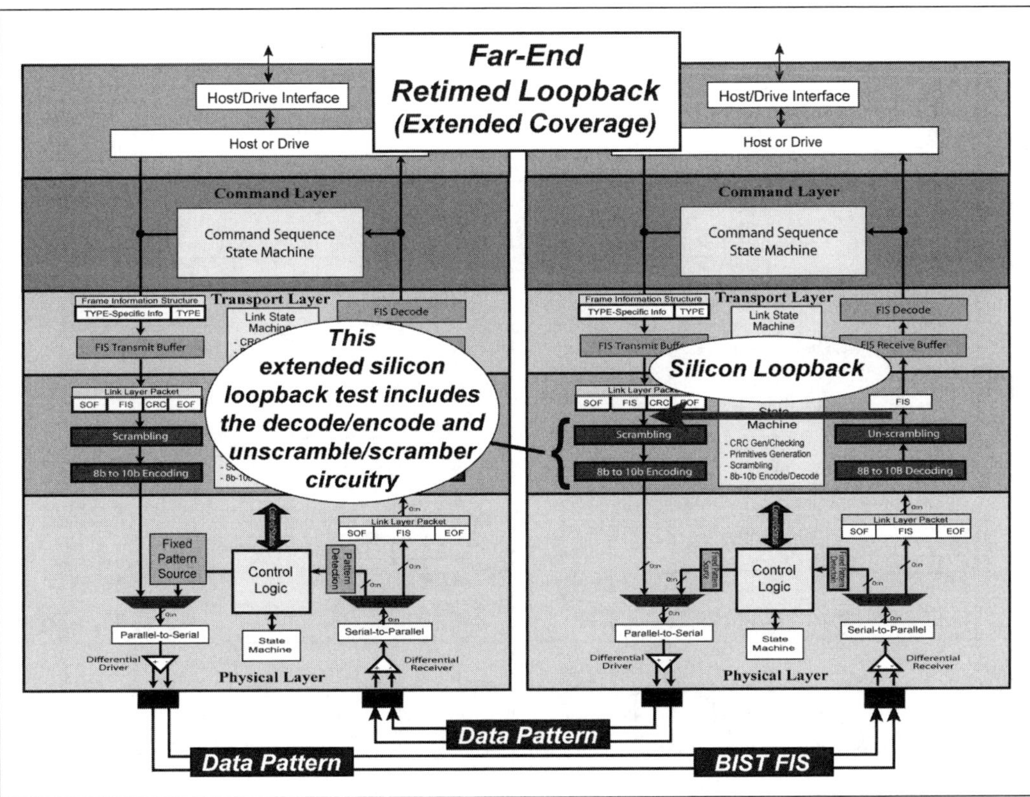

Far End Analog Loopback

The Far End Analog Loopback is entered when a BIST FIS is issued. The BIST Pattern Definition field is shown in Table 23-4. This silicon feedback loop simply routes the receive data directly to the transmitter. The incoming data is not processed in any way as illustrated in Figure 23-4.

Table 23-4: Pattern Definition for Far End Analog Loopback

BIST Mode	F	L	T	P	A	S	V
Far End Analog Loopback	0	1	0	0	0	0	0

Figure 23-4: Far End Analog Loopback Test Actions

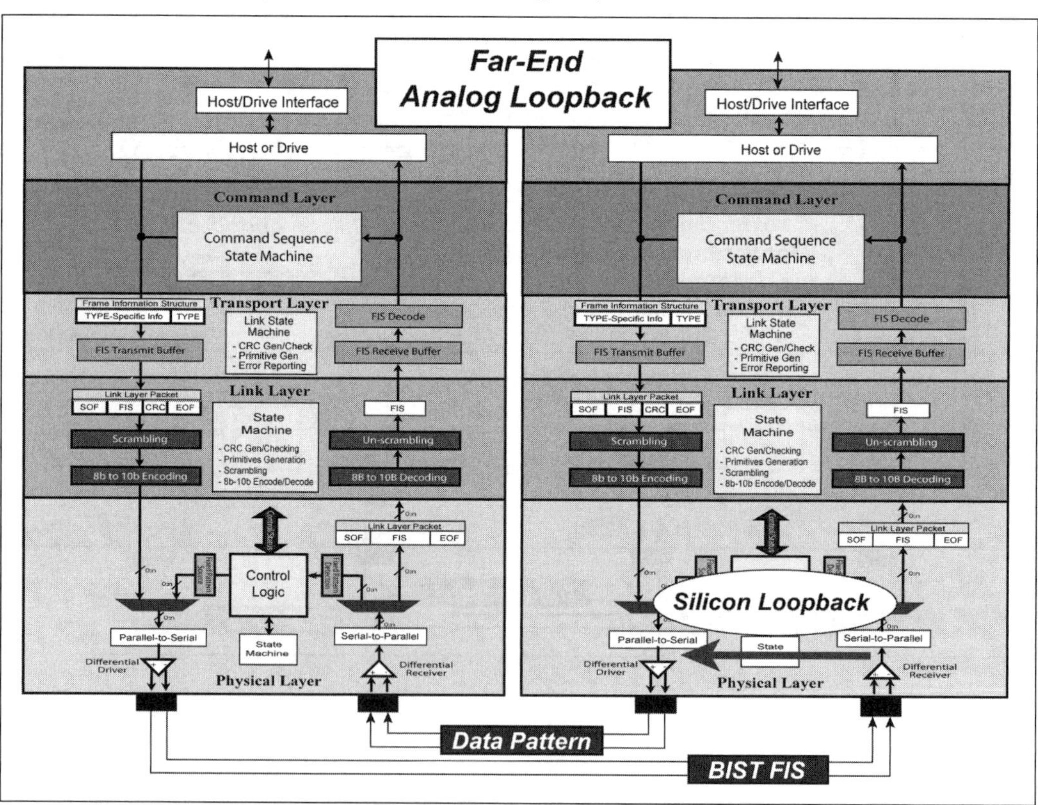

Far End Transmit Only

The Far End Transmit Only mode places the far-end node into a transmit only state. Figure 23-5 illustrates the BIST entry into the Far End Transmit Only mode. The BIST FIS contains the Data 1 and Data 2 fields that carry the data or patterns to be transmitted to the origination node. The BIST FIS includes a number of qualifiers within the Pattern Definition field that specify how the Data 1/2 fields are to be interpreted and delivered. In some modes data are returned, while other modes return only primitives. The following two sections address data and primitive transmission respectively.

Figure 23-5: Far End Transmit Only Test Activation and Actions

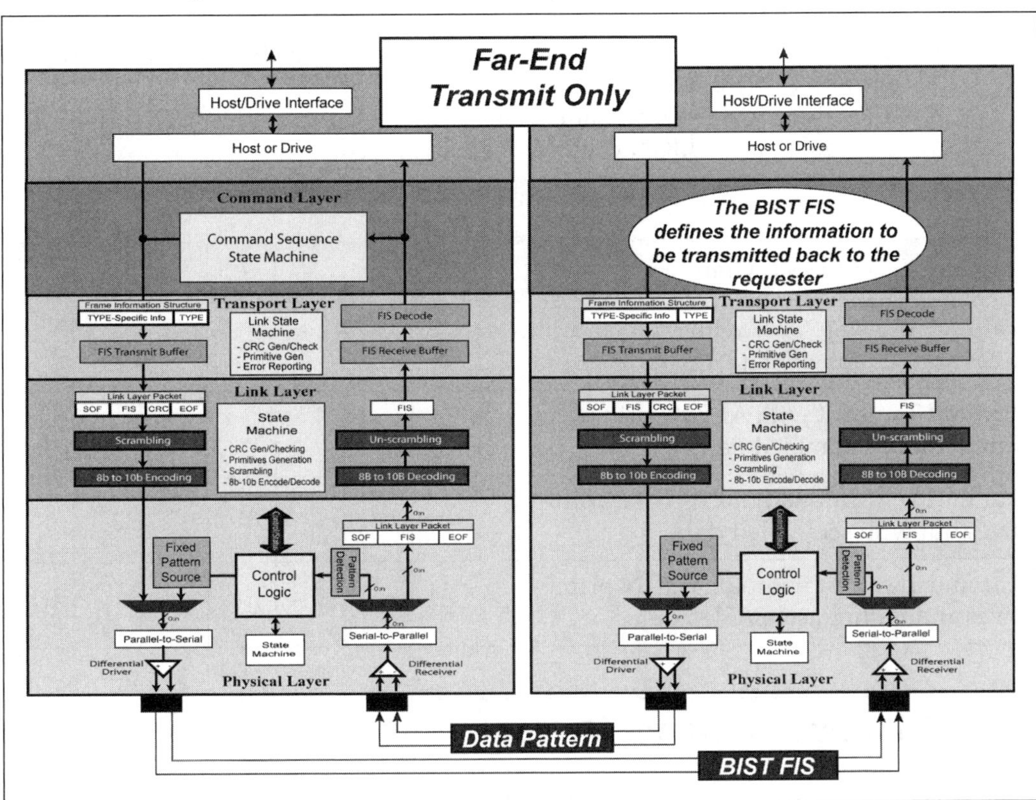

Data Transmit Modes

The data stream transmitted by the far-end node is the same data received in the BIST FIS's Data 1 and Data 2 fields. The data delivered can be test patterns defined by the specification, or any other data pattern that the near-end node's application chooses. The variations associated with the transmission of data depend on the qualifying Pattern Definition bits as follows and as shown in Table 23-5.

- T=1, S=0, A=0 — When none of the qualifying bits are set, the far-end node delivers the data stream (Data 1/Data 2 continuously repeated) with the data scrambled and ALIGN primitives injected into the bit stream every 256 bit times.
- T=1, S=1, A=0 — The same data stream is transmitted except the Scrambler is bypassed.
- T=1, S=0, A=1 — The same data stream is transmitted except the ALIGN primitives are bypassed.
- T=1, S=1, A=1 — The same data stream is transmitted except both the Scrambler and ALIGN primitives are bypassed.

Table 23-5: Data Stream Qualifiers

BIST Mode	F	L	T	P	A	S	V
Far End Transmit Only with ALIGN primitives and scrambled data	0	0	1	0	0	0	0
Far End Transmit with ALIGN primitives but without scrambled data	0	0	1	0	0	1	0
Far End Transmit without ALIGN primitives but with scrambled data	0	0	1	0	1	0	0
Far End Transmit without ALIGN primitives and without scrambled data	0	0	1	0	1	1	0

Primitive Transmit Modes

When the "p" or primitive bit is set, the contents of the Data 1 and Data 2 fields are interpreted as Primitives. Byte zero of the Data 1 and Data 2 fields includes a data value that is interpreted as a control value; either BCh (K28.5) or 7Ch

(K28.3). The addition three bytes are the data values that define the specific primitive being sent. See Table 23-6 for the complete list of possible values. Once again the 8-bit values loading into the Data 1 and Data 2 fields of the BIST FIS must contain the 8-bit values (shown in parenthesis) that when encoded yield the Dxx.y values represented in the table.

Table 23-6: Primitive Definitions

Name	Byte 3	Byte 2	Byte 1	Byte 0
AlIGN	D27.3 (7Bh)	D10.2 (4Ah)	D10.2 (4Ah)	K28.5 (BCh)
CONT	D25.4 (99h)	D25.4 (99h)	D10.5 (AAh)	K28.3 (7Ch)
DMAT	D22.1 (36h)	D22.1 (36h)	D21.5 (B5h)	K28.3 (7Ch)
EOF	D21.6 (D5h)	D21.6 (D5h)	D21.5 (B5h)	K28.3 (7Ch)
HOLD	D21.6 (D5h)	D21.6 (D5h)	D10.5 (AAh)	K28.3 (7Ch)
HOLDA	D21.4 (95h)	D21.4 (95h)	D10.5 (AAh)	K28.3 (7Ch)
PMACK	D21.4 (95h)	D21.4 (95h)	D21.4 (95h)	K28.3 (7Ch)
PMNAK	D21.7 (F5h)	D21.7 (F5h)	D21.4 (95h)	K28.3 (7Ch)
PMREQ_P	D23.0 (17h)	D23.0 (17h)	D21.5 (B5h)	K28.3 (7Ch)
PMREQ_S	D21.3 (75h)	D21.3 (75h)	D21.4 (95h)	K28.3 (7Ch)
R_ERR	D22.2 (56h)	D22.2 (56h)	D21.5 (B5h)	K28.3 (7Ch)
R_IP	D21.2 (55h)	D21.2 (55h)	D21.5 (B5h)	K28.3 (7Ch)
R_OK	D21.1 (35h)	D21.1 (35h)	D21.5 (B5h)	K28.3 (7Ch)
R_RDY	D10.2 (4Ah)	D10.2 (4Ah)	D21.4 (95h)	K28.3 (7Ch)
SOF	D22.1 (36h)	D22.1 (36h)	D21.3 (75h)	K28.3 (7Ch)
SYNC	D21.5 (B5h)	D21.5 (B5h)	D21.4 (95h)	K28.3 (7Ch)
WTRM	D24.2 (58h)	D24.2 (58h)	D21.5 (B5h)	K28.3 (7Ch)
X_RDY	D23.2 (57h)	D23.2 (57h)	D21.5 (B5h)	K28.3 (7Ch)

Table 23-7 lists the Pattern Definitions for primitive delivery during the Far End Transmit Only tests.

Table 23-7: Legal Pattern Definition Bit Combinations

BIST Mode	F	L	T	P	A	S	V
Far End Transmit primitives with ALIGNs	0	0	1	1	0	na	0
Far End Transmit primitives without ALIGNs	0	0	1	1	1	na	0

Near End Analog Loopback

This test mode simply performs a silicon loopback directly between the receiver and transmitter. Prior to the device enabling this test mode the far-end device must first be placed into an electrical idle state (e.g., placed into the Partial or Slumber state).

The BIST FIS not used to initiate entry into this test mode. Furthermore, no method is defined by the specification for initiating the transition to this state.

Figure 23-6: Near End Analog Test Actions

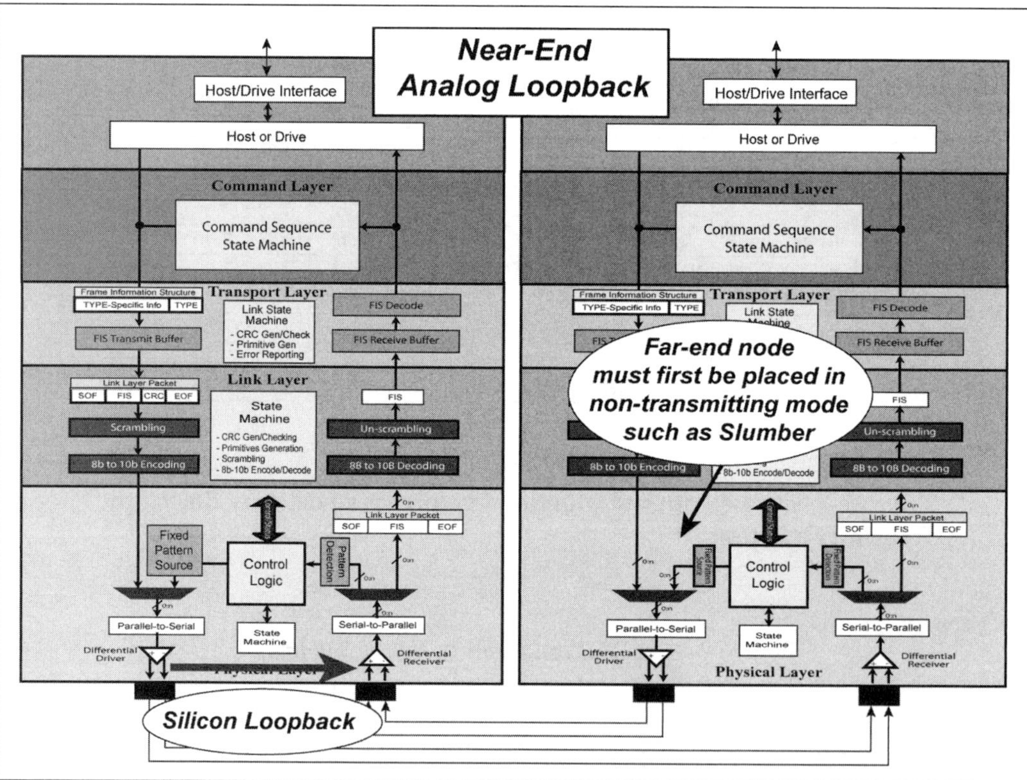

Test Patterns

The specification defines both compliant and non-compliant test patterns. Their intended use is as follows:

- Non-compliant patterns are simply a set of encoded values that are repeated continuously and need not presented in a standard Data FIS format. This is because only the physical layer, link, and connectors are being tested. The intended use on the non-compliant patterns is for jitter measurements, electrical parameters tests, and signal quality assessment across the physical environment.
- Compliant patterns are presented in a standard frame format as illustrated in Figure 23-7. Also, the ALIGN primitives are also injected into the data stream as required. These patterns are intended for frame error rate evaluation and in-system testing.

Figure 23-7: Format of Compliant Test Pattern

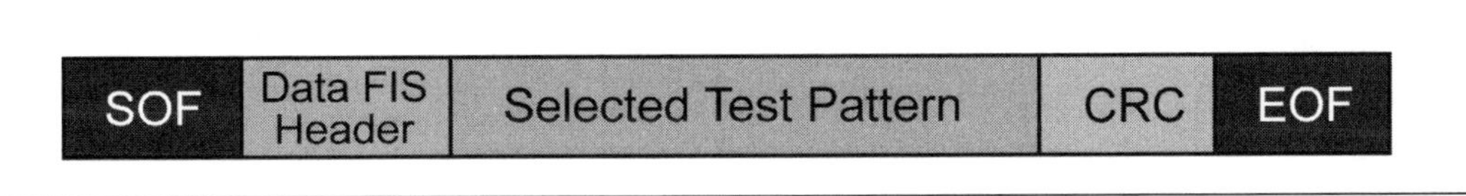

Non-Compliant Patterns

The non-compliant test patterns are intended for use in perform a wide variety of electrical tests. Four patterns are defined as listed below:

- Low Frequency Test Pattern
- Mid Frequency Test Pattern
- High Frequency Test Pattern
- Lone bit patterns

Compliant Patterns

The compliant test patterns are delivered within the frame structure and consequently involve the upper layers of the SATA interface.

- Compliant lone bit patterns
- Compliant composite patterns

Appendices

Appendix A
8b/10b Encoding Tutorial

8b/10b Encoding

The terminology used in this chapter is as follows:

- 8-bit values — data bytes and control bytes referenced by hexidecimal numbers.
- 10-bit values — data and control characters referenced using the Dxx.y and Kxx.y convention or using a 10-bit binary value.

General

The HBA and SATA device transmitters implement the 8-bit to 10-bit encoding mechanism that is widely used in high-speed serial bus implementations. The encoder converts 8-bit data and control bytes into 10-bit characters. The coding scheme is documented in the ANSI X3.230-1994 document, clause 11 (and also IEEE 802.3z, 36.2.4) and US Patent Number 4,486,739 entitled "Byte Oriented DC Balanced 8b/10b Partitioned Block Transmission Code"

Purpose of Encoding a Byte Stream

The primary purpose of this scheme is to embed a clock into the serial bit stream that is typically transmitted using differential signaling. Consequently, this eliminates the need for a high frequency 1.5 or 3.0 GHz clock signal for the link, which would generate significant EMI noise and would be challenging to route on a standard FR4 board. Link wire routing between the HBA and SATA device is made much easier given that there is no clock to route, thus removing the need to match clock length to Lane signal trace lengths.

Below is a summary of the advantages of 8b/10b encoding scheme:

- **Embedded Clock.** Creates sufficient 0-to-1 and 1-to-0 transition density (i.e., signal changes) to facilitate re-creation of the receive clock on the receiver end using a PLL (by guaranteeing a limited run length of consecutive ones or zeros). The recovered receive clock is used to clock inbound 10-bit characters into an elastic buffer. Figure A-1 on page 410 illustrates the the conversion of 00h to 1101000110b, where an 8-bit value with no transitions converts to a 10b character with five transitions. These transitions keep the receiver PLL synchronized to the transmit circuit clock:
  - Limited 'run length' means that the encoding scheme ensures the signal line will not remain in a high or low state for an extended period of time. The run length does not exceed five consecutive 1s or 0s.
  - 1s and 0s are clocked out on the rising-edge of the transmit clock. At the receiver, a PLL can recreate the clock by sync'ing to the leading edges of 1s and 0s.
  - Limited run length ensures minimum frequency drift in the receiver's PLL relative to the local clock in the transmit circuit.

Figure A-1: Example of 8-bit Value of 00h Encoded to 10-bit character

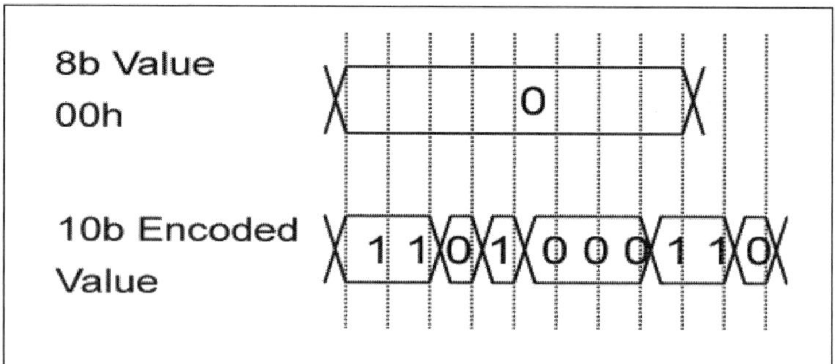

- **DC Balance.** Keeps the number of 1s and 0s transmitted as close to equal as possible, thus maintaining DC balance on the transmitted bit stream to an average of half the signal threshold voltage. This is very important in capacitive- and transformer-coupled circuits.
  - o Maintains a balance between the number of 1s and 0s on the signal line, thereby ensuring that the received signal is free of any DC component. This reduces the possibility of inter-bit interference. Inter-bit interference results from the inability of a signal to switch properly from one logic level to the other because the Lane coupling capacitor or intrinsic wire capacitance is over-charged.
- **Encoding of Special Control Bytes.** Permits the encoding of special control ('K') bytes that can always be recognized by the receiving node. These bytes are always used as the first character of each four character primitive.
- **Error Detection.** A secondary benefit of the encoding scheme is that it facilitates the detection of most transmission errors. A receiver can check for 'running disparity' errors, or the reception of invalid characters. Via the running disparity mechanism (see "Disparity" on page 413), the data bit stream transmitted maintains a balance of 1s and 0s. The receiver checks the difference between the total number of 1s and 0s transmitted since link initialization and ensures that it is as close to zero as possible. If it isn't, a disparity error is detected and reported, implying that a transmission error occurred.

The **disadvantage** of 8b/10b encoding scheme is that, due to the expansion of each 8-bit value into a 10-bit character prior to transmission, the actual transmission performance is degraded by 25% or said another way, the transmission overhead is increased by 25% (everything good has a price tag).

Properties of 10-bit (10b) characters

- For 10-bit character transmissions, the average number of 1s transmitted over time is equal to the number of 0s transmitted, no matter what the 8-bit value to be transmitted is; i.e., the character transmission is DC balanced.
- The bit stream never contains more than five continuous 1s or 0s (limited-run length).
- Each 10-bit character contains:
  - o Four 0s and six 1s (not necessarily contiguous), or
  - o Six 0s and four 1s (not necessarily contiguous), or
  - o Five 0s and five 1s (not necessarily contiguous).

- Each 10-bit character is subdivided into two sub-blocks: the first is six bits wide and the second is four bits wide.
  - o The 6-bit sub-block contains no more than four 1s or four 0s.
  - o The 4-bit sub-block contains no more than three 1s or three 0s.
- Any character with other than the above properties is considered invalid and a receiver consider this an error.
- An 8-bit value is submitted to the 8b/10b encoder along with a signal indicating whether the byte is a Data (D) or Control (K) byte. The encoder outputs the equivalent 10-bit character along with a current running disparity (CRD) that represents the sum of 1s and 0s for this transmission link since link initialization. See "Disparity" on page 413 for more information.
- The specification defines Control bytes that encode into two Control characters: (see "Control value Encoding" on page 420).

Preparing 8-bit/10-bit Notation

8b/10b conversion lookup tables refer to all 10-bit characters using a special notation (represented by Dxx.y for Data characters and Kxx.y. for Control bytes). Figure 2 on page 413 illustrates the notation equivalent for any 8-bit D or K value. The steps below covert the 8-bit (hex) value to 10-bit (Dxx.y) value.

In Figure 2 on page 413, the example Data byte value is 6Ah.

1. The bits in the data byte are identified by the capitalized alpha designators A through H
2. The byte is partitioned into two sub-blocks: one 3-bits wide and the other 5-bits wide
3. The two sub-blocks are flipped
4. The written form of the 10 bit value begins with either Dxx.y (Data) or Kxx.y (Control)
5. xx = the decimal value of the 5-bit field
6. y = the decimal value of the 3-bit field
7. The example value is represented as D10.3 in the 8b/10b lookup tables

Figure A-2: Preparing 8-bit value for Encode

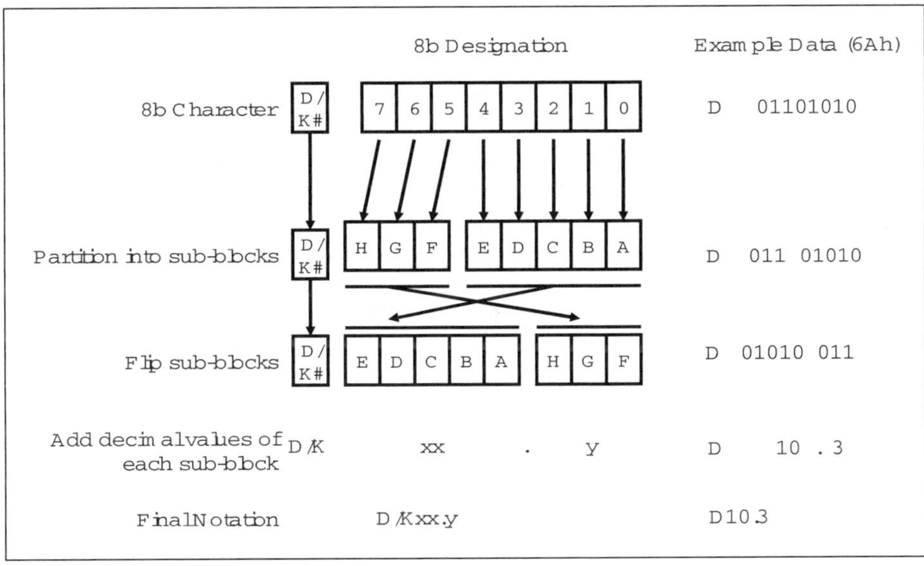

Disparity

value disparity refers to the difference between the number of 1s and 0s in a 10-bit character:

- When a character has more 0s than 1s, the character has negative (–) disparity (e.g., 0101000101b).
- When a character has more 1s than 0s, the character has positive (+) disparity (e.g., 1001101110b).
- When a character has an equal number of 1s and 0s, the character has neutral disparity (e.g., 0110100101b).
- Each 10-bit character contains one of the following numbers of ones and zeros (not necessarily contiguous):
    - Four 0s and six 1s (+ disparity).
    - Six 0s and four 1s (– disparity).
    - Five 0s and five 1s (neutral disparity).

There are two categories of 8-bit values:

- Those that encode into 10-bit characters with + or – disparity.
- Those that encode into 10-bit characters with neutral disparity.

CRD (Current Running Disparity)

The CRD reflects the total number of 1s and 0s transmitted over the link since link initialization and has the following characteristics:

- Its current state indicates the balance of 1s and 0s transmitted since initialization.
- The CRD's initial state (before any values are transmitted) can be + or –.
- The CRD's current state can be either positive (if more 1s than 0s have been transmitted) or negative (if more 0s than 1s).
- Each value is converted via a table lookup with the current state of the CRD factored in.
- As each new value is encoded, the CRD either remains the same (if the newly generated 10-bit value has neutral disparity) or it flips to the opposite polarity (if the newly generated value has + or – disparity).

8b/10b Encoding Procedure

Figure A-3 on page 415 illustrates a simplified view of the lookup tables (for both data and control values) used to produce the 10-bit value. Note that a double lookup is actually performed in parallel for each table as discussed next.

The encode is accomplished by performing two table lookups in parallel. This parallel lookup is performed as follows:

- 5-bit Lookup (values A through E) — Three elements are included in the lookup:
    - o The 5-bit portion of the 8-bit value (bits A through E).
    - o The Data/Control (D/K#) indicator.
    - o The current state of the CRD (positive or negative).

  The table lookup yields the upper 6-bits of the 10-bit character (bits abcdei). Table A-2 on page 418 and Table A-4 on page 420 provides a sample of the 5-bit lookup for data and control values.

- 3-bit Lookup (values FGH) — Three elements are submitted to a 3-bit to 4-bit table for a lookup:
    - o The 3-bit portion of the 8-bit value (bits F through H).
    - o The same Data/Control (D/K#) indicator.
    - o The current state of the CRD (positive or negative).

  The table lookup yields the lower 4-bits of the 10-bit character (bits fghj). Table A-3 on page 419 and Table A-5 on page 420 lists the 3-bit lookup table content for data and control values respectively.

The 8b/10b encoder computes a new CRD based on the resultant 10-bit character and supplies this CRD for the 8b/10b encode of the next value. If the resultant 10-bit character is neutral (i.e., it has an equal number of 1s and 0s), the polarity of the CRD remains unchanged. If the resulting 10-bit character is not neutral (+ or –), the CRD flips to its opposite state. It is an error if the CRD is currently + or – and the next 10-bit character produced has the same polarity as the CRD (unless the next character has neutral disparity, in which case the CRD remains the same).

The 8b/10b encoder feeds a Parallel-to-Serial converter which clocks 10-bit characters out in the bit order 'abcdeifghj' (shown in Figure A-3 on page 415).

Figure A-3: 8-bit to 10-bit (8b/10b) Encoder

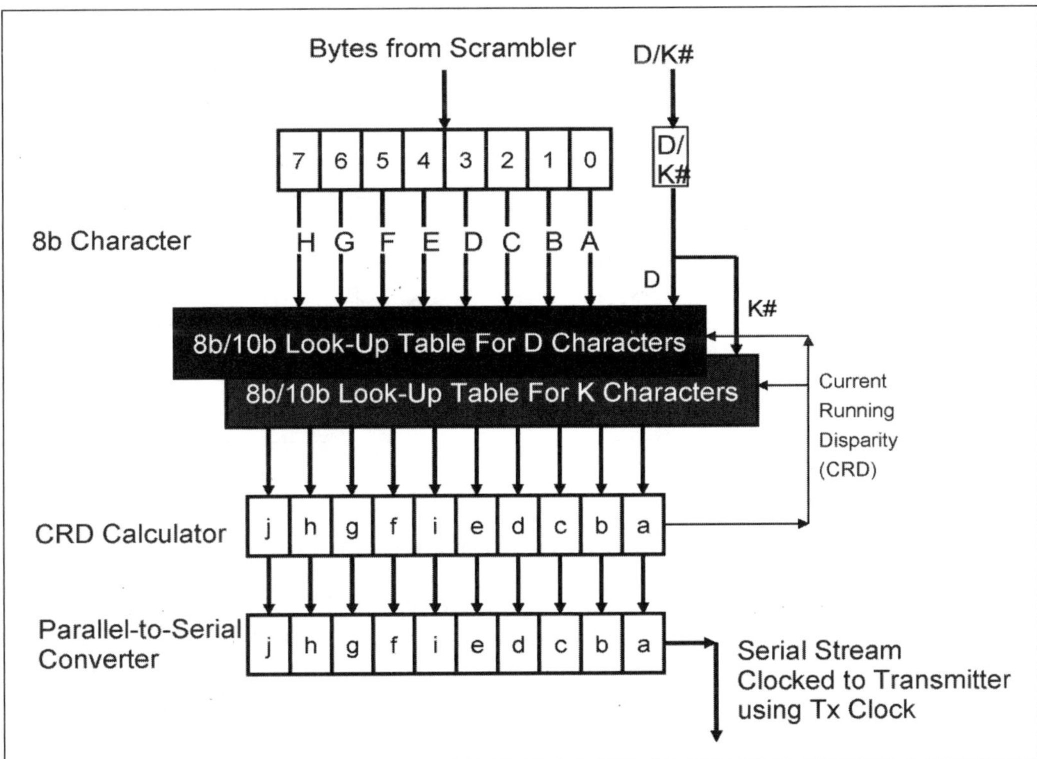

Example Encodings

Figure A-4 on page 416 illustrates some example 8-bit to 10-bit encodings.

Figure A-4: Example 8-bit/10-bit Transmission

Use these two characters in the example below:

D/K#	Hex Byte	Binary Bits HGF EDCBA	Byte Name	CRD - abcdeifghj	CRD + abcdeifghj
Control (K)	BC	101 11100	K28.5	001111 1010	110000 0101
Data (D)	6A	011 01010	D10.3	010101 1100	010101 0011

Example Transmission

	CRD	Character	CRD	Character	CRD	Character	CRD
Character to be transmitted		K28.5 (BCh)		K28.5 (BCh)		D10.3 (6Ah)	
Bitstream transmitted	-	Yields 001111 1010 CRD is +	+	Yields 110000 0101 CRD is -	-	Yields 010101 1100 CRD is neutral	-

Initialized value of CRD is don't care. Receiver can determine from incoming bitstream

Following is an explanation of the conversion of the 8-bit Data value 6Ah:

- The 8-bit value is broken down into its two sub-blocks: 011b and 01010b.
- The two sub-blocks are flipped and represented as the D10.3 value. The binary-weighted value of the 5-bit block is 10d and the value of the 3-bit field is 3d.
- The two blocks are submitted to the data value lookup tables (Table A-2 on page 418 and Table A-3 on page 419 are for D lookups) along with the current state of the CRD).
- The last two columns show the 10-bit character produced by the two parallel table lookups (Table A-2 on page 418 and Table A-3 on page 419) when the CRD is negative or positive.

Table A-1: Example 8-bit/10-bit Encodings

D or K value	Hex Value	Binary Value HGF EDCBA	Byte Name	CRD - abcde fghj	CRD + abcde fghj
Data	6A	011 01010	D10.3	010101 1100	010101 0011
Data	1B	000 11011	D27.0	110110 0100	001001 1011
Data	F7	111 10111	D23.7	111010 0001	000101 1110
Control	BC	101 11100	K28.5	001111 1010	110000 0101

Example Transmission

Figure A-4 on page 416 illustrates the encode and example transmission of three values: the first one is the control value BCh (K28.5), the second value is also BCh (K28.5) and the third value is the data value 6Ah (D10.3):

- If the initial CRD is negative at the time of the encode, the K28.5 is encoded into 001111 1010b (positive disparity), flipping the CRD from negative to positive.
- If the CRD is positive at the time of the encode, the K28.5 is encoded into 110000 0101b (negative disparity), flipping the CRD from positive to negative.
- The D10.3 is encoded into 010101 1100b (neutral disparity). The CRD therefore remains unchanged (negative) for the next encoding (not shown).
- Notice that the resulting character stream is DC balanced over two values.

The Lookup Tables

The following four tables define the table lookup for the two sub-blocks of 8-bit Data and Control values.

Data Lookup Tables

Table A-2: 5-bit to 6-bit Encode Table for Data values

Data Byte Name	Unencoded Bits EDCBA	Current RD – abcdei	Current RD + abcdei
D0	00000	100111	011000
D1	00001	011101	100010
D2	00010	101101	010010
D3	00011	110001	110001
D4	00100	110101	001010
D5	00101	101001	101001
D6	00110	011001	011001
D7	00111	111000	000111
D8	01000	111001	000110
D9	01001	100101	100101
D10	01010	010101	010101
D11	01011	110100	110100
D12	01100	001101	001101
D13	01101	101100	101100
D14	01110	011100	011100
D15	01111	010111	101000
D16	10000	011011	100100
D17	10001	100011	100011
D18	10010	010011	010011
D19	10011	110010	110010
D20	10100	001011	001011

Table A-2: 5-bit to 6-bit Encode Table for Data values (Continued)

Data Byte Name	Unencoded Bits EDCBA	Current RD – abcdei	Current RD + abcdei
D21	10101	101010	101010
D22	10110	011010	011010
D23	10111	111010	000101
D24	11000	110011	001100
D25	11001	100110	100110
D26	11010	010110	010110
D27	11011	110110	001001
D28	11100	001110	001110
D29	11101	101110	010001
D30	11110	011110	100001
D31	11111	101011	010100

Table A-3: 3-bit to 4-bit Encode Table for Data values

Data Byte Name	Unencoded Bits HGF	Current RD - fghj	Current RD + fghj
--.0	000	1011	0100
--.1	001	1001	1001
--.2	010	0101	0101
--.3	011	1100	0011
--.4	100	1101	0010
--.5	101	1010	1010
--.6	110	0110	0110
--.7	111	1110/0111	0001/1000

Control Lookup Tables

Only two control characters are defined by the SATA specification:

- K28.3
- K28.5

Table A-4: 5-bit to 6-bit Encode Table for Control values

Data Byte Name	Unencoded Bits EDCBA	Current RD – abcdei	Current RD + abcdei
K28	11100	001111	110000

Table A-5: 3-bit to 4-bit Encode Table for Control values

Data Byte Name	Unencoded Bits HGF	Current RD – fghj	Current RD + fghj
--.3	011	0011	1100
--.5	101	1010	0101

Control value Encoding

Table A-6 on page 421 shows the encoding of the SATA Control values. These values are not scrambled by the Link layer, but are encoded into 10-bit characters. Because these Control values are not scrambled, the receiver logic can easily detect these characters in an incoming character stream.

Table A-6: Control value Encoding and Definition

8b Name	10b (CRD-)	10b (CRD+)	Description
K28.5 (BCh)	001111 1010	110000 0101	Used only as the first character of the ALIGN primitive
K28.3 (7Ch)	001111 0011	110000 1100	Used only as the first character of all primitives, except ALIGN

Disparity Error Checks

The decoder determines the initial disparity value based on the disparity of the first character received. Thereafter, the calculated disparity for each subsequent value received should toggle between + and - unless the value received has neutral disparity in which case the disparity remains the same value. An error is detected when a non-neutral value is received that matches the current running disparity. This condition results in an error that is reported to the higher layers.

Appendix B
ATA & SATA Commands

Essential Background

The command set for ATA disk drives has been evolving since the early 1980s. When the Serial ATA interface was introduced, a primary goal was maintaining backward compatibility with software written for parallel ATA applications. This meant that the same commands could be issued to either a parallel or serial ATA disk drive and would produce the same results. It was agreed by all parties involved that there should be only one official definition of the command set.

The standards committee for the parallel ATA interface, the T13 Standards Committee of Accredited Standards Committee INCITS, maintains the ATA Command Set document. See References, below, for details.

There are presently four SATA-only commands and three ATA commands that have been modified to include SATA-only information. These new commands and modifications are documented in the SATA specification. They are briefly discussed below in the section on SATA-only Commands (See page 445).

References

ATA/ATAPI-7 Vol. 1 – Register Delivered Command Set, Logical Register Set. Dated 21 April 2004.

The approved final draft of this document can be downloaded from the standards committee website, www.t13.org.

AT Attachment-8 ATA/ATAPI Command Set (ATA-8 ACS)

This is a working document, not yet approved. The most recent version can be downloaded from www.t13.org.

Serial ATA 2.6 is the latest approved version of the SATA specification.

The specification is developed and maintained by the Serial ATA International Organization. Member companies can download the spec from www.sata-io.org. Non-member companies must pay a fee (currently $25) in order to download a copy.

General Characteristics of ATA Commands

All ATA commands have several characteristics in common.

First, all commands are initiated by writing to a set of 1-byte registers in the device. This register set is formally called the Command Block; it is also often informally called the Task File.

Register 7 is used for the command code, which defines the command to be executed. Registers 1 through 6 are used for command parameters. Host software must write any required command parameters to the device before writing the command code because writing to register 7, the Command Register, signals the device to begin command execution. (See note below on shared register addresses.)

Some register names have changed between early and recent versions of the ATA standard. The two name sets are illustrated in Figure B-1 and Figure B-2 on page 425. In normal usage the early and recent names are used interchangeably.

Figure B-1: Legacy Register Names

Cmd Reg	Reads		Writes		Notes
Address	7	0	7	0	
01F0	Data				16-bit accesses
01F1	Error		Feature		8-bit access only
01F2	Sector Count				8-bit access only
01F3	Sector Number				8-bit access only
01F4	Cylinder Low				8-bit access only
01F5	Cylinder High				8-bit access only
01F6	Device	Head	Device	Head	8-bit access only
01F7	Status		Command		8-bit access only
Ctrl Reg					
03F6	Alternate Status		Device Control		8-bit access only

Figure B-2: LBA Address (28-Bits)

Cmd Reg	Reads		Writes		Notes
Address	7	0	7	0	
01F0	Data				16-bit accesses
01F1	Error		Feature		8-bit access only
01F2	Sector Count				8-bit access only
01F3	LBA Low (7:0)				8-bit access only
01F4	LBA Middle (15:8)				8-bit access only
01F5	LBA High (23:16)				8-bit access only
01F6	Device	LBA (27:24)	Device	LBA (27:24)	8-bit access only
01F7	Status		Command		8-bit access only
Ctrl Reg					
03F6	Alternate Status		Device Control		8-bit access only

Command Structure

Each command in the ATA standard is defined in terms of:

- COMMAND CODE – See the table of command codes in Annex B of ATA/ATAPI-7.
- FEATURE SET – See the section entitled "Feature Sets" on page 432 for a description of the ATA feature set.
- PROTOCOL – the type of transport activity that will be used to execute this command. See Table B-1 for a description of different ATA transport protocols.
- INPUTS – the mandatory and optional register contents supplied by the host system when the command is initiated. An example of the Inputs register map for one ATA command is shown in Figure B-3. Descriptive text accompanies the diagram in the ATA standard.

Figure B-3: Inputs – READ DMA command

Register	7	6	5	4	3	2	1	0
Features	na							
Sector Count	Sector count							
LBA Low	LBA (7:0)							
LBA Mid	LBA (15:8)							
LBA High	LBA (23:16)							
Device	obs	LBA	obs	DEV	LBA (27:24)			
Command	C8h							

Normal Outputs . The register contents after the command completes successfully. Register 7, the Status Register, is usually the only register of interest. (See note below on shared register addresses.) An example of the Normal Outputs register map for one ATA command is shown in Figure B-4. on page 427 Descriptive text accompanies the diagram in the ATA standard.

Figure B-4: Normal Outputs – READ DMA command

Register	7	6	5	4	3	2	1	0
Error	na							
Sector Count	na							
LBA Low	na							
LBA Mid	na							
LBA High	na							
Device	obs	na	obs	DEV	na	na	na	na
Status	BSY	DRDY	DF	na	DRQ	na	na	ERR

Error Outputs. the register contents after the command completes with an error. The Status Register and the Error Register are the most important but other registers may contain useful information. An example of the Error Outputs register map for one ATA command is shown in Figure B-5. Descriptive text accompanies the diagram in the ATA standard.

Figure B-5: Error Outputs – READ DMA command

Register	7	6	5	4	3	2	1	0
Error	ICRC	UNC	MC	IDNF	MCR	ABRT	NM	obs
Sector Count	na							
LBA Low	LBA (7:0)							
LBA Mid	LBA (15:8)							
LBA High	LBA (23:16)							
Device	obs	na	obs	DEV	LBA (27:24)			
Status	BSY	DRDY	DF	na	DRQ	na	na	ERR

Multiple Command Protocols

Each ATA command follows a specific template of activity from the time it is issued until it is completed. This sequence is called the transport protocol for that particular command. Altogether, ATA defines ten specific transport protocols for executing commands, plus three others for resets and other non-command situations. Each ATA command is assigned to one of the ten transport protocols and both HBAs and devices are expected to adhere to the rules of that protocol when the command is executed.

All commands are issued by the host system writing command parameters and the command code into the Command Block register set in the device. The command code determines which transport protocol will be followed.

Table B-1 lists the ATA transport protocols.

Table B-1: List of ATA Transport Protocols

Name	Number of commands	Description
Power-on and hardware reset protocol	Non-command protocol	Either device power-on or assertion of the RESET- line in the ATA cable causes a series of mandatory actions internal to the device, culminating in the device becoming ready to operate and making device status available to the host system.
Software reset protocol	Non-command protocol	Similar in effect to a hardware reset but may finish quicker due to less self-test and calibration by the device.
Bus idle protocol	Non-command protocol	This protocol documents the legal entry and exit conditions from the Idle state of the ATA bus.

Table B-1: List of ATA Transport Protocols

Name	Number of commands	Description
Non-data Command Protocol	33	Many commands do not require a separate data transfer phase. All essential information is contained in the Command Block registers. For example, enabling an optional feature requires only the command code and possibly one or 2 bytes of register data.
PIO data-in command protocol	13	Programmed I/O (PIO) was the method used by DOS and early PCs to transfer blocks of data between a disk drive and system memory. Read-type transfers (data-in) were accomplished in two steps under CPU control. First, a 2-byte word was transferred from the disk drive to a CPU register. Then the two bytes were transferred from the CPU register to main memory. Data rate was limited to 5MB/s or less on ISA Bus systems. Today this protocol is primarily used for transferring a single 512-byte block of configuration or control information.

Table B-1: List of ATA Transport Protocols

Name	Number of commands	Description
PIO data-out command protocol	17	Programmed I/O (PIO) was the method used by DOS and early PCs to transfer blocks of data between a disk drive and system memory. Write-type transfers (data-out) were accomplished in two steps under CPU control. First, the CPU fetched a 2-byte word from main memory into a CPU register. Then the two bytes were transferred from the CPU register to the disk drive. Data rate was limited to 5MB/s or less on ISA Bus systems. Today this protocol is primarily used for transferring a single 512-byte block of configuration or control information.
DMA command protocol	7	Direct Memory Access (DMA) became the preferred method of transferring data between a disk drive and main memory with the introduction of the PCI Bus to PC architecture. In a DMA transfer, the CPU is not involved in the movement of data blocks. Instead, a separate system component called the DMA controller or DMA engine manages the transfer. The seven commands in this protocol group are all variations of READ DMA and WRITE DMA.
READ/ WRITE DMA QUEUED command protocol	6	This protocol is a more sophisticated version of DMA that permits more than one command at a time to be outstanding in the device. In SATA this protocol has been replaced by the Native Command Queuing protocol.

Table B-1: List of ATA Transport Protocols

Name	Number of commands	Description
Ultra DMA data-in commands	(6) see description	The original DMA protocol for ATA devices could not be enhanced beyond 16.7MB/sec. A new data transfer protocol, in addition to cable and electrical changes, eventually allowed transfer rates up to 133MB/sec. This set of enhancements was called Ultra DMA. In Ultra DMA operation the transfer rate is set by a single command during drive initialization. The DMA and DMA QUEUED commands will be executed with either basic DMA transfer protocol or Ultra DMA transfer protocol, depending on the initialized transfer rate. Ultra DMA does not add any additional ATA commands. It only changes the way data blocks are transferred.
Ultra DMA data-out commands	(7) see description	See previous description
PACKET command protocol	2	Optical and tape devices can be physically connected to an ATA bus but ATA disk drive commands are generally not valid for those devices. The solution to the problem of issuing a different set of commands to those devices was to define a single ATA-type, register delivered, command called PACKET. This command provides a way to deliver any SCSI command to a device on the ATA bus. The common name for this type of attachment is ATAPI. ATAPI is supported in Serial ATA.

Table B-1: List of ATA Transport Protocols

Name	Number of commands	Description
DEVICE RESET command protocol	1	DEVICE RESET is a command that permits issuing reset to an ATAPI device that shares a cable with an ATA device, without affecting the ATA device. This circumstance is not applicable to Serial ATA.
EXECUTE DEVICE DIAGNOSTIC command protocol	1	The EXECUTE DEVICE DIAGNOSTIC command causes an attached device to run an internal self test and post results in its Command Block registers.

Feature Sets

Grouping ATA commands by Feature Set is more useful for most people than grouping them by transport protocol. ATA-7 defines 21 feature sets, each consisting of a set of related functions and the commands or data fields used to control them. All of these features apply to SATA disk devices as well.

Some feature sets are basic in all modern disk drives; others are optional. The data returned by the IDENTIFY DEVICE command identifies which features are supported and which are enabled on a specific device. See the description of IDENTIFY DEVICE below for more details.

Table B-2 lists all the feature sets defined in ATA/ATAPI-7.

Table B-2: List of ATA Feature Sets

Feature Set	Number of feature specific commands	Purpose	Reported in IDENTIFY DEVICE data	Enabled by SET FEATURES
General Feature Set	16	Define basic commands that must be supported by all devices	Partial	No
Packet Feature Set	3	Allow attachment of optical and tape devices to ATA bus	Yes	No
Power Management	6	Extend battery life on portable computers	No	No
Advanced Power Management	0	Improved control of battery life management	Yes	Yes
Security Mode	6	Password protection for disk	Yes	No
Self-monitoring, analysis, and reporting (SMART)	1 (with 8 subcommands)	Predictive failure analysis	Yes	No
Host Protected Area	4	Create invisible disk save area for host FW use	Yes	No
Compact Flash Association (CFA)	5	Support solid state disk	Yes	Yes

Table B-2: List of ATA Feature Sets

Feature Set	Number of feature specific commands	Purpose	Reported in IDENTIFY DEVICE data	Enabled by SET FEATURES
Removable Media	3	Allow locking or ejecting media. Not used with ATAPI devices.	Yes	Yes
Removable Media Status Notification	2	Notify host SW of media changes. Mainly used with ATAPI devices	Yes	Yes
Power Up In Standby	0	Prevent electrical current surge when multiple drives power up	Yes	Yes
Automatic Acoustic Management	0	Noise reduction for consumer applications	Yes	Yes
48-bit Address	15	Extend disk R/W addressing capability above 137 GB	Yes	No
Device Configuration Overlay	4	Reconfigure factory defaults at power on	Yes	No
Media Card Pass Through Command	4	Embed flash memory card commands within ATA commands	Yes	No
Streaming	5	Multimedia support	Yes	No

Table B-2: List of ATA Feature Sets

Feature Set	Number of feature specific commands	Purpose	Reported in IDENTIFY DEVICE data	Enabled by SET FEATURES
General Purpose Logging	2	Collect usage information gathered by a device	Indirectly through other feature sets	No
Overlapped	2	Allow a slow device to release the ATA bus before command completion for use by a faster device	Only for release and SERVICE interrupts	Yes if release and SERVICE Interrupts are desired
Queued	7, including 2 from Overlapped feature	Allow the host system to issue one or more commands to a device before an earlier command completes. Out-of-order execution by the device is allowed.	Only for release and SERVICE interrupts	Yes if release and SERVICE Interrupts are desired
Long Physical Sector	0	Make more efficient use of disk drive recording area	Yes	No
Long Logical Sector	0	Permit block size greater than 512 bytes, typically to include a user checksum with data	Yes	No

Commands by Function or Feature Set

This section discusses many of the common or important ATA commands and functions. The grouping of topics roughly follows the outline of ATA feature sets but is not rigorous in that respect. See the ATA/ATAPI-7 Volume 1 standard for full details.

Resetting and Initializing a Device

Hardware Reset

ATA uses the term "hardware reset" or "hard reset" to describe the internal initialization that takes place after a device has transitioned to power on state or after the Reset- signal in the ATA cable has been asserted, then de-asserted. The Reset- signal is normally only asserted when the host system experiences a hardware reset.

The SATA interface cable does not have a separate reset signal. The Out-Of-Band Link Reset sequence (COMRESET, etc.) causes the same device reset actions as the Reset- signal does on the parallel interface.

Software Reset

The primary purpose of ATA software reset is to re-initialize the internal state of a device following an error or hang condition. This is accomplished on both parallel ATA and SATA devices by writing a one to the SRST bit of the device's Control Register, followed by writing a zero to the same bit.

Some conditions within a device may be retained following a software reset but will be initialized following a hard reset. In all cases a software reset should return a drive to an operational state. See the ATA/ATAPI-7 standard

Device self-test

Following the initialization portion of a hardware or software reset, a device is expected to run a diagnostic test and post a result code in its Error Register. A code of 01h indicates success.

Status presentation to host system

At the completion of the reset process the device Command Block registers contain two sets of information.

The *Device Signature* is contained in registers 2-5 (Sector Count, LBA Low, LBA Mid, LBA High, for disk drives). The value 01h, 01h, 00h, 00h in these 4 registers indicates that the device is a hard disk drive. A value of 01h, 01h, 14h, EBh indicates an ATAPI device (e.g., a DVD-ROM).

The results of the initialization and self-test are indicated in registers 1 and 7 (Error and Status registers). A successful reset operation will result in these registers containing 01h in register 1 and 40h or 50h in register 7 for an ATA device. An ATAPI device is required to post 00h in its Status register at completion of a reset without error.

The device does not generate an interrupt at the end of reset; the host system must poll the status register until the BSY bit = 0, then read the Status, Error, and signature registers. A SATA device performs the additional step of sending a Register, D->H FIS to update the shadow copy of the Command Block in the HBA. The I (Interrupt) bit in this FIS = 0.

Configuring a Device

There are a few ATA commands that enable or disable specific features, however most features sets or sub-sets are reported in IDENTIFY DEVICE data and controlled using SET FEATURES.

IDENTIFY DEVICE – Finding Supported Features

One of the first commands issued by any host system after a device reset is IDENTIFY DEVICE if the device is a disk drive. IDENTIFY PACKET DEVICE serves the same function for ATAPI devices. In executing this command a device transfers a 512-byte (256-word) data structure to the host system using PIO Data-in transport protocol.

The IDENTIFY DEVICE data contains a great deal of specific information about the device. This includes model number, serial number, firmware level, and storage capacity, as well as many bits indicating which features are supported and which of the supported features is enabled. For example:

- If word 82, bit 1 =1, then the Security Mode feature set is supported.
- If word 85, bit 1 = 1, then the Security Mode feature set is currently enabled.

Considering the large number of features that are possible on an ATA device, this level of detail is essential in order for host firmware or software to properly work with a device.

SET FEATURES – Enabling/Disabling Features

Many of the possible ATA features are not automatically active after a device is powered on. Instead, the host system must enable those features in order to use them. While there are a few exceptions, most features are turned off or on by using the SET FEATURES command. Approximately 30 functions, or sub-commands, are defined for the command, with each sub-command enabling or disabling a feature.

SET FEATURES follows the non-data command protocol. The steps in executing a SET FEATURES command are:

- Host writes the sub-command code into the Feature Register
- Host writes additional parameters, if any, into other registers
- Host writes SET FEATURES command code, EFh, into the Command Register, starting command execution

- Device evaluates the sub-command and performs the requested action
- Device presents ending status indicating that the requested action is complete.

Device Configuration Overlay feature set

This feature is implemented through a single command with 4 subcommands. It allows BIOS or other boot time firmware to reduce the available capacity of a device or to disable certain features or commands. This would permit a system manufacturer, for example, to purchase a high volume of a single model disk drive yet offer two or three different capacities on different model systems.

Host Protected Area feature set

When a PC is put into a Hibernate power management state, an image of memory is written to the hard disk. When the system recovers from the Hibernate state, the memory image is restored to system DRAM. The Host Protected Area feature set is a set of 3 commands with 5 subcommands that reserve and manage an area of a disk that is invisible during normal OS operation. It is intended that only system BIOS or other boot time firmware should use these commands.

READ and WRITE Commands

The full ATA command set includes 10 different read data commands and 13 different write data commands for disk drives (ATAPI devices use SCSI READ and WRITE commands). About half this complexity is due to the matrix of transport protocols and 28- vs 48-bit addressing. The remaining half is due to various other historical and feature-support reasons. SATA adds one more READ and one more WRITE command to the mix.

A current ATA or SATA drive may support all of these commands, however a current OS will probably use only one pair of READ/WRITE commands. This will be READ/WRITE DMA EXT for ATA drives and SATA drives without Native Command Queuing (NCQ) support and READ/WRITE FPDMA QUEUED for SATA drives supporting NCQ.

48-bit Addressing feature set

As disk drive capacity grew over time, the original ATA command format became inadequate to address the full capacity of a disk drive. The Command Block registers contained 28 bits to form a Logical Block Address (LBA). Each block contained 512 bytes. This allowed a maximum addressable capacity of about 137 billion bytes (2*28 x 512 = approx. 137,000,000,000). The solution to the problem had to increase address bits while remaining backward compatible with older host systems and older ATA drives.

Forty eight address bits was selected as an adequate number to allow for many years of growth in capacity. The eventual solution had two parts. First, all commands that use 48-bit addressing have new command codes with new names. Previously existing commands behave as they always have in order to maintain backward compatibility. Second, an expanded Command Block register set was architected to operate correctly with either 28-bit or 48-bit commands. See Figure B-6 for an overview of the architecture change.

Figure B-6: LBA Addressing (48-Bits)

Cmd Reg	Reads		Writes		Notes
Address	7	0	7	0	
01F0	Data				16-bit accesses
01F1	Error		Feature		Two 8-bit accesses
01F2	Sector Count				Two 8-bit accesses
01F3	LBA Low (31:24 then 7:0)				Two 8-bit accesses
01F4	LBA Middle (39:32 then 15:8)				Two 8-bit accesses
01F5	LBA High (47:40 then 23:16)				Two 8-bit accesses
01F6	Device		Device		8-bit access only
01F7	Status		Command		8-bit access only
Ctrl Reg					
03F6	Alternate Status		Device Control		8-bit access only

Streaming Feature feature set

A streaming application is one in which the transfer of data is primarily time critical rather than data integrity critical. Playing a video clip from a hard disk is a common example of this type of application.

This feature set consists of three commands, READ STREAM, WRITE STREAM, and CONFIGURE STREAM. These commands allow several modifications to normal read/write behavior in order to facilitate streaming. Among these modifications are a time limit for command execution and the ability to continue transferring data even after detecting an error.

Tagged Queuing feature set

This feature set is also known as legacy command queuing. It uses five unique read/write command codes. The queued read/write commands present a 5-bit queue tag along with the usual read/write parameters to the target device. Each outstanding command to a device must have a unique tag value. Up to 32 different commands can, in theory, be queued within a device at one time.

Although queuing commands can improve performance, this feature has not been widely used on ATA systems. This is due to the difficulties of managing DMA transfers, interrupts, and device selection when the ATA cable is populated with two devices.

The Native Command Queuing feature of SATA avoids these problems and is widely used.

Power Management feature set

One of the biggest concerns affecting users of portable computers from the earliest portable PCs up to today is extending battery life. In order to minimize power usage by hard disk drives, two lower power states were defined for ATA drives, Standby state and Idle state. In Standby state, the drive spindle motor is turned off for a significant reduction in power usage. Idle state is defined as a condition in which the disk is still spinning but power consumption is somewhat reduced by unspecified means.

The key issue for both designers and users is how to best balance power consumption against performance. Drive activity generally comes in bursts of commands as a file system access is made so we do not want the drive to enter Standby while a burst of commands is in progress as there is a several millisecond delay for a drive to transition from Standby state to Ready state when a new command is received. However, we do want it to spin down when the burst is clearly finished so that battery life is extended.

This feature consists of five commands, STANDBY, STANDBY IMMEDIATE, IDLE, IDLE IMMEDIATE, and CHECK POWER MODE. The STANDBY and IDLE commands both contain a numeric parameter that indicates the number of 5 second increments the drive should wait after completing a command before entering Standby. There is also a value indicating Never Spin Down. A typical factory default value for a notebook computer might be between 30 seconds and 3 minutes. The user can modify this value on most machines through the BIOS or the Windows Control Panel. If a new command is received before the Standby timer expires, then the command is executed and the timer is re-initialized and started again.

Advanced Power Management feature set

By the 1990s, some customers wanted the drive to exercise a more intelligent level of adaptive control over its power management decisions. The Advanced Power Management feature set provided this control. It is activated through the SET FEATURES command.

When the feature is activated, a numeric parameter in the range of 01h – FEh is specified. 01h directs the drive to conserve the maximum amount of power possible, with minimal regard for performance. Values 02h – 7Fh allow increasing degrees of power consumption for better performance, while continuing to use Standby state. Values 80h – FEh do not allow the use of Standby state, while continuing to shift the battery life/performance trade-off toward higher performance.

It is unrealistic to assume that an ATA drive has 254 discrete levels of power management, however, this mechanism does allow drive firmware to support several different, user selectable, power management strategies.

General Purpose Logging feature set

The ATA protocol and command set originally provided the host system with almost no runtime information about device performance or behavior. Beginning with the SMART feature, described below, a number of feature-specific logs have been defined for ATA devices. A typical log consists of counters of various events, such as errors of different types.

This feature set provides two commands, WRITE LOG EXT and READ LOG EXT, to initialize and to retrieve information from individual logs. Each log is 512 bytes long or a multiple of 512 bytes long.

SMART feature set

Self Monitoring and Reporting Technology (SMART) was developed in the late 1990s as a tool to help predict impending device failure so that backup and replacement could be scheduled before a catastrophic failure occurred. Devices implementing SMART were expected to record statistics on such attributes as power on hours, seek retries, soft read errors, and start/stop cycles. The host system could read actual attribute values or simply query whether a predefined threshold of events had been exceeded.

Later, SMART was expanded to include the capability of running various self test and media scan diagnostics.

The SMART feature set provides one command code with eight subcommands to manage the device's SMART behavior. Actual attributes and threshold values are not defined in the ATA standard. These are vendor specific and generally proprietary.

Security feature set

This feature was originally developed as a way to protect data on the disk of a notebook computer in case the computer was stolen. It allows a user and a system administrator to set passwords to control access to the media of the disk drive. When a password protected system is powered on, firmware prompts the user for a password before it attempts to boot the system. Firmware then sends the password to the disk with a special command, SECURITY UNLOCK, to allow access to data on the disk drive.

The feature set consists of six commands to set passwords, lock and unlock the drive, and erase the drive. If a valid password cannot be recalled to unlock the disk drive, the only way to recover use of the device is to erase all data on the disk using the SECURITY ERASE UNIT command.

Packet-delivered Commands (ATAPI)

ATA Packet Interface (ATAPI) was developed in the mid-1990s as a mechanism for connecting CD_ROM devices to a PC system through an ATA HBA and cable. The only widely supported command set for CD-ROM devices at that time was the SCSI multimedia command set. The solution to this design problem was to define a single register delivered ATA-type command, called PACKET, that would allow any standard SCSI command to be transferred to an attached device in a small data packet. This allowed a high percentage of re-use of both device firmware and multimedia device drivers. It also allowed the migration of any SCSI device to the ATA interface with only a moderate amount of redesign. CD-R/W and DVD devices have joined CD-ROM as common ATAPI PC peripherals.

Following delivery of the Command packet, any data transfer required in the execution of the SCSI command is achieved through the PIO or DMA mechanisms of the ATA interface. Figure B-7 shows the Command packet delivery and decode.

Figure B-7: Command Packet Delivery and Decode

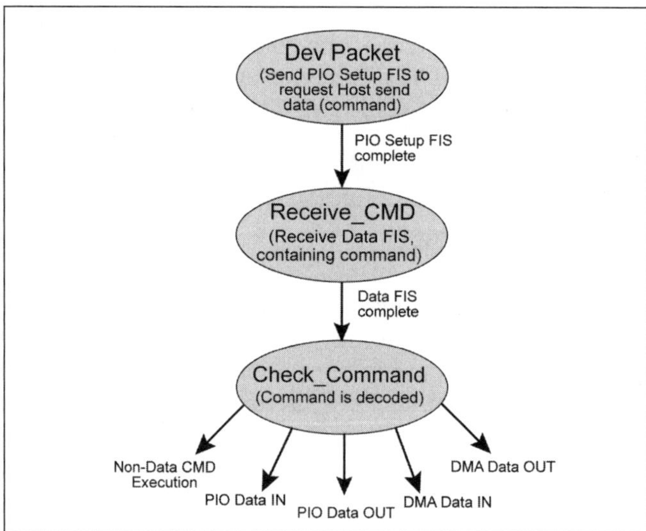

SATA-only Commands

These four commands are discussed briefly here for topical completeness. See other sections of this book for a more complete description of their usage.

READ FPDMA QUEUED and WRITE FPDMA QUEUED

This form of command queuing is also called Native Command Queuing (NCQ). Like the Tagged Command Queuing feature of ATA/ATAPI-7, a 5-bit queue tag is associated with each command outstanding to a device. Beyond that, there is very little in common between the two forms of command queuing.

The most significant protocol difference introduced in NCQ is the mechanism for presenting command completion interrupts. Tagged Command Queuing follows the standard ATA pattern of one ending interrupt per command, with the Status Register containing completion status for that command. NCQ changes this to allow aggregating the completion of several commands into a single interrupt event with the drive indicating which queue tags are now complete, permitting the HBA to indicate to host software which queue tags are still outstanding. These commands are discussed in the section entitled "New Commands" on page 241.

READ and Write PORT MULTIPLIER Commands

A port multiplier (PM) is a switch that allows one SATA host port to access several devices. These two commands are used to configure and retrieve status information from registers internal to the PM. See "PM Read and Write Commands" on page 276 for details regarding these commands.

Appendix C
Commands by Code

ATA Commands By Code

Code	Protocol	Command	No Packet Cmd	Packet Cmd
00h	ND	NOP	O	M
03h	ND	CFA Request Extended Error	O	N
08h	DR	Device Reset	N	M
25h	DMA	Read DMA Ext	O	N
26h	DMAQ	Read DMA Queued Ext	O	N
27h	ND	Read Native Max Address Ext	O	N
29h	PIO-IN	Read Multiple Ext	O	N
2Bh	PIO-IN	Read Stream Ext	O	N
2Fh	PIO-IN	Read Log Ext	O	O
30h	PIO-OUT	Write Sector(s)	M	N
34h	PIO-OUT	Write Sector(s) Ext	O	N
35h	DMA	Write DMA Ext	O	N
36h	DMAQ	Write DMA Queued Ext	O	N
37h	ND	Set Max Address Ext	O	N
38h	PIO-OUT	CFA Write Sectors Without Erase	O	N
38h	PIO-OUT	Write Stream Ext	O	N
39h	PIO-OUT	Write Multiple Ext	O	N
3Ah	DMA	Write Stream DMA Ext	O	N
3Dh	DMA	Write DMA FUA Ext	O	N
3Eh	DMAQ	Write DMA Queued FUA Ext	O	N
3Fh	PIO-OUT	Write Log Ext	O	O
40h	ND	Read Verify Sector(s)	M	N
42h	ND	Read Verify Sector(s) Ext	O	N
51h	ND	Configure Stream	O	O
87h	PIO-IN	CFA Translate Sector	O	N
90h	DD	Execute Device Diagnostics	M	N
92h	PIO-OUT	Download Microcode	O	N
A0h	P	Packet	N	M
A1h	PIO-IN	Identify Packet Device	N	M
A2h	PIO/DMAQ	Service	O	O
B0h	ND	Smart Disable Operations	O	N
B0h	ND	Smart Enable Operations	O	N
B0h	ND	Smart Enable/Disable Autosave	O	N

Code	Protocol	Command	No Packet Cmd	Packet Cmd
B0h	ND	Smart Execute Off-Line Immediate	O	N
B0h	PIO-IN	Smart Read Data	O	N
B0h	PIO-IN	Smart Read Log	O	N
B0h	ND	Smart Return Status	O	N
B0h	PIO-OUT	Smart Write Log	O	N
B1h	ND	Device Configuration Freeze Lock	O	O
B1h	PIO-IN	Device Configuration Identify	O	O
B1h	ND	Device Configuration Restore	O	O
B1h	PIO-OUT	Device Configuration Set	O	O
B1h	DMA	Read Stream DMA Ext	O	N
C0h	ND	CFA Erase Sectors	F	N
C4h	PIO-IN	Read Multiple	M	N
C5h	PIO-OUT	Write Multiple	M	N
C6h	ND	Set Multiple Mode	M	N
C7h	DMAQ	Read DMA Queued	O	N
C8h	DMA	Read DMA	M	N
CAh	DMA	Write DMA	M	N
CCh	DMAQ	Write DMA Queued	O	N
CDh	PIO-OUT	CFA Write Multiple Without Erase	O	N
CEh	PIO-OUT	Write Multiple FUA Ext	O	N
D1h	ND	Check Media Card Type	O	N
DAh	ND	Get Media Status	O	O
DEh	ND	Media Lock	O	N
DEh	PIO-IN	Read Sector(s) Ext	O	N
DFh	ND	Media Unlock	O	N
E0h	ND	Standby Immediate	M	M
E1h	ND	Idle Immediate	M	M
E2h	ND	Standby	M	O
E3h	ND	Idle	M	O
E4h	PIO-IN	Read Buffer	O	N
E5h	ND	Check Power Mode	M	M
E6h	ND	Sleep	M	M
E7h	ND	Flush Cache	M	O
E8h	PIO-OUT	Write Buffer	O	N
EAh	ND	Flush Cache Ext	O	N
ECh	PIO-IN	Identify Device	M	M
EDh	ND	Media Eject	O	N
EDh	PIO-IN	Read Sector(s)	M	M
EFh	ND	Set Features	M	M
F1h	PIO-OUT	Security Set Password	O	O
F2h	PIO-OUT	Security Unlock	O	O
F3h	ND	Security Erase Prepare	O	O
F4h	PIO-OUT	Security Erase Unit	O	O
F5h	ND	Security Freeze Lock	O	O
F6h	PIO-OUT	Security Disable Password	O	O
F8h	ND	Read Native Max Address	O	O
F9h	ND	Set Max	O	O

Appendix D
Commands By Type

ATA Commands By Type

Protocol Type	Command	Code	No Packet Cmd	Packet Cmd
DD	Execute Device Diagnostics	90h	M	N
DMA	Read DMA Ext	25h	O	N
DMA	Write DMA Ext	35h	O	N
DMA	Write Stream DMA Ext	3Ah	O	N
DMA	Write DMA FUA Ext	3Dh	O	N
DMA	Read Stream DMA Ext	B1h	O	N
DMA	Read DMA	C8h	M	N
DMA	Write DMA	CAh	M	N
DMAQ	Read DMA Queued Ext	26h	O	N
DMAQ	Write DMA Queued Ext	36h	O	N
DMAQ	Write DMA Queued FUA Ext	3Eh	O	N
DMAQ	Read DMA Queued	C7h	O	N
DMAQ	Write DMA Queued	CCh	O	N
DR	Device Reset	08h	N	M
ND	NOP	00h	O	M
ND	CFA Request Extended Error	03h	O	N
ND	Read Native Max Address Ext	27h	O	N
ND	Set Max Address Ext	37h	O	N
ND	Read Verify Sector(s)	40h	M	N
ND	Read Verify Sector(s) Ext	42h	O	N
ND	Configure Stream	51h	O	O
ND	Smart Disable Operations	B0h	O	N
ND	Smart Enable Operations	B0h	O	N
ND	Smart Enable/Disable Autosave	B0h	O	N
ND	Smart Execute Off-Line Immediate	B0h	O	N
ND	Smart Return Status	B0h	O	N
ND	Device Configuration Freeze Lock	B1h	O	O
ND	Device Configuration Restore	B1h	O	O
ND	CFA Erase Sectors	C0h	F	N
ND	Set Multiple Mode	C6h	M	N
ND	Check Media Card Type	D1h	O	N
ND	Get Media Status	DAh	O	O
ND	Media Lock	DEh	O	N

Protocol Type	Command	Code	No Packet Cmd	Packet Cmd
ND	Media Unlock	DFh	O	N
ND	Standby Immediate	E0h	M	M
ND	Idle Immediate	E1h	M	M
ND	Standby	E2h	M	O
ND	Idle	E3h	M	O
ND	Check Power Mode	E5h	M	M
ND	Sleep	E6h	M	M
ND	Flush Cache	E7h	M	O
ND	Flush Cache Ext	EAh	O	N
ND	Media Eject	EDh	O	N
ND	Set Features	EFh	M	M
ND	Security Erase Prepare	F3h	O	O
ND	Security Freeze Lock	F5h	O	O
ND	Read Native Max Address	F8h	O	O
ND	Set Max	F9h	O	O
P	Packet	A0h	N	M
PIO/DMAQ	Service	A2h	O	O
PIO-IN	Read Multiple Ext	29h	O	N
PIO-IN	Read Stream Ext	2Bh	O	N
PIO-IN	Read Log Ext	2Fh	O	O
PIO-IN	CFA Translate Sector	87h	O	N
PIO-IN	Identify Packet Device	A1h	N	M
PIO-IN	Smart Read Data	B0h	O	N
PIO-IN	Smart Read Log	B0h	O	N
PIO-IN	Device Configuration Identify	B1h	O	O
PIO-IN	Read Multiple	C4h	M	N
PIO-IN	Read Sector(s) Ext	DEh	O	N
PIO-IN	Read Buffer	E4h	O	N
PIO-IN	Identify Device	ECh	M	M
PIO-IN	Read Sector(s)	EDh	M	M
PIO-OUT	Write Sector(s)	30h	M	N
PIO-OUT	Write Sector(s) Ext	34h	O	N
PIO-OUT	CFA Write Sectors Without Erase	38h	O	N
PIO-OUT	Write Stream Ext	38h	O	N
PIO-OUT	Write Multiple Ext	39h	O	N
PIO-OUT	Write Log Ext	3Fh	O	O
PIO-OUT	Download Microcode	92h	O	N
PIO-OUT	Smart Write Log	B0h	O	N
PIO-OUT	Device Configuration Set	B1h	O	O
PIO-OUT	Write Multiple	C5h	M	N
PIO-OUT	CFA Write Multiple Without Erase	CDh	O	N
PIO-OUT	Write Multiple FUA Ext	CEh	O	N
PIO-OUT	Write Buffer	E8h	O	N
PIO-OUT	Security Set Password	F1h	O	O
PIO-OUT	Security Unlock	F2h	O	O
PIO-OUT	Security Erase Unit	F4h	O	O
PIO-OUT	Security Disable Password	F6h	O	O

Appendix E
Commands By Name

ATA Commands By Name

Command	Code	Protocol	No Packet Cmd	Packet Cmd
CFA Erase Sectors	C0h	ND	F	N
CFA Request Extended Error	03h	ND	O	N
CFA Translate Sector	87h	PIO-IN	O	N
CFA Write Multiple Without Erase	CDh	PIO-OUT	O	N
CFA Write Sectors Without Erase	38h	PIO-OUT	O	N
Check Media Card Type	D1h	ND	O	N
Check Power Mode	E5h	ND	M	M
Configure Stream	51h	ND	O	O
Device Configuration Freeze Lock	B1h	ND	O	O
Device Configuration Identify	B1h	PIO-IN	O	O
Device Configuration Restore	B1h	ND	O	O
Device Configuration Set	B1h	PIO-OUT	O	O
Device Reset	08h	DR	N	M
Download Microcode	92h	PIO-OUT	O	N
Execute Device Diagnostics	90h	DD	M	N
Flush Cache	E7h	ND	M	O
Flush Cache Ext	EAh	ND	O	N
Get Media Status	DAh	ND	O	O
Identify Device	ECh	PIO-IN	M	M
Identify Packet Device	A1h	PIO-IN	N	M
Idle	E3h	ND	M	O
Idle Immediate	E1h	ND	M	M
Media Eject	EDh	ND	O	N
Media Lock	DEh	ND	O	N
Media Unlock	DFh	ND	O	N
NOP	00h	ND	O	M
Packet	A0h	P	N	M
Read Buffer	E4h	PIO-IN	O	N
Read DMA	C8h	DMA	M	N
Read DMA Ext	25h	DMA	O	N
Read DMA Queued	C7h	DMAQ	O	N
Read DMA Queued Ext	26h	DMAQ	O	N
Read Log Ext	2Fh	PIO-IN	O	O

Command	Code	Protocol	No Packet Cmd	Packet Cmd
Read Multiple	C4h	PIO-IN	M	N
Read Multiple Ext	29h	PIO-IN	O	N
Read Native Max Address	F8h	ND	O	O
Read Native Max Address Ext	27h	ND	O	N
Read Sector(s)	EDh	PIO-IN	M	M
Read Sector(s) Ext	DEh	PIO-IN	O	N
Read Stream DMA Ext	B1h	DMA	O	N
Read Stream Ext	2Bh	PIO-IN	O	N
Read Verify Sector(s)	40h	ND	M	N
Read Verify Sector(s) Ext	42h	ND	O	N
Security Disable Password	F6h	PIO-OUT	O	O
Security Erase Prepare	F3h	ND	O	O
Security Erase Unit	F4h	PIO-OUT	O	O
Security Freeze Lock	F5h	ND	O	O
Security Set Password	F1h	PIO-OUT	O	O
Security Unlock	F2h	PIO-OUT	O	O
Service	A2h	PIO/DMAQ	O	O
Set Features	EFh	ND	M	M
Set Max	F9h	ND	O	O
Set Max Address Ext	37h	ND	O	N
Set Multiple Mode	C6h	ND	M	N
Sleep	E6h	ND	M	M
Smart Disable Operations	B0h	ND	O	N
Smart Enable Operations	B0h	ND	O	N
Smart Enable/Disable Autosave	B0h	ND	O	N
Smart Execute Off-Line Immediate	B0h	ND	O	N
Smart Read Data	B0h	PIO-IN	O	N
Smart Read Log	B0h	PIO-IN	O	N
Smart Return Status	B0h	ND	O	N
Smart Write Log	B0h	PIO-OUT	O	N
Standby	E2h	ND	M	O
Standby Immediate	E0h	ND	M	M
Write Buffer	E8h	PIO-OUT	O	N
Write DMA	CAh	DMA	M	N
Write DMA Ext	35h	DMA	O	N
Write DMA FUA Ext	3Dh	DMA	O	N
Write DMA Queued	CCh	DMAQ	O	N
Write DMA Queued Ext	36h	DMAQ	O	N
Write DMA Queued FUA Ext	3Eh	DMAQ	O	N
Write Log Ext	3Fh	PIO-OUT	O	O
Write Multiple	C5h	PIO-OUT	M	N
Write Multiple Ext	39h	PIO-OUT	O	N
Write Multiple FUA Ext	CEh	PIO-OUT	O	N
Write Sector(s)	30h	PIO-OUT	M	N
Write Sector(s) Ext	34h	PIO-OUT	O	N
Write Stream DMA Ext	3Ah	DMA	O	N
Write Stream Ext	38h	PIO-OUT	O	N

Glossary

Term	Description
8b/10b	Shorthand that describes the encoding scheme used by SATA and many other serial transports. Encoding each 8-bit byte into a 10-bit value for transmission introduces some overhead but provides a number of benefits.
AHCI	Advance Host Controller Interface. This controller is used in many PC implementations as the interface between the PCI bus and SATA link.
ALIGN	A primitive used during initialization to help receivers detect aligned 10-bit symbol boundaries. Also used by receivers during normal link operation to manage clock compensation via an elastic buffer.
ATAPI	The ATA Packet Interface protocol that delivers SCSI command to an ATAPI device. CD-ROM, Tape, and DVD drives typically use this protocol. This support is extended to SATA.
Back Bus	A SATA link uses a half duplex signaling scheme using transmit and receive differential pairs. The device transmitting a Frame receives feedback from the receiving node on its back bus (i.e., receive differential pair).
EMI	Electro-Magnetic Interference.
EOF	End Of Frame — A primitive sent at the end of each Frame.
eSATA	External SATA — The interconnect used for external desktop applications.
FIS	Frame Information Structure. A packet of information used for basic communications between the HBA and drive.
Frame	A packet of information transmitted across the link that includes SOF, FIS, CRC, and EOF.

Term	Description
Gen 1	Generation One of the SATA interface based initially on the 1.0a version of the SATA specification. Also, commonly refers to the transmission rate of 1.5Gb/s.
Gen1i	Generation One Internal Connections — refers to the internal SATA interconnect and related electrical specifications for Gen 1 speeds (1.5 Gbps). The maximum cable length can be up to 1 meter.
Gen1m	Generation One Medium Difficulty Environments — refers to External Desktop connections with maximum cable lengths of 2 meters and short backplane applications and related electrical specifications operating at Gen 1 speeds.
Gen1x	Generation One Extreme Environments — refers to long backplane implementations and data center Applications and the related electrical specifications for supporting these environments. The maximum cable length can be greater than two meters.
Gen 2	Generation Two of the SATA interface commonly referred to as SATA II. Also, refers to the SATA II transmission rate of 3.0Gb/s.
Gen2i	Generation Two Internal Connections — refers to the internal SATA interconnect and related electrical specifications at Gen 2 speeds (3.0 Gbps). The maximum cable length can be up to 1 meter.
Gen2m	Generation Two Medium Difficulty Environments — refers to External Desktop connections (maximum cable lengths of 2 meters) and short backplane applications and the related electrical specifications for supporting these environments.
Gen2x	Generation Two Extreme Environments — refers to long backplane implementations and data center Applications and the related electrical specifications for supporting these environments. The maximum cable length can be greater than two meters.
HBA	Host Bus Adapter. The device that acts as a bridge between the system bus (host) and the storage bus.

Term	Description
ISI	Inter-symbol interference - results when the pattern of the previous symbol's bits interferes with proper reception of the current symbol.
JBOD	Just a Bunch Of Disks — a very simple collection of disk drives without a specific organization. See also RAID.
NAS	Network Attached Storage — a server dedicated to file sharing. It allows storage to be added to an existing server network without the need to shut down the network.
NCQ	Native Command Queuing — NCQ permits drives to queue up to 32 commands and execute them in the order that will result in the best overall performance.
Near-line storage	Defined as data storage on removable media, the purpose of near-line storage is to provide inexpensive, reliable, and unlimited backup. The access time for recovery depends on where the needed media resides — it can be slow because the media could be off-line when the data is needed. The combination of near-line and off-line storage accounts for 90% of a typical system's storage allocation. (See also *On-line* storage and *Off-line* storage.)
Off-line storage	Storage of data that must be retained but will rarely be accessed. It is typically stored on slow but reliable tape. (See also *On-line* storage and *Off-line* storage.)
OOB	Out Of Band — defined as communication that is considered outside the normal flow of information because it takes place over the link during initialization.
Overlap	Overlap provides a method for drives (usually slow CD-ROM drives) to relinquish ownership of the shared ATA interface, so that faster hard drives can receive command while the slower device processes the request is has received.

Term	Description
PCI	Peripheral Component Interface. This was developed by several vendors associated with personal computer manufacturing as a new IO bus standard for PC architectures to replace the obsoleted ISA bus (Industry Standard Architecture) developed by IBM. (For more information, see the MindShare book on this topic at www.mindshare.com.)
PCIe	PCI Express. This is essentially a serial version of PCI-X, designed to provide higher bandwidth while retaining software compatibility with PCI. (For more information, see the MindShare book on this topic at www.mindshare.com.)
Partial	Link Power Management state — Link power consumption is reduced by some vendor-specific level and the exit latency back to the PhyRdy state must be 10µs or less.
Port Multiplier	These devices expand the number of ports for attaching and accessing larger numbers of drives via a single HBA port.
Port Selector	These devices permit two hosts to gain access to the same port/drive to allow fail-over implementations.
Primitives	Single-dword information blocks transmitted across a connection for Link Layer communication in support of activities like flow control and reporting successful receipt of a FIS. Primitives are easily recognizable because they are the only legal DWord that contain a control (K) value, which must be the first value in the dword.
RAID	Redundant Array of Inexpensive Disks. This is a more sophisticated collection of disks that has been designed to achieve certain properties of robust operation. See also JBOD.
R_IP	Receive In Progress. A primitive sent by the receiving node to indicate it is receiving the FIS.
R_OK	Receive OK. This primitive is returned from the receiving node to report that the FIS has been received without errors.
Rx	Receiver

Term	Description
Shadow Registers	The Shadow registers, residing in SATA host bus adapters, are a duplicate copy of the ATA registers that reside within SATA drives. These registers are interface registers used for delivering commands to the drive or updating status from the drive.
SOF	Start Of Frame. A primitive sent at the beginning of each frame.
SAN	Storage Area Network - a high speed storage network designed to be attached to server network.
SEMB	Serial ATA Enclosure Management Bridge — This bridge converts SATA transactions (containing enclosure services commands) to I2C transactions that are delivered to a Storage Enclosure Processor.
SEP	Storage Enclosure Processor — The SEP interfaces with the various sensors, actuators, and LEDs to manage the storage enclosure via the SATA interface and SEMB.
Slumber	Link Power Management state — Link power consumption is reduced by some vendor-specific level less than that of the Partial state, and the exit latency from this state must be no longer than 10ms.
SSC	Spread-Spectrum Clocking. This is a method of varying the clock speed slightly but regularly over time to reduce peaks in the EMI generated by a system for any given frequency.
Tx	Transmitter

Index

Numerics

A

C

D

MindShare Press

MindShare Press is constantly looking for high-quality technical material to publish. If you have the desire, experience and ability to author a book on an interesting technical topic, contact MindShare Press to learn about our publishing services and the numerous benefits to having the MindShare name on your book.

Upcoming Titles

- PCI Express 2.0 System Architecture
- Certified Wireless USB System Architecture
- USB Embedded System Architecture
- HyperTransport 3.0 System Architecture
- PC Architecture
- Core and Core2 Processor Architecture
- AMD64 Software Architecture
- Opteron Processor Architecture

MindShare Press - publishing@mindshare.com